DANIEL SMITH DONELSON

DANIEL SMITH DONELSON

SOLDIER, POLITICIAN, TENNESSEAN

Richard Douglas Spence

THE UNIVERSITY OF TENNESSEE PRESS | KNOXVILLE

Copyright © 2023 by The University of Tennessee Press / Knoxville.

All Rights Reserved. Manufactured in the United States of America.

First Edition.

Library of Congress Cataloging-in-Publication Data
Names: Spence, Richard Douglas, 1958– author.
Title: Daniel Smith Donelson : soldier, politician, Tennessean / Richard Douglas Spence.
Description: First edition. | Knoxville : The University of Tennessee Press, [2023] | Includes bibliographical references and index. | Summary: "Richard Douglas Spence has written a biography of Daniel Smith Donelson, a soldier and politician and the nephew of Andrew Jackson. Spence begins with Donelson's upbringing at the Hermitage after Donelson's father died when he was five and follows Donelson's career as a planter, militiaman, state congressman, and finally a general overseeing the Confederate Department of East Tennessee. Fort Donelson was named in his honor, and his brigades fought at Stones River, Perryville, and Murfreesboro before he was transferred to Charleston, South Carolina. He was posthumously promoted to major general after dying of disease on April 17, 1863, at the age of sixty-one"
—Provided by publisher.
Identifiers: LCCN 2023016752 (print) | LCCN 2023016753 (ebook) | ISBN 9781621907404 (hardcover) | ISBN 9781621907411 (pdf)
Subjects: LCSH: Donelson, Daniel Smith, 1801–1863. | Generals—Confederate States of America—Biography. | Confederate States of America. Army—Biography. | Confederate States of America. Army. Department of Tennessee—Biography. | Donelson family. | Legislators—Tennessee—Biography. | Tennessee—Biography. | BISAC: BIOGRAPHY & AUTOBIOGRAPHY / Military | HISTORY / United States / 19th Century
Classification: LCC E467.1.D65 S64 2023 (print) | LCC E467.1.D65 (ebook) | DDC 355.0092 [B]—dc23/eng/20230428
LC record available at https://lccn.loc.gov/2023016752
LC ebook record available at https://lccn.loc.gov/2023016753

To those Meza kids:
Cassy
Mason
Jacob
Joseph
Emma
Philip

CONTENTS

Preface xi

Dramatis Personae xv

CHAPTER ONE
"Fine Material for a Military Man"
June 1801–July 1825
1

CHAPTER TWO
"I Would Sooner See Revolution"
August 1825–March 1833
17

CHAPTER THREE
"A Substantial Farmer of Old Sumner"
April 1833–January 1850
37

CHAPTER FOUR
"Still a Democrat of the Jackson School"
January 1850–March 1861
57

CHAPTER FIVE
"Send Donelson's Brigade"
The War Begins, April 1861–April 1862
95

CHAPTER SIX
"A Most Determined Courage"
Perryville, April 1862–October 1862
115

CHAPTER SEVEN
"More Distinguished Bravery"
Murfreesboro, October 1862–January 1863
137

CHAPTER EIGHT
"An Irreparable Loss"
East Tennessee, January 1863–April 1863
155

EPILOGUE
"Something Peculiarly Appropriate
in the Man for the Time"
171

Notes 177

Bibliography 231

Index 245

ILLUSTRATIONS

Following page 86
Daniel Smith Donelson, 1850
Andrew Jackson
Rachel Jackson
Andrew Jackson Donelson
John Branch
Hazel Path house
Daniel Smith Donelson in Tennessee State Militia Uniform
Robert E. Lee, 1861
Leonidas Polk
Benjamin Franklin Cheatham
Braxton Bragg
Daniel Smith Donelson Near the End of the Civil War
Margaret Donelson

MAPS

The Western Theater 94
The Battle of Perryville 114
The Battle of Murfreesboro 136
East Tennessee 154

PREFACE

Over a century and a half after the guns fell silent, the American Civil War remains as popular and controversial as ever among historians and the general public alike. Every aspect of the war, it seems—from military, political, and economic to social and moral—has been mined extensively and even repeatedly. Few major participants have escaped at least one biography. A notable exception, however, is Daniel Smith Donelson of Tennessee.

Civil War military historians have long appreciated the important role that Donelson's redoubtable brigade played in the battles of Perryville and Stones River (Murfreesboro). Yet Donelson the man, the politician, and the soldier, has eluded a full study. Although he has been the subject of a number of brief treatments, usually among compilations, no book-length biography has ever been published. The impediment that has most likely discouraged an earlier attempt is the dearth of primary sources. Donelson left no body of personal papers. Such that he may have kept were apparently lost or destroyed as Union occupation forces repeatedly pillaged Hazel Path, his home in Hendersonville. What few letters survive, written by or to Donelson, are scattered in the collections of his correspondents, and most of them date to the Jacksonian period, where a Civil War historian might not know to look.[1]

Thus, in many ways, Daniel Donelson can be approached only by way of the historical "back door," through his legendary uncle Andrew Jackson and his brother, Andrew Jackson Donelson, who enjoyed a significant political career in his own right. Moreover, such an approach reveals aspects of his life and career that are in many ways every bit as important as his Civil War record, providing new and fresh perspectives on Jackson's tumultuous presidency and the contentious nature of antebellum politics in Tennessee. Daniel Donelson's relations with his volatile uncle during the Eaton scandal and nullification crisis also open a new window for viewing how complex Old Hickory's personal and public actions could be. The three-way relations between the Donelson brothers and their imperious uncle reveal the intricacies of personal and political allegiances during the Jacksonian and antebellum periods. Ultimately, one brother, Andrew, broke with the Democratic Party which their uncle had founded, but remained loyal to the Union, while the other brother, Daniel, remained loyal to the Democratic Party but broke with the Union. My preceding book, *Andrew Jackson Donelson: Jacksonian and Unionist*, published by Vanderbilt University Press (2017) as part of its New Perspectives in Jacksonian History, examined the course that Andrew took. I now offer this book as its logical follow-up, a companion volume, to examine the course that Daniel Donelson took.

When I quote Donelson and his contemporaries, I retain their original spellings and orthography, using [*sic*] and corrective square brackets only minimally to prevent confusion, and their emphases (underlined when in a manuscript, italicized in print) as in the original. Needless to say, the errors that no doubt remain in this work are my entire responsibility.

Researching and writing a book is never the solitary activity that many who have never attempted it might think. Like everyone who has, I have benefited from the moral and material assistance of many people at every level. Thus, I have accrued a large pile of gratitude that I now take great pleasure in dispensing. My thanks begin with the research phase, going to all the dedicated staff at all the libraries and archives that I have used. I thank again Andrew Jackson ("Jack") Donelson of Bowling Green, Kentucky, who graciously invited me to dig through boxes of Donelson family material in his possession while I was working on my preceding book, some of which I am able to use here, as well. Similarly, I again thank Mark Cheathem, Professor of History at Cumberland University, Lebanon, Tennessee, for his years of support throughout these lengthy Donelson projects.

In terms of field work, it is with great pride that I acknowledge and thank the support of someone who adopted me into his family years ago when he was an undergraduate student of mine. Jose Meza, now an obstetrician/gynecologist in Lawton, Oklahoma, and his oldest son, Mason, then twelve, accompanied me on a most enjoyable summer trip in 2018 to Kentucky and Tennessee. There, we trooped over the battlefields of Perryville and Murfreesboro, and visited (for me, not my first or last time) Rock Castle, Hazel Path, the Hermitage, Tulip Grove, and the First Presbyterian Church of Hendersonville. Mason in particular became quite the expert at deciphering eroded names and dates on crumbling tombstones in the cemeteries at these places, the last in a pouring rain. I express here my appreciation to the valuable contribution that this fine, promising young man made to this project, which inspires the dedication of the result.

Also on that trip, I became much obliged to Chuck Lott, a park ranger at the Perryville Battlefield State Historic Site, and Ren Hankla, a local resident who owns the adjacent private property of Walker Bend, for kindly giving Jose, Mason, and myself an extensive tour of Walker Bend, from which Donelson's brigade launched its attack.

As the manuscript progressed, my old friends Hubert and Debbie Reddin Van Tuyll, respectively professors (now emeritus) of History and Communications at Augusta University, Augusta, Georgia, again contributed support, good visits at their home and mine, and input (Hubert mostly Civil War military, Debbie mostly antebellum Southern politics) that is always informative, illuminating, and appreciated.

Personal thanks again go to all the members of my family for their support and, so they say, interest in these historical projects of mine. My mother still bakes a double-chocolate cake every time I am able to drive across Texas to visit her. She, my sisters Susan Denson and Gail Necker (who keeps badgering me to lay off the Donelsons and start researching the Spence family), Gail's husband James, and my nephews Jordy and Garrett Denson, all loyally swear that they read my preceding book. Perhaps they might read this one, too.

Last, I am very pleased, of course, to thank the good people at the University of Tennessee Press for their help in bringing this project to fruition. Acquisitions Editor Thomas Wells, who expressed interest from the first submission of the manuscript, recognized the need for a biography of Daniel Donelson and served as its advocate throughout the review process. The reviewers encouraged me to expand the work by placing Donelson into a broader contextual history of the antebellum South. Pat Ford, the meticulous copy editor, improved my writing in a number of places. In preparing the excellent maps, Tim Kissel lived up to Thomas

Wells's billing as a "crackerjack cartographer." Jenny Lillich proved to be a diligent and comprehensive indexer, and editorial assistant Jonathan Boggs guided the book to completion.

Doug Spence
May 16, 2023

DRAMATIS PERSONAE

DONELSON FAMILY (PATERNAL LINE)

Donelson, (Colonel) John (1718?–1786), Tennessee pioneer, co-founder of Nashville, paternal grandfather of DSD.

Donelson, Rachel Stockley (c. 1730–1801), wife of Colonel John Donelson, paternal grandmother of DSD.

Children of Colonel John and Rachel Stockley Donelson (among eleven total):

    Donelson, (Captain) John (1755–1830), father of William Donelson, Stockley Donelson, and Emily Donelson, first wife of AJD, all DSD's cousins.

    Jackson, Rachel Donelson Robards (1767–1828), DSD's aunt.
    —First husband: Lewis Robards.
    —Second husband: Andrew Jackson.

    Donelson, Samuel (c. 1770–1804), first husband of Mary Ann (Polly) Smith Donelson Sanders, father of John Samuel (Jacky) Donelson, AJD, and DSD.

SMITH FAMILY (MATERNAL LINE)

Smith, Daniel (1748–1818), Tennessee pioneer and statesman, maternal grandfather of DSD.

Smith, Sarah Michie (c. 1755–1831), wife of General Daniel Smith, maternal grandmother of DSD.

Children of General Daniel and Sarah Michie Smith:

    Smith, George (1776–c. 1833), uncle of DSD.
    —Son: Henry (Harry) Smith, DSD's cousin.
    Smith, Mary Ann (Polly) (1781–1857), mother of DSD.
    —First husband: Samuel Donelson.
    —Second husband: James Sanders.

WIFE AND CHILDREN OF SAMUEL DONELSON

Donelson Sanders, Mary Ann (Polly) Smith (1781–1857), wife of Samuel Donelson; after Samuel's death married James Sanders.
Children of Samuel and Mary Ann (Polly) Smith Donelson:
    Donelson, John Samuel (Jacky) (1797–1817), DSD's eldest brother.
    Donelson, Andrew Jackson (1799–1871), politician, diplomat, DSD's older brother.
    —First wife: Emily Donelson (1807–1836), daughter of Captain John Donelson.
    —Second wife: Elizabeth Martin Randolph Donelson (1815–1871).
    Children of AJD (among twelve total):
        John Samuel Donelson (1832–1863), DSD's nephew.
        Daniel Smith Donelson (1842–1864), DSD's nephew.
Donelson, Daniel Smith (1801–1863), politician, officer in Tennessee state militia, brigadier and major general in Confederate States Army (see below).

SANDERS FAMILY (MARY ANN [POLLY] SMITH DONELSON SANDERS'S SECOND MARRIAGE)

Sanders, James (1764–1836), second husband of Mary Ann (Polly) Smith Donelson Sanders, DSD's mother, and thus DSD's stepfather.
Children of James and Mary Ann (Polly) Smith Donelson Sanders, DSD's half-sisters, and their husbands:
    Sally (?–?), m. Robert Looney Caruthers, jurist, congressman.
    Martha (1811–1830), m. Dr. Thomas G. Watson.
    Mary Ann (?–?), m. Dr. James W. Hoggatt.
    Emily (?–1842), m. Meredith Poindexter Gentry, congressman.

BRANCH FAMILY

Branch, John (1782–1863), governor of North Carolina, Secretary of the Navy under President Andrew Jackson, father of Margaret Branch Donelson and father-in-law of DSD.
Branch, Eliza (Elizabeth) Foort (Fort) (1787–1851), wife of John Branch, mother of Margaret Branch Donelson and mother-in-law of DSD.
Children of John and Eliza Branch (among nine total):
    Branch, Margaret (1811–1871), wife of DSD (see below).

DRAMATIS PERSONAE

WIFE AND CHILDREN OF DANIEL SMITH DONELSON

Donelson, Margaret Branch (1811–1871), wife of DSD.
Children of Daniel Smith and Margaret Branch Donelson, and their spouses:
    Elizabeth Branch (Lizzie) (1831–1918), m. William Williams
    Mary Ann (1834–1916), m. James Glasgow Martin Jr.
    Sarah Smith (1836–1869), m. Dr. William Henry Bradford
    Emily (1838–1931), m. James Edwin Horton
    Rebecca (1840–1911), m. David J. Dismukes
    James Branch (1842–1912), m. Josephine (Jessie) Evans
    Samuel (Sam) (1844–1906), m. Jessie L. Walton
    Martha Bradford (1847–1893), m. John Michael Shute
    Susan Branch (Sue) (1848–1871), m. Marcus Lafayette Dismukes
    John Branch (Branch) (1850–1918), m. Jennie S. Alexander
    Daniel Smith (Dan) (1853–1914), m. Florence Hood

EXTENDED FAMILY BY BLOOD OR MARRIAGE

Burton, Robert M. (1800–1843), husband of Martha Donelson, daughter of William Donelson, a brother of DSD's father Samuel Donelson, and Rachel Donelson Jackson; Robert was thus DSD's cousin by marriage.

Coffee, John (1772–1833), soldier, friend, and confidant of Andrew Jackson, married to Mary Donelson, a sister of AJD's first wife, Emily Donelson, and thus cousin by marriage to DSD.

Eastin, Mary Ann (1810–1847), daughter of William and Rachel Donelson Eastin, she was a niece of AJD's first wife, Emily Donelson, and thus DSD's first cousin, once removed; married Lucius J. Polk, a nephew of James K. Polk.

Hays, Samuel Jackson (1800–1866), son of Robert and Jane Donelson Hays, sister of DSD's father Samuel Donelson and of Rachel Donelson Jackson, and thus DSD's cousin.

Jackson, Andrew (1767–1845), military leader, politician, seventh president of the United States (1829–1837), husband of Rachel Donelson Robards Jackson, and thus DSD's uncle by marriage.

Jackson, Andrew Jr. (1808–1865), adopted son of Andrew and Rachel Donelson Jackson, and thus a cousin of DSD.

POLITICAL ASSOCIATES, RIVALS, AND OPPONENTS

Barry, Thomas R. (1807–1891), Tennessee politician, General Assembly Democratic member from Sumner County, and political rival of DSD.

Bell, John (1796–1869), Tennessee politician, congressman, senator, candidate for president of the United States (1860); initially a Jacksonian, then later a supporter of Hugh Lawson White and a founder of the Whig party in Tennessee.

Brown, Aaron V. (1795–1859), Democratic politician, governor of Tennessee (1845–1847).

Brown, Neill Smith (1810–1886), Whig politician, governor of Tennessee (1847–1849), Speaker of the House of Representatives of the Tennessee General Assembly (1855–1856), and thus a political rival of DSD.

Burford, David (1791–1864), Tennessee politician and legislator, became involved with DSD in the political dispute between Robert M. Burton and Robert Desha.

Calhoun, John Caldwell (1782–1850), South Carolina senator, secretary of war, vice-president of the United States (1825–1832) under presidents John Quincy Adams and Andrew Jackson, respectively, and political mentor of DSD.

Desha, Robert (1791–1849), Tennessee politician and congressman, became involved with DSD in a political dispute with Robert M. Burton.

Eaton, John Henry (1790–1856), Tennessee senator, secretary of war, friend of Andrew Jackson, husband of Margaret (Peggy) O'Neale Timberlake Eaton.

Eaton, Margaret (Peggy) O'Neale Timberlake (1799–1879), wife of John Henry Eaton, source of the social "Eaton affair" during Andrew Jackson's presidency.

Guild, Josephus Conn (1802–1883), Tennessee planter, soldier, politician, Democratic political ally of DSD.

Harris, Isham Green (1818–1897), Democratic congressman, senator, governor of Tennessee (1857–1863), political ally of DSD.

Houston, Sam (1793–1863), soldier, congressman, senator, governor of Tennessee (1827–1829) and Texas (1859–1861), president of the Republic of Texas (1836–1838, 1841–1844).

Johnson, Andrew (1808–1875), Democratic congressman, senator, governor of Tennessee (1853–1857) and ally of DSD, vice-president (1865) under Abraham Lincoln, and seventeenth president of the United States (1865–1869).

Jones, James Chamberlain (1809–1859), Whig politician, governor of Tennessee (1841–1845).

Peyton, Balie (1803–1878), Sumner County politician, congressman, a founder of the Whig party in Tennessee; initially a Jacksonian rival, later became a Whig opponent of DSD.

Peyton, Joseph (Jo) Hopkins (1808–1845), Gallatin physician, brother of Balie Peyton, Whig politician, congressman; opponent of DSD in congressional election, 1843.

Polk, James Knox (1795–1849), Democratic congressman, governor of Tennessee (1839–1841), eleventh president of the United States (1845–1849), ally of DSD.

Richardson, John Watkins (1809–1872), Tennessee politician, DSD's opponent for the speakership of the Tennessee state House of Representatives (1857).

Trousdale, William (1790–1872), soldier, Democratic politician, governor of Tennessee (1849–1851), ally of DSD.

Van Buren, Martin (1782–1862), New York machine politician, secretary of state, vice-president and eighth president of the United States (1837–1841).

White, Hugh Lawson (1773–1840), Tennessee political leader, senator, candidate for president of the United States (1836), supported by DSD.

MILITARY ASSOCIATES

Anderson, Robert (1805–1871), classmate of DSD at West Point, United States Army officer who surrendered Fort Sumter in the opening hostilities of the Civil War.

Anderson, Samuel Read (1804–1883), major general, Provisional Army of Tennessee; brigadier general, Confederate States Army.

Bate, William Brimage (1826–1905), major general, Confederate States Army; governor of Tennessee (1883–1887), U.S. senator (1887–1905).

Beauregard, Pierre Gustave Toutant (1818–1893), general, Confederate States Army, commander of the Army of the Mississippi (later Army of Tennessee) and DSD's army commander.

Bragg, Braxton (1817–1876), general, Confederate States Army, commander of the Army of Tennessee and DSD's army commander.

Cheatham, Benjamin Franklin (Frank) (1820–1886), major general, Confederate States Army and DSD's divisional commander, Army of Tennessee.

Cooper, Samuel (1798–1876), adjutant and inspector general, ranking general of the Confederate States Army.

Davis, Jefferson (1808–1889), schoolmate of DSD at West Point, president of the Confederate States of America (1861–1865).

Johnston, Albert Sidney (1803–1862), schoolmate of DSD at West Point; general, Confederate States Army.

Johnston, Joseph Eggleston (1807–1891), general, Confederate States Army; commander of Confederate States armies in the west and DSD's theater commander.

Lee, Robert Edward (1807–1870), general, Confederate States Army; DSD's commander in western Virginia and South Carolina.

Loring, William Wing (1818–1886), major general, Confederate States Army, commander of the Army of the Northwest in western Virginia.

Marshall, Humphrey (1812–1872), brigadier general, Confederate States Army, subordinate to DSD in East Tennessee.

Pemberton, John Clifford (1814–1881), brigadier and major general, Confederate States army; DSD's commander in South Carolina.

Pillow, Gideon Johnson (1806–1878), major general of the Tennessee state militia; major general, Provisional Army of Tennessee (1861).

Polk, Leonidas (1806–1864), schoolmate of DSD at West Point; major general, Confederate States Army and DSD's corps commander, Army of Tennessee.

Smith, Edmund Kirby (1824–1893), major general, Confederate States Army, DSD's predecessor as commander of the Department of East Tennessee.

Thayer, Sylvanus (1785–1872), superintendent of the United States Military Academy at West Point (1817–1833) while DSD was a cadet there (1821–1825).

Trist, Nicholas Philip (1800–1874), schoolmate of DSD at West Point; U.S. government official and diplomat.

DONELSON'S BRIGADE (MAIN UNITS)

Eighth Tennessee Infantry Regiment, Colonel Alfred S. Fulton, later Colonel William L. Moore, Lieutenant Colonel John H. Anderson.
Fifteenth Tennessee Infantry Regiment, Colonel Robert C. Tyler.
Sixteenth Tennessee Infantry Regiment, Colonel John H. Savage.
Thirty-eighth Tennessee Infantry Regiment, Colonel John C. Carter.
Fifty-first Tennessee Infantry Regiment, Colonel John Chester.
Eighty-fourth Tennessee Infantry Regiment, Colonel Sidney S. Stanton.
Tennessee Light Artillery Company (Carnes's Battery), Captain William W. Carnes.

CHAPTER ONE

"Fine Material for a Military Man"

JUNE 1801–JULY 1825

Daniel Smith Donelson could boast of having some of the most distinguished ancestry in the new state of Tennessee. Both of his grandfathers enjoyed that combination of rough frontier experience and what were called "gentlemanly attainments" that served to carve a civilization out of the raw American wilderness.

The paternal grandfather, John Donelson, descended from a family that originated in Scotland as an offshoot of the clan whose name is more commonly spelled Donaldson. He was born in Somerset County, Maryland, sometime between 1718 and 1725. In 1744 he brought his bride Rachel Stockley to the Virginia piedmont, where they raised eleven children. Over the years, he grew prosperous in land and slaves, and became a surveyor, justice of the peace, colonel of the militia, and delegate to the House of Burgesses from Pittsylvania County. His attention nevertheless remained focused westward. He helped to negotiate the Treaty of Lochaber in 1770 with the Cherokees, then surveyed the treaty line which became known as Donelson's Line, opening Kentucky to settlement. When the Revolutionary War broke out between Britain and the colonies, Colonel Donelson led the Pittsylvania militia to fight Cherokees and Shawnees in the Appalachian mountain valleys. By 1778 he had decided to resettle in what he described as "that western world, *that Land of promise*[,] *that Terrestrial Paradice* and *garden of Eden.*"[1]

Donelson joined with a land agent, James Robertson, to settle the wilderness along the Cumberland River west of North Carolina. While Robertson led some two hundred men overland to a place on the Cumberland River known as French Lick, Donelson led the other group, with the women and children, in a flotilla of flatboats down the Tennessee River.

Casting off in December 1779, the flotilla was plagued by cold, ice, Indian attacks, smallpox, and hunger. Only in April 1780 did the bedraggled survivors arrive at French Lick, but under Donelson's cool leadership, they succeeded in what an early historian pronounced as "one of the great achievements in the settlement of the West."[2]

The main settlement at French Lick was named Nashborough. The Donelsons built a stockade ten miles upriver at Clover Bottom, where Stones River empties into the Cumberland River. The Cumberland settlers, however, remained isolated some two hundred miles west of the main line of settlement. Indians raided crops and stock, and killed several people. In 1781, Donelson moved his family to comparatively peaceful Kentucky. Eventually, as peace and rudiments of civilization came to the Cumberland valley in 1783, the North Carolina State Assembly organized the region as Davidson County. Nashborough was renamed Nashville. Donelson decided to return his family to his Clover Bottom property. In the spring of 1786, he returned to Kentucky from a winter of business in Virginia to find that his family had already departed. He set off after them, but along the way he was shot by unknown assailants in the woods. The mystery of who killed him, whether Indians or renegade whites, remained unsolved. Nevertheless, his legacy was clear: as a soldier, surveyor, peacemaker, and pioneer, John Donelson helped to open a continent.[3]

The maternal grandfather, Daniel Smith, enjoyed a career that was hardly less impressive. He was born in 1748 in Stafford County, Virginia, into a farming family that was prosperous enough to afford an education in a little of everything from "physic" (medicine) to surveying, and even a smattering of law. In 1773, Smith married Sarah Michie, whose father operated the well-known Michie's Tavern in Charlottesville. The couple raised two children—a son George, born in 1776, and a daughter Mary Ann, born April 26, 1781. Smith served with distinction in Dunmore's War, and also fought against the Cherokees on the Appalachian frontier and the British at the Battle of Guilford Courthouse. In 1779, he was appointed to a commission to survey the boundary line between Virginia and North Carolina, west to the Mississippi River. The commissioners slogged their way westward through the wilderness during the same winter that Donelson's flatboats struggled toward their destination on the Cumberland River. Smith grasped the promise of the region and claimed 3,140 acres of rich bottomland several miles upriver from Nashborough, along the mouth of Drake's Creek on the north bank of the Cumberland River. He moved his family there in the fall of 1784 and spent the next ten years erecting an imposing, five-level stone house whose name, Rock Castle, is all the description that is needed.[4]

By 1786, the Cumberland valley had grown populous enough that North Carolina established Sumner County, stretching along the north bank of the Cumberland River and extending northward to the Kentucky line. The new county was named in honor of General Jethro Sumner, a North Carolina hero of the Revolutionary War. As he constructed Rock Castle, Daniel Smith became one of the most prominent residents of the new county. "Old Sumner" immediately took its place as the predominant county in the Cumberland valley, behind only Davidson County with Nashville itself.[5]

Considering their distance from the main body of settlements, in 1788 North Carolina grouped the Cumberland communities into the District of Mero, elected Daniel Smith as brigadier general of the district militia, and established a separate court district. Appointed to attorney general for the Mero District was a tall, wiry, hawk-faced young lawyer with a shock of reddish hair and volatile temper—Andrew Jackson.[6]

Born on March 15, 1767, in the frontier Waxhaws settlement straddling North and South Carolina, Jackson was the posthumous son and namesake of an Irish immigrant from Ulster. His life was hard from the start and thus his sharp temper, domineering personality, and combative nature developed early. Cornwallis's army swept through the Carolinas in 1781, leaving Andrew orphaned with his mother and two brothers dead, and himself scarred by a British officer's sword. Growing up on his own, Jackson studied law and, at age twenty, was licensed to practice law in North Carolina.[7]

After John Donelson's death, his widow Rachel Stockley Donelson established the family at the Clover Bottom stockade. Most of the children, even those who were grown and married, stayed nearby, although daughter Rachel lived in Kentucky with her husband Lewis Robards. When Andrew Jackson arrived in the Cumberland valley, he took lodging at the Donelson stockade. He fit right in with the large, boisterous Donelson clan, but complications arose with Rachel's arrival after her marriage to Robards had broken down. Rachel and Jackson soon fell in love, and Robards filed for divorce. Subsequent events became, and remain, controversial. Hearing that Robards had obtained a divorce, Jackson and Rachel married in the autumn of 1791. In December 1793, word arrived that Robards had been granted the divorce only that September, on grounds that "Rachel Robards . . . hath and doth Still live in adultery with another man." Jackson and Rachel were married again in January 1794. The Donelsons, despite their social standing in the community and their traditional close-knit family ties, took the episode in stride. Far from becoming outcasts, the Jacksons became pillars of the Cumberland community.[8]

Meanwhile, Rachel's younger brother Samuel Donelson, who was born about 1770, reached his adulthood and staked a position in Cumberland society that was to be expected of an ambitious son of Colonel John Donelson. In November 1794 he was licensed to practice law. He and his brother-in-law Andrew Jackson became best friends and partners in a number of joint endeavors. They purchased land together and opened a general store which was profitable until their creditor in Philadelphia defaulted on his notes. They took a considerable financial beating, but their political stars were rising. When Tennessee gained statehood in 1796, Jackson was elected as the new state's congressman. Samuel became a candidate to succeed Jackson as attorney general for the Mero District. The new state legislature, however, elected Howell Tatum into the office. When Tatum appeared in court on the first day of the term to decline the office, the court appointed Samuel Donelson as attorney general *pro tempore*, a position that he held until the next session of the General Assembly elected a permanent successor.[9]

Best of all, by this time Samuel had fallen in love. The object of his affection was the daughter of Daniel Smith, Mary Ann, whom everyone called Polly. At the time, she was fifteen, with fair hair and blue eyes. Samuel and Polly were soon very much in love, but her father objected to the romance. Jackson attempted to intercede on their behalf but got nowhere. On the night of June 20, 1796, Polly opened her bedroom window at Rock Castle in response to a prearranged signal. Samuel waited below with Jackson and a ladder. They rushed to the Jackson home, Hunter's Hill, where Rachel had arranged for a parson to be present. Thus, Samuel and Polly were married despite her father's objections.[10]

Others gave the newlyweds their best wishes. Judge Joseph Anderson predicted "that a Grand Son, will put a period to the old General[']s pouting." Indeed, the next year, 1797, the birth of a boy named John Samuel Donelson worked wonders on Smith's attitude. He gave several slaves to Polly, and to Samuel and Polly together he gave a tract of 1280 acres along the east bank of Drake's Creek in Sumner County as a belated wedding gift, provided that they would move there. This Samuel agreed to do, although he and his new family were already settled on a 600-acre tract in Davidson County not far from the Jackson home, Hunter's Hill. He set about clearing the new tract, building a cabin and a mill, and planting an orchard. These improvements took time, however, and Samuel and Polly were still living in the cabin on his Davidson County tract, when, on August 25, 1799, a second son was born to them. In honor of Samuel's brother-in-law, he was named Andrew Jackson Donelson.[11]

By the first year of the nineteenth century, the young Donelson family was living on their Sumner County tract. There, the master of Rock Castle was pleased to see, at last, a grandson who was named after him—Daniel Smith Donelson—born on June 23, 1801.[12]

Samuel's affairs prospered as his family grew, but he speculated in land that soon exceeded his ability to pay for it properly. His debts increased, as did the consequent problems. No doubt he trusted that, given time, he could untie his knotted affairs, but in July 1804, while he was visiting the Jacksons at Hunter's Hill, Samuel Donelson fell ill suddenly and died, intestate and thousands of dollars in debt.[13]

Polly was left a widow at twenty-three to care for three young boys. John Samuel, who was called "Jacky" by the family, was seven, Andrew was nearly five, and Daniel was three. Both Polly's father and the large Donelson clan were prepared to offer whatever support and assistance that she needed. Ultimately, she turned to her husband's most trusted friend. Donelson family tradition holds that as Samuel lay on his deathbed at Hunter's Hill, Jackson promised to look after the boys. Appointed as executor of the estate, Jackson began the long, complex task of settling Samuel's affairs. What help Daniel Smith could provide diminished when in 1805 he departed for Washington, D.C., as senator from Tennessee. He wrote Jackson in February 1806 to express his "very grateful impressions" that "you have shown Mr. Donelson's children" and hoped in future to repay him. "I acknowledge your friendship and benevolence to my daughter and her children," he repeated that spring, in regard to selling some of Samuel's property to raise funds.[14]

Jacky, Andrew, and Daniel became Jackson's wards, and he and Rachel assumed the major duties of raising them, despite their own financial difficulties. Jackson soon had to sell the well-developed Hunter's Hill plantation, and moved to the undeveloped Hermitage property. It was clear by now that the Jacksons would never have children of their own. Eventually, they became parents by adoption. On December 4, 1808, Elizabeth Rucker Donelson, the wife of Rachel's brother Severn, gave birth to twin boys, but was unable to nurse both babies. Severn and Elizabeth turned one of them over to the Jacksons, who christened the baby Andrew Jackson Jr.[15]

In keeping with the usual practice of frontier society, Polly Smith Donelson did not long remain a widow. On February 26, 1806, she married widower James Sanders, a prominent resident of Sumner County. Unfortunately, Polly's sons took an instant dislike to their stepfather. According to one family story, Sanders had acquired a nickname, Jimmy Dry, which he detested. When young Andrew once "sassed" Sanders, calling him Jimmy Dry to his face, Sanders thrashed him. The tragedy of Polly's marriage to a man whom her sons disliked was that she became increasingly estranged from them, a circumstance that was all the sadder because the boys, especially little Daniel, could scarcely have retained many real memories of their father.[16]

Schooling began for Jacky and Andrew at a local school, after which Jackson sent them to a school in Nashville. Less is documented about younger son Daniel's schooling, but it apparently proceeded along a similar course. In a typical letter, Jackson assured Smith that "your little grandsons are learning well, and, often speak of you—" When they stayed at Rock Castle, the boys enjoyed the use of Smith's library, which was reputed to be one of the best in the West.[17]

In 1812 war broke out between the United States and Great Britain. First as major general of the Tennessee state militia, then in the regular U.S. Army, Jackson led his forces initially against the Creek Indians, and then against the British. For his toughness, his men bestowed on him an admiring nickname, "Old Hickory." On January 8, 1815, at New Orleans, Jackson's backwoodsmen routed a veteran British army, gaining the greatest victory of the war. Hard on the heels of the triumph, word came from across the Atlantic Ocean that a peace treaty had been signed in Ghent. To Americans, the two events became indelibly linked. Andrew Jackson was now more than just Old Hickory—he was now a national hero.[18]

When Old Hickory and his victorious army returned to Nashville, the city threw them a delirious welcome. The arrangements committee escorted Jackson to the courthouse. Lined up on the steps as a sort of honor guard, resplendent in their academic gowns, were the students of Cumberland College. Among them stood Daniel Donelson's older brother Andrew. Cumberland College functioned as both a finishing school for the young gentlemen of Tennessee and a preparatory school for those who might go on to a university. Virtually all records of Cumberland College have vanished; it is now unclear whether young Daniel attended before chronic financial problems forced the college to close in 1816. By then, however, thanks to the pull of his uncle, the Hero of New Orleans, Andrew had received an appointment to the United States Military Academy at West Point, New York.[19]

For whatever reason, attending a university was not for Daniel's oldest brother. Instead, following in the footsteps of both grandfathers, Jacky became a surveyor on an expedition led by W. Purnell Owen into the former Creek country of Alabama. There, he "was attacked by a desperate cough and high fevers . . . in the wilderness where medical aid could not be procured," Owen recounted, and died on February 22, 1817. "This was a shock," Jackson wrote Smith, "Prepare the mind of his tender mother for the shock, before you communicate it, & keep from her [the] knowledge, for the present, that he wanted for any thing in his illness." The manner in which Polly handled the news of Jacky's death provides a striking example of the distance that had grown between her and her sons. She left it to Smith and Jackson to break the news to Andrew, who had only just arrived at West Point, then waited nearly two weeks before writing herself. Even then, the tragedy merited one sentence in a short letter that was otherwise devoted to trivial family gossip: "You know [*sic*] doubt my dear Andrew have heard the fatal news of your Brother's death, that news which has and will be forever a source of regret to your Mother." This is the only known letter between Polly and any of her sons.[20]

Grandfather Smith was himself soon in rapid decline. In his letter to Andrew breaking the news about Jacky, he had noted that he was not well. By December 1817 Jackson wrote Andrew that Smith "is wasting away very fast." When Andrew wrote his grandfather in March 1818, Smith was too weak to answer and asked Daniel to reply. "Grandfather is in a very low state of health and considerably worse than when you left him," Daniel accordingly wrote his brother in his earliest known letter, "if there is not an alteration very shortly he cannot live much longer for he has become almost as a corpse. He scarcely eats anything worth mentioning." Smith lingered through the spring, dying on June 16, 1818. His death struck the grandson who had been named for him particularly hard. "He has gone from our sight but his memory lives," Daniel wrote Andrew, and attempting to keep his own spirits up, expressed that "it is my sincere wish that we may never be so delighted with the follies and vices of the world as not to pursue Grandfather[']s instructions and advice."[21]

At the time of Smith's death, Daniel reported to Andrew, "I still continue to go to school with Mr. Wright and am reading homer and blair[']s lectur[e]s. There is a probability that I will go to some college next session." Instead, he came under the tutelage of James Priestley, the president of Cumberland College before it closed and who continued afterward to instruct pupils at his home, Montebello, outside Nashville. Until that time, Daniel had not been impressed with the course of his education. "So for myself I can say that I have spent a great deal of my time to no purpose with different teachers that knew very little concerning languages," he complained to Andrew in January 1819. "And now I have commenced school with Dr. Priestley and am much pleased with him and his method [of] teaching but the fare is astonishing to a man that possesses as much wealth as he does, we have two meals a day, and our chief motto is hog meat and hominy and that has a very disagreeable smell." "Daniel is with Doctor Priestl[e]y," Jackson wrote Andrew in May, "progressing in his studies well—and is a boy of fine promise—" "I am very much pleased with Dr. Priestly," Daniel repeated that spring, "but it is a very lonesome place and the fare is extremely bad." Cumberland College reopened the next year, 1820, and perhaps Daniel resumed his formal schooling, but if so, it was a brief return. The college closed again in February 1821, following Priestley's death.[22]

Meanwhile, Andrew graduated from the military academy. An excellent student throughout, he completed the usual four-year curriculum in just three, ranked second in his class of 1820, and placed into the prestigious Corps of Engineers. Upon returning home, Brevet Second

Lieutenant Andrew Jackson Donelson must have been an impressive sight in his new blue uniform. No doubt he was an inspiration to Daniel, who was now nineteen. The two brothers were both described as being "of commanding and superb presence," but while Andrew had a ruddy complexion with dark eyes and hair, Daniel was different. "He was a man of fine personal appearance," recalled the historian W. W. Clayton, who may have known him personally, "tall and large, fair complexion, blue eyes and sandy hair."[23]

It seemed natural for Daniel to attend the military academy, too, and the expense was now a primary consideration. Jackson had suffered serious financial reversals resulting from the Panic of 1819. He had invested thousands of dollars in land speculation in Alabama and West Tennessee. Desperate to collect money from wherever he could obtain it, he brought suit on scores of people who owed him. When the Tennessee General Assembly proposed bills to stay the collection of debts and set up loan offices for the relief of debtors, Jackson opposed the move. He even joined with several other prominent neighbors in submitting a memorial to the legislature that the bills would create "an inequitable distinction between the *debtor* and *creditor*," which would be ruinous to the latter, including him.[24]

Consequently, West Point offered the great advantage of providing an education for free. "I wrote you sometime since, on the subject of obtaining a warrant for Daniel S Donelson to enter the Military Academy," Jackson explained to Secretary of War John C. Calhoun in December 1820, adding, "he is an orphan and without means of his own to finish his education. I wish him to finish his education at the Military Academy. He is fine material for a military man—large, portly, and a good constitution—"[25]

"The application in favor of DS. Donaldson to be a Cadet is on file," Calhoun assured Jackson, along the way misspelling the surname, as it so frequently would be, Donaldson, "and shall receive attention when the next appointments are made which will be in the next month." The decision was probably easy, considering the favorable legacy that Andrew had left at the military academy. "I enclose an appointment as Cadet for your nephew," an obviously pleased Calhoun informed Jackson in March, "who I hope will equal his brother in his standing at the institution."[26]

Daniel's appointment precipitated a flurry of preparations for departure, as the entrance examination would be administered in June. "I recd.

a warrent for Daniel," Jackson informed Andrew, then in New Orleans to report on fortifications in Louisiana, "he will leave here for west Point about the middle of april, If we can procure eastern funds for him." The funds were in some way acquired, and Daniel bade good-bye to the uncle and aunt at the Hermitage who had raised him. As a parting gift, his proud uncle presented him with "a handsome gold watch." Daniel would carry the watch for the rest of his life, and it would be handed down among his descendants.[27]

Daniel arrived in Washington, D.C., mid-May 1821, and stopped by the Department of War to pay his respects to the secretary of war. "Your Nephew passed through this place a few days since," Calhoun informed Jackson. "He spent but a part of a day, tho I was very urgent for him to remain here for several days, as he had ample time. He declined, as he had made an arrangement to meet a friend in Baltimore, which would not admit his making a farther delay." Calhoun was nevertheless pleased with Old Hickory's second Donelson nephew, noting, "His appearance and conversation make a very favorable impression, and I hope he will realize your fondest anticipations."[28]

The identity of the friend in Baltimore remains unknown, but afterward Daniel proceeded to West Point. The academy at that time was still a smallish, spartan affair with only a few buildings and about two hundred cadets, but it was already undergoing a major transformation under its redoubtable superintendent, Major Sylvanus Thayer. Daniel's brother, Andrew, had arrived at West Point four years earlier just in time to witness a lax superintendent, Captain Alden Partridge, replaced by the academically rigorous and militarily strict Thayer. By the time Daniel arrived, Thayer's system was working smoothly and efficiently. Each cadet was ranked in his class and his proficiency was graded in every category from mathematics to the drill field. Under Thayer, a cadet boasted, "the academy became a great school of military science," competing "with the best in the world."[29]

Upon arriving at West Point, Daniel faced taking the entrance examination. He could not have found it to be difficult. "Each cadet, previous to his being admitted a member of the Military Academy," read the Rules and Regulations, "must be able to read distinctly and pronounce correctly; to write a fair legible hand; and to perform with facility and accuracy the various operations of the ground rules of arithmetic, both simple and compound; of the rules of reduction of single and compound proportion, and also of vulgar and decimal fractions." To judge from his extant letters of this period, Daniel already wrote well, although like many people he never knew where to put an apostrophe. He frequently sprinkled his letters with Latin words and phrases. Curiously, throughout life he tended to add a superfluous "e" to words that end in "k" ("riske," "sicke"). More difficult than the examination was understanding how it applied to admission to the academy. This was another innovation that Thayer made after Andrew had been through the process. As Jackson attempted to explain to Andrew, "the regulations are so changed, that the Cadets stand an examination in June for admittance, and in January next when [or] if the[y] Pass the examination [in January] the[y] receive their commission as a Cadet back in June—" The consequence of failure was final: "if the student does not pass his examination in January, he is dismissed [from] the school and receives no pay—"[30]

Fortunately, Daniel passed the entrance examination and thus began his studies as a first-year "plebe" in what was formally called the Fourth Class. His academic load consisted of introductory courses in English grammar and composition, French, and mathematics that covered logarithms, algebra, plane geometry, ratios, and proportions. French was taught largely because the few extant textbooks on military science were written in that language. The cadets' day was full and rigidly controlled. Reveille woke them at dawn. Summers they drilled until breakfast. Classes began at eight o'clock in summer, nine in winter, until dinner at one, then resumed at two and continued until four, when afternoon drill was held, followed by supper. Lights were extinguished at nine.[31]

Daniel soon made friends among his fellow cadets. The upperclassmen would have known his brother before Andrew graduated. Among these was Nicholas P. Trist, a Virginian with good family connections (he would marry a granddaughter of Thomas Jefferson). Andrew wrote to Trist, asking him to look after his younger brother: "I trust you found in him an honest and sincere heart, and though somewhat rough and blount [*sic*] in his deportment, yet a sensibility enabling him to appreciate your attentions." As would plebe Donelson, some of these upperclassmen would find themselves fighting a fratricidal war forty years in the future. Joseph K. F.

Mansfield, who had been appointed from Connecticut, would be mortally wounded leading his corps at Antietam. Isaac R. Trimble of Kentucky would lose a leg at Gettysburg.[32]

In January 1822, at the end of his first term, Daniel passed his examinations and, according to Thayer's new regulations, he was formally admitted as a cadet in the United States Military Academy, effective the preceding July 1, 1821. Cadet Donelson now became subject to another of Thayer's regulations. Hitherto, many cadets had viewed the academy largely as a vehicle for receiving a first-rate, free education at government expense. They then resigned their new officers' commissions soon after graduation. Andrew Donelson, unenthusiastic about the limited career prospects in a peacetime army, had with Jackson's encouragement just submitted his own resignation, in order to attend law school at Transylvania University in Lexington, Kentucky. In an attempt to stop such attrition, Thayer instituted a regulation that cadets agree to serve at least five years in the army upon graduation. Following Daniel's formal admission to the academy, Thayer thereupon sent a letter to his guardian asking consent to the five-year commitment. Jackson readily agreed.[33]

Once he was settled at West Point, Cadet Donelson never wrote home often enough to satisfy his uncle. "I have not heard from Danl since I wrote you," Jackson wrote Andrew in April 1822, "but from his last letter [I] have full confidence that he will do well." Jackson believed that his wards merited encouragement, and that it should be a family effort. Therefore urging, "I wish you to write him often & encourage him to application, and a strict attention to the obedience of all legal, and usual orders in the ro[u]tine of di[s]cipline there—I shall do likewise—I have a great desire that his education should be complete." "I have recd a letter from Danl," wrote Jackson, finally able to tell Andrew that summer, "he is well. I intend in my answer to scold him a little" for not writing more often.[34]

In September Cadet Donelson advanced to the second year, or Third Class, which meant a slate almost entirely in mathematics: plane and spherical geometry, conic sections, and drawing. The only break from mathematics was a continuation of French. As late as October everything seemed to be proceeding smoothly. "I have wrote to Danl. and am gratified to learn that he is doing so well," Jackson assured Andrew.[35]

Then Daniel precipitated a crisis. In November he abruptly submitted his resignation from the military academy. After a round of examinations he was angered to be ranked only thirteenth in his class. To his uncle, he claimed that he knew the lessons better than some who had been ranked ahead of him and announced his decision to transfer to Yale College. Thayer, who by now was accustomed to handling disgruntled cadets, refused to accept the resignation until Jackson granted permission. Taken aback, Jackson thought that Daniel was acting precipitously but turned to Andrew for advice. "Daniel has become much dissatis[fied with] the military school," he wrote, "and has tendered his [resi]gnation," to which Jackson would not agree "untill I hear from you." Put on the spot, Andrew's careful reply emphasized practical considerations. An education at the military academy was free. Yale cost money. Obtaining these funds would require that Daniel sell land that had been left to him by their father. "If you are of the same opinion with myself," Andrew concluded, "Daniel can continue at W. Point until the receipt of such funds as will be suitable." Andrew hoped that the prospect of parting with their father's land would give Daniel pause.[36]

Jackson also consulted Daniel's grandmother, Sarah Michie Smith, and his stepfather, James Sanders. He then accordingly advised Daniel that the prevailing opinion among the family was that his place was at West Point, but if he remained determined to resign his commission then funds could be arranged for his return home—as opposed, tacitly, to an immediate transfer to Yale. If, thereafter, Daniel still insisted on Yale, then Jackson would do everything that he could to provide funds, short of selling Samuel Donelson's lands. The impasse continued into the early months of 1823. Daniel still wanted to resign but beneath his family's superficial support he could not fail to see the underlying opposition. Jackson asked Andrew to write Daniel directly and say that "if he is still dis[s]atisfied at the m. academy tell him from me, that he shall be supported at Yale college . . . still I would be gratified if he could remain contentedly at the M academy. I believe it the best school in the world, but without [feeling] he is contented there . . . he cannot improve his mind."[37]

To the relief of the whole family, Daniel decided to remain at West Point, although not without occasional grumbling. After the summer examinations, he remained in thirteenth place, with the top twelve getting all the honors. Thayer attempted to ease the humiliation by describing Donelson's class "as decidedly superior to any other ever admitted into this Institution." Eventually, Daniel admitted to his uncle, "I have considered the subject well and do acknowledge that I was much to blame," regarding his hasty resignation.[38]

Daniel still did not write often enough to satisfy family members, who gathered information as best they could. "If you can spare the time I should be thankful for a letter from you," Andrew wrote Thayer directly in July 1823, "—telling me . . . what is the standing & progress of my Brother—He is the only Brother I have, and I feel a deep interest in his welfare—" In September 1823 Daniel advanced to the Second Class, which was considered to be the most difficult academically, with a focus on the physical sciences, engineering, and military drawing. The last course was a practical one, designed to teach army officers how to use surveying instruments and draw maps, fortifications, and topographical plans. Try as he might, however, Daniel showed no artistic talent, grousing that "application in my opinion has but little to do in that science." That summer he was able to report to his uncle that he had passed his June examinations, although he did not yet know his consequent standing in his class. "I think however it will be much the same as it was last year," he sighed, "as that science *drawing* still continues to be a plague to me."[39]

Daniel was not so absorbed in his studies as to be unaware of family and political events back home in Tennessee. Andrew completed his legal studies at Transylvania University in the spring of 1823, returned home to the Hermitage, and opened a law practice in Nashville. More spectacularly, their uncle Andrew Jackson was thrust into state, and then quickly national politics. A group of Tennessee politicians headed by John Overton, one-time roommate of Jackson at the Widow Donelson's blockhouse, John H. Eaton, one of the U.S. senators from Tennessee, and William B. Lewis, a wealthy neighbor near the Hermitage, arranged for the Tennessee General Assembly to nominate Jackson for the office of president of the United States in the upcoming presidential election of 1824. The General Assembly not only did so, but also elected Jackson to fill Tennessee's other Senate seat. Jackson's presidential nomination was intended to be only a tactic as part of a power play by the Overton-Eaton-Lewis faction in state politics, but to their surprise it precipitated a popular bandwagon for Old Hickory across the South and West and as far north and east as Pennsylvania. Almost overnight, the Hero of New Orleans was a leading contender for the presidency of the United States.[40]

Amid these breathtaking events on the national stage, Cadet Donelson quietly trudged through his time at West Point, indeed essentially without surviving records, and largely isolated from family and political events. In September 1824, his brother Andrew married a cousin, Emily, daughter of their late father's brother, Captain John Donelson. Later that fall, the young couple accompanied their uncle Andrew and aunt Rachel Jackson to Washington, where Senator Jackson would attend the session of Congress. Andrew worked as his uncle's secretary while Emily served as the social arm of her pious, reclusive aunt Rachel. While the Jacksons and Donelsons were in Washington, the presidential election was held. Old Hickory won a plurality in both the popular and electoral votes in a four-way race but because no candidate won a majority, the election was decided by the House of Representatives, which chose runner-up John Quincy Adams. The country as a whole was surprised and Jacksonians were shocked. Then, President-elect Adams selected as his secretary of state Speaker of the House Henry Clay, who seemed to have played an almost suspiciously influential role in how the House had voted. Outraged, Jacksonians thundered about a "corrupt bargain." Almost as soon as the Jacksons and Donelsons departed Washington for home, after Congress adjourned and Adams was inaugurated president, Old Hickory's followers began to prepare for the election of 1828.[41]

"The science of War and Fortification," as Andrew had described the subject that dominated the fourth year, or First Class, culminated in a cadet learning the essentials of military leadership and engineering—gunnery, how to attack and defend a fortified position, and how to build batteries, redoubts, fortified lines, field works, forts, and bridges, including calculations of the amount of time, labor, and material that would be needed for their construction. Whatever had led earlier to his being ranked only thirteenth in his class, Daniel apparently excelled in these courses of practical military application. The final examinations were held in June. When he was graduated, on July 1, 1825, he had risen to rank a very respectable fifth in a class of thirty-seven. He received his commission in the U.S. Army as brevet second lieutenant, and was assigned to the Third Artillery Regiment. Unlike his brother, Daniel had not ranked high enough to obtain a commission in the elite Corps of Engineers, but the artillery was regarded as ranking second in prestige.[42]

Others in Daniel Donelson's graduating class would gain future distinction in the army and other fields. The cadet who was graduated first in the class, Alexander Dallas Bache of Pennsylvania, a great-grandson of Benjamin Franklin, would appropriately carve a distinguished career for himself as a physicist and chemist, and become the first president of the National Academy of Sciences. Others would eventually find themselves fighting in the same war as would Donelson. Robert Anderson of Kentucky, who graduated fifteenth in the class, would suffer the indignity of surrendering Fort Sumter at Charleston harbor. Charles F. Smith of Pennsylvania, nineteenth, would play a major role in capturing the fort on the Cumberland River in Tennessee that would be named in honor of his classmate Donelson.[43]

Still others among the lower classes, whom Cadet Donelson as an upperclassman would have known before his graduation, would also cross his future military career. Albert Sidney Johnston of Louisiana, class of 1826, one year behind Donelson, would command all Confederate forces in the West until he was mortally wounded in 1862 at Shiloh. Leonidas Polk of North Carolina, class of 1827, two years behind Donelson, would command the corps in which Donelson became a brigade commander. Jefferson Davis of Mississippi, class of 1828, who was a plebe when Donelson was a First Classman, would become president of the Confederate States.[44]

By any measure, and despite the occasional difficulty, Daniel Donelson had done well for himself and had every right to take pride in his accomplishments at West Point. Time would show that the United States Military Academy had given him a splendid education and excellent training in his life ahead, both military and civilian.

CHAPTER TWO

"I Would Sooner See Revolution"

AUGUST 1825–MARCH 1833

Upon his graduation from the United States Military Academy, a new officer received a furlough of two months before being ordered to his first assignment. Brevet Second Lieutenant Daniel Smith Donelson thus returned home to the family he had not seen in four years. Unhappily, a feud erupted immediately, pitting the Donelson brothers against their stepfather, James Sanders.

When Samuel Donelson died, he still owned the 600-acre tract in Davidson County, where older brother Andrew had been born, in addition to the 1280-acre tract in Sumner County that had been a wedding gift to Samuel and Polly from her father Daniel Smith, and where younger brother Daniel had been born. As executor of the estate, Andrew Jackson was loath to part with the land and had cleared Samuel's debts chiefly by selling Samuel's slaves. Through the years, Sanders retained possession of the Sumner tract on the grounds that no deed had been transferred between Smith and Samuel. In a family agreement after the death of his oldest brother, John Samuel ("Jacky"), in 1817, Daniel signed over his share of the Davidson tract to his remaining brother, Andrew, in exchange for one-half (640 acres) of the Sumner tract. Smith accordingly wrote his will on the assumption that Andrew would be the sole inheritor of the Davidson tract, and thus Daniel became the chief beneficiary of Smith's estate. Smith's will provided that the Sumner tract be held in trust by James and Polly Sanders until Daniel reached twenty-one.[1]

On his return home from West Point, now age twenty-four, Daniel, with Andrew, applied to Sanders and their mother to convey the Sumner tract to him. At first, they agreed, but when Andrew and Daniel presented them with the paperwork, Sanders refused to sign. He asserted that "there was no obligation upon him to convey," and that he had a life estate on the property and the mill that had been constructed on it. Sanders claimed that Daniel's absence at West Point on his twenty-first birthday abrogated Daniel's right to the property and entitled Sanders to a life estate.[2]

Andrew and Daniel were outraged, and an argument ensued. Sanders even insisted that the brothers hand over the whole Sumner tract to him as a life estate; they would get it back after he died. Most galling was his insistence that the transfer be regarded, as Andrew put it, "as a gratuitous favor extended to us, *not* as an acknowledgement of any *separate right* of ours." Polly was in a quandary. She believed that Daniel was entitled to the property, but she would not oppose her husband. Andrew, who was now a lawyer but still young, emotional, and personally involved, drafted a scathing missive to Sanders: "Little did I ever think that the absence of my Brother would be attempted to be wielded against him, or made the cause of his disinheritance. . . . My father built the mill, cleared the land, planted the orchard, put up the dwelling house, leased part of the premises, and died—is this a title *for you,* and are his orphan children to be driven to the Parish?" Obviously, two well-educated young men from the cream of Cumberland society were hardly being thrown onto the charity of the public, but the wrath in the letter shows that while they were growing up at the Hermitage, the Donelson boys had picked up some of Old Hickory's temper.[3]

Sanders was unmoved. He was happy, he told Andrew, "to leave our matters of dispute to Judges of Law." The brothers were suspicious of Sanders's smugness and doubted their ability to obtain a fair judgment in Sumner County, where he was an influential citizen. Instead, they suggested that he choose one, and they choose one, from a list of five judges. "We will not leave the case to County Court Lawyers," Andrew insisted.[4]

Sanders adopted the tactics of delay. He knew that Daniel had received his orders from the army. Something, Andrew insisted, "should be done before Danl is compelled to leave here." Feeling "much regret," or so they said, the brothers were "compelled" to resort to legal counsel, "believing it was our last alternative—" They received some respite when Daniel succeeded in having his furlough extended to January 1826.[5]

Sanders began to falter. He told John C. McLemore, Andrew's brother-in-law (McLemore had married a sister of Andrew's wife, Emily) that he was willing to submit the matter to a disinterested party. McLemore hurried to tell this to Andrew, who renewed his offer to Sanders that they agree on two judges and a third as referee should the first two disagree. Sanders made one last show of asserting his due. He still insisted on "Reserving to me a Life Estate in the mill" that had been built on the property. Assisted by a young attorney, Ephraim H. Foster (a future senator), the Donelson brothers and Sanders agreed on two Nashville judges as arbitrators, who without further deliberation awarded the Sumner County tract to Daniel.[6]

Happily, the family estrangement did not extend to the four Sanders half-sisters. As they grew up and took husbands, Andrew and Daniel became close friends and associates of their brothers-in-law: Robert Looney Caruthers, a rising jurist, married Sally Sanders in 1827; Dr. Thomas G. Watson married Martha in 1829; Dr. James W. Hoggatt married Mary Ann in 1831; and Meredith P. Gentry, a rising lawyer, married Emily in 1838.[7]

A more immediate result of the dispute was Daniel's resignation of his army commission. The reasons, if there were any beyond the lengthy dispute with Sanders, are undocumented. Nor is it clear how he was able to escape the five-year service commitment that Superintendent Sylvanus Thayer required of West Point graduates. At any rate, he submitted his resignation and it was accepted, effective January 22, 1826. As a consequence, Daniel Donelson never served a day of active duty in the United States Army.[8]

Now out of the army, Donelson turned to developing the property that he had just acquired from the Sanders dispute, apparently living in the house that his father had built there and in which he had been born. He soon began construction on a home of his own. He located it about a mile north of Rock Castle and about a mile south of the Gallatin Pike through Hendersonville. More handsome and sturdy than elegant, the house was built of handmade brick reflecting Virginia Tidewater influence, standing one and one-half stories tall, two rooms wide and one room deep on each floor, with four bays on the façade and, typical of a Southern home, a detached kitchen. Donelson named his new house Eventide.[9]

The opportunity soon arose to acquire even more land, this time in Alabama, which saw the culmination of a forty-year-old story. In 1784, Georgia had appointed commissioners, among them Colonel John Donelson, to open to settlement the Big Bend of the Tennessee River in what became

Alabama, but a promised payment to each commissioner of 5,000 acres in the region was never granted. After the war of 1812, the surviving children of John Donelson appointed Jackson as their attorney to push Congress for the land that they asserted was theirs as the colonel's heirs. They were joined in their efforts by Thomas Carr, the last surviving commissioner, and the heirs of the others to obtain their due. After a mound of testimony and lengthy consideration, in 1818 a congressional committee recommended payment. Nevertheless, Congress continued with glacial slowness to consider the claims during subsequent sessions. As late as 1822, Jackson fumed to Andrew Donelson that he was still "waiting for the act of Congress if finally passed" so that he could go to Alabama to "enter your & Danls. Interest." Not until 1824 did Congress, with Jackson now pressing in the Senate, award the contracted land to the commissioners or their heirs. Part of John Donelson's 5,000 acres passed to Andrew and Daniel.[10]

The Donelsons were fortunate to have John Coffee on the spot to see to their interests. In the years after Samuel Donelson's death, Coffee had become Jackson's best friend, even part of his personal and military family. He had married one of Captain John Donelson's daughters and commanded Jackson's cavalry during the war of 1812. Coffee was surveyor general of federal lands in Alabama and could ensure that the Donelson claimants were allotted the best lands. Andrew Donelson accordingly requested in April 1826 that if Coffee took some of the forfeited sections and "if there be yet time to take the same course with regard to the claim of my Brother and self, I should be very glad if you could so arrange it as to have it done." When the allotted land became objects of dispute with rival claimants, the Donelson brothers announced their intent to fight in the courts if their claims were disputed. Andrew even offered Coffee to let "Daniel & myself" share with him "the expense of the prosecution, which we will cheerfully do." Within a year, however, whether because of the legal difficulties or financial necessity, Andrew and Daniel lost their original enthusiasm. "I have lately conversed with my brother respecting the claim to the land granted by congress & he is anxious, if it is worth anything, to sell it," Andrew informed Coffee.[11]

Daniel's attention turned elsewhere. Resignation of his commission from the army by no means meant the end of his military career. He soon entered that obligatory society of Southern and Western gentlemen, the state militia. He rose quickly and in 1827 was commissioned as a brigade major in the Tennessee state militia, pulling even with his brother. Andrew, however, was so involved in their Uncle Jackson's political career that he would never make the effort to rise higher in rank and thus he would remain Major Donelson the rest of his life. Daniel would soon rise higher. Within a year he was promoted to the rank of colonel and appointed assistant adjutant general on the staff of Major General John W. Simpson of the Second Division of the Tennessee state militia.[12]

By now the Jackson campaign for the presidential election of 1828 was in full swing. The Donelson brothers were usual members of their uncle's "suite" at various dinners and tributes for the general that his supporters frequently held. Among Jackson's opponents, however, the campaign quickly became dirtier than any that were ever waged before. Old Hickory's controversial and often bloody career provided a large target for mudslinging. To answer such charges, Jackson's campaign managers needed all the help that they could get, even at the mundane level of messengers and intermediaries. Daniel Donelson was happy to assist as he was able. When Nathaniel W. Williams, a Tennessee circuit court judge, published correspondence insinuating Jackson's role in the Aaron Burr conspiracy, Jackson had Daniel carry his objection to Williams's home in Sparta and bring back the judge's reply. Inevitably, accusations arose about Jackson's marriage to Rachel. Not even accusations of treason or murder wounded and infuriated Jackson more than these attacks upon Rachel's "Sacred Name." His campaign managers scoured the countryside for surviving family and friends who could vouch for Rachel's character and the legality of her marriage to Jackson. Daniel took a statement from Grandmother Sarah Smith, who recollected that Lewis "Roberts" was "a man of irregular habits, and much given to jealous suspicions." But as for Rachel, Sarah had "never been acquainted with a lady more exemplary in her deportment, or one to whom a greater share of the respect and regard of friends and acquaintances can be awarded."[13]

Daniel was more directly associated in a campaign dispute involving a cousin, Samuel Jackson Hays. "Sam," as Daniel addressed him, was at risk of "the rascal" William Gibbes Hunt, editor of the *National Banner and Nashville Whig*, presenting a "piece" that Sam had written to William Preston Anderson, an enemy of Jackson's. As Daniel cautioned him, "By no means suffer yourself to be in the wrong."[14]

The election results confirmed that Jackson won a smashing victory. Everyone in the family exulted, except Rachel. Over the years, her health had deteriorated as she grew obese and retreated into a pious solitude. Crushed by the revelation of the slanders that had been cast against her, Rachel's overburdened heart failed. On December 22, 1828, she found the peace that she had sought for so long. Thousands converged on the Hermitage for her afternoon funeral on Christmas Eve. His iron will almost broken by the death of his beloved, Jackson leaned on the ever-faithful John Coffee. A cloud of grieving Donelson relatives attended. Daniel was surely among them, as he would not have missed bidding farewell to the kind-hearted woman who had taken in her brother's boys and in many ways had been a better mother to them than their own.[15]

His heart heavy with grief, Jackson departed in January 1829 for Washington, where he was inaugurated on March 4 as the seventh president of the United States. Accompanying him were Andrew Donelson, who would serve as his uncle's presidential secretary, and Andrew's wife, Emily, who would serve as hostess of the President's House. As did other family members and friends, Daniel kept the family in Washington informed of events at home. Very soon, there was sensational news to report.[16]

Daniel Donelson had known Sam Houston since the years after the war, when Houston was a young officer on Jackson's staff at the Hermitage. Under Old Hickory's mentorship Houston had risen high. In 1823, he was elected to Congress, and in 1827 as governor of Tennessee. In January 1829, he married Eliza Allen, daughter of a Sumner County planter, seemingly another step up the ladder of success. His fall was swift and spectacular. Within three months, he returned his bride to her father, resigned the governorship, and left the state to take refuge among the Cherokees in Arkansas Territory. Everyone in Tennessee had a pet theory as to what had happened. The most commonly held rumor was that Eliza was in love with another man but had been pressured by her socially ambitious family to marry the rising governor instead. When Eliza finally confessed, Houston reacted more with indignation than jealousy. Given the local prominence of the Allen family, Houston's political rivals in Sumner County gleefully exploited the crisis.[17]

Daniel Donelson thought that he knew the truth. Most people believed Houston to be deranged "upon the subject of jealousy—" he wrote his brother, using his bad West Point French, "but Andrew (enter nos) I cannot believe in *derangement*." Daniel came to this "unbelief" from some conversations that Houston had with him "soon after he was married, say three weeks—I mean the revolution of Texas." According to Daniel, Houston believed that he possessed the means and popularity to carry out this "grand scheme" and, by confiding in Daniel, his "object evidently was to get me to join him, but he dared not name it. From this time forward I lost all confidence in him and believed him then as I do now a *scoundrel;* that he married Miss Allen to leave her, in order to have a justification for his leaving the U. States." The marriage was thus another of Houston's shams, Daniel believed, a cruel but necessary step in his reach for glory. "I cannot believe in derangement," he concluded. "I may be mistaken; may I be?" Daniel was surely mistaken, but Houston's subsequent career was, nonetheless, a remarkable coincidence.[18]

Sam Houston's star may have set, but Daniel Donelson's was rising. In the summer of 1829, Congressman Robert Desha resigned as brigadier general of the Fourth Brigade of the Tennessee state militia that was constituted for Sumner, Smith, and Williamson counties. Donelson announced his candidacy to succeed Desha, as did the rising young Gallatin attorney Josephus Conn Guild, who was colonel of the Sumner County militia regiment. "I am electione[e]ring hard for Donalson," Gallatin barber David Twopence assured President Jackson, adding, "although I am Not allow'd a vote in that," as he was a free black man. When the election was held in December, Donelson was victorious. At the age of twenty-eight he now not only outranked his older brother in the state militia but had reached the top echelons of the social structure in Tennessee.[19]

Donelson took his duties seriously, even the paperwork. What little survives concerns personnel records, such as reporting elections of subordinates to the Tennessee secretary of state and requests to issue their commissions. He took pleasure in writing letters of recommendation, such as for "my young Friend" Reuben P. Pryor of Nashville for an appointment to the United States Military Academy at West Point. He exercised his prerogative to appoint friends and family to the brigade staff, for example Balie Peyton, a rising young Gallatin attorney, as aide-de-camp, and as quartermaster Thomas S. Watson, whose farm adjoined Donelson's Eventide and who was the father of his brother-in-law Dr. Thomas G. Watson.[20]

Donelson was unable to travel to Washington until the Jackson presidency was nearly a year old. He finally arrived for an extended visit in

February 1830, staying, of course, at the President's House with his old guardian, brother, and sister-in-law. He reveled in being at the center of government. For the first week or so, as he wrote a friend, he was "a constant attendant at both houses of congress," but then something else captured his attention. Her name was Margaret Branch, daughter of Secretary of the Navy John Branch.[21]

A wealthy planter from Enfield, in Halifax County, North Carolina, John Branch had served first as governor of and then senator from his state. He and his wife, Eliza (or Elizabeth) Foort (or Fort) Branch, were the parents of nine children. Margaret was born August 4, 1811, making her only eighteen when she was introduced to Daniel Donelson. The early Tennessee historian W. W. Clayton, who apparently knew her, described her as being "of fine personal appearance, of polished manners, of accomplished education . . . and a devout Christian." Daniel was smitten. Unfortunately, by falling in love with Margaret Branch, he risked becoming entangled in a bitter social and political feud that was raging in Washington parlors and offices and which threatened to tear apart Jackson's administration and family.[22]

The problem began with another Margaret—Margaret O'Neale Timberlake Eaton, the new wife of Secretary of War John H. Eaton, one of Jackson's longtime friends and political cronies. The daughter of a Washington boardinghouse keeper, Margaret was pretty, vivacious, and forward. She never had developed the demure reserve of "ladies," even after her marriage to John B. Timberlake, a navy purser. Timberlake was often away at sea, and soon Washington gossip was rife with Margaret's alleged affairs, including with Eaton, a widower. In 1828 Timberlake died aboard the U.S.S. *Constitution,* rumored a suicide upon hearing of his wife's infidelities. Then, with discomfiting rapidity, Eaton married Margaret. The ladies of Washington were shocked. A tavern keeper's daughter with a bad reputation was now the wife of one of the highest officials in the government! The new Mrs. Eaton, they decided, would not be allowed into the genteel society of the capital.[23]

Regrettably for the new president, the new hostess of the President's House, Emily Donelson, joined ranks with the ladies who refused to socialize with the new Mrs. Eaton. Emily's decision, as she herself recognized, became "a great source of mortification to our dear Old Uncle." Mortification turned into anger and righteous indignation. As the social scandal mounted, coming to be known by such names as the Eaton affair and the petticoat war, Old Hickory's chivalrous instincts rose to defend Margaret Eaton. She became in Jackson's mind, infused as it was with memories of his sacred Rachel, the innocent victim of groundless slander. The presidential family fractured. Jackson insisted that Emily, as hostess of the President's House, socialize with Mrs. Eaton. Emily stood on her principles and resisted her imperious uncle. Andrew Donelson decided that his duty was to his wife, thereby becoming yet another target of his uncle's wrath and sense of betrayal.[24]

Worse, what began as a social scandal soon entered the political arena. The question of who would succeed Jackson as president was already gathering importance. The heir-presumptive was Vice President John C. Calhoun, but Jackson's secretary of state, Martin Van Buren, also harbored presidential ambitions. From years of running a New York political machine, Van Buren had acquired a reputation of being cunning, opportunistic, and duplicitous. The cabinet split in ways that reflected not only social views about the Eatons but political leanings as well. The wives of Secretary of the Treasury Samuel D. Ingham, Attorney General John M. Berrien, and Secretary of the Navy John Branch were among those who refused to socialize with Mrs. Eaton. Their husbands were friends and associates of Calhoun. By contrast, Van Buren enjoyed the advantage, under the circumstances, of being a widower and thus had no wife to dictate his social network. Quickly assessing the prospects before him, he ostentatiously aligned with the Eatons. This pleased Jackson and Van Buren's star began to rise in Old Hickory's estimation.[25]

Jackson and Calhoun were drifting away from each other on other grounds. The rift began with the high "Tariff of Abominations" of 1828, which arose from Henry Clay's ambitious American System to foster American industry and pay for an expensive list of government-financed projects. In protest, Calhoun asserted as a constitutional right that an individual state might, to protect its own vital interests, declare a federal law to be "null and void." Jackson was no political philosopher, but his ample common sense told him that if a state could nullify any law that displeased it, then the federal government would soon be unable to enforce its own authority.[26]

Such was the potentially treacherous state of social and political affairs when Daniel Donelson fell in love with the daughter of a cabinet member with whom the president was increasingly at odds. To be sure, the budding romance between Daniel and Margaret Branch was never at risk of suffering from the petticoat war. Jackson's bellicosity and tendency to see conspiracies were only part of his complex personality and often masked his sentimentality and love for his family. For example, however strained their relations became over the Eaton affair, the bonds between Jackson and Andrew and Emily Donelson held. Similarly, Jackson was an inveterate matchmaker. He delighted in seeing young couples in love and gave them every blessing and assistance—as in his role in the elopement of Samuel Donelson and Polly Smith all those years ago. At any rate, Daniel soon reached an understanding with Margaret and her parents, who had no reason to object to an engagement between their daughter and this tall militia general from one of the leading families of Tennessee.

Daniel departed for home at the end of April. Jackson gave him $100 to help with travel expenses. After Daniel arrived home, the courtship continued through letters that were exchanged through a proper intermediary—in this case Mary Ann Eastin, a niece of Emily Donelson's who was living at the President's House to assist Emily in her duties. Daniel soon received a letter from Mary quoting Margaret, who longed to "have it from his own sweet lips" his expressions of love and devotion. John C. McLemore thereupon urged Daniel to "start forthwith for Washington." Until then, Daniel could only thank Mary for her intermediary role with Margaret, "whom I love most affectionately." He enclosed a letter to "Margaret herself. You can judge its contents," he told Mary, who exercised the prerogative on how to handle it, "treating wholly upon our destined union."[27]

As long as Daniel's connection with the Branches remained purely personal, there was little to fear. If, however, he became involved in the wider political difficulties, then there was potential for a serious rift with his uncle. And he quickly got a lesson in the boundaries of the petticoat war. Despite its dominance of Washington society, neither Jackson nor anyone else who was involved wished the knowledge of the affair to spread. While he was in Washington, Daniel saw and heard much. On returning home he told his cousin Samuel Jackson Hays, evidently in confidence, that Eaton was so angered over Emily's treatment of his wife that "it was with some difficulty" that Jackson "prevented Major Eaton from making it a serious matter with Andrew," which was language that implied Eaton might challenge Andrew to a duel. Hays divulged this information to Emily's brother Stockley Donelson, who then told his and Emily's mother, which upset her greatly. When the story got back to Washington, Old Hickory was furious. Strangely, he singled out the middleman Hays, not Daniel or Stockley, to receive the lecture: "My D[ea]r Saml, you ought to have had more prudence than to communicate any thing that would have given any pain to that amiable old lady—"[28]

Nevertheless, the difficulties between Jackson and Andrew and Emily Donelson were soon an open secret among family and friends. Worse, when they all returned home on vacation in July 1830, the petticoat war relocated to Tennessee. Jackson's faithful old friend, honest and steady John Coffee, and John C. McLemore, both of whom were also Andrew and Emily Donelson's brothers-in-law, attempted gamely but unsuccessfully to mediate. Daniel Donelson quickly took the opportunity to escape. On August 10, he departed for Washington to make wedding plans. As evidence of how Daniel's romance with Margaret remained immune from the president's difficulties with her father, Jackson wrote ahead instructing that the White House be made available for Daniel to stay there. He nevertheless gave Emily an ultimatum: either socialize with Margaret Eaton in Washington or remain in Tennessee. When Andrew accompanied his uncle on their return to Washington in September to resume his secretarial duties, Emily proudly remained at her mother's home.[29]

By the time when the presidential party reached the White House, Daniel had been there several weeks. He and Margaret and her family had by then agreed on a wedding date. A pleased Jackson thus announced on the last day of September, *"Genl Daniel Donelson is to marry Miss Branch this day fortnight."* Margaret was more specific with regard to the date but remained demurely ladylike in naming the event and her fiancé. "Mr. Donelson" and she "have appointed the 14th of October for the day of our———" Jackson gave Daniel $300 on October 9, either as a wedding gift, to help with expenses, or both. Despite these plans, the wedding ultimately took place on October 19, 1830, having been, as Jackson explained, "pos[t]poned by the Sickness & death of her unkle Mr. Southall—" The good news reached home in early November, when the *National Banner and Nashville Whig* announced: "MARRIED—At Washington, on the 18th [*sic*] ult. Gen. Daniel S. Donelson of Tennessee to Miss Margaret Branch, daughter of the Hon. John Branch, Secretary of the Navy." Meanwhile, on the morning after the wedding, the couple left on a honeymoon trip to New York.[30]

When Daniel and Margaret returned to Washington in early November, they stayed at the White House. With the newlywed couple there, Jackson and Andrew put on their best faces, but in reality, they were by now hardly speaking to each other. Andrew was lonely for his wife and young children and resentful of their exile in Tennessee. Old Hickory was irascible and self-righteous over what he considered to be Andrew's and Emily's disloyalty. No doubt the newlyweds felt the tensions, but neither were they in any hurry to leave. In part, they wanted to make the most of the social season, in what Margaret called the *"Big City."* At the end of November, she wrote Mary Eastin, whom she now felt comfortable addressing as "my dear *cousin*," that they had enjoyed "a great deal of gayety for the last four week[s] partys almost every night." And partly because Margaret was hesitant about "being seperated [sic] from my dear Father & Mother but when I think of you and my [new] sister[-in-law] Emily and all my new relations I become quite reconciled to the seperation."[31]

The newlyweds initially planned to start for Tennessee in early December, because "Mr. Donelson," as Margaret continued to refer formally to her husband, "is getting anxious to get home." For whatever reason, they did not depart until December 20. The timing strikes as being curiously bad. Had they departed when Daniel originally wished, then they would have arrived in time to celebrate Christmas in their new home. Conversely, had they remained in Washington only a few more days, then they could have enjoyed the holidays in comfort among their new, blended family. As it was, they committed themselves to spending their first Christmas on the road somewhere. They traveled first by private carriage to Wheeling, then by steamboat down the Ohio River and up the Cumberland River. Daniel carried with him a dress that was a present from the Washington family for Mary Eastin, "some *hickory nutts*" from Old Hickory to Andrew Jackson Jr., with directions to plant them around Rachel Jackson's tomb, and a letter from Andrew to Emily expressing both his loneliness for his family as well as determination in not allowing the Eatons to dictate their social relations. For her part, Margaret had written Mary that "I have not the least doubt but that I will be pleased with my new home."[32]

Daniel and Margaret settled happily into married life in Tennessee. He soon bought her a "pleasure carriage." Meanwhile, in Washington, the petticoat war continued but was gradually subsumed by the truly more serious nullification controversy. By now President Jackson had cut his last ties with Vice President Calhoun, who was not only the leader of the nullifiers but, Jackson believed, also headed the faction that refused to socialize with Margaret Eaton. Jackson included in this group Andrew and Emily, and Daniel's new in-laws, the Branches. Meanwhile, as Martin Van Buren rose in Jackson's estimation, enemies accused him of manipulating both crises to his advantage. If this is so, then by the spring of 1831 he had concluded that his new position as Jackson's successor was secure. To ensure that he was not destroyed by any backlash, Van Buren had to end the petticoat war. In April 1831, he resigned as secretary of state and convinced Eaton to resign as secretary of war. Their resignations gave Jackson the pretext that he needed to demand the resignations of Secretary of the Treasury Ingham, Attorney General Berrien, and Secretary of the Navy Branch. Jackson's purge of his cabinet cut the Gordian knot of the Eaton affair by rendering moot the question of socializing with the Eatons, but bad feelings would soon fester.[33]

Given their new connection through Daniel and Margaret, the Donelson and Branch families had successfully managed to avoid entanglement in the petticoat war while it raged, only to have bitterness emerge in its aftermath. The troubles began earlier, with Daniel meddling in local Tennessee politics. In the fall of 1829, he had supported his Sumner County neighbor William Trousdale over Robert Desha in a congressional race. That in itself would not have displeased Jackson. As a young officer, Trousdale had fought in Old Hickory's Creek and New Orleans campaigns and was already viewed as a rising star in the Jackson camp. Besides, the president was inclined to suspicion and had already fingered Desha at the local level, as making "the first public movement under the conspiracy here [against Eaton] on the great political chess board." Moreover, the seed of a later difficulty was planted when Daniel spoke to Robert M. Burton, an ambitious young attorney. Burton was married to Martha Donelson, the daughter of William Donelson who was a brother of Rachel Jackson and Daniel's father, Samuel Donelson— which made Burton a cousin to Daniel by marriage. As Daniel later revealed to his brother-in-law Robert L. Caruthers, he confessed to Burton that he had "pursued an impolitic course in supporting Trousdale in preference to Desha," who could better reward his friends. A Trousdale supporter with political ambitions of his own, Burton leaked this information. Trouble consequently ensued between Burton and Desha, although Daniel Donelson again, for the time being, escaped trouble. Rather, what apparently bothered him was "the manner which this was said," giving Daniel the impression that Burton "had not acted in good faith to Maj Trousdale." Alas for Trousdale, perhaps because of such divided support, he lost the election to Desha.[34]

The next year, 1830, Burton announced his candidacy for Desha's seat in Congress. At a public meeting at the Sumner County courthouse in Gallatin in October, Burton and Desha got into an argument that progressed to fisticuffs. Burton drew his pistol but it misfired, whereupon he thrashed Desha with his cane. Desha was so publicly humiliated that in his stead his friends chose to run General William Hall, who had served as interim governor following Sam Houston's resignation.[35]

Trouble began for Daniel Donelson when word of Burton's candidacy reached the White House. Jackson was by now denouncing Desha privately as being "a strong Calhounite" whose "inveterate hostility" was being directed against himself and Eaton. Old Hickory was therefore pleased that Burton had challenged Desha, but when rumors began to circulate that the president had solicited Burton to run he was quick to deny them. At that time it was still important that the president of the United States be seen as rising above local political squabbles. A local solon, David Burford, undertook to ferret out the story for Jackson. Unfortunately, the source of the public rumor of Jackson's partisanship proved to be Daniel Donelson. As Daniel rather sheepishly explained to Burford, while he had been in Washington in the fall of 1830 for his wedding to Margaret, he showed his uncle a Gallatin newspaper recounting the "affray" between Desha and Burton. From Old Hickory's reaction, as Burford reported back to Jackson, Daniel "*infer[r]ed that you was in favour of Burton—*" Once he returned to Tennessee, Daniel let his inference get out that Jackson favored Burton.[36]

Rumors circulated, all with Daniel's role in these difficulties coming into question. Finally, Caruthers asked him for an explanation. "I know you too well to doubt the truth of anything you have or will state," he added supportively, "nor do I suppose that anyone will be found to question your veracity on the subject." Already facing public embarrassment over his actions thus far, Donelson compounded his indiscretion. That spring, Desha asked him to support Hall against Burton. Donelson obliged, even providing a certificate to Desha that revealed private matters that could be injurious to Burton. Suddenly it was a family affair. When word of Daniel's actions reached the White House, Old Hickory was aghast. As Jackson saw it, Daniel had betrayed family trust and solidarity. As he told Andrew, "be assured, *Daniel* will derive no credit from this thing." "I never knew any thing but disgrace to a family," he clucked, "where it united with strangers to disgrace its own kindred."[37]

As the bitter feelings from the aftermath of the Eaton affair festered, Jackson fumed that Daniel had played into the hands of his enemy Desha. "I . . . regret to see what a ridiculous situation my young friend placed himself," he sighed to the Reverend Hardy M. Cryer. He similarly moaned to Mary Eastin, "how I regret to see Daniel Donelson arrayed . . . against the husband of a favorite daughter of his deceased uncle." "If injury accrues to Burton it reflects upon himself as part of the family," he groused about Daniel to Coffee, "and have what effect on Burton it may, it will injure Daniel in the eyes of all honorable men." Connecting, as he saw it, his recent triumph in the Eaton affair with the difficulties that his Donelson relations were putting him through, Jackson brooded to Emily Donelson that "my enemies can do me no harm, unless thro a division of my Household, and 'a House divided against itself cannot stand.' When you see Danl. bring him in mind of this."[38]

Worse happened. "Genl. Daniel S. Donelson has stated [that] you desired him, Donelson, to support the election of Mr Burton in preferance to Genl. Hall," Burford reported to Jackson. Old Hickory was livid. "I never spoke with Daniel on such a subject," he insisted, also claiming that Daniel's statement "is positively untrue, but it is intended to rouse the hostility of Hall against me." People wondered why Daniel would so embarrass the president. Some concluded that he had been greatly angered by the cabinet purge, and took an opportunity for revenge. As Burford asked Jackson, "has the dismissal of his farther[*sic*]-in-law Branch changed his feelings towards you, and would he now be willing to injure you for the purpose of sustaining Mr. Branch?" Burford confronted Daniel, who not only stuck to his story but accused Burton of reading, or pretending to read, letters of support from Jackson in his campaign speeches. If Burton read any such letters aloud in his speeches, then they did him no good. When the election was held in August, Hall was the victor. Burton saw himself as being the victim of a family plot. "The whole Donelson con[n]exion of Davidson & Sumner [counties] did every thing they could against me," he complained to Jackson.[39]

In the aftermath, Burford became more convinced than ever of "the reason assigned by Gen. Donelson for making this stat[e]ment" about Old Hickory's partisanship: "the answer is too plain—" he explained to Jackson, "it must have been to injure you, it could injure no one else . . . and to favour the views of Mr Calhoun and his farther in law Govr. Branch. I know Sir, that Gen. Donelson is a relation of yours but believing as I do and many others that he has not acted the part of a friend, but on the contrary that his course . . . was calculated, and as I then and now think was intended to injure you—"[40]

Except for his February 1831 letter to Caruthers, which preceded the purge of his father-in-law from the cabinet, no explanation of his actions survives directly from Daniel Donelson. Everything else is reported second- or third-hand. It is therefore difficult to assess his motives. Caruthers chose to judge his brother-in-law charitably. "He is an honest man of the strictest veracity & no one who knows him would think of questioning any thing he would say, but like all other men is liable to mistake & err innocently." Old Hickory, nevertheless, felt that he had been ill-served by the sons of Samuel Donelson—Andrew in the Eaton affair, and Daniel in the quarrel between Burton and Desha. "The course taken by A. J. Donelson & Daniel have filled me with much & sincere regret," he pouted.[41]

Amid these difficulties, one last distraction occurred, and from a rare source. "Our mother," as Daniel put it to Andrew, appeared at Eventide one day in August. One of her daughters from her marriage to James Sanders had recently died as a young bride, and Polly suddenly had need of her well-educated sons. She handed Daniel the "information with regard to our sister Martha Watson," which he related to Andrew in a passage where, tellingly, he inserted "our" with a caret in front of "sister," whom he identified formally by her married surname. He shoved the assignment onto Andrew. "I wish you to write a short inscription of about 300 letters to be placed on her tombstone," he instructed without apology. "Do not forget this."[42]

Daniel's curt treatment of the incident perhaps resulted from a very different family distraction. He was about to become a father. On August 25, 1831, Daniel and Margaret Donelson's first child was born, a daughter, who was named Elizabeth Branch Donelson. Within the family she would be called Lizzie.[43]

Daniel Donelson's anger over the dismissal of his father-in-law from the cabinet flared again when the Eatons returned to Tennessee in October. Seeking redemption for what had happened to him and his wife in Washington, Eaton challenged Felix Grundy, an old Jackson stalwart, for his Senate seat. "I blush for my country," Daniel spat to Andrew about Eaton's actions, "when I take a retrospective view of the rise and progress of the *unpleasant affair*, and how wholly it is misunderstood by the Amer-[ican] people." Daniel made clear that his own preference was for Grundy. Many feared that the president "will use his influence in favor of Eaton," he clucked, "if so . . . I should regret such a step." In the end, Daniel could take satisfaction that Eaton's Senate challenge failed.[44]

The petticoat affair faded, but the nullification crisis festered. If nothing else, as with many of Jackson's supporters, especially among Southerners and Westerners, Daniel remained suspicious of Van Buren, whom Jackson wanted as his vice-presidential running mate when he ran for a second term in 1832. Daniel went so far as to attend one of the many meetings that were being held across the South in support of Philip P. Barbour of Virginia, a one-time Speaker of the U.S. House of Representatives, as an alternative to Van Buren. In every other significant issue, it should be emphasized that Daniel remained a solid supporter of his uncle Jackson's policies. A case in point was Jackson's landmark veto message of the bill to recharter the Second Bank of the United States. "The view taken by the President in that document meet[s] with my entire approbation," Daniel affirmed to Andrew, with whom he agreed that "it must and will add greatly to his popularity." While Daniel assured Andrew that "my vote [will] be recorded for him [for] President," his other vote would be not for Van Buren, but "Barbour [for] v. Pres." His uncle's landslide victory over Henry Clay, with Van Buren on the ticket, produced ambiguous feelings. "I am glad to see the overwhelming vote by which the General is elected," Daniel wrote Andrew, "but regret exceedingly the combination of circumstances that have caused V.B. to be the V. President."[45]

The nullification crisis soon approached its climax. In South Carolina, a state nullification convention passed an ordinance on November 24, declaring the tariffs of 1828 and 1832 to be null and void within the state, and specified that any attempt by the federal government to coerce the state would constitute just cause for secession from the Union. The legislature prepared to raise an army, purchase arms, and defend the state's borders. When Congress convened in December, the president's annual message was admirably restrained. A few days later, however, he issued his Proclamation on Nullification. A bold, vigorous statement, the proclamation breathed spirit and fire that was pure Jackson. "Disunion by armed force is *treason*," he asserted. Never in the short history of the republic had the Union been in as much danger as during the winter of 1832–1833. Fortunately, for the administration, the other states rallied to the Union. Many passed resolutions praising the president's proclamation. South Carolinians discovered that even their southern neighbors abhorred nullification if it put the Union in danger.[46]

As with everything involving Jackson, the nullification crisis had its personal side. Even the family split. Branch, who was still bitter, leaned toward the nullifiers. Daniel Donelson decided that he would stand by his father-in-law. "I do not approve of all the acts of the nullifiers of S. Carolina," he wrote Andrew while he was visiting Branch's home in Enfield, North Carolina, in February 1833, "but my feelings are wholly with them. . . . I would say nothing about the proclamation of the President, but for the ultra federal doctrines contained in it, which if acted out would make this [country] a great consolidated empire," against which "I would sooner see revolution itself." A few weeks later he reiterated his position. "I cannot disguise the fact to you that I go with Mr. Calhoun. I cannot say to the full extent as far as nullification is concerned because I have not been enabled to understand the practical application of it, but with him [goes] all my heart with regard to the rights of the States in contradistinction to those doctrines in the proclamation bearing the signature of the President." Daniel feared that in his uncle's determination to save the Union, Old Hickory would destroy the very things that the Union stood for.[47]

Not only was Daniel Donelson at odds with his uncle and brother over the nullification crisis, he proved to be so with the majority of his Sumner County neighbors. A public meeting in Gallatin in December 1832 heartily supported Old Hickory and the Nullification Proclamation and adopted resolutions asserting that South Carolina "has not the right to annul or void an act of Congress" and that no state "has the right nor can be permitted to dissolve its connections with the other states."[48]

Jackson offered a carrot in the form of a bill to reduce the tariff to such low rates that protectionists accused the president of surrendering to the nullifiers. A few days later, Old Hickory wielded the stick. He requested that Congress grant him the authority to use the military to collect federal revenue and suppress armed rebellion. The whole country held its breath. The last hope was that the nullifiers would yield to this "Force Bill" and accept the compromise tariff. South Carolina, realizing its isolation, backed down, and suspended the nullification ordinance. Old Hickory achieved the decisive victory. Having let Jackson do all the fighting, Henry Clay stepped forward to negotiate the peace. Clay's proposed tariff bill was not nearly as sweeping as Jackson's, but Calhoun, who preferred to surrender to Clay than to Jackson, accepted it. Two days before his second inauguration, Jackson signed both the Force Bill and Clay's tariff into law. The Union was saved.[49]

Daniel Donelson had been fortunate to escape the family repercussions of the petticoat war despite marrying the daughter of one of the men whom Jackson considered to be among the instigators of the plot against him, as he saw it. Rather, it was in the aftermath of the Eaton affair, by his own meddling in Tennessee politics, that he gained the ire of his imperious uncle. Ultimately, the nullification crisis demonstrated that Daniel, influenced by the fate his father-in-law had suffered, leaned farther south than either his uncle Jackson or his brother Andrew. The peaceful settlement of the nullification crisis meant that the issue was not further pressed within the family. If the sectional crisis would be renewed in the future, however, then it might be revealed just how far Daniel Donelson's views of the Union diverged from those of his uncle and brother.

CHAPTER THREE

"A Substantial Farmer of Old Sumner"

APRIL 1833–JANUARY 1850

Little is known of Daniel Donelson's farming endeavors during this period, aside from some minor purchases and sales of land. He was apparently making no money and growing restless. "I might live here where I am for years with a few working hands and maintain my own with difficulty," he groused to his brother, Andrew, in November 1833, adding, "this I have tried long enough and am now determined to seeke my fortune elsewhere." He then announced, "I have made an important move which will probably be disapproved of by you—I have sold my farm to Tho. S. Watson for $15 per Acre." Half of the amount was to be paid by Christmas 1834 with the remainder in annual installments.[1]

Until then, he and the family could remain at their home, Eventide, but Daniel planned to set out after the new year "to looke out for a country where I can make money by planting, if Florida should prove healthy I will probably go there, if not I shall expect to live in Mississippi 9 months in the year the remaining 3 in some healthy clime." His father-in-law, John Branch, along with several of Margaret's brothers, had recently bought a plantation near Tallahassee, Florida Territory. In an effort to ship and sell his crop that fall to earn money, Daniel had been "exerting every thing to the utmost to set out my cotton and send the Negroes I had in my possession to Florida—this I effected a week ago, and they are now upon the way—"[2]

Before the Donelsons could depart for Florida, a number of personal and professional details required attention. Daniel's cousin Henry (Harry) Smith, the son of his mother's brother, George Smith, "deeded" twenty-one slaves jointly to him and his cousin William Donelson "to secure them from financial responsibility," in settling the elder Smith's estate. In turn,

Daniel and William Donelson endorsed a note to Harry for $7,924.08. Daniel also resigned his commission as major general of the Fourth Brigade of the Tennessee state militia, and was pleased to see his brother-in-law Robert L. Caruthers elected as his successor. Daniel and Margaret were still at Eventide on August 14, 1834, when she gave birth to their second child, another daughter. She was named Mary Ann, perhaps in honor of Daniel's mother, however cool their relations otherwise were.[3]

The Donelsons departed for Florida on December 1, 1834. They had a "very unpleasant time of it," Daniel confessed to Caruthers. Rain fell for half the days of their trek, the roads were consequently muck, and accommodations along the way were so rare or terrible that they camped out six nights. Remarkably, nobody fell ill. Not until January 6, 1835, did they arrive at their destination. Donelson had rented a farm about two miles outside of Tallahassee that had a good dwelling house, outbuildings, and two hundred acres of cleared land, on which he planned to plant 130 acres of cotton. However unwittingly, he was attempting to make his own small contribution toward the expansion of slave country and cotton kingdom into the region that was coming to be called the Deep South.[4]

Things quickly turned bad. In March, before he had even planted his cotton, Donelson joked grimly to Caruthers, "there is no *danger* of my becoming *dangerously rich* soon," especially when local prices demanded one dollar for a bushel of corn. While the family lived on the rented farm, he purchased another five miles away that he considered to be "an excellent bargain," with the arrangements being made by his brother Andrew and a Colonel Williams in Washington. Daniel assured Andrew that the advance payment of $840 "shall be promptly made." He further wrote that if Williams had not already taken care of the payment, then "inform me and the amount shall be forwarded forthwith."[5]

By July, Daniel was moaning to Andrew, "this is the most sickly if not the most deadly country extant; I have seen more sickness for the last two months than I ever witnessed before during my whole life." He was discovering what so many pioneers during this period encountered as they left their old homes for new lands, where the climate was often far different from that to which they were accustomed. Given the medical understanding of the time, newcomers even expected a certain amount of sickness as they went through a period of acclimation to the native ailments of their new surroundings.[6]

What surprised Donelson was how brutally the Florida climate struck. His overseer arrived on June 15 but a week later "died of bilious fever, leaving a wife and 3 helpless children, all now and some[ ]time before his death sicke—" Being left "pretty much without an Overseer," Donelson commuted every day between his two farms. This left him "a good deal exposed to the hot sun," and consequently he felt "no surprise at my own sickness." What truly astonished him, however, was that his "black family," as he was often pleased to style them, suffered as severely as did his "white family." Of fourteen field hands, only three or four on any day were healthy enough to work. It was not supposed to be this way. Whites were expected to suffer under the harsh sun of the Deep South. Slaves, however, descended from those who had been imported from equatorial Africa, and were thought to be inured to such an oppressively hot and humid climate. For Southerners, this belief provided a major justification for slavery. If Donelson perceived this flaw in the system, then he made no mention of it. What worried him more immediately was that the costs from the Florida climate to both his white and black families were consuming his anticipated profits. "My expenses will therefore be heavy in the way of Doctor's bills, etc.," he complained.[7]

By midsummer, Daniel was already reconsidering his original decision to relocate in Florida. "I sometime[s] begin to think," he admitted to Andrew, "that if I were again in Ten. I should be content to remain there," adding that he "would greatly have prefer[r]ed it had I gone to Mississippi," where he would have been within "rideing distance of a healthy region," but he was not yet ready to give up. "Having however," he sighed, "left the land of our nativity in search of wealth I must riske something," although "this enterprise [is] perhaps too hazardous for one in my circumstances."[8]

"When I left Ten. I resolved in my own mind to have as little to do with the political world as possible," Daniel assured Andrew, but events had transpired in his absence. His move to Florida occurred simultaneously to the political struggles that gave rise to the Democratic and Whig parties. While President Andrew Jackson retained his overwhelming personal popularity, a portion of his initial supporters developed reservations over some of the major policies of his administration. The original clique led by John Overton, John H. Eaton, and William B. Lewis that had first pushed Jackson into politics now found itself in eclipse—partly because of

Eaton's resignation from the cabinet and Overton's death in April 1833, and partly because many of them had extensive interests in the Nashville branch of the Bank of the United States, as did much of the Nashville mercantile community. Conversely, supporters of Jackson's Bank War rose in the Old Hero's estimation. This group included old stalwarts such as Senator Felix Grundy along with younger men such as Congressman James K. Polk. Daniel's brother, Andrew, was naturally a member of this group.[9]

So far, the Eaton-Lewis faction in Tennessee by no means constituted an opposition party. They were still solid Jackson men, but merely chafed at their displacement by the Grundy-Polk faction. Their opportunity to re-establish their dominant status in the president's party came when they found a challenger to Polk, Jackson's hand-picked candidate, for the House of Representatives speakership when Congress convened in December 1833: Congressman John Bell, who represented Jackson's own congressional district in Tennessee. Delighted to exploit this rift among the Jacksonians, the Whigs and nullifiers in Congress threw their support to Bell, who was elected Speaker. The "regular" Jacksonians were shocked by the unexpected challenge, and denounced Bell as an apostate.[10]

Worse, there was a similar group of men throughout the South and Southwest who were also true Jackson men, aside from their inability to stomach Van Buren. As early as December 1833, Andrew Donelson sensed that these dissatisfied Jacksonians were thinking of running "a *no administration candidate*" for the presidency in 1836 in an attempt to displace Van Buren as Old Hickory's successor. They soon identified their candidate. The highly respected Senator Hugh Lawson White of Tennessee offered almost everything that anti-Van Buren Jacksonians sought. He opposed nullification and the Bank of the United States, and was overall "an unquestionably pure Jacksonian." By early 1834 newspapers in Tennessee and across the Southwest were pushing White as a presidential candidate. For John Bell, whose lunge at the Speaker's Chair left him politically isolated, joining the White movement offered him a new political base.[11]

The White movement took the Jacksonians by surprise. Further, they were mortified by the appeal of the White movement and how rapidly it spread. Worst, in the state and local elections in the summer and fall of 1834, the Whigs were so badly beaten in New York, New Jersey, and Pennsylvania that they realized the necessity of supporting, as John Tyler of

Virginia declared, a Southern man "who will unite the whole South, and thereby ensure to himself the support of all the anti-Van Buren states." Overnight, White became the candidate not only of anti-Van Buren Jacksonians, but also many Whigs and nullifiers. Daniel Donelson, whose father-in-law had been an apparent victim of Van Buren's machinations, was a classic example of a "pure" Jackson man who found White to be preferable to the New Yorker. "I feel deeply for the permanency of our free institutions," Donelson told Caruthers. "Van B. is the man to whom *you know* I allude, seeing then [that] this character universally attaches to him, would it not be best to select some individual equally Jacksonian, say Judge White, who is not so deeply involved in the New York Tactics, corrupt and corruption[?]"[12]

Daniel Donelson was not the only member of Jackson's family who found the White movement to be appealing. "I am informed," the president pouted to Mary Eastin Polk, that her new husband, Lucius J. Polk, a cousin of James K. Polk, no less, "has become one of the modern White Whiggs [*sic*]—say to him he is in bad company—" When Andrew Donelson criticized White for "manifestly surrendering to the malice of the opposition" in a letter to his and Daniel's brother-in-law Caruthers, who was a candidate for the General Assembly from Wilson County, he did so because Caruthers had given a speech suggesting support for White. The loyal Robert M. Burton similarly discerned that Caruthers "took up with Whiteism" and feared that it marked "the end of anything like Jacksonism" in him.[13]

Andrew Donelson became a central figure in the feud between the Jacksonians and the Bell-White faction when, in July 1835, Washington Barrow, editor of the Bell-White *Nashville Republican*, accused him as the president's secretary of abusing the president's franking privilege. The accusations were reprinted in White and Whig newspapers across the country, but Andrew discerned the real villain behind the controversy. "Bell is the great rascal," he spat to Polk. "He is the prompter of these vile attacks upon me."[14]

The controversy reached a point that a rumor made the rounds. Daniel Donelson heard it even in Tallahassee. Robert Butler, an old childhood friend who had also been a ward of Jackson's, told him that Andrew was about to come into "an unpleasant affair," which meant a duel. Daniel asked if it was to be with Bell. Butler replied, "no, Barrow." Butler told

Daniel that Andrew wished to keep the dispute with Barrow a secret from Jackson, "until it was settled upon the *field*." Andrew and Daniel might have found themselves on the opposite sides of nullification and the presidential succession, but their personal loyalty as brothers still trumped political differences. Angered over the rumored development, Daniel wrote Andrew opining that such a duel would be against the wrong person. "Bell," he asserted, "is the man who should be punished," while "Barrow is an Editor whose avocation it is to lie and misrepresent, therefore nothing can be gained from having an affair with him." However the story originated, no duel resulted.[15]

The results of the August 1835 state elections in Tennessee shocked the Jacksonians. Newton Cannon, the Bell-White candidate, was elected governor, as were nine candidates among the thirteen congressional districts. The Jacksonians regrouped, however, and when Congress convened in December they succeeded in electing Polk as Speaker.[16]

By this time Daniel had given up on his Florida enterprise. In October 1835 he informed Andrew, "I am making my arrangement to leave here for Mis. as soon as my crop is gathered[;] my white family will I expect set out next month for Ten.—the S. Carolina Negroes will go directly to Mis." The sickly Florida climate had defeated him, although what precisely precipitated his decision is not known. Margaret's unrecorded opinions were surely important, perhaps for the most tragic of reasons, even too painful to make their way into any of the surviving family correspondence. In July, Daniel had written Andrew that Margaret "and our youngest child" had been "sicke." When Daniel and Margaret finally departed Florida, they left behind them an infant whose name, birth, and even sex are unrecorded except for a gravestone in Bradford-Eppes Cemetery outside Tallahassee that reads simply, "UNKNOWN DONELSON."[17]

Donelson's letters suggest that he still had not decided whether to return his family permanently to Tennessee, move permanently to Mississippi, or split their time between the two locations. The return to Tennessee, at least temporarily, is not documented until June 1836, when Stockley Donelson, Emily's brother, mentioned in a letter to Andrew that "Cousin Daniel and Lady and family has [*sic*] arrived and will remain here the summer out." Their return was soon followed by one family blessing and two tragedies. Although a birth date has not been found in the surviving records, sometime during the year 1836 Margaret gave birth to their third daughter (not counting, perhaps, the "unknown Donelson" who had died in Florida). She was named Sarah Smith Donelson, apparently in honor of Daniel's maternal grandmother, Sarah Michie Smith, who had died five years earlier.[18]

James Sanders, the stepfather whom Andrew and Daniel so detested, died on August 24, 1836. Daniel, who was by then back at Eventide and thus nearby, saw to the needs of their mother, Mary (Polly) Smith Donelson Sanders, who at age fifty-five became a widow for the second time. Andrew Jackson and Andrew and Emily Donelson were home for the summer, but Andrew did not visit his mother during her bereavement, probably because at the time of Sanders's death he was too worried over Emily's health, which had taken a sudden turn for the worse. Emily remained too weak to return to Washington at the end of the summer. A worried Andrew remained at her side at their new home, Poplar Grove, down the lane from the Hermitage. As he set out for the capital alone, Jackson stopped in Gallatin to pay the requisite call on Polly Sanders.[19]

By early October, Emily had recovered enough that Andrew departed, though reluctantly, for Washington. Daniel and Margaret promised to come down to Poplar Grove to check on her. Unfortunately, on the scheduled day for the visit, Daniel had to send his regrets, "Per Boy." As he explained to "My Dear Sister," both his mother and his wife were themselves indisposed, "the former has been dangerously ill but we think her better this morning—the latter had a child last night with fever during the night, but better this morning." Whether Daniel and Margaret were ever able to visit later is unrecorded. In December, Emily's health collapsed. Andrew, who remained unaware of how seriously she was failing, was detained by his duties in Washington, then his attempt to race home was impeded by an icy winter. He arrived home two days after her death on December 19, 1836.[20]

By now, Daniel Donelson had decided to remain in Tennessee, as the early Tennessee historian W. W. Clayton recorded, on "the farm where he was born." What happened with Thomas Watson's purchase of the farm is not recorded; Donelson and Watson might simply have canceled the sale. "Being a thoroughly practical business man," Clayton, who may have known Donelson, noted, "he was enabled at different times to add to this farm and make it one of the best in the State." In 1837, with his family outgrowing the modest Eventide, Donelson began to build a fine plantation house of stone and brick that were quarried and fired on the estate. Elm Tree, as he first called the new home, would grow larger and grander over the next twenty years, and he would eventually rename it Hazel Path. In October 1839, he purchased 432½ acres along Drake's Creek and the turnpike from J. B. Hall and A. G. Payne for $5,762. In February 1840, he purchased the "Hendersonville tract" of 182 acres "by court decree" from the estate of his stepfather, James Sanders, for $364. He also continued to purchase slaves. On January 3, 1840, he purchased a slave girl, Charity, from E. K. Withers for $400; the nature of the transaction suggests that he bought her to be a personal servant for one of his daughters, probably Lizzie, who would turn nine that year. Three days later he received five slaves from Watson for $5.00 "and other considerations to be held as security" for a debt of $1,125 that Watson owed to Elmore Douglass that would come due January 1, 1842. In the 1840 Census, Donelson reported owning twenty-eight slaves, which placed him among the elite Southern society of planters.[21]

Donelson also returned to the orthodox Jacksonian fold, even to accepting Martin Van Buren. Old Hickory successfully withstood the White challenge, ensured the election of his designated successor, and retired to the Hermitage in the spring of 1837. In October business took Andrew Donelson on a trip to Washington. He left his children with Daniel and Margaret at Elm Tree. "Present me kindly to Mr. Van Buren," Daniel enjoined him, "and say to him that I am a well wisher to the success of his administration." By the next spring, Daniel was so well settled back among his original neighbors that he was exchanging routine gossip on county court business with his brother-in-law Caruthers.[22]

Nevertheless, the Democrats continued their struggle to hold Tennessee against the surging Whigs, who absorbed many among the Bell-White group. In the 1837 gubernatorial election, however, not even war hero Robert H. Armstrong, who had commanded Jackson's artillery during the Creek War, could unseat the colorless incumbent, Newton Cannon. Redeeming Tennessee in the state elections of 1839 therefore became imperative. The Democrats were obliged to draw upon their leading member to lead the charge. After seven terms as congressman, including two terms as Speaker of the House of Representatives, James K. Polk came home to make the Democratic run for the governorship. A Herculean effort by all, including a grueling statewide speaking tour by Polk, achieved success at last. Polk was elected governor, and the Democrats doubled their representation in Tennessee's thirteen congressional seats from three to six.[23]

Daniel Donelson was surely pleased to see Polk assume the governor's chair. In his inaugural address and subsequent message to the General Assembly in October 1839, Governor Polk invoked all the Jacksonian Democratic nostrums that he hoped to implement during his administration: strict Jeffersonian adherence to the Constitution in federal-state relations and, at the state level, tight control of the state banks and economic progress in state-sponsored internal improvements, such as the construction of turnpikes and railroads. At the more personal level, Donelson made good use of his connections to the governor. In December 1840, he was one of a group of Sumner County citizens who signed a petition to Governor Polk to post a reward for the apprehension of Willis G. Carroll, who was accused of murder. In May 1841, he wrote and was the first signatory on a second petition to Polk to post a reward for the apprehension of an escaped slave, Charles, who belonged to Priestly Bradford, for an attempted rape.[24]

Unfortunately for Daniel Donelson and all Tennessee Democrats, the Whigs redoubled their efforts to reclaim the state in the elections of 1841. To contest the efficient but relentlessly serious Polk, they put up as their candidate tall, spindly James C. Jones, whose entertaining style on the stump came right out of the ballyhoo campaign that had ejected Van Buren from the White House and swept Whigs William Henry Harrison and John Tyler—"Tippecanoe and Tyler, Too"—into office in the presidential contest the year before. Despite another exhausting campaign tour, Polk was narrowly defeated for reelection by "Lean Jimmy" Jones and his "coonery and foolery" antics.[25]

Little is documented about Daniel Donelson's financial affairs, but they apparently compared favorably to those of his brother. Indeed, a running theme between the two brothers during these years is Daniel's frequent embroilment in Andrew's chronic indebtedness. He was even a witness to an incident that was, for Andrew, the ultimate indignity. On October 1, 1839, Andrew was visiting his brother, "when lo! and behold!" as Daniel reported to Caruthers, the sheriff of Sumner County appeared at Elm Tree and served a writ on Andrew to appear in court at Gallatin "to answer to a *bill* which was presented by . . . *one Nathaniel Sanders* of

Montgomery Ct." Daniel begged Caruthers to "arrange this matter" for Andrew. Caruthers did, although it involved both the sheriff and Daniel shuffling debts and cash to square matters on Andrew's behalf.[26]

In November 1841 Andrew remarried, to Elizabeth Anderson Martin Randolph, a young widow who was a niece of his first wife, Emily. Shortly after, he renamed his home Tulip Grove. He may have restored his family situation but his finances were still desperate and Daniel still found himself becoming entangled in them. Robert Henderson of Leesburg, Virginia, tried to collect $1,600 toward payment of a $4,500 bond to the late Thomas R. Mott. Henderson finally wrote Daniel, who served as security for his brother. Daniel urged Andrew to pay, but the best that he could get was a promise to pay $800, half of what was asked, ten months hence. Whether it was compensation, when Elizabeth bore a son in December 1842, the boy was named Daniel Smith Donelson, to honor Andrew's brother as much as their maternal grandfather.[27]

Daniel's family also continued to grow, although spotty records render precise birth dates for several of the children difficult to ascertain. On February 19, 1838, Margaret gave birth to their fourth child and daughter, whom they named Emily, perhaps in honor of their recently deceased sister-in-law. In (no date) 1840 she gave birth to a fifth consecutive daughter, whom they named Rebecca. In July (no date) 1842, when Margaret presented him with a sixth child, Daniel finally welcomed the birth of a son. They named him James Branch Donelson, apparently in honor of a brother of Margaret's who had died in Florida in 1839. In January 1843 Daniel made arrangements for Lizzie, nearly twelve, to attend a school for girls in Lebanon, where she boarded with "Uncle Robert" and "Aunt Sally" Caruthers, with her father contributing $25 for her board for each term.[28]

Meanwhile, politics took a surprising turn, but confirmed that Donelson had been accepted back into the fold of regular Jackson Democrats. In August 1842, Thomas R. Barry, a Democrat, resigned his seat representing Sumner County in the Tennessee House of Representatives. A special election was called for September 8, 1842, to fill the seat before the General Assembly would convene for an extra session on October 3. A meeting of Sumner County Democrats in Gallatin announced "Gen. Daniel Donelson" as the Democratic candidate. "Daniel Donelson will be elected easily in place of Barry," Daniel Graham assured James K.

Polk. "Some fellow named Daughtr[e]y is running against him." Indeed, in some unspecified way, Joel H. Daughtrey's candidacy was unplanned and unwelcome; as the *Nashville Union,* the Tennessee state Democratic organ, asked, "Is it possible that Mr. Daughtrey is running against Gen. Donelson without having obtained a pledge?" At any rate, although details of the campaign, such as it might have been, are vague and even the vote totals were not released, Donelson was elected by what the *Union* assured its Democratic readers was "an overwhelming majority."[29]

For several reasons, Governor Jones had called the Twenty-fourth General Assembly to meet in special session on October 3, 1842: to consider relief measures to ease lingering hard times from the Panic of 1837, to draw new congressional and state legislative districts based on the results of the 1840 U.S. Census, and to elect two United States senators. The last item was to correct a fiasco that carried over from the preceding regular session of 1841. In another example of the acrimony between the two parties in the state, the thirteen Democratic state senators—the "Immortal Thirteen," as their supporters proudly christened them—thwarted all attempts to elect two Whigs to fill the U.S. Senate seats.[30]

In the absence of a state capitol building, for which funding of its construction had yet to be authorized, the General Assembly met in the Davidson County courthouse. As a new legislator, Donelson was not conspicuous. He was appointed to no committees, gave no speeches, and took no part in debates. Once, he presented a "petition," a second time "memorials," and on a third occasion "remonstrances" from his Sumner County constituents who were seeking "relief," and once he inquired of the chair for the committee on relief on the status of a "validation law." Otherwise, in a repeat performance of the regular session, the Immortal Thirteen Democrats again successfully blocked the election of any Whigs as U.S. senators. For two years, Tennessee remained unrepresented in the United States Senate.[31]

At the national level, Martin Van Buren remained the presumptive Democratic nominee for president in 1844, but his defeat for reelection in 1840 encouraged rivals. He was alarmed in December 1842 to hear a rumor that Jackson had turned his support toward John C. Calhoun for the presidency. The perpetrator was "young John Branch," who was in Tennessee visiting his sister Margaret Donelson. Branch claimed that he got his story straight from Jackson, but Old Hickory recalled only a brief conversation of "a few minutes & in company with Genl. Daniel S. Donelson." Andrew Donelson admitted to Van Buren that young Branch was "a friend of Mr. Calhoun, but he is without influence," and was unaware of "how ridiculous the truth would make his statements appear."[32]

Meanwhile, elections would be held in the summer of 1843 for state offices, including governor and the General Assembly, as well as for Tennessee's representatives in the United States Congress. The elections would be critical for the Democrats, who were attempting to wrest the state from the Whigs. Polk would again attempt to reclaim the gubernatorial chair. Thomas Barry, who had resigned the state House seat into which Donelson had been elected, now decided that he wanted it back. Apparently bad blood had developed between Donelson and Barry, whose solution was to make his old House seat available by attempting to kick Donelson upstairs. "Barry wishes Donelson to run for the Senate (that he may be beat)," is how Robert Armstrong put it to Polk.[33]

For Donelson, a better opportunity arose. The recent special session of the General Assembly had grouped Davidson, Smith, and Sumner counties into the Eighth Congressional District. Josephus Conn Guild was the first choice of the Democratic party to run for Congress from the district. Another possibility was William Trousdale, whom Donelson had supported for Congress in 1829 in the episode that ballooned into his difficulties with Robert M. Burton and Robert Desha. Trousdale had since gained distinction in the Seminole War. This time, moreover, Donelson's name appeared on the list of possible candidates. In February 1843, Guild declined to run. "Trousdale is the man if he will accept," Armstrong then informed Polk, but added, "Donelson would do far better." Burton agreed, telling Polk, "The next best chance is Genl. Donelson."[34]

On January 23, "a large and respectable meeting" of Sumner County Democrats called for a convention to meet in Gallatin to nominate their delegates to the district convention. Davidson county Democrats met on February 11 to select their delegates; Andrew Donelson was one of them. The district convention was held in Gallatin on February 20, and nominated Daniel Donelson as the Democratic candidate for Congress. "A good selection," beamed the *Nashville Union*, "—one which we have strong confidence will insure the success of the democracy of the District. . . . One strong and united effort, and Gen. D. will be our Representative." The *Union* immediately placed Donelson's name on its masthead, just under that of Polk for governor. David Burford, another ghost from Donelson's difficulties with Burton and Desha, received the nomination as the Democratic candidate from Sumner County for the state Senate. "What says Wilson County in respect to Major Donelson?" Van Buren asked Jackson when he heard the news, but he had his Donelsons and congressional districts confused. "It is not Major A,J. Donelson who has been called out to represent this District in congress—" Old Hickory explained, "it is his brother, Genl. Danl. S. Donelson of Sumner—the District being changed."[35]

Donelson's opponent was Joseph Hopkins Peyton, a medical doctor in Gallatin, and brother of Balie Peyton who had once served as aide-de-camp to Donelson when he was brigadier general in the state militia. Like Donelson, the Peyton brothers had been attracted to the Hugh Lawson White movement but, unlike Donelson, who had subsequently returned to the Jackson camp, they became Whigs. While Balie had advanced to represent their district in Congress during the Jackson administration, where he became an ally of John Bell, "Jo" Peyton had held various local offices and served a term in the General Assembly. Not coincidentally, the Peytons were brothers-in-law to Thomas Barry, who had engineered Donelson's ejection from his seat in the House. Against such a formidable phalanx, Donelson nevertheless entered the race, as Armstrong assured Polk, being "highly pleas[e]d with his prospects." The campaign opened when Donelson and Jo Peyton held a public debate at Rome, in Smith County, on March 11. "Among the egregious blunders" that the doctor made, reported the *Nashville Union*, was to assert that "Judge White was in favor of a U. States Bank." Donelson immediately set his opponent and the audience straight. As the *Nashville Union* drolly commented, "The General is more than a match for the Doctor." In contrast to the favorable account in the Democratic *Union*, the Whig *Republican Banner* predictably sneered that Donelson's speech was "so disjointed, unconnected, scattering and in short order such a motley of nonsensical jargon, that it was impossible to get the *hang* of it."[36]

Statewide attention focused on the race for governor, but many of the congressional races were also fought intensely, including the one in the symbolically important Eighth District, which included not only Nashville but also the home of Old Hickory. Donelson and Peyton engaged in a series of seven debates, one per day (Sunday excepted) from June 10 through June 17 in critical Davidson County. The partisan newspapers exhorted their readers into a frenzy. The *Nashville Union* reminded voters that "DANIEL S. DONELSON is an upright and substantial farmer of Old Sumner; a man well acquainted with the wants of the people and measures necessary to preserve their rights and advance their prosperity." Years later, a supporter proudly recalled how Donelson "responded to the call and entered the canvass as though he was certain of success, dealing heavy blows upon the opposition from every political stump in the district." For a while, the result looked promising. "Donelson is gaining daily," Armstrong assured Polk in May, adding, "All we hear is *good* and looks well." By June, he added, "The Prospect for Donelson and Burford is good."[37]

Tennessee state election days were held on the first Thursday of August. When the votes were counted, Polk failed by four thousand to recapture the governorship. There was a small consolation that the Democrats elected six of the eleven congressional representatives. Donelson was not one of them. The only good news was that in the contest between native sons, Sumner County preferred Donelson over Peyton by a vote of 1,663 to 781. Conversely, its large mercantile community made Nashville a Whig city, which tilted Davidson County toward Peyton; Donelson lost even the Hermitage precinct, 57 to 82. Worse, Smith County favored Peyton by a three-to-one majority. The total vote for the Eighth District race was 4,851 for Peyton to 3,803 for Donelson. At least Donelson retained his sense of humor, quipping to Caruthers, "I will only say as far as I am concerned that 'veni vidi *non* vici.'" Nevertheless, in his race, a supporter recalled that Donelson "proved himself a man of noble bearing, of great energy, and worthy [of] the confidence of the people."[38]

Daniel Donelson's political aspirations were dashed, at least temporarily, although he remained active at the local level. He served as a Sumner County delegate to the 1843 Democratic state convention which met in Nashville that November to select delegates to the 1844 national convention, scheduled to meet at Baltimore in May for selecting the Democratic nominees for president and vice president. At the state convention he also served on the resolutions committee, as a member for the Eighth District.[39]

Texas resurrected Polk's political aspirations, and offered Andrew Donelson his next opportunity for public service. American settlers who had flocked to the Mexican province rose in revolt and achieved independence for Texas in 1836 at the Battle of San Jacinto under the leadership of Sam Houston—a remarkable confirmation of Daniel Donelson's earlier claim of Houston's plan after the breakup of his first marriage in 1829. Most Texans, being expatriate Americans, preferred annexation to the United States, but the issue proved to be too controversial for American politics. Southerners and Westerners, especially Democrats, strongly favored Texas annexation, while Northerners and Easterners, especially Whigs, objected just as strongly to acquisition of more slave territory into the Union. Having been expelled from the Whig party, President John Tyler began searching for a campaign issue on which to base a run for the presidency in 1844, and seized on the annexation of Texas. At first it seemed that Tyler's strategy might work, as both front-runners, Whig Henry Clay and Democrat Martin Van Buren, refused to endorse annexation. As a result, in a dramatic turnaround, considering his legendary loyalty to his friends, Jackson dropped his longtime support of Van Buren. In a daring maneuver, the origins of which were hatched at the Hermitage and finessed by Andrew Donelson at the Democratic National Convention in Baltimore in May 1844, the Democrats abandoned Van Buren. Instead, the convention nominated Polk, who strongly endorsed annexation. Meanwhile, Tyler pushed to complete annexation before his term expired. In September he appointed Andrew Donelson chargé d'affaires to the Republic of Texas, where his connections to Old Hickory and President Houston were critical to see that annexation was successfully accomplished.[40]

Daniel Donelson's role was a familiar one: guarding his brother's financial interests. In the process he managed to cross his aging but still-formidable uncle. In January 1845 Elizabeth Donelson resolved to meet her husband in New Orleans when he returned on a leave from Texas. She asked Daniel to make the travel arrangements and draw $600 for expenses. Old Hickory was horrified, and enumerated reasons why she should not go, ranging from the risk of steamboat accidents to the low price of cotton, which made them all too poor "even to meet our pressing pecuniary matters, let alone trips of pleasure." Somehow Jackson persuaded Elizabeth to stay home, leaving Daniel in the embarrassing position of having been a culprit in an abortive enterprise of which his uncle disapproved. When Andrew arrived home in February, Daniel and Jackson had to inform him what a disastrous year 1844 had been for their crops; at New Orleans their cotton had drawn only four cents per pound. Further, at Andrew's other cotton plantation in Chickasaw County, Mississippi, Daniel reported that the overseer was drinking and might have to be dismissed.[41]

Polk was elected president in November 1844, which the Democrats interpreted as representing a national mandate for the annexation of Texas. The only disappointment was that even in victory Polk lost his own state of Tennessee to Clay by only 113 votes, which Jackson attributed to "the vilest frauds that have ever been practised." Even more frustrating, no sooner had Polk taken office in March 1845, than he was besieged by office seekers. Andrew Donelson suggested to his brother that he apply for a lucrative sutler's position in the U.S. Army. Sutlers were civilian merchants whom the army licensed to sell luxuries to soldiers that the Commissary Department did not supply. Shady sutlers charged greatly inflated prices, but even honest sutlers could make handsome profits, as soldiers eagerly bought their fare. Daniel accordingly submitted an application in a letter to Polk that was remarkably tactless. He declined to enclose letters of recommendation that would attest to his "fitness, habits, qualifications etc[.,]" believing them to be "wholly unnecessary, you being personally acquainted with me." He also declined to come to Washington to ask Polk in person, believing that would be "somewhat derogatory to my own character." He did not receive the appointment.[42]

By late spring 1845 Andrew Jackson was clearly on his deathbed. On May 29, Daniel went to Nashville on business. On his way back home, he visited Elizabeth Donelson at Tulip Grove and his dying uncle next door at the Hermitage. It was the last time that Daniel would see the man who had raised him like a father.[43]

The long-dreaded family tragedy came on Sunday, June 8, 1845. Family and friends gathered at the Hermitage during all that long spring afternoon, so as to be there at the end. Sam Houston, whose term as president of the Republic of Texas had recently ended, was visiting relatives in the United States, and happened to be in Nashville. He arrived shortly after Old Hickory breathed his last. Neither of Samuel Donelson's sons were present. Andrew was still in Texas, awaiting a convention of the people of the Republic to approve annexation. From Elm Tree, Daniel was a bit too far away to arrive in time. He was especially sensible of Andrew's absence.

"I wish you could have been here, during his last days of existence," he wrote wistfully to Andrew afterward but, stating with his usual brevity, "I do not doubt it would have been for the best, could it have been so— I will not say more on this subject. Elizabeth, I know has written you already in relation to it."[44]

Whatever ill feelings Daniel Donelson had for Houston as a result of his failed marriage, political disgrace, and ostensible designs to revolutionize Texas back in 1829, had long dissipated by the time of Houston's return in 1845. Because of the difficult circumstances at the Hermitage in the wake of Old Hickory's death, Elizabeth Donelson welcomed Houston at Tulip Grove, along with his new wife, their small son, and their retinue. Daniel was now pleased to visit the Hero of San Jacinto there. "I was with Genl Houston and family at your house," he wrote Andrew, practically beaming that "they have been well received in Ten." Given the possibility that the former president of the Republic of Texas could be elected president of the United States, Daniel crowed that "he is undoubtedly a Democrat."[45]

With annexation having been secured, Polk rewarded Andrew with another diplomatic mission, this time as full minister to a Great Power, Prussia. Elizabeth and the children would accompany him overseas, so Andrew gave his brother power of attorney over his affairs. Andrew and family were hardly away in April 1846 when Daniel was beset by Andrew's many creditors. For the next three years, Daniel wrote his brother regularly, detailing Andrew's debts and pleading for guidance on how to address them. In reply, he received mostly silence. In the fall of 1848, he complained to Elizabeth's brother James Glasgow Martin Jr., that he had not heard from Andrew in over two years. "Cousin Daniel says his hands are perfectly tied," James wrote Elizabeth, "and that the Majs Estate is in a very precarious situation if he cannot get relief from some source."[46]

In turn, Daniel was not very informative regarding family matters at home. For example, only at the end of a lengthy letter itemizing Andrew's debts did he append a few personal sentences. "Our relations are generally well. Our mother looks badly, with an affliction of the Bowels, which I fear will result before a great while, fatally." Polly Sanders survived, information that Daniel did not subsequently relate, nor did he report the births of several more children during this period. His seventh child, and second son, Samuel ("Sam") Donelson, was born on December 15, 1844, followed by two more daughters, Martha Bradford Donelson, on February 19, 1847, and Susan Branch ("Sue") Donelson, on October 18, 1848. Daniel's and Margaret's oldest daughter, Elizabeth, or "Lizzie," who was not yet eighteen, married William Williams on May 9, 1849.[47]

Daniel Donelson's apparent habit of writing few letters (certainly few survive) and his brief treatment of family matters in those that he did write in no way hint at either an introverted personality or problems to hide. On the contrary, everything that can be discerned from what he said and wrote, and the accounts of people who knew him well, suggest that he was open, personable, and well-liked. As a young man, he was subject to impulsive actions and indiscreet gossip, as revealed by his misfired resignation from the Military Academy, quixotic move to Florida, and bungling through the Burton-Desha episode. As he matured, however, he settled down, learned when silence was best, and to measure his words when he did speak. He was well educated for his time and place, it shows in his speeches and writings, but he was never a man of the world. Unlike his brother Andrew, whose diplomatic career took him as far afield as frontier Texas and the palaces of Europe, Daniel never traveled broadly. Except, probably, for occasional visits to his Branch in-laws in Florida and North Carolina, he stuck pretty closely to his home world of the Cumberland Valley, and remained simply, as the *Nashville Union* had labeled him, "an upright and substantial farmer of Old Sumner." He and Margaret seem rarely to have been separated, which would explain at least in part the absence of a single surviving letter between them. The few surviving accounts suggest that they enjoyed a happy, close, and stable marriage. In an era when politics could become viciously personal, Donelson's opponents never found any mud to sling at him. He obviously impressed his friends, neighbors, and political associates. If he learned over time when to be serious, to command respect, and even to project an air of gravitas, neither did he ever lose that eye-twinkling, self-deprecating sense of humor that shines from his surviving personal letters. In the eyes of his contemporaries, Daniel Donelson was, in a word, admirable.

Nevertheless, considering his obvious high profile among the elite of Sumner County, and his years of service in the Tennessee state militia, it is curious that Donelson did not participate when war broke out between the United States and Mexico in the spring of 1846. Many of Donelson's Sumner County neighbors rallied to form two companies that were designated as the Tenth Legion. As part of the First Regiment of Tennessee Volunteers, they fought gallantly in the battles around Monterey, at the siege of Veracruz, and on the road to Mexico City. Donelson's political colleague William Trousdale earned particular distinction, rising to the rank of brigadier general, and in the state elections of 1849, the governor's chair. On all this blood and glory, Donelson missed out. Not a word survives from his sparse papers to explain why he remained at home.[48]

Within the civilian sphere, however, Donelson continued to play the role of the patriotic public citizen. While he did not serve in Mexico, in October 1846 he represented Sumner County on a committee to commission and erect a monument to honor the Tennessee Volunteers who fell at Monterey. The next spring, he served on a relief committee to send "money, sacked corn, or barreled flour" from Sumner County to famine victims of the potato blight in Ireland.[49]

Politics finally intervened to relieve Daniel from the pressure of dealing with his brother's creditors, when in 1849 the new Whig president, the Mexican War hero Zachary Taylor, recalled minister Donelson. When Andrew and his family arrived home in January 1850, he claimed that he brought from Europe enough money to relieve his most "*pressing debts,*" but Daniel insisted that the best way for his brother to get out of debt was to sell his extraneous property. Andrew, Daniel claimed, would then "have it in his power to say I am a *free man.*" Worse, Andrew returned home in the middle of a sectional crisis. However difficult managing Andrew's financial affairs had been, the Donelson brothers now faced a vastly more daunting crisis, one that threatened the survival of the Union itself.[50]

CHAPTER FOUR

―――― ★ ――――

"Still a Democrat of the Jackson School"

JANUARY 1850–MARCH 1861

For Daniel Donelson, times were good. In the 1850 Census, he reported the value of his farm at $22,000. His wealth now included ownership of some fifty slaves. "The times would seem to be improving," he noted with satisfaction at the beginning of the year, with "Lands, Negroes, and almost every species of property rising in value owing to the rise in Cotton." In January, "Gen. Donaldson" was a member of a delegation of prominent Sumner County citizens who petitioned the Tennessee General Assembly to charter the Louisville and Nashville Railroad, which would run through the county.[1]

"My own family," Donelson wrote his father-in-law John Branch, in February, "both white and black has been unusually healthy for near 12 months, no case assuming in any way alarming excepting my own." He was still recovering from a "long indisposition" that had confined him for two months "stretched on my *Cholera bed*." Donelson's jocular brush-off of what might have been his near-death made too lightly of a deadly cholera epidemic that ravaged Tennessee during the summer of 1849. Hundreds fled Nashville. One of its victims there was James K. Polk, dying barely three months after his term of office ended, already weakened and prematurely aged from overwork. Sumner County suffered heavily; perhaps one hundred died in Gallatin, the county seat.[2]

Yet, despite unprecedented growth and prosperity, the Union was tearing itself apart. North and South were at odds over the one question that eluded a solution—the future of slavery, especially the question of whether slavery should be allowed into the territories that had been acquired following the Mexican War. Particularly worrisome to Southerners, the Gold Rush of California had increased the population in the territory to the point that the new inhabitants, who came overwhelmingly from Northern states, were agitating for admission to the Union as a free state. A meeting in Jackson, Mississippi, in October 1849 called for a convention of Southern states to meet in Nashville to "adopt some mode of resistance" to various Northern "aggressions." The Mississippians volunteered Nashville, apparently due to being located in a moderate Southern state, to allay Northern fears, and to evoke reassuring images of the great unionist Andrew Jackson.[3]

In the host state, Tennessee, the selection of delegates fell victim to its partisan divisions. The Democratic House of Representatives authorized Democratic governor William Trousdale to appoint delegates, but the Whig Senate objected. As a result, the process devolved onto local initiatives. Daniel Donelson presided over the meeting at the courthouse in Gallatin on May 6, 1850, to select delegates from Sumner County for the convention. On the same day, Andrew Donelson presided over the Davidson County meeting. Both brothers were selected by their meetings as delegates.[4]

When the Nashville Convention met in June 1850, the moderates prevailed and successfully kept the fire-eaters at bay. The convention adopted a set of mild resolutions that took stands on issues on which few southerners disagreed, particularly denying congressional authority to exclude slavery from the territories. Neither Donelson brother played a conspicuous role. As unionists remained in control of the convention, they were probably content to watch the proceedings with quiet satisfaction.[5]

Daniel, for one, was pleased so far with the administration of President Zachary Taylor. Because Taylor "is the owner of a large number of slaves," he opined to his father-in-law, "it is sufficient for the South to give him their support." His approval of Taylor was largely personal, not political. Daniel remained otherwise a staunch Democrat. Moreover, his comment, though fleeting, provides a rare glimpse into his views on slavery as an institution. What little substantive information is known about Daniel Donelson as a slave owner must be gleaned mostly from such dry, unilluminating records as census data and slave purchases. Unlike many planters, including his brother, Daniel seems to have been largely immune to the mania for land speculation. Such frantic purchases of land, often as additional plantations in one of the Deep South states, were fueled by the imperative to grow more of the inevitable cash crop, cotton, which in turn drove the purchase of more slaves. Rather, once he returned from his brief Florida adventure, Daniel was content to develop his Sumner County farm with minimal additional land purchases, never owning more than half as many slaves as did Andrew.[6]

Even more frustrating is the dearth of surviving information regarding Donelson's personal relations with his slaves. The brief reference in his February 1850 letter to his father-in-law, to "my own family, both white and black," suggests at least the type of happy, even familial, harmony that so many slave owners flattered themselves into believing truly existed. No family anecdotes survive to support one way or the other such a supposition in Donelson's case. Otherwise, little more can be said beyond the conclusion that he regarded himself as being a typical slave owner. He evidently accepted the institution as being the best arrangement for both whites and blacks. As late as 1856, as executor of the estate of a deceased neighbor, Donelson blandly placed a card in Nashville newspapers that he would conduct a sale at public auction of "a Negro Woman named FRANKEY . . . for cash."[7]

In this early phase of the sectional crisis, he was clearly not yet alarmed that either the Union or slavery were threatened by the results of the first Nashville Convention or the subsequent passage by Congress of the package of bills that constituted the Compromise of 1850, which included, to the gratification of most southerners, a more effective Fugitive Slave Act. Indeed, as with many delegates, Daniel did not even attend the second session of the Nashville Convention when it reassembled in November. Why is not recorded, but he could claim a family distraction. That month, although the date has not been identified, Margaret gave birth to their tenth child and third son, John Branch Donelson, who would be called "Branch" in the family. Whatever the reason, Daniel missed the much more dramatic second session. The fire-eaters seized control of the convention, calling for a Southern congress with full authority to resist Northern aggressions and maintain Southern rights, even to the point of secession. In response, with the unionist citizens of Nashville cheering him from the galleries, Andrew Donelson denounced the "UNWORTHY" convention, asserting, "I wish to PROTEST against its UNHALLOWED PURPOSES!"[8]

The Southern fire-eaters would never forgive Andrew Donelson for the humiliation that he inflicted on them at the second Nashville Convention.

Neither Donelson brother could know it at the time, but from that event, propelled by the currents of the sectional crisis, their public careers would take diverging paths. Before too many years, they would scarcely be speaking to each other, except when they were quarreling, often publicly, from opposite camps.

The new darling of the unionists, Andrew Donelson's star reached its zenith. He was rewarded by being made the editor of *The Daily Union,* the newspaper in Washington, D.C., that functioned as the national organ of the Democratic party. Politically, he was charged with reuniting the two extreme wings of the party, the Northern free-soilers and the Southern states' rightists, with the moderate center. A personal incentive for Andrew was that if the *Union* was awarded the congressional printing contract, then he could make enough money to allow him to wipe out years of chronic debt. On both counts he failed. The states' rights men refused to be reconciled and conspired to keep the printing contract from him. By the summer of 1852, he was home, wondering if he had a future in the Democratic party which, in his view, had been irredeemably hijacked by the sectional extremists.[9]

Meanwhile, Daniel Donelson focused on his community, farm, and growing family. He continued to be an active advocate for the Louisville and Nashville Railroad, helping to establish a bond issue of three hundred thousand dollars to fund construction of the route through Sumner County. On May 3, 1850, his eldest daughter Elizabeth, or "Lizzie," who had married William Williams a year before, presented Donelson with his first grandchild, a girl named Margaret. A family tragedy occurred, albeit distantly, on January 19, 1851, when Margaret Donelson's mother, Eliza Foort Branch, died at the Branch home outside Tallahassee. More happily, on November 20, 1851, his second daughter Mary Ann married James Glasgow Martin Jr., a brother of Andrew Donelson's wife, Elizabeth. On May 13, 1853, they presented the Donelsons with their second granddaughter, also named Margaret. The grandparents were not to be outdone. Six months later, on November 15, 1853, Daniel and Margaret welcomed their eleventh child and fourth son, Daniel Smith Donelson II. "Dan," as he was called in the family, would be their last. Neither parent was young anymore—Daniel was now fifty-two, Margaret was forty-two.[10]

All during this time, Daniel Donelson remained a silent spectator to the avalanche of events that ripped off the fresh bandages that the

Compromise of 1850 had pasted over the sectional wounds. If compromise is the art of leaving both sides equally dissatisfied, then the Compromise of 1850 succeeded all too well. At best, many Southerners merely acquiesced to its provisions, which they viewed as being overly harsh to their region. Worse, the provision that they regarded as being the only sop that they received, the Fugitive Slave Law, provoked so much outrage and resistance in the North that it became almost impossible to enforce. Like the Democrats before them, the Whig party was rent asunder, splitting into a moderate group, the "Cotton" Whigs, who supported the Compromise as providing the best means of preserving sectional harmony, and the more radical "Conscience" Whigs in the North, who opposed any concessions to the slave states.[11]

Amid such unrest, the country entered the presidential contest of 1852. The bitterly divided Democrats met in their national convention in Baltimore. After the delegates who supported the leading contenders—Lewis Cass of Michigan, James Buchanan of Pennsylvania, Stephen A. Douglas of Illinois, and Sam Houston of Texas—balloted into deadlock, the nomination went to a compromise candidate, Franklin Pierce of New Hampshire. Uniting around this amiable nonentity, Democrats carried the election to a landslide victory for Pierce over his Whig opponent, General Winfield Scott. Unfortunately for Tennessee Democrats, theirs was one of only four states that Scott carried.[12]

Perhaps because Tennessee remained, in essence, a moderate, conservative Middle South polity that eschewed the extremist elements of both North and South, the two-party system that had been established during Jackson's administration continued to operate in the state, even as it began to break down nationwide. Much of this political balance resulted from the geography of the state, and the economic and social patterns that developed therefrom. To paraphrase Julius Caesar, Tennessee is divided into three distinct parts, or Grand Divisions, as they are formally styled. East Tennessee is a rugged land of parallel spurs of the Appalachian Mountains separated by intervening valleys. Such terrain was not conducive to large slave-based plantations. Thus, East Tennessee remained a region of rough mountain folk and hardy small-scale farmers—exactly the type of common people for whom Jacksonian Democracy held appeal. At the opposite end of the state, the broad and generally flat terrain of West Tennessee was as well suited to the cultivation of King Cotton as were the

Black Belts of Alabama and Mississippi. The commercial class of its great river metropolis, Memphis, was staunchly Whig but its rural mixture of slave-owning planters and yeoman farmers leaned toward their states'-rights Democratic brethren of the Deep South. In between, Middle Tennessee was the most economically diverse section. Large cotton plantations certainly abounded and slaves made up a quarter of the population, but the fertile soils of the Cumberland Basin allowed freeholding yeoman farmers to cultivate a wide variety of market crops from grain to tobacco. With its central location on the navigable Cumberland River, Nashville dominated the region economically and politically, and both its mercantile and agricultural interests were heavily Whig.[13]

As a consequence, the Whig party remained as strong in Tennessee as the Democratic party. Election after election produced an even balance. The governor's office alternated between the parties during this period with each biennial election. The Whig James C. Jones, who had wrested the governor's chair from James K. Polk, was succeeded in 1845 by the Democrat Aaron V. Brown, who, in turn, was succeeded sequentially by Whig Neill S. Brown in 1847, Democrat William Trousdale in 1849, Whig William B. Campbell in 1851, and Democrat Andrew Johnson in 1853. Similarly, the houses of the General Assembly changed hands just as frequently but with neither party ever holding a majority of more than a few votes. Such evenly balanced politics produced an active, engaged, and informed electorate with high percentages of voter turnout, but also resulted in bitter partisan divisions and frequent governmental paralysis, of which the shenanigans of the Immortal Thirteen and the inability to agree on an official state delegation to the Nashville Convention were among the most conspicuous, embarrassing examples.[14]

At the national level, rather than partisan peace and domestic unity, the feckless Pierce administration in Washington precipitated another cascade of sectional discord. In 1854, under the guidance of Senator Stephen A. Douglas and pressure from President Pierce to make it a test of Democratic loyalty, a bitterly divided Congress passed the polarizing Kansas-Nebraska Act. One of its provisions instituted "popular sovereignty," whereby the inhabitants of these territories could decide for themselves whether to allow or prohibit slavery. Southern ultras leaped at the opportunity to open the region to slavery. The North erupted into a paroxysm of fury. Thousands of angry Northern Whigs and anti-Nebraska Democrats deserted their parties and formed the Republican Party, which was dedicated to restricting the further spread of slavery into the territories.[15]

Also exacerbating the territorial issue was a simultaneous reaction against the recent huge influx of foreigners, among them many Irish and German Roman Catholics who were fleeing famine and political unrest at home. The Democratic party historically welcomed immigrants, partly because it was the traditional advocate for the poor and downtrodden, and partly because it sought their votes to strengthen its base in the burgeoning industrial cities of the North. The nativists, more likely to be Whigs, took alarm. During 1853, an obscure, secret fraternal organization, the Order of the Star Spangled Banner, gained prominence and a nickname that stuck. Its members responded to questions about the Order by answering, "I know nothing," which prompted critics to label them derisively as "Know-Nothings." While the sectional crisis merged with the backlash against immigrants and Catholics, the Know-Nothing faction somehow became the populist vehicle to address all these concerns, transforming it into a national political movement.[16]

The Know-Nothings gained members even among Southerners, who feared that uneducated immigrant voters would fall under the control of demagogues—which meant to them, in a word, abolitionists. Furthermore, the movement attracted thousands of Democrats and Whigs who were deserting their parties in disgust but had nowhere else to go. As elsewhere, Tennessee Know-Nothings capitalized on voter dissatisfaction. In the fall of 1854, candidates who were backed by the Order won local elections, including the mayor's offices in Nashville, Memphis, and Clarksville. By early 1855, the Know-Nothing movement formed itself into the American party, an alternative third party whose goal was to wrest control of the government from the corrupt, incompetent Democrats and Whigs, and save the Union.[17]

The sectional crisis destroyed the party system that had governed the Union for twenty years and, ironically, not only provided the background for a revival of Daniel Donelson's political career but also led to a permanent rupture with his brother. In May 1855 Andrew Donelson announced his break with the Democratic party, which he now viewed as being dominated by his Southern states' rights enemies, and their pliant Northern doughface allies, including President Franklin Pierce. Not surprisingly, Democrats were shocked at his apostasy and attacked him viciously, attributing his desertion of the party to "disappointed ambition and failure to obtain an office" from Pierce.[18]

Complicating Andrew's break with the Democratic Party were the resultant family disruptions. These were compounded when the Donelsons' brother-in-law and ex-Whig congressman Meredith P. Gentry became the American party candidate for Tennessee governor. Daniel Donelson remained a loyal Democrat and, at least partly as a counterweight to his familial defections, his standing in local and state Democratic ranks began to rise. On March 12, 1855, he was among the Sumner County delegation selected to attend the Democratic state convention that would convene on March 27 in Nashville. There, the Democrats of Tennessee "unanimously" elected him as president of the convention and nominated Governor Andrew Johnson for a second term. On June 2, the Democrats of Sumner County met again. On Donelson's motion, officers were elected, then he offered resolutions which were "unanimously adopted" that endorsed the Democratic state platform and local candidates.[19]

To counter the threat that they perceived was posed by the Know-Nothing movement, the Democrats sought the best candidates for local races. Originally, three Democrats announced their candidacy for the Sumner County seat in the state House of Representatives. Then, on July 17, an obviously surprised *Nashville Union and American* announced, "We hear from Gallatin that the candidates for the Legislature in Sumner County have withdrawn, and that Gen. DANIEL S. DONELSON, has consented to become a candidate." In an era when it was still desirable that a candidate appear to be reluctant, Donelson felt compelled to explain to the public what had happened, in a "Circular" published in the local newspapers. The original candidates were "all good and true men," but "in view of the extraordinary state of things," arising from the threat of the Know-Nothing movement, "it was believed that we were in danger of defeat." A group of Sumner County Democrats met at the courthouse in Gallatin, "without any previous arrangement, as I understand," Donelson insisted as a disclaimer. There, "my name was put in nomination, and the vote was unanimous for my taking the field." He received the notification by mail at his home, Elm Tree, on July 16, and the next day rode to Gallatin, where he was informed that the other candidates had "withdrawn." Only then did he accept the nomination.[20]

Donelson immediately published in the local newspapers a "CIRCULAR to the Voters of Sumner County" in which he affirmed his adherence to Democratic principles. "I have from the first opposed this political monster," he wrote, in reference to the Know-Nothing movement, "believing that . . . no good could result from it," even to fearing that "the dissolution of our glorious Union might . . . be the consequence." "Men may, and do change," he conceded in a clear reference to his brother, "but principles are immutable; they are old Jackson principles as I understand them; for these principles I contend now, and expect ever to contend as long as I have an existence."[21]

Already late to the field, the new candidate wasted no time joining the hustings. Only two days after Donelson announced his candidacy, the Democrats of Sumner and Davidson counties announced a "Democratic Rally" that was scheduled for Walton's Campground on July 28. "GEN. D.S. DONELSON" was especially "invited to speak." The Democrats of Sumner County hosted six "Public Barbecues" between July 24 and August 1. At the "glorious rally" at Shallow Ford on July 25, notwithstanding the "severe inclemency" of the weather, Donelson spoke to about 400 people. "I shall not attempt a sketch of his able and eloquent speech," reported "Spectator" to the *Nashville Union and American*. "He proved himself still a democrat of the JACKSON and JEFFERSON school, and defies mortal man to show where himself or his party had ever departed from their time-honored principles. The General is a brother of Maj. DONELSON, and is much the best speaker of the two. He has a splendid voice. His manner is bold and animated. He is just the man to show up wooly-headed *Sam*," the report said, using a contemptuous term for the Know-Nothings, whom the Democrats refused to dignify as the American party. The fashionable resort complex at Castalian Springs hosted one of the last rallies of the campaign, with Donelson again among the speakers. "Gen. Donelson . . . is an able advocate of our great principles," observed "Spectator" once more, "and will no doubt be elected."[22]

Election day was Thursday, August 2. In many areas, counts and recounts continued for days, but in one county the vote was so decisive that only two days after the election the *Nashville Union and American* could trumpet, "SUMNER COUNTY . . . the whole county heard from. Donelson elected by 500." In the other state and local elections, the results were closely divided. Sumner County had gone Whig in the preceding governor's race in 1853, but Donelson's candidacy now helped the Democrat

Johnson to carry it by some 350 votes. Statewide, Johnson eked out a narrow but important victory over Gentry, becoming the first governor of either party to be elected to a second term since Whig James C. Jones a dozen years earlier. The Democrats and Americans elected five congressmen each from the state's ten congressional districts, and split the General Assembly, with the Americans gaining a three-vote majority in the Senate and the Democrats a one-vote majority in the House of Representatives.[23]

Democrats nevertheless made the most of their victory and recognized those who had helped to make it possible. However narrow their majority in the House, a West Tennessean declared that they were "entitled" to elect the speaker, and he saw an obvious candidate. "Mr. DONELSON . . . is a gentleman of fine ability, a good voice, and an independent, gentlemanly, generous deportment, that endears him to all who know him, and renders him entirely worthy of the position." "MIDDLE TENNESSEE" also gave his "hearty concurrence." Donelson, he agreed, "is a man of fine memory, quick apprehension, prompt action, inflexibly just, and fearless in the execution of his purpose."[24]

The Thirty-first General Assembly of the State of Tennessee convened on Monday, October 1, 1855. After Donelson had served his brief term in the special session of 1842, the majestic state capitol building had since begun to rise, commanding a view over the entire city of Nashville. Though still under construction, the building was usable–but barely.[25]

The Senate, where the Americans enjoyed a majority of fourteen to eleven, organized quickly. Among the seventy-five members of the House of Representatives, the Democrats clung to an ostensible bare majority of 38 to 37. As expected, they nominated Donelson for speaker, while the Americans nominated former Whig governor Neill S. Brown of Davidson County. The balloting quickly went awry for the Democrats. Normally, in a traditional act of courtesy, each candidate voted for the other, thus canceling their votes and leaving the true decision to the remaining members. Brown, however, "failed throughout the calls of the roll" to vote for Donelson, who in turn did not feel obliged to vote for Brown. Worse, two members who claimed to be Democrats voted for Brown. Four days of fruitless balloting ensued. Finally, claiming that he had no wish to impede the proceedings, Brown withdrew his name. Immediately Donelson did the same, insisting that he had been nominated by his friends in the first place, "against his wishes." The Americans then all voted anyway for

Brown who, on the forty-sixth ballot, was elected speaker by one vote. Although one member of the House praised equally the "patriotic and magnanimous conduct" of both candidates, precisely what happened was never explained. When the *Nashville True Whig* accused the *Nashville Union and American* of insinuating that Brown had "schemed and planned" to secure his election to the speakership, the *Union* called the accusation "scurrilous."[26]

The House finally began its business. In contrast to his inconspicuous role during the special session of 1842, this time Donelson was appointed to three committees: Education and Common Schools, Agriculture and Manufactures, and Public Roads. Curiously, despite his years as a general in the state militia, he was not appointed to the committee on Military Affairs; with his rival for the speaker's chair making the committee assignments, this was perhaps not merely an oversight. He was also appointed to a joint committee to oversee the progress on the capitol building and its grounds. The new steam furnace in the cellar did not work properly, making the cavernous House chamber smoky and requiring that the windows in the upper gallery be opened even on cold days to improve ventilation. Even worse was dealing with Alfred Royal Wynne, a merchant and land speculator who owned the "grounds adjoining" the building. A year later, Donelson was still negotiating with Wynne, doing "all in my power to effect a sale of your grounds to the Commissioners of the State Capitol."[27]

If Donelson emerged as one of the Democratic leaders in the General Assembly, he understood that it was not necessary to talk too much. He seldom spoke, participated in few of the interminable debates, and focused instead on the business of his committees and Sumner County constituents. Across the session he introduced charters for a number of commercial and educational institutions, especially if they were to be located in Sumner County: the Sumner Manufacturing Company, the Gallatin Building and Loan Association, the Sumner Cashmere Company, "[for growing the cashmere shawl goat]," the *Nashville Union and American* helpfully explained in square brackets, the Howard Female Institute in Gallatin, and the Hartsville Female Institute.[28]

Jacksonian Democrats had long opposed federally funded internal improvements as not authorized according to their strict interpretation of the United States Constitution, but they regarded such funding at state levels as entirely appropriate. Tennessee at this time was caught up in the national mania for building railroads and stringing telegraph lines. Amid a plethora of proposed bills to charter or fund railroad construction in the state, Donelson insisted on a "well-regulated" system of internal improvements to restrain the worst excesses. "He had ever been an internal improvements man upon judicious principles," wrote the *Nashville Union and American*, paraphrasing, in third person, one of his rare speeches, "and now, having a system of improvements, he preferred to wait awhile and see its workings, rather than go headlong into the adoption of every scheme for extending it, at the imminent hazard of the credit of the State."[29]

Donelson saw no contradiction in taking an active role to seek state funding for the Tennessee section of the Louisville and Nashville Railroad. When he opposed a fellow House member's efforts to obtain state aid for the East Tennessee and Virginia Railroad to build bridges, the member retorted that "the gentleman from Sumner" was "the peculiar advocate of the Louisville and Nashville [Rail]road." Donelson, "interrupting," asserted that he had asked for "bridge-aid" across the Cumberland River only in order "to connect his constituents in Sumner County with Nashville" within Tennessee, rather than see their trade directed northward by the railroad in the absence of the bridge, and head out of the state toward Louisville in Kentucky. Donelson, indeed, prided himself on the consistency of his positions and the straightforward nature of his dealings. On another issue, that of obtaining state funds for statues to be placed in the new capitol building of George Washington, Andrew Jackson, James K. Polk, John Sevier, and Hugh Lawson White, a member accused him of using his influence. Donelson held his tongue until he could stand it no longer. "He never made bargains in legislation—" as the *Nashville Union and American* reported his outburst. "He never log-rolled any in his life—and he never would."[30]

Otherwise, in the tradition of bitter, closely divided Tennessee politics, the Americans in the House of Representatives directed most of their effort at thwarting the legislative program of Democratic governor Johnson. On the numerous occasions when Neill S. Brown descended to the floor so that he could engage in the debates, he was at least generous in distributing the speaker's chair among the members, and on several occasions to his former rival Donelson. For his part, when the lengthy session finally adjourned on March 3, 1856, in a traditional gesture Donelson sponsored the resolution of the House thanking Brown "for the able, impartial and dignified manner in which he has presided over its deliberations, and performed the arduous duties of the Chair." Donelson's role in the legislative session also merited appreciation. "The people of Davidson and Sumner are greatly indebted to Gen. DONELSON for his services in this particular," the *Nashville Union and American* editorialized, especially with respect to the Louisville and Nashville Railroad.[31]

"Hereafter we shall be able to devote our columns to matter[s] of more general interest than Legislative proceedings," the *Union* sighed in obvious relief. At virtually the same time, for example, word arrived in Nashville that at the American party national convention in Philadelphia, Daniel's brother, Andrew Donelson, had received the vice-presidential nomination as running mate to Millard Fillmore.[32]

Andrew's new prominence in the upstart party reinforced Daniel's position in the state Democratic party, almost as a rebuke of his brother for his apostasy. On January 4, 1856, while the legislature was still in session, Daniel Donelson chaired a meeting of Democratic legislators that adopted resolutions endorsing the actions of the Democratic members of the Tennessee delegation in the United States House of Representatives "who believe in those purely democratic doctrines of 'civil and religious liberty,'" which was another swipe at the principles of the detested Know-Nothings, "and in the principles contained in the Nebraska-Kansas act." Donelson was likewise a delegate representing Sumner County at the state Democratic convention, which met in the State House chamber on January 8.[33]

As the campaign unfolded, Donelson was in great demand to attend and address Democratic rallies across the state. On published lists of those who had been "invited and are expected to be present," his name sometimes appeared as high as third, beneath only Governor Andrew Johnson and Ex-Governor Aaron V. Brown, a revealing measure of how high he now stood in the state party. He rarely if ever attended events that required extensive travel, although at a rally in Weakley County a speaker "read a patriotic letter from Gen. D.S. Donelson, (brother of the know nothing candidate for the Vice Presidency), [and] it breathes the right spirit." Closer to home, however, he enthusiastically lent his time, energy, and voice in person. He and brother-in-law Robert L. Caruthers were among the speakers at a rally in Castalian Springs on July 22. In

Hendersonville on October 16, "Gen. Donelson" and Ex-Governor Brown spoke at "a very handsome and well arranged barbecue."[34]

Donelson joined in issuing a call to Sumner County Democrats to march to a massive rally in Nashville on October 21, where, as a "patriot citizen and unfaltering democrat," he proudly led the company of Sumner County cavalry. "A finer set of men were never led by a braver or more gallant Captain," enthused the *Nashville Union and American*. Immediately following in the order of the parade through the streets of Nashville were "thirty-one young ladies, as beautiful as e'er the sun shone on, handsomely mounted in riding costume with badges," each representing one of the states. Representing California was "Miss Donelson, daughter of General Donelson, of Sumner County."[35]

Denunciations from Democrats of Andrew Donelson spread, "and as usual in such cases," he understood, "there is a plentiful supply of malignant gossip and scandal to take the place of reason and common sense." He could handle those. "Nothing however can ever alter my view of the conduct of my Brother." In Andrew's view, Daniel "has shown an utter want of fraternal affection and must in the end lose the confidence and esteem of even those who are making capital out of his hostility to me. I cannot account for it unless it be that he is operated upon by the old nullifying feeling of the Branches." Sympathetic to the views of his wife's family, Daniel had always leaned farther south than Andrew. "Genl. Jackson dismissed Branch from his cabinet," Andrew claimed, "and always told me that I would live to see the day when the nullifiers would strike me down if they could." Others shook their heads over the very public strife within the Donelson family. "I think it is strange that the General is taking such an active part against his brother," clucked Mary Trousdale, adding "he never goes in a democratic crowd but what he hears him [Andrew] abused."[36]

The Democratic victory in the presidential election of 1856 changed the political fortunes of the Donelson brothers. The American party defeat effectively ended Andrew's political career. Conversely, Daniel's importance to the state Democratic party promised to rise even higher. He served as one of the Sumner County delegates to the state convention that met in Nashville on April 15, 1857, to nominate a candidate for governor to succeed Johnson, who had announced that he would not seek a third term. At a preliminary meeting of party leaders, Donelson was appointed to a committee to recommend officers and rules for the convention. When the convention assembled, he presented both reports and was elected as one of the three vice presidents. The convention nominated former state senator and congressman Isham Green Harris as the Democratic candidate for governor.[37]

In the state campaign of 1857, prospects looked brighter for the Democrats than at any time in recent memory. The American defeat in the 1856 presidential election had sent the party into steep decline both nationwide and in Tennessee. The victorious Democratic candidate James Buchanan even carried the state, the first presidential candidate of Andrew Jackson's party to do so since Martin Van Buren in 1840. Although the Whigs had remained strong and retained their party organization in Tennessee far longer than they had nationwide, the collapse of the American party carried them down along with it. While many "Old Line Whigs" such as John Bell and Balie Peyton remained staunchly proud of their heritage and principles, the remnants of the Americans and Whigs in Tennessee were lumped together and labeled simply as the "Opposition" to the surging Democrats.[38]

As the Democratic incumbent representing Sumner County, Daniel Donelson's candidacy for reelection to the state House of Representatives was apparently taken for granted. He seems to have had no Opposition party opponent but the easy Democratic prospects did produce rivals within his own party, which threatened to split what would otherwise be a united vote. Accordingly, on June 2, Donelson, along with B. F. Allen and J. S. Dyer, signed a card addressed "To the Democrats of Sumner County" announcing that they "have agreed for the present to withdraw their names as candidates for the Legislature." "We are induced to take this step from a sincere desire to preserve good feeling and harmony in the democratic ranks," they explained, and called on Sumner County Democrats to meet in Gallatin on June 15 to "determine who shall be the candidate for the Legislature."[39]

Whatever the intervening obscure details, Donelson again became the Democratic candidate from Sumner County for the state House of Representatives. Several major campaign events were held, including a "GREAT RALLY OF THE DEMOCRACY OF SUMNER COUNTY" that featured several speakers, but it is unrecorded whether Donelson was one of them. As weak as the Opposition had become, the campaign did not lack controversy. Harris denounced the revenue bill that had been passed by the preceding General Assembly. Instead he pushed a scheme whereby the federal government would transfer the millions of acres of public lands that it held nationwide to the states. With the revenue that would be raised from selling its share of these public lands, Harris argued, Tennessee could eliminate its debt, build schools, and fund internal improvements. The Opposition *Daily Nashville Patriot* pointed out that many Democrats had voted for the bill, including Donelson, who had been "esteemed worthy of the leadership of the House." Attempting to sow disagreement between Harris and Donelson, the *Patriot* demanded, "It is important that Donelson should be placed right before his constituents." Nevertheless, when the results became available after the election on August 4, Donelson was listed as being the winner in Sumner County, although the vote tallies were not reported. The apparent ease of his victory was reflected by an unprecedented Democratic sweep across the state. The Democrats won seven of the ten congressional districts, majorities of 42 to 33 in the House of Representatives and 18 to 7 in the Senate, and every elective state office, including the governorship, which Harris won by a majority exceeding 11,000.[40]

On August 29, "Sumner" in the *Nashville Union and American* again recommended "Gen. Donelson" as the man who "most deserve[s] the Speakership." "Added to fine capacity and a liberal experience in parliamentary usage," "Sumner" wrote, "he has a frankness of manner and decision of character which peculiarly adapt him for the position." In praising Daniel, the letter referred to the differences between the brothers. "Yes, at the sacrifice of family pride and feeling, he battled with all the powers of his vigorous nature against the election of his brother to the Vice Presidency, and for the political faith in which he had been schooled, by the iron nerve of his uncle of the Hermitage. This incident well illustrates the political nerve and integrity of the man." Over the next several days, the *Union* received additional letters urging "that sterling Democrat and tried patriot, Gen. Donelson," for the speakership.[41]

That his brother's political star was rising, while his own had set, so bitterly rankled Andrew Donelson that he foolishly precipitated the sorriest spectacle of his career. On September 3 an unsigned reply in the *Daily Nashville Patriot* denounced as "farcical" Daniel's attachment to Old Hickory, reminded readers that he was the son-in-law of John Branch, whom Jackson had "dismissed" from his cabinet, and accused him of having opposed Jackson's reelection and participated in "an indignation meeting designed to break down Jacksonism." Although he had been defeated then, Daniel "waited until he saw the flag of State rights unfurled by the nullifiers and abolitionists.... Let Gen. Donelson be rewarded" by the Democrats, "but let it not be done in the name of friendship to Gen. Jackson, or what is equally untrue, of regret for the position of his brother, Maj. Donelson."[42]

"A more causeless assault we do not remember to have seen," frowned the *Union*. At first Daniel intended to let matters pass "*sub silentio*" but he realized that he needed to rebut the charge, politically fatal to a Democrat, that he had opposed Jackson's administration. Replying in the *Union* on September 8, he reminded readers that his father-in-law had not been dismissed from Jackson's cabinet but resigned for "*personal*" reasons, a tactful reference to the Eaton scandal. As for the "indignation meeting," it had simply been one of many meetings that had been held across the South supporting Philip P. Barbour of Virginia as Jackson's running mate in 1832. "If there was any hostility manifested to Jacksonianism in this meeting," Daniel insisted, "I was not aware of it." After Barbour declined to be considered for the vice-presidential slot, "I gave an ardent support" to Martin Van Buren, Daniel claimed, which was true but only after Van Buren became president. Before closing, Daniel asserted, a bit plaintively and perhaps with telling circumlocution, that "it may not be improper to say that I have indubitable evidence of the confidence and friendship of Gen Jackson as long as he lived." He also hinted that he suspected who the author of the anonymous *Patriot* article was, and suggested that bygones be bygones. "The Democratic party might even resolve him into 'fellowship' with proper evidence of his sincere contrition."[43]

On October 2 another article appeared in the *Patriot* under the headline "THE SHAM DEMOCRACY AND ITS SHAM GENERAL DONELSON," and signed "Anti-Nullifier," which related more of Daniel's actions during the nullification crisis. "Gen. Donelson at that period went further than Calhoun" and "declared that revolution was better than submission to the doctrine of Gen. Jackson." Now, Daniel's "chief merit in the eyes of the Democracy, seems to be that of opposition to his brother." This *Patriot* article was even "more bitter and malignant than the first," Daniel complained in his reply "To the Public," which was published in the *Union* on October 4. The fact that the *Patriot* article discussed "matters connected with family history" convinced him that Andrew was the author. When Daniel confronted the editor of the *Patriot*, he admitted as much. "Every feeling of my nature forbids my entering into a political contest" with his brother, Daniel replied. "Whatever charges he may make against me shall *go unanswered*. I will not open to public gaze the brotherly correspondence of former years, or reopen with him difficulties over which the ashes of oblivion ought to be spread." With that, Daniel closed his part of the exchange.[44]

Andrew did not. Dropping the veil of anonymity, he attacked Daniel's "pretensions which decks him with the plumage of Jackson Democracy," because how he stood during the nullification crisis "is not a matter of conjecture. I have in my possession proofs without number of his cooperation with the nullifiers and abolitionists, and of his opposition '*to the iron nerve of his uncle in the Hermitage*'" and, in contrast to Daniel, Andrew was not averse to publishing brotherly correspondence. He chose the letter that Daniel had written from Branch's North Carolina home in Enfield in February 1833, which declared that his feelings were "wholly with" the nullifiers, and objected to Jackson's Nullification Proclamation "for the ultra federal doctrines contained in it, which if acted out would make this a great consolidated empire," against which "I would sooner see *revolution itself*."[45]

The young Nashville attorney Randal W. McGavock spoke for nearly everyone when he pronounced Andrew Donelson's attacks on his brother to be "disgraceful—and will consign him to everlasting disgrace." Worse, if Andrew's goal was to sabotage his brother's political career, then he failed.[46]

The Thirty-second General Assembly convened on Monday, October 5, 1857. In the House, William C. Dunlap, Democrat of Shelby County, was elected speaker *pro tempore* to preside over the election of the permanent speaker. George W. Rowles, Democrat of Bradley County, "nominated Gen. Daniel S. Donelson, of the county of Sumner." Dr. John W. Richardson of Rutherford County was nominated by the as-yet unnamed Opposition. In contrast to the interminable balloting of the preceding session, the Democratic majority was now so overwhelming that the result was decided in one ballot: Donelson received 37 votes to Richardson's 29. "The Speaker pro tempore thereupon declared Mr.

Donelson to be duly elected Speaker of the House of Representatives of the General Assembly of the State of Tennessee." Donelson was escorted to the chair and, ascending to the high point of his political career, addressed the House as the new speaker. "Permit me to return my heartfelt thanks for the honor you have conferred in selecting me your presiding officer," he began graciously. "You know full well my want of experience in the business of legislation," and "knowledge of parliamentary rule and rules governing deliberate bodies." Following this requisite statement of modesty, he turned to the task before them. He called, "most earnestly," on the members to turn their "undivided attention" to the improvement of the state legal system, the "careful management" of state finances, and to "our charitable institutions," as well as the other "great interests of the State." For his part, he stated, "I, gentlemen, shall endeavor to give you all the aid in your deliberations which I may have the ability to do; and I make no request but that you will, in return, give me all the assistance in your power."[47]

In organizing the House, the Democrats determined to make the most of their huge majority. With Speaker Donelson providing his promised "assistance" from the chair, they elected all the clerks and doorkeepers, while he selected the membership of the standing committees, which of course reflected Democratic dominance. In joint session with the Senate, the *Nashville Union and American* was awarded the state contract for public printing. Another joint session elected lame-duck Governor Johnson to the U.S. Senate to succeed Whig James C. Jones, whose term had expired. The *Union* smiled that "the Legislature has never been composed of a more intelligent body of men," beginning with its leadership: "Gen. DANIEL S. DONELSON, the Speaker of the House, is well-known to the people of the State as a Democrat who has seen hard service in all our past contests with the opponents of the Democracy. His election was a compliment due alike to these services and to his eminent position as a safe and prudent counsellor and as a man of sound, practical judgement."[48]

The large Democratic majority, with its presumed ability to push its legislative agenda, had initially led nearly everyone, including Donelson in his opening remarks as speaker, to hope that the session would be a short one, perhaps even adjourning before Christmas. These hopes would soon prove to be overly optimistic. As the *Daily Nashville Patriot* suspiciously observed, "From the intimation of Mr. Speaker DONELSON, we imagine that the democracy have a vast amount of labor cut out," and thus it feared a lengthy session. For one thing, the very dominance of the Democrats drove them to acts of unprecedented ambition. Not content to elect Johnson to the Senate seat that had just expired, they turned to the seat that was occupied by the hated John Bell, whose term would not expire until March 1859. On the pretext that the next General Assembly would not convene until October of that year, seven months after Bell's term would expire, Democrats determined to elect his successor preemptively during the current session. A plethora of aspirants for the seat resulted in unexpected dissension. Although it took the Democratic caucus sixteen ballots to nominate former senator Alfred Osborne Pope Nicholson, once his name was presented to a joint session of both houses, he was easily elected over the Opposition attempt to reelect Bell.[49]

Financial issues were even more divisive. The economic boom of the 1850s had been driven by land speculation and the mania for railroad construction. In August, the collapse of an Ohio insurance company precipitated the Panic of 1857, leading many banks to close or suspend specie payments. In the wake of Old Hickory's destruction of the Second Bank of the United States and the Panic of 1837, Tennessee, then under Whig control, had chartered the state-regulated Bank of Tennessee. The wave of suspensions reached the Bank of Tennessee in October just as the General Assembly convened, which revived the reservations that Jacksonian Democrats harbored about all banks. Always sensitive to the concerns of his constituents, Donelson could not have failed to notice a public meeting in Gallatin on October 19 on the issues regarding the banks, the currency, and debt relief. Although the most radical resolutions called for "the utter abolition of the banking system in Tennessee," the milder resolutions that were adopted trusted "to the wisdom of the Legislature" to adopt "such relief measures for the people, as they shall deem most prudent."[50]

Members of both parties produced a flurry of bills to address these issues, which led to divisions even among the Democrats. Amid the resulting debates, on November 3, Harris was inaugurated as governor. It was Speaker Donelson's privilege to escort the incoming and outgoing governors through the ceremony at the state capitol. In his first formal message to the General Assembly, Governor Harris added to the legislative confusion by proposing a number of financial reforms, which ranged from the removal of small denominations ($20 and smaller) of paper bank notes from circulation in favor of gold or silver coins, to repeating his predecessor's suggestion of liquidating the Bank of Tennessee.[51]

Overall, Donelson worked to move the House efficiently through such actions as ruling a speaker or motion to be in or out of order, or seeing to it that the clerks read all the bills, resolutions, and petitions that came before the House, and a calendar of business was prepared at least a week in advance. Unlike the political creature that his predecessor Neill S. Brown was, Donelson never made a partisan speech, rarely participated in debates, and usually surrendered the chair only when his obligations of representing his Sumner County constituents superseded his duties as speaker.[52]

Donelson kept to his chair whenever possible, even in the face of a looming family tragedy. His brother Andrew returned in late November from Bolivar County, Mississippi, where he had recently purchased a cotton plantation, to learn that their mother was gravely ill. Dutifully, he rode to Gallatin on November 29, a Sunday. Daniel was already there. So assiduous was Daniel to his duties as chair that he had made the trip from Nashville without being absent from the House for either the preceding Saturday session or the following Monday session. With their brother-in-law Robert L. Caruthers, who was now a judge on the Tennessee State Supreme Court, Andrew and Daniel arranged their mother's will. Even then the ice held. Polly Sanders left all of her property to her daughters by James Sanders. Her sons and twenty-one Donelson grandchildren were ignored, except for a tract of 580 acres on Drake's Creek which had belonged to her father, Daniel Smith, that she had deeded as "a gift" to Daniel in 1856 and she now "made secure to him."[53]

As Christmas approached, Donelson stepped out of his role as chair to support a resolution that the General Assembly adjourn for the holidays. During the preceding session, he recalled, the House had never formally adjourned, but so many members went home anyway that, for two weeks, no business was conducted for lack of a quorum. "In common with other gentlemen, I would like to spend Christmas day with my family," he now explained, but if the House did not formally adjourn, then "I shall be compelled as Speaker, to be here on Christmas" as well as every other day over the holidays. The General Assembly duly adjourned, formally, but Donelson spent a sad holiday. Having lingered another month, Polly Sanders died on December 29, 1857, at the age of seventy-six. When the

General Assembly reconvened on Monday, January 4, 1858, Donelson was not present; he was "detained at home . . . having lost his mother," the House journal noted. It is unclear whether he had returned by the next day, January 5, as the session adjourned for lack of a quorum, but he was certainly back in the chair the day after, on January 6. Throughout the rest of the lengthy session, he took only two more absences. He presided over the morning session of Saturday, January 23, but for the afternoon and evening sessions he asked for "leave of absence till *Monday* on account of indisposition." During the session of Wednesday, February 3, he announced that "business of an imperative character" required him to take a leave of absence "perhaps, till Monday." In both instances, he was back in the House on the appointed Monday.[54]

Meanwhile, the session ground on. Debates grew acrimonious and tempers flared. At least two fistfights erupted between assemblymen. In an oblique reference to one of the fistfights, the *Nashville Union and American* understated January 28 as "an exciting day in the deliberations of the House," when a bank bill was finally approved that embodied most of Governor Harris's recommendations. "Having disposed of the Bank Question," sighed the *Union* in relief, "the Legislature will now proceed to dispose of those questions both of local and general importance before it, about which there is less division and feeling." Again, these expectations proved to be optimistic. Even routine legislation, such as funding for state asylums for the blind and insane or finishing work on the capitol building, became mired in debate and delay. Worse, the bank bill that had been approved was resurrected and subjected to further acrimony and revision. On top of everything else, a commission of legal experts that had been created by the Twenty-ninth General Assembly of 1851–1852 to revise and codify the plethora of "Statutory enactments of the State of Tennessee" had finally completed its massive task; reading through and approving the "Revised Code of Laws" became another interminable but necessary duty that devolved onto the current General Assembly, and the beginning of each daily session came to be allocated to review a section of the Code.[55]

Through it all, Donelson tried to maintain order. Along the way, he demonstrated that he could be flexible on matters that ranged from minor points of procedure to major principles of Jacksonian ideology, if flexibility advanced constructive legislation. On one occasion, a member appealed his ruling that an amendment was out of order by reading from

"Jefferson's manual." In turn, Donelson "cited a case in which he was sustained by a constitutional provision," but, under the circumstances, "he was willing to yield to the authority quoted," and allowed the amendment. Not only had the tortuously debated bank bill not liquidated the Bank of Tennessee as governors Johnson and Harris both recommended, it also chartered two additional branches, one each in Knoxville and Memphis, to serve East and West Tennessee, and furthermore required an equal amount of "accommodation paper" with bills of exchange. As a Jacksonian, Donelson was a hard-money man and wary of the proliferation of banks. Nevertheless, as he explained to the House, "in view of the present indebtedness of the people" and the need to sustain the Bank "in the present monetary crisis, he was willing to forego [sic] his objections, and vote for the bill."[56]

At last, adjournment was set for March 22, 1858. As per tradition, Dr. Richardson, the defeated candidate for speaker, submitted a resolution, "That the thanks of the House of Representatives are hereby unanimously tendered to the honorable Daniel S. Donelson, for the fidelity and impartiality with which he has discharged the duties of presiding officer." "My last official duty is at hand," Donelson began in reply, in his "valedictory" address; he first "expressed my heartfelt thanks" for the resolution tendering "your approbation of my course, as presiding officer of this House." "We have accomplished much," he continued, "which a majority of this General Assembly believe[s] will conduce to the best interest of the people of the State." In particular, he thanked the committee that had labored so long and hard on the Revised Code of Laws. "I am pleased to know that whatever bad feelings have arisen in this House," he closed, "have disappeared . . . and we part as brothers." With that, he brought down the gavel. "I now pronounce this House adjourned, *sine die*." Randal McGavock judged that Donelson's valedictory was "a good speech."[57]

The overwhelmingly Democratic Thirty-second General Assembly thus adjourned "after a laborious session" of 155 days, exactly tying the length of what the *Nashville Union and American* had denounced as the preceding "Know Nothing Legislature of 1855–6," and only demonstrating that party dominance does not necessarily lead to efficient government. "Generally," the *Union* nevertheless conceded, "we think the people will approve the leading acts of their representatives." It was a fair assessment—the Revised Code of Laws proved to be particularly enduring, not requiring revision again until 1932. As speaker of the House, Donelson played no small role in the legislature's overall success.[58]

Almost as though from exhaustion, state politics remained quiet for the rest of the year. Democrats were confident in their ability to retain the state, and Governor Harris's nomination and election to a second term were assured. "Our people have commenced talking about the probable candidates for the Legislature," the Democratic Gallatin *Examiner* was able to report by February 1859, adding that "We do not know whether . . . Gen. Donelson again desires the honors of the county." "Sumner" remained his advocate and now pushed him for even higher office as the Democratic candidate for Congress from the Fifth District, where Sumner County had been placed subsequent to 1850 Census redistricting. "Gen. Donelson is a man of large experience, not only in matters of State, but in the tested fields of Democracy. . . . Under all circumstances, and at all times," "Sumner" exhorted, "he has ever stood forth [as] the bold and daring advocate of his political faith, and if the Democracy of this district will bring out Donelson, they cannot fail of success."[59]

However, for whatever reasons, Donelson decided not to be a candidate for a third consecutive term in the legislature or seek higher office, although he continued to be politically active at the local level. When the state Democratic convention met in Nashville on March 17, 1859, to nominate incumbent Harris for a second gubernatorial term, Donelson attended as a delegate. Otherwise, family matters both happy and sad dominated his attention.

On January 23, 1856, the Donelsons' third daughter, Sarah, had married Dr. William Henry Bradford, a Tallahassee neighbor of their Branch kin. The first Bradford grandchild, Sarah Jane, was born on July 31, 1859. Tragically, however, two previous, unnamed Bradford grandsons, possibly twins, were stillborn or died almost immediately. Meanwhile, second daughter Mary and her husband James Glasgow Martin at last presented her father with a namesake grandson, Daniel Donelson Martin, born in 1859 (date unknown) while they were apparently visiting or residing briefly in San Antonio, Texas. Also, on October 16, 1860, fourth daughter Emily married James Edwin Horton.[60]

It was during this period that Donelson also completed construction on the house that he began years before, and changed the name from Elm Tree to Hazel Path, after the hazel trees that lined the entrance. This fine plantation house of native red brick in the popular Greek Revival style boasted a portico with four square columns, double chimneys on each side, and the usual large central hall with sweeping staircase to the second floor. In all, the new home radiated both prosperous grandeur and homey warmth. In the Census of 1860, the reported value of his Hazel Path farm, which now encompassed 1,094 acres, was $43,600 and his personal estate was $45,170, although he modestly gave his occupation as "farmer." The number of his slaves had increased only slightly over the preceding decade, to fifty-three.[61]

During these years, Daniel's relations with his brother continued to be complex. In 1858, Andrew sold Tulip Grove in a last desperate attempt to clear his debts and moved his family to a house that he bought in Memphis. By that time, too, Andrew Jackson Jr., had run the Hermitage so deeply into debt that the state of Tennessee purchased it in hopes of saving it, but attempts to sell it to the United States government, for turning into a Southern version of West Point, were unsuccessful. Then Andrew's and Daniel's cousin William Donelson proposed to "unite" with Andrew to buy the Hermitage. In the spring of 1860, the legislature considered a bill that would reinter Andrew Jackson's body at the state capitol. William, believing that removal would make the sale of the Hermitage more likely, lobbied for passage, supported by Andrew and Daniel, who agreed at least on this issue. Andrew Jr. and his family understandably opposed it. Governor Harris assured young Samuel Jackson, Old Hickory's grandson, that the bill "to remove the remains of dear Grand Pa . . . would not be passed." The bill was indeed rejected. "Old Billy Donelson, the *Major* & Daniel Donelson were the only ones that had given any consent," sniffed Andrew Jr.'s daughter. The state allowed the Jacksons to remain on the property as caretakers. The Donelson brothers thereby lost an opportunity for a more permanent rapprochement.[62]

The sectional crisis instead carried the Donelson brothers along divergent paths. Tensions between North and South became ever sharper. President James Buchanan's fecklessness split the Democratic party into warring factions. The presidential election of 1860 promised to be decisive in determining the future of the Union, and both Donelson brothers would play a role, albeit for conflicting causes.

The state Democratic convention met in Nashville on January 18, 1860, to select delegates for the national convention. At a planning meeting just prior to the convention, Daniel Donelson was selected to serve on the committee that would nominate officers for the state convention. Then the convention was "called to order . . . by the Hon. DANIEL S. DONELSON, Speaker of the lower House of the last General Assembly." The convention endorsed Andrew Johnson as its first choice to be the Democratic candidate for president. Two delegates and two alternates were selected from each congressional district to attend the national convention; Donelson was selected as one of the alternates from the Fifth District.[63]

Being an alternate, Donelson did not attend the Democratic national convention, which convened in Charleston, South Carolina, on April 23. As a result, he missed one of the most tumultuous events of the era. Southern fire-eaters were determined to block the nomination of the front-runner, Senator Stephen A. Douglas of Illinois, whom they loathed because of his break with the Buchanan administration over its attempts to foist slavery onto Kansas. After a week of obstruction and discord, the delegations from the Deep South states walked out, which prevented the nomination of Douglas or anyone else. The Tennessee delegates held little love for Douglas, but however they might have sympathized with their Deep South brethren, they remained loyal, for now, to the main party. Party leaders could only agree that the convention would reconvene in Baltimore on June 18.[64]

Before the Democrats could meet again, two other parties met in convention and nominated their presidential candidates. On May 9, Andrew Donelson was among those who convened the Constitutional Union party, which proclaimed its dedication to preserve the Union from Northern Republicans and Southern States' Rights Democrats alike, and nominated for the presidency Andrew's old antagonist John Bell. A week later, the supremely confident Republicans nominated as their candidate for the presidency Abraham Lincoln of Illinois.[65]

Democrats in many states wondered whether their initial body of delegates should remain intact to attend the rescheduled convention or new delegates should be chosen. For the Tennessee delegation, the *Nashville Union and American* opined that "if possible," the delegates who attended the Charleston convention should go to Baltimore, because "None others can so well understand or so fully appreciate the exact conditions of the business done and to be done by the Convention." For whatever reason, however, J. W. Avant, one of the two original Fifth District delegates in

Charleston, was unable to attend the rescheduled convention. Attending in his place in Baltimore was listed "D.S. Donaldson."[66]

Having missed the initial party rupture in Charleston, Donelson was present at the final breach when the Democratic national convention reconvened in the Front Street Theatre in Baltimore. Several days were spent with the delegates quarreling over whether new pro-Douglas delegates from the Deep South states should be seated in place of those whose original delegations had bolted at Charleston. This time the delegates from the Upper South departed to join their fellow insurgents from the Deep South. The rump convention of northern Democrats was finally able to nominate Douglas. The Southern delegates, including Donelson among the Tennessee delegation, convened at the Maryland Institute down the street and nominated Buchanan's vice president, John C. Breckinridge of Kentucky, as its candidate for president and General Joseph Lane of Oregon for vice-president. "The disruption of the Democratic National Convention is complete," the *Nashville Union and American* announced. For this, the paper blamed "the friends of Mr. Douglas" while the "Conservative Democrats," as the *Union* now dignified the southern insurgents, had saved the party by nominating Breckinridge and Lane.[67]

After he departed Baltimore, Donelson passed through Virginia and then spent several days in North Carolina, apparently to visit his Branch in-laws, but he was home in time for a "Grand Rally" in Nashville on June 30 to ratify the Breckinridge and Lane nominations. Governor Harris gave the first speech, followed by two others who also had served as delegates at Baltimore. The fourth speaker was "Gen. DANIEL S. DONELSON of Sumner." Recounting the course that the Tennessee delegates had taken in the first Baltimore convention at the hands of Douglas supporters, "Gen. D. showed that they had submitted to continued wrong until further submission would have [branded] them as traitors to justness, fair dealing [and the] interests of the Democracy of Tennessee."[68]

Voters went to the polls on November 6, 1860, solemn with a sense that the fate of the Union was at stake. Despite the efforts of Donelson and other Breckinridge Democrats, Bell carried Tennessee, along with Kentucky and Virginia. Breckinridge carried every other slave state, save for Missouri. The decisive theater, however, was in the North, where Lincoln secured his victory. For Southern fire-eaters, the moment that they had long warned against had come to pass—a purely sectional party that opposed the extension of slavery had elected a president. On December 20, South Carolina seceded from the Union, followed during January and February 1861 by every other state of the Deep South. A convention of seceded states met in February in Montgomery, Alabama, organized the Confederate States of America, and elected Jefferson Davis as interim president.[69]

The actions of the fire-eaters in the Deep South threw the Upper South into a quandary. Unionists there vastly outnumbered outright secessionists, but the latter group at first seemed to have fervor and momentum on their side. Characteristically, Tennessee offered all opinions. As the Deep South states seceded, Governor Harris called the General Assembly to meet in special session in January 1861. Although a political colleague described Harris as being "not a disunionist for the sake of disunion," the governor's message to the Assembly was a litany of wrongs that the North had committed against the South that justified secession and called for a state convention so that the citizens of Tennessee could decide the issue. But rather than calling for a state convention to vote directly on secession, the Assembly approved a measure that merely called for a referendum to be held on February 9, on whether such a convention should be held. By that time, the state's unionists, largely Old Line Whigs and Conservative Democrats, had recovered their footing. Although West Tennessee heavily approved holding the convention and Middle Tennessee split almost equally, East Tennessee rejected the convention overwhelmingly, ensuring an overall statewide majority to reject the convention. Should the convention have been approved, even West and Middle Tennessee voted to elect unionist delegates.[70]

Nevertheless, although Tennesseans had asserted their unionist preferences, like their brethren across the Upper South they did not constitute a monolith. Many were to various degrees what were called "conditional unionists." They denounced secession and the fire-eaters of the Deep South for precipitating the crisis, but conceded that secession was an extra-constitutional revolutionary right of last resort. They hoped that a peaceful resolution to the crisis could be reached. Most important, they were therefore equally determined to denounce any attempt by the federal government to suppress the seceded states by force. Even Andrew Donelson, who strongly opposed secession, insisted that Tennessee "will never abandon any rights deemed necessary to the safety of the South."[71]

For the Donelson brothers, the secession crisis was heart-rending, and evidently more so for Andrew. He had absorbed his love of the Union at the side of Old Hickory, and his public career during the preceding decade had been dedicated to its preservation. Daniel was no fire-eater, and he, too, had grown up at the Hermitage, but the nullification crisis and the fate of his father-in-law John Branch, as a consequence of perceived opposition to Jackson, had pulled him farther south than his brother. Daniel surely wished to have preserved the Union, but he supported the Union only insofar as the rights of the Southern states were respected and he would tolerate no coercion by the federal government. No contemporary accounts record his views directly but historian W. W. Clayton, who may have known Daniel Donelson and been privy to his thoughts, wrote two decades later, "No one deplored it more than he did," meaning the dissolution of the old Union, "but with a prophetic eye he saw war, inevitable war, and, believing the South to be right, he was willing and ready to resist."[72]

This portrait by George Dury, ca. 1850, depicts Daniel Donelson in his prime, as a prosperous Sumner County planter and prominent Tennessee political leader. (Courtesy Historic Rock Castle, Hendersonville, TN.)

Andrew Jackson, ca. 1828, portrait by R. E. W. Earl. The colossus of the era named for him, Old Hickory remains controversial even after two centuries, but his father-son relationship with his Donelson nephews, occasionally tempestuous but also loving and supportive, illuminates some of his best traits. (Courtesy Andrew Jackson's Hermitage, Nashville, TN.)

Rachel Donelson Jackson, miniature by Louisa Catherine Strobel. Her controversial marriage to Andrew Jackson left emotional scars that never fully healed, but she was, in effect, the second mother to her Donelson nephews. (Courtesy Andrew Jackson's Hermitage, Nashville, TN.)

Andrew Jackson Donelson, ca. 1830, portrait thought to be by Francis Alexander. In their youth, Andrew and Daniel Donelson were as close and supportive as any brothers, but during the sectional crisis they split both politically and personally over the course of the Democratic party and fate of the Union. (Courtesy Andrew Jackson's Hermitage, Nashville, TN.)

John Branch, secretary of the navy in Andrew Jackson's first cabinet and, as father of Margaret Branch Donelson, Daniel Donelson's father-in-law. Daniel supported his father-in-law when Branch resigned from Jackson's cabinet over the notorious Eaton Affair.

Hazel Path, Daniel Donelson's elegant home, remains a prominent landmark in Hendersonville. Begun as a more modest structure called Elm Tree, Donelson spent twenty years enlarging and remodeling the house. Federal occupation forces repeatedly pillaged the house and plantation during the Civil War.

This photograph of Daniel Donelson was apparently taken in the spring of 1861, after Tennessee's secession from the Union but before joining the Confederate States. Donelson is wearing his elaborate uniform as brigadier general of the Tennessee State Militia while he served in the Provisional Army of Tennessee.

At the time Daniel Donelson served under him during the western Virginia campaign in the fall of 1861, General Robert E. Lee still looked much like this photograph taken when he was an officer in the United States Army, clean-shaven with only a mustache, before the gray hair and beard by which Lee later became universally famous. (Library of Congress.)

Major General Leonidas Polk, depicted here in his Episcopal clerical robes, commanded the corps in the Army of Tennessee in which Donelson's brigade was assigned. Polk's zeal for the Confederate cause exceeded his military prowess. (Library of Congress.)

(*Left*) Major General Benjamin Franklin "Frank" Cheatham commanded the division in the Army of Tennessee in which Donelson's brigade was assigned. Donelson's immediate superior was a bold fighter but subject to rumors that he was frequently drunk on the battlefield. (Library of Congress.)

(*Right*) General Braxton Bragg remains one of the most controversial figures of the Civil War. He could exhibit real strategic insight and displayed tactical aggressiveness, but his abrasive personality led to clashes with his officers and on the battlefield he suffered from a unique ability to snatch defeat from the jaws of victory. (Library of Congress.)

This photograph of Confederate States general Daniel Donelson was apparently taken in February or March 1863 after his assignment as commander of the Department of East Tennessee. Compared to the photograph taken only two years earlier, the decline in Donelson's health is visibly obvious.

It is a pity that the only known image of Margaret Branch Donelson is this portrait, artist unknown, dating from her last years. Margaret is depicted here as a dignified widow dressed in black wearing a cameo of her late husband. (From a private collection as seen on tnportraits.org, a project of The National Society of the Colonial Dames of America in the State of Tennessee.)

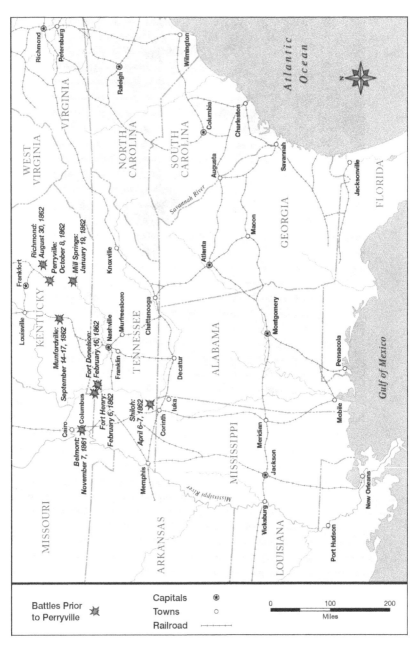

The Western Theater in the American Civil War. Map by Tim Kissel.

CHAPTER FIVE

"Send Donelson's Brigade"

THE WAR BEGINS,
APRIL 1861–APRIL 1862

The political storm soon became a military one. On April 12, 1861, Confederate batteries bombarded Fort Sumter in Charleston harbor. Major Robert Anderson, who had graduated with Daniel Donelson from the U.S. Military Academy back in 1825, commanded the small Federal garrison there and endured the indignity of lowering the Stars and Stripes. In response to the attack, President Abraham Lincoln issued proclamations calling for troops to "suppress" the "insurrection." His actions constituted the coercion that many Southern unionists had maintained would precipitate their complete break with the old government. The loyalty of the Upper South states to the Union was broken at a snap.[1]

In Tennessee, a tide of revolutionary fervor swept the state, especially the middle and western Grand Divisions. Governor Isham G. Harris again called the General Assembly into session on April 25. This time the Assembly scheduled a popular referendum for June 8 to vote on whether Tennessee should remain in the Union. Even now, however, under the influence of the state's Old Line Whigs and Conservative Democrats, questions over the constitutionality of "secession" were avoided. Instead, following the tradition of their Revolutionary forefathers, Tennesseans were asked to approve a "Declaration of Independence" from the United States. The terminology mattered little; the result of the vote was everything. The turnaround in public opinion from the first referendum of the preceding February, in which a majority of voters rejected a convention even to consider secession, was dramatic. When the second referendum was held in June, an even larger proportion of Tennesseans approved the

"Declaration of Independence." Traditionally-balanced Middle Tennessee voted even more heavily for "independence" than did Southern-leaning West Tennessee. Only mountainous East Tennessee remained staunchly unionist but was heavily outvoted by the other two Grand Divisions.[2]

Even long before the vote was held, Gideon J. Pillow, the senior major general in the Tennessee state militia, called on Tennesseans to "organize as rapidly as possible," and within days military units were forming. "The people of Sumner are thoroughly 'fired,'" the *Nashville Union and American* crowed, as just one example. By the first week of May, three companies of "Sumner boys" were drilling in camp at the fairgrounds outside Nashville. These companies formed the core of a regiment that was soon sent by rail eastward to Virginia under the command of William B. Bate, a rising young Sumner County attorney, General Assembly member, and Mexican War veteran.[3]

On May 8, the General Assembly passed a bill to "raise, organize and equip, a provisional force of volunteers for the defence of the State," up to 55,000, and an officer corps to command it. The next day, Governor Harris appointed Pillow and Samuel R. Anderson, another long-serving officer in the state militia and Mexican War veteran, as the two allotted major generals, five brigadier generals, and as "*Adjutant General*—Daniel S. Donelson."[4]

Many among Donelson's immediate and extended family flocked to the colors. His oldest son, James Branch Donelson, nearly nineteen and listed as a student, was commissioned as a second lieutenant in Company E of the Seventh Tennessee Infantry Regiment. Donelson's son-in-law James Edwin Horton, daughter Emily's husband, became captain of Company H, Ninth Alabama Infantry Regiment. Despite their father's vociferous unionism, both of Andrew Donelson's sons of military age volunteered for service; John Samuel Donelson and Daniel Smith Donelson became officers in the One Hundred Fifty-fourth Senior Tennessee Regiment. Even Old Hickory's grandsons joined the rebellion: Andrew Jackson III commanded a battery in the Artillery Corps of Tennessee, while Samuel Jackson commanded a company in the Forty-fourth Tennessee Infantry Regiment.[5]

Tennesseans prepared to defend their state from invasion. On May 6, Governor Harris ordered Daniel Donelson "to establish a camp of Instruction for the troops raised in Montgomery and Stewart Counties." In compliance with these orders, on May 9, Donelson bade farewell to his wife Margaret and the children who were still at home, and rode away to begin his part in the war. He would never see his home, Hazel Path, again.[6]

Donelson soon arrived at Dover, where on May 18 he mustered in three companies from Stewart County. Nearby, Adna Anderson, a civil engineer for the Edgefield and Kentucky Railroad, selected two sites for forts to be built along the border between Tennessee and Kentucky, which for now remained with the Union but declared its "neutrality" in the coming hostilities. One site guarded the approaches along the Tennessee River, the other site guarded the Cumberland River, as each stream crosses the boundary between the two states. Wishing that a professional soldier provide a corroborating opinion, Harris directed Donelson to examine the sites. Donelson approved the Cumberland River site but, not liking Anderson's original site on the Tennessee River, selected another that was more clearly on the Tennessee side of the state line. On May 31, he wrote Pillow, whom Harris had appointed as commander of the Provisional Army of Tennessee, "as to the number and character of guns that would be required" to arm the forts. The fort guarding the Tennessee River was named Fort Henry, in honor of Gustavus Adolphus Henry, a longtime Whig politician from the area, a descendant of the Revolutionary patriot Patrick Henry, and just selected as a senator from Tennessee to the Confederate States Congress. The fort guarding the Cumberland River was named Fort Donelson, in honor of the officer who approved its site.[7]

When Tennessee state forces were formally incorporated into Confederate States service on July 9, Governor Harris forwarded to President Jefferson Davis the names of Pillow, Anderson, and Donelson as brigadier generals, evidently in that intended order of seniority, an action that simultaneously relieved Donelson of his appointment as adjutant general. On August 1, Davis transmitted to the Congress of the Confederate States a list of appointments, including that of Daniel Smith Donelson as brigadier general in the Provisional Army of the Confederate States. Donelson's appointment was confirmed on August 29, to date from July 9. According to a Donelson family legend, at a dinner party in Memphis honoring Daniel and Brigadier General Benjamin Franklin Cheatham, Andrew Donelson, whose relations with his brother seem to have been exacerbated by secession, had the effrontery to attend intoxicated.[8]

Daniel Donelson was soon given a field command. On July 24, Anderson arrived in Lynchburg, Virginia, to take command of Tennessee forces that were already gathering there. By the next day three Tennessee regiments had arrived, and two others had been ordered up from Bristol, in East Tennessee. Donelson arrived that same day, without a command, or as Anderson phrased it, "without incumbrance." On July 27, however, General Samuel Cooper, Adjutant and Inspector General of the Confederate States Army, ordered Donelson to "Proceed immediately to Staunton and take command of the two Tennessee regiments ordered to Huntersville." Donelson's son-in-law Major James Glasgow Martin accompanied him as his assistant adjutant general.[9]

The folks back home were pleased to learn of Donelson's new command. The *Nashville Union and American* cheered, "it may be truly said that he is the right man in the right place . . . firm and unbending in the discharge of duty, submitting cheerfully to privation and labor, he is just the man to inspire his soldiers with patience, zeal and endurance in their country's cause." Moreover, perhaps as yet unrealized, at sixty, Donelson became the oldest officer of the rank of general to have a field command in the Confederate States armies.[10]

Huntersville, which was described ungenerously by a Confederate chaplain as "a most wretched and filthy town," was located in the valley of the Greenbrier River, which flows southwest between the Allegheny Mountains to the east and the parallel Greenbrier Mountains to the west on its way to join the Kanawha River. Like mountainous East Tennessee, mountainous western Virginia remained staunchly Unionist. For United States forces, here was a back-door entrance to the heart of secessionist Virginia. For the Confederate States, here was a vulnerable region that had to be defended against invasion.[11]

Military operations, however amateurish, soon began in the isolated but strategically important mountain valleys of western Virginia. The commander of Ohio's state troops, the brash and ambitious George B. McClellan, rushed several regiments of raw volunteers into the region. By the middle of July, they had occupied Rich Mountain and the surrounding passes. In response, on July 20, General Robert E. Lee, who commanded all military forces in Virginia, placed Brigadier General William W. Loring in command of the troops, about 4,500 effectives, who were retreating before McClellan's forces. It was to this force, which was now styled the Army of the Northwest, that the regiments at Huntersville under the command of "Gen. Donnleson" were directed.[12]

Lee himself soon arrived in Huntersville, where Loring had established headquarters. "There are but few of your acquaintances in this Army,"

Lee wrote his wife, Mary. Among them, "Genl Daniel S. Donelson is in command of a Tennessee regiment." When and where the Lees and Donelsons were previously acquainted can only be conjectured. Rather than being placed in command, Lee had been sent merely as President Davis's military adviser to facilitate, through his well-known tact and persuasiveness, some unity of action among the disparate commands in the region. Loring resented Lee's presence, while over the next several weeks Lee grew impatient with Loring's reluctance to take the offensive against the Federals, who for the moment seemed to be content to occupy the mountain crests along the northern end of the Greenbrier River valley. While keeping the touchy Loring in formal command of the Army of the Northwest and punctiliously forwarding all of his directives through him, Lee began to plan a campaign to drive the Federals out of the mountains of western Virginia. Lee's object was to duplicate the same victory in the mountains of western Virginia what Confederate States troops under Generals Joseph E. Johnston and Pierre G. T. Beauregard had recently accomplished in eastern Virginia at the Battle of Manassas (Bull Run).[13]

By early September, Loring's Army of the Northwest consisted of nineteen regiments, large and small, plus cavalry and artillery, perhaps 15,000 men in total, grouped into six brigades. Donelson commanded the Third Brigade, comprised of the Eighth and Sixteenth Tennessee Infantry regiments, the First and Fourteenth Georgia Infantry regiments, the Greenbrier Cavalry company, and a section of the Hampden Artillery battery. The Eighth and Sixteenth Tennessee Infantry regiments would constitute the core of the brigade that Donelson would lead for as long as he held a field command. The Eighth, which was commanded by Colonel Alfred S. Fulton, had been organized at Camp Trousdale north of Gallatin in Sumner County in May and arrived at Huntersville a few days before Donelson. The Sixteenth, organized in June at Camp Harris outside of Nashville, had arrived in August. Most of its men were rough farming types from Putnam, Warren, and neighboring counties in the rugged Eastern Highland Rim that straddled East and Middle Tennessee, and were described by H. H. Dillard, a company captain, as being "what you might call mountain-men." Its commander, Colonel John H. Savage, a native of McMinnville in Warren County, was a hard-bitten veteran of the Mexican War, wounded at Molino del Rey, and a former Democratic congressman; he could also be irascible, critical, and insubordinate. Among the men in the ranks, there was "universal rejoicing" when it was announced that Donelson "was to be our foreman," Surgeon J. W. Gray of Fulton's Eighth Tennessee Infantry Regiment reported, "for all who had ever had a knowledge of his profound judgment and unmistakable courage, were at once willing to follow him on the bloodiest field of battle."[14]

The major impediment to a campaign was the weather. An unusually cool, wet summer produced twenty-seven days of rain between July 24 and August 22 and even frost on the night of August 14–15. The men, cold, wet, and miserable, huddled around campfires. "A Tennessee hog pen would scarcely be more uncomfortable," one officer complained. Savage's Sixteenth Tennessee and the Fourteenth Georgia Infantry regiments "were compelled to work on the roads, so as to keep them passable for supplies." Nearly half of Loring's command were sick "from typhoid and bilious fevers and other diseases" and unfit for combat. Not liking the squalor and bad water of the Huntersville camp, Savage asked Donelson to move his command to a higher, healthier location. Donelson denied the request but Savage moved his regiment anyway. Donelson quickly acknowledged his error, telling him, "Col Savage, I like your encampment." He relocated his entire command accordingly and within days most of the men regained their health, but Savage quickly formed a poor opinion of Donelson as being a political general who lacked any practical field or battle experience.[15]

Amid the rain and mud, Lee developed a plan to attack the Federals, who were now commanded by Brigadier General William S. Rosecrans, after McClellan had been called East to take command of the Army of the Potomac. Lee's plan, which he carefully delivered through Loring, required precise timing and coordination among several columns. From the Confederate base, the valley of the northward-flowing Tygart Valley River ran along the western slope of Cheat Mountain. By a flank march, Colonel Albert Rust's Third Arkansas Infantry Regiment would turn the Federals out of their position on the crest of Cheat Mountain. Anderson's Second Brigade, constituting the center of the force, would advance northward down Tygart Valley along the western slope of Cheat Mountain. Donelson would march his brigade alongside Anderson's left flank.[16]

Anderson's brigade, which had the longest march, set out on the morning of September 10. Donelson's oldest son, James, marched in the Seventh Tennessee Infantry Regiment as part of Anderson's command. Movement and coordination were hampered by rain, mud, and the forested mountainous terrain, compounded by the inexperience of officers and men.

Donelson started his brigade that afternoon. His objective was to turn left, or west, to descend Becky Run to cross and cut the Huntersville-Huttonsville Road. There, he would be in a position either to guard Anderson's flank or block a Union movement southward from Huttonsville that might threaten the Confederate base at Huntersville. His brigade was soon struggling. Their northward track required crossing a series of short creeks, or "runs" in Virginia parlance, that flowed westward toward the Tygart Valley River, then climbing and descending the ridges that formed the watersheds between them. An officer in Fulton's Eighth Tennessee Infantry Regiment compared Donelson's crossing of the "Alleghanies" to Bonaparte's crossing of the Alps. Two men from each company went ahead, armed with axes, picks, spades, and shovels "to make passways for the troops," recalled an anonymous memoirist. Donelson was nevertheless soon compelled to leave his artillery behind, while the men "had absolutely to crawl part of the way," recounted a member of Fulton's regiment, known only by the initials J. C. C., who wrote home, "we were either going up or down a mountain the entire route . . . hundreds of men with not a shoe on their feet." Guiding the brigade was Dr. Oscar Butcher, a local "who was thoroughly acquainted" with the area.[17]

Donelson's brigade struggled all the day of September 11, but enjoyed what historian Douglas Southall Freeman pronounced as being "an exciting day for green troops." First, his skirmishers sighted Federal pickets manning a house that belonged to a family named Matthews. Forty years after matriculating at West Point, Donelson faced his first hostile action. Having no delusions about his experience, or rather the lack thereof, he held a "council of war" with Fulton and the veteran Savage. As he related in his report following the action, Donelson took a position "to have a full view of the house." He then "gave the command 'charge,'" as Surgeon Gray reported. Fulton and Dr. Butcher advanced and captured four pickets, who were, as Donelson reported, "taken by surprise, no gun fired." Donelson's men then "double quicked" a mile or so down the run. They soon came upon another picket post, killing two and taking several more prisoners. Another two miles along, they surprised the main post at the Simmons house. As Donelson laconically put it, they "arrested" the captain of a company and took "forty-eight prisoners." This first real military action that Donelson experienced, Surgeon Gray reported, "seemed to call back many years of our brave old General's life." The captured officers surrendered their swords and small arms. Savage, Butcher, and

Donelson's aide and son-in-law James G. Martin each accepted a sword, while Donelson accepted a fine Enfield rifle. Donelson then sent the prisoners to the rear.[18]

After his men bivouacked for the night, Donelson reconnoitered ahead personally, establishing a pattern that he would follow, to verify a situation by his own observation and leaving nothing to mischance that might endanger his troops. He found that his command had bivouacked uncomfortably close to another Union outpost. As a result, he ordered that no fires be lit, despite the nighttime cold, and the men were forbidden to speak above a whisper. The rain finally stopped, but September 12 dawned foggy. The men were cold and hungry, as the rain had prevented the delivery of rations or ruined what they carried, but the various units of Lee's little army had reached their destinations. The ever-critical Savage thought that Donelson had advanced three or four miles too far, putting his brigade at risk of capture or destruction. The carefully planned and long-expected attack was to begin with the musket volleys of Colonel Rust's attack to seize the crest of Cheat Mountain.[19]

Nothing happened. Only silence drifted from the direction of Rust's intended attack. A few scattered shots then came instead from Becky Run. Lee, who with his staff had camped the night in "some hay-stacks," rode to investigate. They stumbled into being nearly captured by a Union cavalry patrol, when the timely arrival of Donelson's pickets drove off the Federals. This was not yet the Lee of later legend, of gray hair and beard, but nevertheless his first appearance among Donelson's troops riveted attention. "He is a fine portly looking man about six feet one inch high," Surgeon Gray related home, "well proportioned, with round limbs and firm muscles. His eyes are black and penetrating, his hair black with traces of gray. His mustache . . . is heavy, while the balance of his face is kept clean shaved." Once he arrived safely inside Donelson's lines, Lee learned to his chagrin that the shots came from green soldiers who decided that firing their guns was an easy way to discharge damp powder. In so doing, they had only alerted the Federals to their presence.[20]

In the absence of action or intelligence from Rust, Lee decided to initiate the battle where he was. Conferring with Donelson, who told him that Anderson's men were within supporting distance, Lee declared, "we will send for them and attack the enemy," but then he asked Donelson about the state of his provisions. Donelson "hesitatingly" admitted, "my soldiers are hungry and without food." "Then it must not be done," Lee replied, "it would not only be unmilitary but inhumane to make the attack." Instead, he ordered Donelson to retire his brigade to be provisioned. Before the withdrawal could begin, however, word came that Federals were gathering in a nearby field. Lee canceled the withdrawal and ordered the attack to proceed. Donelson responded with alacrity and threw units of the Eighth and Sixteenth Tennessee Infantry regiments across a creek and into the woods on the other side. After each side had fired a volley, he ordered, "charge on them and give them hell," whereupon his men "gave a yell" and rushed forward. Savage, Donelson reported, "charged gallantly the enemy [who], as soon as charged, retired in confusion." The short firefight drove off the Federals, killing perhaps twenty and capturing about as many, with the loss of private Alf Martin, the first man in Donelson's command to be killed on the field of battle.[21]

This limited action was all that there would be. Lee was unable to move any of his other officers. Each had an excuse. Loring's command could not ford a stream that was running too high. For most others, it was enough that their men were cold, wet, and hungry. Rust had failed to attack because captured pickets frightened him into believing that the Federals on Cheat Mountain were prepared for his attack. Putting out feelers for continuing the campaign by moving to the west around the Union flank revealed that all the passes were well guarded. Eventually, Lee ordered his columns back to their starting point at Valley Mountain. With that, the Battle of Cheat Mountain came to an end. At least the Federals showed no inclination to abandon their mountain fastness to pursue the retiring Confederates.[22]

If little glory had been won for anyone, even Lee, at Cheat Mountain, then at least Donelson was one of the few officers who had performed creditably. Despite hard marching in difficult terrain and weather, he had succeeded in delivering his brigade to its assigned objective by the appointed time. Wherever Donelson's men encountered Union troops, they responded with alacrity and aggressiveness, and the prisoners whom they captured – sixty-seven total, by Donelson's count – were virtually the only fruits that the Confederates gained from the campaign. If the impulsive action of his men discharging their weapons, thereby precipitating unplanned hostilities, was a mark against his full control over his command, then he redeemed himself by his instant willingness, alone among Lee's commanders, to commit his troops to the new battle plan that Lee improvised. Whatever the failure of others, all agreed that "Gen. Donelson with his Brigade, was at his post." In the bickering afterward, an officer in Anderson's brigade could assert, "Of the other Tennessee brigade, commanded by Gen. Donaldson, I can only say that they executed their orders promptly." An officer in Fulton's regiment agreed: "But let it be recorded that Donelson's brigade executed every order, however, difficult, however dangerous, to the very letter."[23]

Lee took note. Habitually reserved and sparing of praise, on this occasion Lee "complimented us highly," J. C. C. recalled of the assault on Cheat Mountain that Lee saw Donelson's men conduct, "—said we were the best troops in the world—that we were up precisely to the time and place, and ten miles ahead of the general movement." Lee's praise may have been uncharacteristically fulsome, but it was not insincere. It became his command style that officers who disappointed him were transferred elsewhere while he retained and even sought to bring under his command officers who gained his confidence. Lee would send for Donelson and his brigade to serve under him again in the future.[24]

Lee's muddled campaign had at least cowed the Federals on Cheat Mountain into quiescence, but to the west Rosecrans was advancing up the valley of the Great Kanawha River, threatening two small Confederate States forces under the commands of Brigadier Generals John B. Floyd and Henry A. Wise, both of whom were former governors of Virginia, with Floyd also having served as secretary of war under President James Buchanan. On September 20, barely a week after the fighting fizzled on Cheat Mountain, Lee ordered Loring to move most of his force to join Floyd and Wise.[25]

Donelson's brigade, along with that of Brigadier General Henry R. Jackson, were retained to guard against any Federal movement along the Greenbrier River. By early November the lines in the Greenbrier River valley had stabilized while Floyd's sector remained threatened. On November 5, Loring was accordingly ordered to send Donelson's brigade to join Floyd at Lewisburg. Floyd was instructed to make arrangements to "afford him such facilities as may be in your power" to assist Donelson's men. They needed the assistance. "All the boys in camp look well," a visitor to Donelson's headquarters wrote, "tho' they are very ragged and dirty—their clothes have never reached them."[26]

Donelson's brigade waited at Lewisburg for over a week, camped "in a heavy forest without tents." "I have at last succeeded in sending to your aid three fine regiments," Acting Secretary of War Judah P. Benjamin chided Floyd on November 15 for his failure to use them, including "two Tennessee regiments under Brigadier-General Donelson." Meanwhile, Colonel J. Lucius Davis, commanding the First Virginia Cavalry Regiment at Meadow Bluff and coming under perceived threat, appealed to the nearby Donelson for help. While he was eager for action, Donelson explained that "I have two regiments under my command that are without clothing, blankets, shoes, &c." Nevertheless, he added, "I shall not hesitate to take the additional responsibility . . . to come to you, until I can communicate with General Floyd on the subject and know his wishes." The next day, Floyd directed him to remain with his brigade "at some good place until further orders." Despite the frustrations of immobility, the exchanges demonstrated two aspects of Donelson's growing military character—his solicitude for his troops' basic needs and his unhesitating willingness to assume responsibility, the latter no doubt a legacy of his uncle Andrew Jackson.[27]

Through the rest of November, Donelson and his brigade waited at Lewisburg, along with the Sixtieth Virginia Infantry Regiment under the command of Colonel William E. Starke. Winter settled in, with "a big snow on the ground," as Captain H. H. Dillard of Savage's Sixteenth Tennessee Infantry Regiment complained. Happily, "a bountiful supply of winter clothing and blankets" soon arrived from home, "together with an immense amount of letters and nicknacks from mothers, wives, and sweethearts." Their assignment and mission remained unclear. Captain C. C. Brewer heard vaguely that the brigade "will act in concert with the forces in East Tennessee, during the present winter." Worse, Donelson was suffering from the effects of field command under such miserable conditions. "My health is far from good," he admitted to his father-in-law John Branch, explaining, "I have suffered much within my Bowels & stomach, but have not lost an hour from duty."[28]

Then, on December 2, Donelson and Starke received orders from Adjutant and Inspector General Cooper that were as unexpected as was their telegraphic brevity: "Retire with your respective commands to the nearest point on the Virginia and Tennessee Railroad, and proceed thence to Bowling Green, Ky., and report to General A. S. Johnston." Donelson was "pleased," as he wrote Branch, to receive the order to transfer his brigade to Bowling Green. For one, General Albert Sidney Johnston, who commanded all Confederate States forces west of the mountains, was an old acquaintance. Donelson no doubt remembered him from West

Point, where Johnston graduated the year behind him. Better yet, Bowling Green would put Donelson and his men closer to home. As he wrote to Branch, "I would then have had an opportunity to spend a day or two with Margaret and [the] children, and arrange my domestic affairs, somewhat out of condition from my long absence."[29]

Unfortunately, even as the railroad cars were being readied, everything changed. On December 6, the Adjutant and Inspector General's Office in Richmond revoked the previous orders. Instead, "the Tennessee brigade under General Donelson and the regiment under Colonel Starke . . . will immediately proceed to Charleston, S.C., and report for duty to Gen. R.E. Lee, commanding." The message was "much to the surprise of every one," recorded Captain James J. Womack in the Sixteenth Tennessee Infantry Regiment. This time it was clear that the new orders were not subject to change. When Richmond had no confirmation four days later that the movement had begun, Cooper ordered Donelson directly, "Proceed without delay with your brigade and Starke's regiment to Charleston, S.C., and report to General R.E. Lee." On the same day Cooper was reassured that "Donelson's brigade, 1,300 strong, moves today for Petersburg."[30]

Donelson was disappointed that the orders to Bowling Green were canceled, although he was "glad to leave the mountains of Va. where for four months, we have suffered much from exposure to incessant rains, cold weather, and the worst roads in America." He worried that being posted to South Carolina would separate him even farther from his family, who were situated dangerously near the Union lines in Kentucky. He declared that "if the Enemy makes a forward move, and should be successful in and about Bowling Green, then I must go to the *rescue*, of them who are dearer to me than life itself."[31]

What had happened to precipitate this flurry of orders that first sent Donelson's brigade to Johnston's army at Bowling Green, then just as suddenly in the opposite direction, to Charleston? It was clear to authorities in Richmond that winter had forced a halt to operations in the mountains and the inactive forces could be better employed elsewhere. As Cooper explained to Floyd, "For this reason it is that the Department has ordered Anderson's [Donelson's] brigade and Starke's regiment (originally intended to re-enforce your command) to South Carolina."[32]

The order to send Donelson's brigade to Bowling Green made good sense, as it would be nearer their homes in Tennessee. The surprise was the sudden reversal of direction, and specifically of Donelson's brigade, to the distant shores of Charleston, plus the insistence that the move be made without delay. The inference was that the change originated with Robert E. Lee, who had been ordered to organize the coastal defenses of South Carolina and Georgia. In early November a United States fleet had landed over 12,000 troops under the command of Brigadier General Thomas W. Sherman on the coast of Port Royal Sound, South Carolina, threatening both Charleston and Savannah, Georgia.[33]

For Lee, who was assembling troops to defend the coast, only the best units would do. Apparently, he recalled that amid the confusion and missed opportunities at Cheat Mountain there was one commander who moved his troops as directed and did not hesitate to attack—Brigadier General Daniel S. Donelson, precisely the kind of officer that Lee wanted under his command. No letter has been found from Lee that specifically requests Donelson's brigade to be sent to him in South Carolina, but the existence of one can be inferred in a December 8 dispatch from Secretary of War Benjamin to Lee. Benjamin assured Lee "that measures had been taken to re-enforce you with . . . three regiments of infantry." Had any reinforcements satisfied Lee, or had he not specified which units, then Benjamin's following clarification would have been unnecessary: "the three on the way to you are Donelson's brigade, of two Tennessee regiments, and Starke's regiment." Even Savage, the prickly commander of the Sixteenth Tennessee Infantry Regiment, was "satisfied that these regiments made this movement under the orders or by request of General Lee."[34]

Donelson and his staff arrived in Charleston on December 15 and took rooms at the Charleston Hotel, near the Mills House where Lee and his staff were staying. His brigade camped about fifteen miles outside of town. "Tennessee regiments arrived," Lee confirmed to Secretary of War Benjamin by telegraph, in which brevity did not obscure the apparent specificity of Lee's original request or his relief that they were now at hand. He immediately ordered Donelson to "proceed with your brigade" to Coosawhatchie as soon as the quartermaster "can furnish you with the necessary transportation." At Coosawhatchie, on December 24, Donelson received "By order of General Lee" the following assignment: "Brig. Gen. D.S. Donelson, commanding the Tennessee Brigade, and Col. W.E. Starke, commanding Sixtieth Virginia Volunteers, will report their commands to Brigadier-General Pemberton for duty in the Fourth Military District of South Carolina."[35]

John C. Pemberton was a Pennsylvanian who had cast his lot with the Confederate States apparently out of a greater loyalty to his Virginia-born wife than to the United States. Having won two brevets for gallantry in Mexico, at this point in the war he seemed to be an officer of great promise. Lee placed him in command of the Fourth Military District, as it fronted Port Royal Sound, the place where the Federals had established their lodgment on several coastal islands. Lee wanted to make sure that he posted commanders and troops of known reliability at the point that was closest to the invading enemy.[36]

Testing Lee's prescience, Donelson's brigade was at its new post barely a week before the Federals attempted an incursion onto the mainland. On New Year's Day, 1862, a force of about 3,000 Federal troops launched a raid where the Port Royal Ferry crossed the Coosaw River, intending to destroy a Confederate battery that threatened United States ships in the channel. Gunboats provided cover fire. Guarding that stretch of coast was the Fourteenth South Carolina Infantry Regiment under the command of Colonel James Jones. Alerted by the sound of gunfire, Pemberton ordered Jones to attack "the moment an opportunity should offer, and, if compelled to fall back, to do so fighting." Pemberton also ordered forward troopers from Colonel William E. Martin's Mounted Regiment, four companies of the Twelfth South Carolina Infantry Regiment, and Donelson's brigade to help Jones to repel the incursion.[37]

Along the way, Donelson, marching at the head of eight companies of the Eighth Tennessee Infantry Regiment, was met by Colonel Martin. Making use of Martin's "local knowledge," Donelson soon arrived at Jones's camp, whereupon he "assumed command of the entire force," as a South Carolinian related in obvious relief. Ever meticulous, Donelson wrote, "[I] halted my command . . . until I could make a personal reconnaissance by going into the field . . . with the view to taking position and to co-operate with the forces of Colonel Jones." Donelson and Martin advanced so that they "could survey the open field through which Colonel Jones' regiment was then retiring." Alas, as the Federals withdrew to the protection of their earthworks and gunboats, Donelson concluded that there was nothing more that he could do. Shellfire from the gunboats "could do us much injury without any ability on our part to return the enemy's fire." By now the short winter day was ending. Donelson ordered the entire command to fall back beyond the range of the gunboats.[38]

That ended the "Engagement at Port Royal Ferry," for it was too small an action to be classed as a battle or even a skirmish. Casualties were light on both sides, with none among Donelson's troops. Both sides claimed victory—the Federals because they neutralized the Confederate battery that had been harassing their shipping, and the Confederates because they believed that they had repulsed an attempted invasion. For Donelson there was little battlefield glory. By the time when he arrived on the field, the action was over and he knew that he could do nothing against troops who were protected by gunboats. Otherwise, he again performed creditably. He began marching his brigade immediately on receiving orders from Pemberton. Upon arrival on the field, he made use of Colonel Martin as a local guide. As the ranking field officer, he assumed command of all the available forces, and as he had done during the Cheat Mountain campaign, he surveyed the field in person, ahead of his troops. Recognizing Donelson's efficiency and aggressiveness, the best that Pemberton could say in his report was that "though moved with the utmost promptitude, the brigade was disappointed in its desire to meet the enemy."[39]

Afterward, the Federals remained quiet. Donelson's men were able to relax and enjoy the mild South Carolina winter. "Supplies were plentiful and the boys found that their task was easy," recalled an officer in Savage's regiment. Donelson, however, never relaxed his vigilance along his sector of the coast. Lieutenant Christopher C. McKinney of the Eighth Tennessee Infantry Regiment wrote his wife back home on a wet February day, complaining that "not withstanding the weather, I . . . rode all day in the rain in company with Genl Donelson around our line of opperation and inspecting our fortifications &c I dont think we will have any fighting here now as the spring tide is over and no Yankees dare to venture on our side of the water."[40]

Beyond their primary duty of guarding against incursions along the coast, Donelson's men were also instructed to prevent the escape of slaves from mainland plantations to the Union-held islands which beckoned barely a thousand yards offshore. The Federals even sent escapees "stealthily" back across the channel "in small skiffs as spies through the country." As Captain H. H. Dillard of Savage's Sixteenth Tennessee Infantry Regiment recalled, "We had strict orders to stop it." Finally, one night the pickets fired on and killed one or two escaped slaves as they fled after being halted. "After that we had no further trouble from this source with the negroes."[41]

Donelson's headquarters was evidently a happy and organized place. He was as generous as duties allowed with leaves and other freedoms, and his staff officers clearly liked and respected him. For example, when his aide and son-in-law Major James Glasgow Martin fell "sicke" from "an attack of Typhoid fever" just as the brigade was departing western Virginia, Donelson granted him leave of absence for thirty days "to go home for the benefit of his health," and then to rejoin them in Charleston. Quartermaster George Washington Winchester was close enough to Donelson in age (Winchester's son also served on the staff) to get away with referring to him, with irreverence but no disrespect, as "the great mogul." Similarly, Thomas R. S. Elliott wrote his father that Donelson "is quite a fine old cock & gives me leave of absence when ever I wish it," time that Elliott spent running a business of transporting and ginning cotton on the side.[42]

When the Federals turned aggressive it was not along the coast, but disturbingly close to home. On January 19, 1862, two small armies, Union and Confederate, clashed at Mill Springs on the Cumberland River, in the mountains of eastern Kentucky just north of the Tennessee border. The Confederates were routed and their commander, Brigadier General Felix K. Zollicoffer, a onetime newspaper editor and congressman, was killed.[43]

Among the other dead was Lieutenant Balie Peyton Jr., son and namesake of Daniel Donelson's longtime Sumner County neighbor and political rival. At this early stage in the war, there was still room for gallantry and ceremony. The Union commander, Brigadier General George H. Thomas, ordered the return of Zollicoffer's and Peyton's bodies. On February 1, Governor Harris and the bereaved elder Peyton led a procession of notables that escorted the bodies to a funeral service in the state capitol building in Nashville. Young Peyton was buried the next day in the family cemetery outside Gallatin. It is not recorded whether Margaret Donelson attended the burial service but, past political differences aside, Peyton's death had a sobering effect on the people of Sumner County. Who might be next? How much closer to home might the war come?[44]

Though the death of Lieutenant Peyton was a personal tragedy for the people of Sumner County, on a larger scale, the defeat at Mill Springs was a strategic disaster for the Confederate States. The eastern anchor of Albert Sidney Johnston's thin defensive line along the Kentucky border collapsed. From Donelson's view along the distant Carolina coast, Sumner County, and his family, suddenly lay dangerously exposed to the front lines.[45]

The war came to Middle Tennessee in February. A flotilla of United States gunboats, cooperating with a land force under the command of Brigadier General Ulysses S. Grant, captured Fort Henry on the Tennessee River on February 6. The next week, Grant forced the "unconditional surrender" of Fort Donelson on the Cumberland River. The entire Confederate defensive position along the border between Kentucky and Tennessee became untenable. Johnston's army evacuated Bowling Green and withdrew south. A Union army occupied Nashville on February 25 and fanned out across the Cumberland valley. Located between the Kentucky line and Nashville, and lying athwart the strategically vital Louisville and Nashville Railroad, Sumner County came under occupation. Margaret and the children fled southward to the safety of her Branch relatives, leaving Hazel Path in the care of their overseer. Lieutenant Daniel Donelson, son of Andrew Donelson, who was with Johnston's retreating army, wrote his father on March 7 that he saw "Aunt Margaret" as they were passing through Murfreesboro. Andrew similarly reported to his wife, Elizabeth, that "Danls property in [Middle] Tennessee is in the utmost danger of being lost." The commander of the occupation force in Hendersonville took possession of Hazel Path and removed the forage, farming implements, and furniture.[46]

It fell to Captain Dillard to break the news to Daniel Donelson at their camp in South Carolina of the events back home. He had just received a newspaper from Charleston when Donelson rode by. He read the dispatch to Donelson while the general leaned forward on his horse, as Dillard recounted, "gazing at me as a man hearing a death-knell." Easing back on his saddle, "with his eyes fixed without object," Donelson replied "in subdued tones, 'Well, well, well! That is the saddest piece of news that ever fell upon my ears during life.'" "His parental heart was touched," Dillard perceived. "His house was doomed; his dear wife and defenseless daughters at the mercy of the enemy; his fine estate sacked; and Tennessee subjected to all the ravages of the war. He saw all this at a glance, and it weighed down his soul."[47]

Donelson chafed at his station along the Carolina coast as his home in Tennessee was plundered and his wife and children were forced to flee, but duty kept him where he was. Indeed, his responsibilities were enlarged. On March 2, President Davis recalled Lee to Richmond. Pemberton was promoted to major general and assumed command of the Department of South Carolina and Georgia. On March 19, Donelson was placed in command of the Fifth Military District of South Carolina. Happily, Margaret soon joined him. After she and the children fled Hazel Path, seventeen-year-old Sam escorted "the girls"—Martha, Sue, and Rebecca—to the Branches in Tallahassee, but Margaret kept the two youngest boys, Branch and Dan, eleven and eight, respectively, with her. Their arrival no doubt did wonders for Donelson's spirits. Otherwise, with little activity by the Federals, the Confederates had time to squabble among themselves. Donelson even had the irascible John Savage arrested, ostensibly "for disobedience of his orders in West Virginia." The details remain so vague that at the court martial even Savage admitted that he "had no defense," and he was suspended briefly from the command of his regiment.[48]

Harassing actions by Union forces continued to prick the coast. On March 20, the day after Pemberton reorganized his department, a regiment of Federal troops landed in the Sixth Military District, adjacent to Donelson's district. Before Donelson could arrive with reinforcements, the Federals withdrew. Another rumored incursion two days later proved to be a false alarm, and Donelson's troops remained in camp. No Union threat subsequently developed in Donelson's sector.[49]

Instead, disaster struck in the west. The Battle of Shiloh, as the Federals called it, or Pittsburg Landing, as the Confederates called it, was fought April 6–7 on a scale hitherto not seen during the war, with massive casualties incurred on both sides. Johnston was mortally wounded and was succeeded in command by General Pierre G. T. Beauregard. Grant's heavily-reinforced army counterattacked and compelled the exhausted Confederates into abandoning what little they still held of Middle and West Tennessee.[50]

Confederate States authorities scrambled to rush reinforcements to Beauregard, who had retreated to Corinth, Mississippi. At last Donelson received the orders that he had hoped to receive months before, and they originated from an unsurprising source:

RICHMOND, *APRIL 10, 1862.*
Major-General PEMBERTON:
Beauregard is pressed for troops. Send, if possible, Donelson's brigade of two regiments to Corinth. If Mississippi Valley is lost Atlantic States will be ruined.

Very respectfully,
R.E. LEE

Lee was normally the master of cool understatement. Such a telegram breathing disaster spoke to how seriously the Confederate States high command viewed the crisis. The same day, Pemberton's headquarters issued the requisite orders: "Brig. Gen. D.S. Donelson, commanding Fifth Military District, with the Eighth and Sixteenth Regiments of Tennessee Volunteers, will proceed with as little delay as possible and report to General Beauregard at Corinth, Miss., for duty."[51]

Donelson received the orders at 9 o'clock that evening and immediately began preparations to start the next morning. The orders threw Margaret into a quandary— Sam had rejoined them, but Branch was ill. Although she had written her father that she would join him at Enfield as soon as young Branch was well enough to travel, considering the new orders, she determined to accompany "Mr. Donelson & go with him as far as I can." After thirty years of marriage, she still referred to her husband that formally, even to her own father.[52]

Donelson's four months in South Carolina had involved little action. Within the limited opportunities that were afforded him, he had successfully built upon the reputation that he had established in western Virginia. He remained vigilant to possible enemy movements, even to conducting reconnaissance himself, regardless of the weather. He was quick to spring to action, marched his troops rapidly, and at their head. Nevertheless, the assignment must have been frustrating. Commanding the Fifth Military District of South Carolina may have sounded impressive, but this stretch of coast had become a strategic backwater that trapped Donelson and his men far from home even as the enemy invaded, pillaging their homes and farms, and driving their families out as refugees. At last, now they were returning to face their foe.

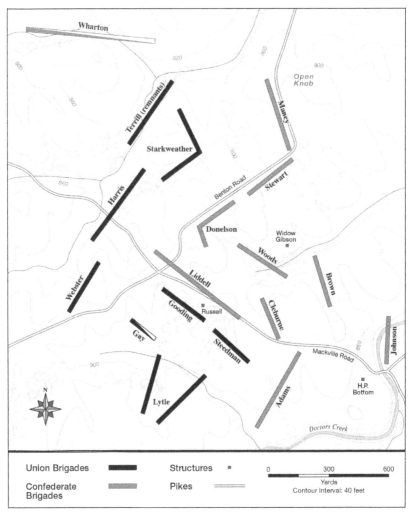

The Battle of Perryville. Map by Tim Kissel.

CHAPTER SIX

"A Most Determined Courage"

PERRYVILLE,
APRIL 1862–OCTOBER 1862

On the morning of April 11, 1862, only hours after Brigadier General Daniel S. Donelson received General Robert E. Lee's orders, his men marched out of their camps at Pocotaligo, South Carolina. From the railhead at Grahamsville, Donelson's brigade traveled through Charleston and Augusta, Georgia, to arrive in Atlanta on April 14. En route to Chattanooga the next day, through some confusion of orders, their trains were stopped, ordered back to Atlanta, and then directed to proceed to Corinth by way of Mobile, Alabama. Along the way, a train carrying the Sixteenth Tennessee Infantry Regiment ran off the track, killing six horses and one man. For whatever reasons—whether orders, general confusion, or perhaps her son Branch was still too ill to travel any farther—Margaret remained in Atlanta while her husband continued on with his brigade. Only on April 22, eleven days after departing their camps in South Carolina, did Donelson's regiments arrive at Corinth.[1]

The Army of the Mississippi, as it was designated, was still in disarray following the grievous losses in men and materiel that it had suffered at Shiloh. General Pierre G. T. Beauregard scrambled to rebuild his shattered army and arrange for the defense of Corinth, a strategic railway-crossroads town in the northeastern corner of Mississippi, from the inevitable advance by United States forces. By the end of April, he could muster somewhat over 45,000 troops. The influx of so many troops produced a bewildering series of reorganizations to his army. There was some uncertainty, for example, where to assign Donelson's troops. After several transitory assignments that were superseded almost as soon as they were implemented, Donelson and his two regiments were eventually assigned to the First Corps, commanded by Major General Leonidas Polk. There, Donelson's units were formally styled the First Brigade of the Second Division, commanded by Major General Benjamin Franklin Cheatham.[2]

Donelson was back among friends. He had known Leonidas Polk, a distant cousin of the late president, as a cadet who was two years behind him at the Military Academy. Eschewing a military career, Polk had entered the ministry and rose to the office of Episcopal Bishop of Louisiana. Throwing off his clerical vestments at the outbreak of war, he was appointed immediately to the rank of major general by his loyal friend, also from West Point days, President Jefferson Davis. Polk's enthusiasm for the Confederate cause exceeded his martial skills, however. Against orders and the stated defensive policy of his government, Polk had advanced north out of West Tennessee in September 1861 to occupy Columbus, Kentucky. This placed the Confederate States in the role of aggressor and welded Kentucky to the United States, an action that was later judged to be "one of the greatest mistakes of the war."[3]

The more experienced commander was Benjamin Franklin Cheatham. Like Donelson, Frank Cheatham had years of service as a brigadier general in the Tennessee state militia and, when the war began, he was appointed as brigadier general in the Confederate States Army. From there, their careers diverged. Cheatham fought with distinction at the Battle of Belmont in November 1861, was promoted to major general in March 1862, and was given command of a division, while Donelson remained stuck in the South Carolina backwater. If Donelson felt any chagrin at now being outranked by and serving under a man who was nearly twenty years his junior, no record survives.[4]

After Shiloh, Major General Henry W. Halleck, commander of the United States Department of the Mississippi, took personal direction of the armies of Major Generals Ulysses S. Grant and Don Carlos Buell. Although the combined armies doubly outnumbered Beauregard's army, Halleck, essentially a desk soldier, advanced cautiously, taking a month to cover the thirty miles from Pittsburg Landing to Corinth.[5]

To defend Corinth, Beauregard deployed his army in an arc covering the eastern, northern, and western approaches to the town. Donelson's brigade was posted on the western extremity. In addition to the Eighth and Sixteenth Tennessee Infantry regiments that he brought from South Carolina, his brigade was augmented by the Second and Fifteenth Tennessee

Infantry regiments, the One Hundred Fifty-fourth Senior Tennessee Infantry Regiment, and Carnes's artillery battery. Commanded by Colonel Joseph Knox Walker, nephew and private secretary of the late President Polk, the Second Tennessee fought at Belmont in November 1861 but had suffered so heavily at Shiloh that, after only a few weeks, it was removed from Donelson's brigade and consolidated with another regiment. Also a veteran unit of Shiloh, the Fifteenth Tennessee under its commander, Colonel Robert C. Tyler, would enjoy longer service with Donelson's brigade. Captain William W. Carnes had recently assumed command of the Tennessee Light Artillery Company. The assignment of the One Hundred Fifty-fourth Senior Tennessee Regiment under Donelson's command included his nephew John Samuel Donelson, captain of Company E, the Hickory Rifles. As with the Second Tennessee, however, the assignment with Donelson's brigade was brief, and the One Hundred Fifty-fourth Senior, too, was soon transferred.[6]

By early May, Halleck's huge but plodding force had crossed the state line from Tennessee into Mississippi. On May 6, Captain W. C. Bacot, commanding a company of cavalry out on reconnaissance, reported to Donelson that his scouts had fired on an advance party. Donelson immediately reported to his division commander Cheatham, "that the enemy are advancing in force with infantry and cavalry." Cheatham in turn reported to his corps commander, Polk, that he had ordered Donelson "to send forward all the cavalry, [and] to keep us posted."[7]

Back in Middle Tennessee, quartermasters from the United States occupation forces purchased, by requisition, produce from Donelson's Hazel Path farm, through the overseer whom Margaret had left in care of the place. The *Daily Nashville Union,* which was now being published as a pro-Union newspaper in the occupied city, took the opportunity for sarcastic propaganda. "Daniel S. Donelson, Brigadier General in the Confederate service," the paper sneered on May 15, "while ordering his troops to burn *other people's cotton and rice,* in the Southern States, recently *sold his own* . . . for Yankee Gold and 'greenbacks.'—What a self-sacrificing Southern patriot is Gen. Donelson." The next day the *Union* printed an appeal from Beauregard to *"Planters South"* to burn their cotton rather than risk it falling into the hands of the Yankees. "Brigadier [General] Daniel Donelson, do you hear?" asked the *Union,* which then resorted to the scurrilous stereotypes that somehow seemed to come more easily to the critics of, rather than slave owners themselves. "Call Cuffy, Dinah, Sambo, Topsy and Aunt Milly and tell each of them to place a lighted torch to your cotton bales to keep it from the hands of the Yankees! A gallant Southerner would scorn to touch Lincoln gold in exchange for it. Oh, we forgot, General! You sold your crop the other day, we believe.—Beg your pardon, sir!"[8]

Donelson's response, if there was one, was never printed in the newspaper. Considering his location and circumstances, he may not even have known about the sale. He would scarcely have been in a position to prevent it, anyway. More happily, once he had settled his brigade in Corinth, he sent for Margaret, who had gone to stay with her father, John Branch, at Enfield, North Carolina. Now, "in compliance with the wishes of Gen. Donelson," Branch reported, she set out for Corinth, "Taking along with her the two little boys."[9]

Beauregard remained alert for any opportunity to strike at Halleck's slowly advancing force and, on the morning of May 22, it appeared that one had developed. As he reviewed his brigade, which had assembled in lines by regiments, Donelson delivered to his troops "a stirring, patriotic speech." In "eloquent tones," as a soldier in the Sixteenth Tennessee Infantry Regiment recalled, Donelson spoke of "the arduous task before them to be performed this day," but he had "the fullest confidence in the valor" of his men. "They were fighting for their homes and all they held dear, which they would wrest from the hand of the invader, but it was a work that would involve much sacrifice and the loss of many lives." In the absence of surviving correspondence from his own hand, such paraphrased recollections nevertheless affirm Donelson's devotion to the Confederate cause. Alas, Major General Earl Van Dorn was so tardy marching his troops to their assigned positions that Beauregard canceled the attack without a shot being fired. It was all rather anticlimactic.[10]

On May 28, Halleck's forces opened a brisk fire with his long-range guns on the Eighth Tennessee Infantry Regiment, commanded by Lieutenant Colonel William L. Moore, which was serving as the "advanced picket-post" of Donelson's brigade. As "directed" by Donelson, the regiment charged the Federals, but "by some misunderstanding," Moore reported, it then fell back to its former lines, "the enemy shelling us very heavily with an enfilade fire." The only casualty was Moore, who was wounded in the hand.[11]

By now, Beauregard decided that Corinth was not worth holding. It was an unhealthy spot with bad water, and soon, more men were falling ill and dying than had been killed at Shiloh. It was better to evacuate than be trapped in such a place under siege. Without notifying his superiors in Richmond, Beauregard began to withdraw the army on May 30. It had settled into its new defensive position around Tupelo, fifty miles to the south, by June 9. Donelson established his brigade headquarters about three miles out of town. President Davis, who had long since lost all confidence in Beauregard and was angered by the unauthorized retreat, relieved him and appointed newly-promoted General Braxton Bragg to the command of the Army of the Mississippi.[12]

Halleck accommodated Bragg's transition by not pursuing the Confederates. Indeed, he broke up his huge, consolidated force into its original components and sent Buell with his Army of the Ohio heading eastward across northern Alabama. Buell moved as slowly as had his superior, Halleck, but by the end of June he was threatening Chattanooga, which had become a strategically vital location—with the fall of Nashville, it was now the seat of government of what remained of Confederate Tennessee. In July Governor Isham G. Harris arrived in Tupelo to persuade Bragg to send reinforcements. "I succeeded in getting the general to send two brigades of Cheatham's division of Tennessee troops (General Maury's and General Donelson's) to this place," Harris reported on July 28, upon his return to Chattanooga.[13]

Donelson's brigades departed Tupelo for Chattanooga on July 22, repeating in reverse the roundabout route that they had traveled through Mobile and Atlanta, including another boxcar wreck that injured several men. Once Halleck relinquished the initiative, Bragg seized it himself. He followed up the transfer of Dabney H. Maury's and Donelson's brigades by transporting the bulk of his army eastward to Chattanooga. The remaining part of the army remained at Tupelo, under Major General Sterling Price, to resist any move by Grant. By the middle of August, Donelson's brigade was reunited in Chattanooga with the rest of Cheatham's Division as part of what Bragg now styled the "Right Wing" of the Army of the Mississippi under Polk's command. Along the way, Donelson's brigade gained the Thirty-eighth Tennessee Infantry Regiment, another veteran unit of Shiloh commanded by Colonel John C. Carter, and the Fifty-first Tennessee Infantry Regiment, commanded by Colonel John Chester.[14]

Cheatham's division was posted several miles outside of Chattanooga. The nearness to the home counties of many of Donelson's troops allowed for leaves of absence, with more troubles arising from the contentious Colonel John Savage. Captain James Womack returned from a leave in McMinnville to visit his new bride and family, to find that Savage had relieved him of command of his company. To Womack, Savage's action had "every appearance of malice, and . . . ill will toward me," although Savage never specified the charges. Womack applied to "Genl. D.S. Donaldson to be restored to my command," to which Savage objected "in extense." After examining the papers, Donelson sent a letter in Womack's defense to division commander Cheatham. Donelson and Cheatham restored Womack to his command but the episode only confirmed to Womack his opinion he had "long entertained," that Savage "is corrupt and will not do to rely upon."[15]

The threat from Buell's slowly advancing columns put an end to such internal squabbling. Polk directed Cheatham to advance Donelson's brigade to counter Buell, but no Union attack came. Buell's advance sputtered to a halt. When cavalry raids led by Nathan Bedford Forrest and John Hunt Morgan in Middle Tennessee disrupted his supply lines, Buell abandoned his offensive, withdrew from northern Alabama, and took up defensive positions around Nashville.[16]

Buell's withdrawal handed Bragg the breathtaking opportunity to redraw the strategic map of the war by marching north to redeem Kentucky, as Southerners saw it, for the Confederate States. Already, Major General Edmund Kirby Smith, who commanded a smaller force as a separate command in East Tennessee, was marching through the Cumberland Gap into eastern Kentucky. With active operations commencing, Margaret and sons Branch and Dan departed to rejoin her father at Enfield, although Sam, who would not turn eighteen until December, joined his father's staff as "Lt Saml Donelson my aid[e]." Bragg's army, totaling 30,000 men, began its march north from Chattanooga on August 28.[17]

The troops slogged over the Cumberland Plateau, with Cheatham's division in the lead, to Sparta, where they arrived on September 3. The march carried the Sixteenth Tennessee Infantry Regiment through its home counties, upon which "many of the boys broke ranks and went home," much to Donelson's consternation. He also attempted without success to cut off the supply of whisky that was arriving from visiting friends and relatives. As he became increasingly "wrothy," some regimental officers assured him that before the army resumed its march "every man would be in place at the proper time." And every man was.[18]

In Sparta, Bragg received the heartening news that Kirby Smith's force had already reached the Kentucky Bluegrass region. Indeed, when the cavalryman Forrest reported that Buell was "rapidly evacuating Nashville," Bragg now feared that Buell, who was moving north toward Bowling Green, would strike Kirby Smith's smaller, isolated force. Bragg's march now became one to stay between Buell and Smith. Accordingly, he ordered Polk on September 10 to march his corps to Tompkinsville, just over the Kentucky line. There, Carnes's battery was able to obtain "some fine artillery-horses." On September 12, Donelson's brigade, the leading element of Cheatham's division, marched into Glasgow, east of Bowling Green.[19]

Donelson's men were enthusiastically received there. "The welcome to Kentucky was cheering," the brigade's quartermaster Major George Winchester wrote in his diary, "as the waving Kerchiefs and—the smiling faces of men & women & even children announced the grateful welcome, with which all Kentucky received the Southern soldier." After resting his men two days in Glasgow, Bragg marched his army north to Munfordville, then to Bardstown, keeping between Buell's army which continued its retreat northward to Louisville, and Kirby Smith whose army had occupied Lexington and the Kentucky state capital of Frankfort. The movement involved a grueling night march. Stragglers and confusion multiplied in the darkness, most tragically in Donelson's brigade, when some men accidentally shot one of their own officers, mistaking his party for Union cavalry.[20]

On September 28, Bragg departed for Lexington to confer with Kirby Smith. He placed Polk in command of the Army of the Mississippi, setting in motion a series of officers moving up to temporary command of the next higher unit. Replacing Polk, the senior division commander Cheatham assumed command of the Right Wing. Accordingly, his senior brigade commander, Donelson, took Cheatham's place to lead what was renumbered as the First Division, while Colonel John Savage stepped up from the Sixteenth Tennessee Infantry Regiment to become First Brigade commander. Until Bragg returned and resumed command of the army, restoring the original hierarchy of command, the First Division was frequently referred to as Donelson's division.[21]

Bragg's plan to unite with Kirby Smith's force was disrupted when Buell's army marched out of Louisville toward them. Buell's columns fanned out along four roads that ran from due east, threatening Frankfort, to due south, but the last three roads could all easily converge on Bardstown. Perceiving only the threat to Frankfort, Bragg sent orders to Polk to march his army north and strike Buell in the flank while Kirby Smith attacked from the front. Polk, seeing the columns that were converging on his position at Bardstown, replied that Buell's approach made "compliance with this order not only eminently inexpedient but impracticable." He convened a council of his wing and division commanders, none of whom he named but presumably included Donelson as temporary commander of the First Division, and reported to Bragg that they "unanimously" endorsed his (Polk's) views. Polk instead ordered a retreat eastward toward the main Confederate supply depot at Danville. The army began its march the next day, October 4, with Donelson's division in the lead.[22]

Polk's message caught Bragg in Frankfort inaugurating a Confederate state governor, which pleased Kentucky's Confederate sympathizers, although it did nothing to remove the Bluegrass State from the Union. At first, Bragg proceeded with his planned concentration and ordered Polk to march "both divisions of the right wing (Withers' and Cheatham's)" to Versailles to join Kirby Smith. On October 6, Major General William J. Hardee, commanding the Left Wing of the Army of the Mississippi, stopped his troops at Perryville. The next day, he became aware of Federal troops approaching from the northwest and requested reinforcements to deal with them before continuing his march. Bragg accordingly ordered Polk to send "Cheatham's division" to Hardee's support and "give the enemy battle immediately; rout him and then move to our support at Versailles." Neither Hardee nor Bragg anticipated more than sweeping aside an outlier of the Union army so that the Confederates could continue their consolidation, but under the busy circumstances it is understandable if it twice slipped Bragg's mind that, in his absence, Cheatham's division was now Donelson's division.[23]

In compliance with Bragg's directive, Polk ordered the division of Brigadier General James Patton Anderson of Hardee's Left Wing to rejoin the rest of Hardee's force at Perryville. He also ordered "General Cheatham, with Donelson's division of his wing," to follow Anderson, while the other division of Cheatham's Right Wing, commanded by Major General Jones M. Withers, continued as originally ordered to Versailles. "Donelson's (known as Cheatham's) division," as the army understood the command structure, accordingly left Harrodsburg at 7:00 p.m. and arrived at Perryville about midnight. Donelson had marched them with characteristic rapidity, leaving their baggage train behind and bringing along only the ambulance and ammunition trains. Nevertheless, the men marched enthusiastically and brimming with confidence.[24]

Hardee's defensive line faced west, running along the east bank of the Chaplin River, which ran north through the town of Perryville. As reinforcements arrived during the night of October 7, Polk placed Anderson's division to the left, or south, of the division led by Major General Simon Bolivar Buckner, and "that of General Donelson, of the right wing," to the left of Anderson. Polk calculated that this force "did not exceed 15,000."[25]

As dawn broke on October 8, what Polk saw of the Union force that faced him west of Perryville shocked him. Instead of a small outlier that could be easily brushed aside, he realized that his three understrength divisions faced at least a corps. Polk again called "a meeting of the general officers," again unnamed but apparently including wing commanders Hardee and Cheatham and division commanders Buckner, Anderson, and Donelson. In view of the size of the Federal force that confronted them, the officers "resolved . . . to await the movements of the enemy, and to be guided by events as they were developed."[26]

Events developed into a battle. Converging on Perryville from the west were three roads: Mackville Pike approached from the northwest, Springfield Pike from due west, and Lebanon Pike from the southwest. Approaching Perryville from the northwest along the Mackville Pike was the I Corps, commanded by Major General Alexander McD. McCook. Marching along the Springfield Pike was the III Corps, commanded by Acting Major General Charles C. Gilbert, while marching from the southwest along the Lebanon Pike was the II Corps, commanded by Major General Thomas L. Crittenden—in sum, three Union Corps, each of which by itself outnumbered Polk's entire force.[27]

When Bragg, rushing back from Frankfort, arrived in Perryville about 10:00 am, he held to his belief that Polk faced only an outlier of the Union army, and determined to attack anyway. Significantly, he declined to resume command. His decision formally retained Polk as commander of the Army of the Mississippi, implicitly retaining Cheatham in command of the Right Wing and Donelson as commander of the First Division.[28]

Bragg nevertheless "suggested" that Polk make some changes in the placement of his units. McCook's Corps, advancing from the northwest along the Mackville Pike, had the potential to flank the Confederates on their right, to the north, cutting them off from their intended march northward to join Kirby Smith's force. The Confederate attack therefore would throw McCook's column back, in order to keep the line of march open. Considering the placement of Polk's line, however, no troops in that sector were available to make the attack. Bragg therefore determined that Donelson's division would pull out of the far left, or southern, end of the line and march behind the other two divisions, northward through Perryville. Polk ordered Cheatham "to move the whole of his command from the left to the right of our line." With Withers's division in Versailles, the whole of Cheatham's command that was present at Perryville was the First Division, which was still commanded by Donelson.[29]

The redisposition of Donelson's division entailed a circuitous march of about two miles, and it needed to be made quickly before the Federals along the Mackville Pike were alert to the gap in the Confederate right flank and attacked to exploit it. Fortunately for Bragg's plan, Donelson was experienced at marching his troops rapidly and efficiently. After he received the order, the men of the division pulled out of the main line. Leading the march was Donelson at the head of his old brigade. The troops marched "at the double quick" northward through Perryville, crossing to the west side of the Chaplin River, and passing behind the brigade of Brigadier General S. A. M. ("Sam") Wood which occupied the right or northern end of the main Confederate line.[30]

Along this stretch of road, the artillery battery of Captain William Carnes ran into difficulty. While "passing through a farm gate," one of his caissons ran afoul of a gate post. To get around the obstruction, the infantrymen tore down a nearby section of fence and continued. Just as Carnes freed the gun, Polk rode by and directed him to take his battery and support Wood. The two trailing units of Donelson's brigade, the Eighth and Fifty-first Tennessee Infantry regiments, were likewise diverted to support Carnes and Wood. Once it was unlimbered on the hill that Wood occupied, Carnes's battery began an artillery exchange with a Union battery that occupied a rise to the west.[31]

When the division reached its objective, Polk and Cheatham formed the division into a column of brigades facing west. In the process the generals, evidently without any formal notice, reinstated their original command structure, with Cheatham resuming command of his division and Donelson of his brigade. Minus the Eighth and Fifty-first Tennessee Infantry regiments, which were detached with Carnes's battery supporting Wood's brigade, Donelson's weakened brigade, consisting of only the Fifteenth, Sixteenth, and Thirty-eighth Tennessee Infantry regiments, formed the first line. Behind them, at intervals of 150 yards, were lines formed by the other two brigades of Cheatham's Division, commanded by Brigadier Generals Alexander P. Stewart and George E. Maney.[32]

Just before the attack was to begin, with Donelson's brigade in the lead, Colonel John A. Wharton "of the Texas Rangers," as Cheatham described him, whose cavalry was screening the Confederate right flank, reported a previously unnoticed Federal column advancing from the northwest down the Mackville Pike. This was disturbing news. If the Confederate assault was launched from its present position, this additional Union column could still hit their right flank even while the Confederate line was attacking its original target. In order to get past and flank the approaching column, Cheatham's division was set to march even farther north. "This order was promptly executed," Donelson wrote in his battle report. The division crossed the Chaplin River again—easy enough, as the riverbed was nearly dry from an unusual drought—to regroup in a westward-projecting tongue of land called Walker's Bend, formed by an oxbow loop of the river. The brigades re-established their original lines, with Donelson's brigade in front and Stewart's and Maney's brigades behind, arrayed across the wide fields surrounding the fine Walker house.[33]

While the troops waited, Donelson dispatched his assistant adjutant general, his son-in-law Major James G. Martin, to retrieve "if possible," the detached Eighth and Fifty-first Tennessee Infantry regiments so that they could add their weight to the anticipated assault. Martin found and obtained permission from, in sequence, Generals Cheatham, Polk, and Bragg, then rode off to find the regiments "just as the order was given" for Donelson's command "to move rapidly in the direction of the Enemy."[34]

In response, the Fifteenth, Sixteenth, and Thirty-eighth Tennessee

Infantry regiments that constituted Donelson's partial brigade advanced from their starting position in Walker's Bend. This involved crossing what Donelson called Chaplin Creek for the third time. As they ascended the western bank they were obliged to climb heavily wooded bluffs. As Donelson wrote in his report, "The movement however was accomplished with great promptness and the line formed in an open field" on the west side of the bluff. Ever thorough, Donelson and his staff rode forward to examine the ground over which his brigade would attack, accompanied by the three regimental colonels—Robert Tyler of the Fifteenth, John Savage of the Sixteenth, and John Carter of the Thirty-eighth Tennessee Infantry regiments. In particular deference to the veteran Savage, "whom he always consulted on critical occasions," acknowledging his experience in war, Donelson conversed with his officers about what they were facing. From their vantage point, the ground to the west sloped down to the valley of Doctor's Creek, a northward flowing tributary of the Chaplin River. Beyond Doctor's Creek the land ascended to another rise, atop of which a Federal battery was visible.[35]

As Donelson reported, "I soon ascertained from the fire of another Battery of the Enemys further on our right that I did not have the proper direction. I accordingly gave orders for a change of direction further to the right." His colonels were already returning to their regiments, so Donelson sent a staff officer to order Savage on the far right of the line "to halt when in the proper direction, until I could bring up the other two Regts in line of battle." At this point, Donelson's and Savage's accounts diverge. According to Donelson, "this order was not obeyed because as I have since learned one of Genl Cheathams Staff ordered said Regts to move forward rapidly." Savage, instead, recalled that Donelson directed him to attack the Federal battery alone. Savage balked at what he saw as being literally a murderous assignment. Donelson rode to Savage to clarify matters. "Colonel, I am ordered to attack," he explained. Savage did not respond. Donelson repeated the order twice. "General," Savage finally replied, "I will obey your orders but if the Sixteenth is to charge that battery you must give the order." At that, Donelson, as Savage described it, stood in his stirrups, "raised his voice in a rather loud and excited tone" and cried, "Charge."[36]

"Forward," Donelson then shouted. The men charged, sounding the rebel yell or shouting "Victory." From his vantage point, Cheatham admired how "these brave men rushed forward with a determination and impetuosity which not even superior numbers or advantage of position could resist." An Atlanta newspaperman agreed: "the whole line moved forward in beautiful battle order." The Thirty-eighth Tennessee Infantry Regiment followed the Sixteenth to add weight to its attack, with the Fifteenth to its right.[37]

Ahead of them the terrain gradually descended for almost four hundred yards toward the hollow formed by Doctor's Creek, beyond which the ground rose again through cornfields and a belt of trees to the far ridge. The Federal column toward which Donelson's partial brigade was marching was no mere outlier but all or parts of three brigades. His three regiments, perhaps 1,200 men, were attacking a force that outnumbered them almost five to one. Nevertheless, he reported proudly, "Although Shot and Shell fell in profusion there was no faltering on the part of men or officers, the three Regts moving forward at a double quick step amid Yells and Cheers at every step."[38]

Savage's interpretation of the orders added to the confusion. He rushed his regiment directly at the Federal battery, advancing far out in front of the Fifteenth and Thirty-eighth Tennessee Infantry regiments. This rapid, unsupported move is what apparently led Savage later to convince himself that his regiment had been ordered to attack the battery alone. "The Consequence," Donelson reported, was that when Savage's men "came within range of the Enemys small arms, they received the first shock of the Enemys fire." Worse, the battery that they were charging opened a devastating fire on Savage's isolated men. They nevertheless pushed forward, with Savage riding in front. When they reached shelter in the hollow, Savage halted them momentarily in order to dress his lines. Then, artillery began to rake his men from the righthand or northward battery that Donelson had seen earlier and had tried to order Savage's regiment to attack instead. This second battery, on what became known as the Open Knob, had a clear field along the length of the hollow and enfiladed Savage's men with deadly accuracy.[39]

Eventually, the Fifteenth and Thirty-eighth Tennessee Infantry regiments caught up and entered the hollow to Savage's right, finally providing him the support that he had outrun. Donelson's charging men stopped only one hundred yards from the Union line at the edge of the trees, stabilized their line as much as possible, and fired the first of several volleys. The Federal lines replied with murderous fire. The Tennesseans charged toward "a House and small cornfield," as Donelson described their objective, belonging to the Widow Gibson. Savage's horse went down and Savage suffered wounds to his leg and back, obliging him to hand command of his regiment to its second-in-command, Lieutenant-Colonel D. M. (Dick) Donnell, whose own horse was soon killed. The brigade could advance no farther against the murderous fire. Donelson confessed, with little understatement, that "at this point the Cornfield was exceedingly hot and obstinately contested."[40]

"At this critical moment" in the struggle, Donelson continued with almost laconic brevity, Maney's Brigade "came to the rescue." Cheatham had realized that Donelson's "daring and desperate charge" was suffering a "most serious loss." Accordingly, he ordered Maney to "attack and carry" the Federal battery on the Open Knob on the right that had "almost destroyed Genl Donelson's Command on my left." Maney and his "gallant line . . . rushed rapidly forward, silencing the Battery and driving the gunners from their pieces."[41]

Bragg still seemed to be unaware that he had not struck an isolated column but had blundered into the left wing of the entire Army of the Ohio. Rather than disengage from a contest that he did not realize was so unequal, he continued to think that committing more troops would throw the enemy back so that he could resume his original plan. Quite without understanding what he was getting his army into, Bragg was turning the Battle of Perryville into the decisive contest for Confederate fortunes in Kentucky.[42]

With his northern, Right Wing having been fought to temporary exhaustion for only limited results, Bragg now had Hardee hurl his southern, Left Wing at the Federals along the Mackville Pike. Of most immediate relevance to Donelson's brigade, the attack by Colonel Thomas M. Jones's Mississippians, the rightmost brigade of Hardee's Left Wing and therefore immediately to Donelson's left, drew fire away from his exhausted regiments. Better yet, "at this opportune moment Genl Stewart . . . came to the rescue," Donelson reported with evident relief. Stewart's regiments plugged the gap to Maney's left, Cheatham reported, "and to the relief of Gen. Donelson."[43]

To support Maney's and Stewart's assaults on the right, the Confederates also renewed their efforts on their center and left. Buckner sent in the hard-hitting veterans of Patrick R. Cleburne's brigade, supported by the brigade of Brigadier General John Calvin Brown and the reserve regiments of Wood's brigade, to Brown's right. Wood's brigade at last formed a link between Hardee's wing on the left and Cheatham's division on the right, with Donelson's depleted brigade being located just to the right of the linchpin formed by Wood's brigade.[44]

Donelson's men were fought out, at least for the moment. With Stewart's veteran brigade now engaging the Federals, Cheatham ordered Donelson to retire his broken regiments to "re-form" in the Doctor's Creek hollow that was now located about one hundred yards to their rear. There, Donelson directed that his men be resupplied with ammunition, but they were obliged to use "the Cartridge boxes of the wounded and dead men." Martin had yet to return with the two detached regiments, so Donelson took the opportunity of this lull to dispatch two more aides to expedite the search.[45]

While Donelson's brigade had been engaged in its first charge, Martin had located the Eighth and Fifty-first Tennessee Infantry regiments, which were still supporting Carnes's battery. Before Martin could return the wayward units, however, Cheatham intercepted the group. At his direction, Martin and cavalryman Wharton selected a hilltop position far on the Confederate right that provided a commanding field of fire over the entire Union left. From there, Carnes "opened a flanking fire" on the Federal left flank, which he claimed caused "them to break and flee in complete rout."[46]

By this time, the two aides whom Donelson had sent to find the wayward regiments met Martin, who was finally leading the units back to rejoin the brigade in "double quick time" just as the original three regiments were reforming their lines. Donelson placed the two fresh regiments behind his original line, adjacent to the left of Stewart's brigade. "Again we formed . . . and charged them a third time," Captain Womack of the battered Sixteenth Tennessee Infantry Regiment enthused. Reinforced with perhaps eight hundred fresh troops, Donelson gave the order for "a forward movement upon the Enemy," which "with Yells and Cheers [was] most promptly obeyed." Donelson's men thus again charged forward alongside Wood's brigade to the left and Stewart's brigade to the right.[47]

The Federal battery yet again served as a focal point for their assault. At the same time that Donelson's brigade began its third charge, he reported that the Union troops were "making a forward movement in the direction of the captured Battery evidently with a view to retake [it]." Exhausted of ammunition and energy, however, the Federals were in no condition to withstand this third charge, which Donelson described as "moving forward all the time. The Enemy gave way," retreating into the woods behind the Widow Gibson's house, abandoning the battery that had cost Donelson's brigade so much blood. As they advanced, Donelson's and Wood's men tore down the rail fence and raced past the abandoned guns and over the Federal dead and wounded in pursuit. "The Enemy . . . were driven back with great Slaughter for more than a mile," Donelson reported. He ended the account of his brigade's final charge almost with a sigh: "The evidence were to[o] plainly to be seen . . . that we had committed sad havoc in killing and wounding large numbers."[48]

Pressing the Union retreat was the last contribution of Donelson's brigade to the Battle of Perryville. It had been considerable, but it was left to other, fresher units to continue to drive the Federals until darkness put an end to the carnage. In the immediate rush of events, Donelson and his men could exult in what looked for the moment to be a sweeping victory. When Captain Carnes and his long-lost battery finally rejoined the brigade at the end of the day, Donelson was even in a mood to tease them about their absence without his permission: "Nothing succeeds like success," he winked, adding jocularly, "It's all right with your commanding Generals *now*, since the unauthorized movement succeeded; but if you had failed, or got into trouble, you would all have been dismissed for acting without orders."[49]

Despite the initial euphoria, once the accounting was made, the cost in blood and men had been enormous. Later calculations report that of the 15,000-odd men who were available to Bragg that day, 510 were killed, 2,635 were wounded, and 251 were missing, for a total casualty bill of 3,396, a loss rate of over 20 percent.[50]

Donelson's brigade had suffered as much as any unit on either side. The Eighth and Fifty-first Tennessee Infantry regiments, which had been diverted behind Carnes's battery, missed all but the last stages of the battle and their casualties were consequently light. Of the 436 effectives in the Eighth, four were reported as killed and twenty-nine were wounded, an aggregate loss of thirty-three. The Fifty-first reported nine killed and twenty-five wounded, an aggregate loss of thirty-four. Carnes reported four wounded in his battery. Of the three regiments that were engaged all day, the Fifteenth Tennessee Infantry Regiment reported nine killed and twenty-five wounded, a total of thirty-four casualties. The Thirty-eighth Tennessee Infantry Regiment suffered somewhat more, with five reported killed and thirty-eight wounded, a total of forty-three casualties. It was Savage's Sixteenth Tennessee Infantry Regiment that suffered by far the most horrendous casualties in Donelson's brigade. Of the 370 men whom Savage had led into battle, forty-one were reported killed, 151 wounded, and seven missing, an aggregate loss of 199, a staggering loss-rate of 54 percent. Savage's regiment accounted for over 60 percent of the dead in Donelson's entire brigade (sixty-eight total killed) and 57 percent of the total losses (347 casualties of all types), a bloody testament to how difficult a task Savage had faced charging the Union battery. Of the 1,553 effectives who had been reported the week before the battle, in what was then Savage's brigade, while Donelson commanded the First Division and Cheatham the Right Wing, total losses exceeded 22 percent. More recent calculations, which count only 1,429 effectives in Donelson's brigade on the day of the battle but 374 total casualties, produce a casualty rate of 26 percent.[51]

Whatever the exact numbers, all bloody day long on October 8, 1862, Donelson's men fought, according to Polk's battle report, "with a most determined courage." Everyone praised Donelson as commander. Cheatham referred to him as "this Gallant Leader" who moved his brigade "forward in admirable order and most gallant style." "Polk, Cheatham, Donelson, and all our leaders," recalled Colonel Tyler of the Fifteenth Tennessee Infantry Regiment, "were everywhere seen cheering on our troops with reckless exposure of their persons to the hottest fire of the enemy." After the day's action, Donelson, characteristically, saw to the welfare of his men. He reconnoitered the ground "in person" on which his exhausted troops bivouacked and detailed fifty men to take care of the wounded.[52]

The conspicuous exception amid all the praise was the habitually critical Savage. For reasons unknown, in the decades after the war, the battle reports for Perryville that were submitted by Cheatham, Donelson, Maney, Stewart, and others were not published in *The War of the Rebellion: A Compilation of the Official Records of the Union and Confederate Armies*, the huge compendium of 130 serial volumes that sought to publish every important document related to the entire conflict. The horrific casualties suffered by Savage's regiment, in his mind, warranted scapegoats, and he saw the omission of battle reports in the *Official Records* as constituting evidence of a coverup. Accordingly, he devoted twenty pages in his memoirs to a vitriolic attack on Cheatham and Donelson, accusing them of ordering his regiment to make a suicidal charge in the deliberate hope that he would be killed.

Savage wrote his autobiography, bearing the main title *The Life of John H. Savage: Citizen, Soldier, Lawyer, Congressman*, forty years after the events, and long after his targets were safely dead. It was clear, however, that time had not softened the hatred that still boiled in the type of man whose mindset could pen the lengthy subtitle: *Before the War Begun and Prosecuted by the Abolitionists of the Northern States to Reduce the Descendants of the Rebels of 1776, who Defeated the Armies of the King of England and gained Independence for the United States, Down to the Level of the Negro Race.*[53]

Savage traced the origins of the difficulties between Donelson and himself to "no good feeling" that had arisen in western Virginia the year before. Savage claimed that it was "difficult to form a satisfying opinion" as to what induced Donelson and Cheatham to order his regiment, "solitary and alone, to charge the main line of battle at the Yankee Abolition army." To Savage, it was not enough to attribute Donelson's and Cheatham's orders merely to "excitement and stupidity or dullness," or in a word, to incompetence. Rather, he asked, "was it a purpose to sacrifice a disobedient and insubordinate officer?"[54]

Heedless of inconsistencies and often at demonstrable variance with contemporary records, Savage expanded his criticisms to whether Cheatham and Donelson were ever on the battlefield, or whether they were drunk. Cheatham's reputation for drinking was widely known. His modern biographer enumerates four times during the war when Cheatham was recorded as drinking or drunk but, perhaps significantly, the battle of Perryville was not one of them. No word survives in the sparse records that describe Donelson's drinking habits, but during the march through the home counties of Savage's own men, his attempts to interdict the supplies of whisky that were being brought in by friends and relatives were consistent with the actions of a man who was himself not a heavy drinker.[55]

In Savage's recollection, Cheatham's and Donelson's actions explain why they did not file battle reports. Several times he asserts that they did not even write reports, and goes so far as to state that "a blank space" appears in the relevant volume of the *Official Records* that had been left for Cheatham's report. More seriously and frequently, rather, Savage accused Cheatham and Donelson of suppressing not only their own reports but those of Maney and Stewart. That they did this, Savage declared, constituted "conclusive proof that Cheatham and Donelson willfully, wrongfully, violating military law, suppressed all reports." For suppressing the truth about their actions, Savage concluded baldly that Donelson and Cheatham ought to have been "dismissed from the service or shot by court-martial."[56]

And yet despite all of Savage's hyperbole—he compared the charge of his regiment to the charge of the Light Brigade at Balaclava, even quoting two stanzas from Tennyson's poem—he was incorrect on his primary charge: Cheatham and Donelson did indeed write and submit reports on the battle of Perryville. For whatever reason, these reports, along with those of Maney and Stewart, remained filed among Bragg's military papers, most likely a simple oversight by one of Bragg's staff officers. This is something that Savage never knew, but it is characteristic of the man that he would construe a mere absence of evidence as constituting evidence of a conspiracy against him.[57]

Ironically, in their reports neither Donelson nor Cheatham expressed any criticism of Savage. True, there is an air of dismissiveness in Donelson's report that, during the attack, "Col. Savage received a flesh wound in his leg and an injury to his back." If, however, Savage truly thrice refused Donelson's order to attack, as he himself recounted in his memoirs, then Donelson not only had grounds to relieve him on the spot of the command of his regiment but also did Savage an inestimable favor by not remotely alluding to his insubordination in his report. Otherwise, Donelson included Savage and his regiment in his "highest commendation of both Officers and men during the entire engagement." Cheatham, in his more grandiose phrasing, referred to Savage as being among "the most valuable officers in the command" who "received a serious wound ... while gallantly leading his men against the enemy line."[58]

For all their gallantry, the Confederates had gained at best only a limited tactical success at Perryville. During the night, as Bragg took stock, he realized that it had taken his entire Army of the Mississippi (less Withers's division at Versailles) to defeat one corps of the Army of the Ohio. Worse, the other two corps, which had largely missed the battle, were now at hand. Most threatening, Crittenden's Third Corps to the south was in a position to flank Bragg and cut the Confederates off from their line of retreat to the Cumberland Gap. The next morning, the Army of the Mississippi began to withdraw eastward toward Harrodsburg. On October 12, Bragg made the decision to abandon Kentucky entirely. His army crossed through the Cumberland Gap and re-entered Tennessee on October 20, with Kirby Smith's force following two days later. The Kentucky campaign would prove to be the high-water mark of the Confederate States in the West.[59]

The recriminations then began, and most of the obloquy fell on Bragg. The generals split into feuding camps of Bragg supporters and detractors. Leading the attacks against Bragg, often simply to deflect valid criticism against themselves, were the two wing commanders, Polk and Hardee. Although Cheatham fell among the critics, most of the lower divisional and brigade commanders supported Bragg. Only brief, peripheral references indicate where Donelson stood. He was apparently a quiet supporter of Bragg. It was not in his nature to be bombastic, plus he was otherwise too good a soldier to show such disloyalty, and he understood that a major part of an officer's duty is discretion.[60]

Bragg in turn recognized Donelson's demonstrated abilities. The military disasters that had struck the Confederate States during 1862 had exposed a number of weaknesses in their command structure. In response, on October 13, the Confederate States Congress passed an act "to relieve the army of disqualified, disabled, and incompetent officers." Accordingly, on November 8, Bragg directed that an "examining board," consisting of Hardee, Buckner, and "Major-General Donelson," convene to investigate suspect officers. Bragg's selection of Donelson of all the brigade commanders speaks to his regard for him. The examining board carried out its charge "to weed out these officers of funguous growth," as was reported in the Atlanta *Southern Confederacy*, in an efficient and dispassionate manner. Within a week, Bragg was able to report on the reassignment or dismissal of several officers for reasons that ranged from incapacitating illness to drunkenness and incompetence.[61]

Beyond the selection of Donelson to serve on the examination board, the slip of the pen referring to him as "Major-General" further revealed Bragg's intentions. A survey of the general officers in the western theater that month listed Donelson as ranking second in seniority among forty-seven brigadier generals. Now, his dogged tenacity in battle won plaudits from the army's high command. Contemplating the re-organization of his army in the aftermath of the Kentucky campaign, Bragg considered not merely the "dead weights" to be cashiered, but also those officers who were eminently worthy of promotion. Accordingly, enclosed in the same batch of reports, Bragg submitted the names of Daniel S. Donelson and the equally hard-fighting Patrick R. Cleburne for promotion to major general. "Donelson is the senior," Bragg noted in his recommendation of both men, "a graduate of West Point, and much the older man. He is ever devoted to duty, and conspicuously gallant. Cleburne is young, ardent, exceedingly gallant, but sufficiently prudent; a fine drill officer, and, like Donelson, the admiration of his command as a soldier and gentleman."[62]

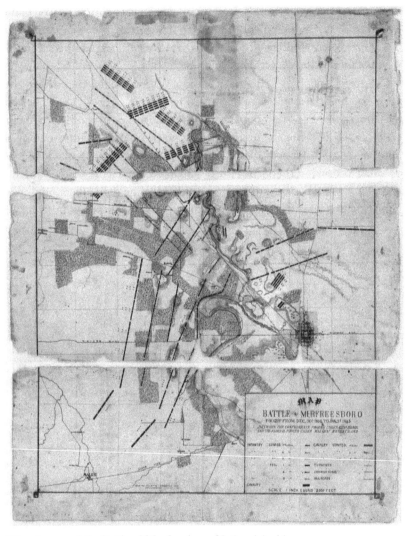

Historic map of the Battle of Murfreesboro. National Archives.

CHAPTER SEVEN

"More Distinguished Bravery"

MURFREESBORO,
OCTOBER 1862–JANUARY 1863

Promotions of general officers, upon being forwarded by the president, were then subject to approval by the Congress of the Confederate States. This could take time. While Brigadier General Daniel Smith Donelson awaited word of his promotion to major general, General Braxton Bragg proceeded with the refit and reorganization of his battered army. Not least, he gave it an appropriate new name, the Army of Tennessee. Gone was the "wing" designation, replaced by corps that were named according to their commanders, as were the divisions, although brigades kept their numerical designations. Thus, Donelson now commanded what was formally designated as the First Brigade, Cheatham's Division, Polk's Corps. His brigade retained the Eighth, Fifteenth, Sixteenth, Thirty-eighth, and Fifty-first Tennessee Infantry regiments, and Carnes's Artillery battery.[1]

With the general disruption that Bragg had succeeded in causing to United States army deployments by his Kentucky campaign, Union occupation forces had withdrawn from all of Middle Tennessee south of Nashville. Before they could return from Kentucky to regain their hold on the area, Bragg advanced his army toward Murfreesboro. There, at the geographic center of the state, he could claim that he had redeemed much of Middle Tennessee and, at only thirty miles from Nashville, he could give the appearance of hemming the Federals into their defenses.[2]

Accordingly, at the end of October the Army of Tennessee marched northward from Chattanooga toward Tullahoma and then on to Manchester, noted Captain James Womack of the Sixteenth Tennessee

Infantry Regiment, with "Donaldson's Brigade being in the van of the army." "Great anxiety" arose, however, continued Womack, among the officers and men in Donelson's brigade who were again very near their homes and agitating for leaves of absence to visit their families. The resultant low morale among the men "was ripening into a source of frequent desertions, and was very annoying indeed." Nevertheless, Donelson's brigade continued its march and reached Murfreesboro on November 24. The men pitched their tents about a mile beyond town, near a small creek that ran along the Nashville and Chattanooga Railroad.[3]

On December 3, orders came through Leonidas Polk's headquarters that "Major-General Cheatham will hold two brigades of his command ready to move at an hour's notice, with three days' cooked rations." The next day, Frank Cheatham advanced Donelson's and George Maney's brigades to Lavergne, within fifteen miles of Nashville. He left Maney's brigade there "on outpost duty" and returned with Donelson's brigade to Murfreesboro. While the *Memphis Daily Appeal,* which was now publishing in exile from Jackson, Mississippi, portrayed the movement as being "a dash on the enemy," for Donelson's men it was nothing but a hard slog through several inches of snow.[4]

The reconnaissance toward Nashville had brought Donelson almost as close to his home of Hazel Path. Even as he was retreating from Kentucky with the rest of Bragg's army, Union foragers had again raided his farm, "getting as much subsistence as they could bring away—indeed, bringing everything belonging to General Donelson, except the overseer and negroes, amounting to over 300 cattle, 300 sheep, 300 hogs, and turkeys, chickens, etc., in abundance, besides 600 wagonloads of corn, oats, etc." This time there was no mention of payment. The raid aside, the numbers speak volumes about the ability of Donelson's overseer and slaves to maintain production even in the midst of wartime depredation.[5]

If Bragg's purpose was to goad the Union army to come out of Nashville and fight, then he was having a hard time achieving that goal. United States President Abraham Lincoln had replaced the skittish Don Carlos Buell with Major General William S. Rosecrans. An efficient organizer, Rosecrans shared Buell's caution, and resisted the increasingly shrill directives from the Lincoln administration to advance before winter weather shut down major operations. Things looked so quiet that Donelson granted

Christmas leave to his aides, son Lieutenant Samuel Donelson and son-in-law Major James Glasgow Martin.[6]

Meanwhile, Bragg's army was visited by two distinguished officials. The dire situation in the West had resulted in the appointment of General Joseph E. Johnston as overall commander of the entire region between the Appalachian Mountains and the Mississippi River. Johnston arrived in Murfreesboro on December 5 to inspect the army and confer with Bragg. A week later, President Jefferson Davis arrived to join the consultation. During the long, busy day of December 13, Davis met with Johnston, Bragg, and the corps and division commanders, then reviewed each division of the army, at the end of which he and Johnston departed by train for Chattanooga.[7]

Donelson thus received a shock the next day, December 14, when Bragg's headquarters released the promotions of the new major and brigadier generals. Patrick Cleburne was duly announced as major general, but Donelson's name was conspicuously absent. What had happened? Bragg had discussed his recommended promotions with Davis, but without stating his reasons, Davis struck three names from the list, including Donelson's. As field officers, major generals typically commanded divisions; perhaps Davis did not approve Donelson's promotion simply because there was no vacancy at that time among division commanders in Polk's Corps. In the meantime, the recent transfer of Major General Simon Bolivar Buckner to command of the defenses at Mobile had left a vacancy in Hardee's Corps, allowing Cleburne to ascend to divisional command within his original corps. Conversely, the president was notoriously touchy; he was stubbornly loyal to his friends, could be meanly petty to his enemies, real or perceived, and meddled in military details far below his station. Donelson, in some unrecorded way, might have become a victim of guilt by association. Davis would have known that Daniel Donelson was the brother of Andrew Jackson Donelson. During the sectional crisis of the 1850s, Andrew, first as editor of the Washington *Union* and then as a leading member of the American party, had been among the harshest critics of the Southern States' Rights branch of the Democratic party, and had directed considerable vitriol against Davis. Still an unrepentant Unionist, Andrew criticized the Confederate States government and President Davis so strongly that in August 1862 he had been arrested on charges of sedition. Major General Earl Van Dorn dismissed the charges as being frivolous and ordered that Andrew be released, but Davis may have received word of the affair, and he was not above rejecting the promotion of his gadfly's brother. Arthur M. Manigault, one of the colonels who did not receive his recommended promotion to brigadier general, likewise believed that this was due to his own criticism of the Davis administration in a letter which then had been published without his permission in the newspapers.[8]

On the day after Christmas, Rosecrans finally began his advance on Murfreesboro. The most direct route between the two cities was the eponymous Nashville-Murfreesboro Pike. Maney's brigade was still on its "outpost duty" near Lavergne. Federal columns advanced through cold wind and rain, as Maney's infantry and Joe Wheeler's cavalry skirmished but steadily fell back from Lavergne. In placing his troops, Bragg was hampered by the geography of the Murfreesboro area. Stones River looped northwesterly as it passed west of town, which required him to split his units on opposite sides of the river. He placed Polk's Corps on the southwest bank, forming the left wing of the army, while Hardee's Corps took a position as the right wing on the opposite, or northeast, side of the river.[9]

The troops prepared for battle. The men of Donelson's brigade cooked three days' rations and sent their wagons to the rear. At dawn on December 29, the troops assumed their line of battle. Polk's Corps faced roughly northwest, with its right flank on Stones River, and extending leftward across the Nashville-Murfreesboro Pike and the Wilkinson Turnpike. Withers's division formed the front line, then Cheatham's division formed the second line behind Withers. Donelson's brigade formed the righthand side of Cheatham's division. The two rightmost companies of Colonel John Savage's Sixteenth Tennessee Infantry Regiment extended across the Nashville and Chattanooga Railroad, which paralleled the Nashville Pike, so that the right of Donelson's brigade was anchored on Stones River. The leftmost regiment, Colonel John Carter's Thirty-eighth Tennessee Infantry Regiment, extended across the Wilkinson Pike and rested on the right of Alexander Stewart's brigade at Donelson's left. To the left of Stewart was Maney's brigade, and to the left of Maney was Preston Smith's brigade. In Smith's brigade was the One-Hundred Fifty-Fourth Senior Regiment of Tennessee Volunteers, in which Donelson's nephew,

Captain John Samuel Donelson, his brother Andrew's son, commanded Company E, the Hickory Rifles.[10]

Sometime during the army's move to Murfreesboro, the Fifteenth Tennessee Infantry Regiment was detached from Donelson's brigade, apparently held back in Knoxville or Chattanooga. As compensation, on the morning of December 29 Donelson had assigned to his brigade the Eighty-fourth Tennessee Infantry Regiment under the command of Colonel Sidney S. Stanton. Reporting only 276 men, the regiment had been organized only weeks earlier from areas of Middle Tennessee that had been liberated by the Kentucky offensive that autumn. Unfortunately, the men arrived in Murfreesboro without blankets or arms and received their muskets only upon arrival. Stanton spent the next two days drilling his men to impart a semblance of experience. For Donelson, this green, understrength unit was hardly adequate replacement for a veteran regiment, but he accepted it without comment.[11]

During the day of December 30, Rosecrans's forces approached the Confederate position. "Rainy, cold & disagreeable. Heavy, and, at times, very brisk skirmishing all through the day," is how Captain Womack of the Sixteenth Tennessee Infantry Regiment summarized the day and the action. Cheatham detached the One Hundred Fifty-fourth Senior Tennessee Infantry Regiment to support the artillery battery of Captain Felix Robertson. Three Union regiments rushed Robertson's battery, but were repulsed by canister from the battery and "a well-directed volley" from the Seniors. The regiment "lost considerably in this engagement," Cheatham reported, "but behaved themselves most gallantly." John Samuel Donelson was wounded in the shoulder.[12]

As dark fell, Polk ordered Donelson's brigade forward to relieve the brigade of Brigadier General James R. Chalmers of Withers's division, which had been posted in the front line for three days. While Donelson's brigade held its forward position, the usual silence of the night was replaced by music from regimental bands that was audible to the men of both sides. In short order, Union bands struck up such patriotic tunes as "Yankee Doodle" and "Hail, Columbia," while Confederate bands answered with "Dixie" and "The Bonnie Blue Flag." When one band began playing "Home, Sweet Home," all the others on both sides joined in, with Yankees and Confederates alike singing the sentimental lyrics.[13]

By dawn the next morning, Chalmers's brigade "resumed its place" on the front line and Donelson's brigade returned to its position in the support line. While Donelson's and Chalmers's brigades were exchanging places during that cold, drizzly night of December 30–31, Bragg had resolved to attack Rosecrans's army. "The character of the country" that was occupied by Withers's division in front and Cheatham's division behind, divided as it was by the Wilkinson Turnpike and a copse of woods, would render it "impossible for the division commanders to give that immediate, personal supervision" of their entire lines. Accordingly, as Withers described, "it was agreed" that they divide the command of their two divisions. Cheatham would take the left, with "immediate control" of Withers's two leftmost brigades in addition to his own brigades behind them, while Withers would have "the direction" of Cheatham's two rightmost brigades, those of Donelson and Stewart, in support behind his own. Accordingly, that night Donelson received orders from his formal superior, Cheatham, "directing me to obey any orders which I might receive from Major-General Withers," in addition to any orders from corps commander Polk.[14]

Donelson's brigade had barely returned to its original support position on the cold, foggy morning of New Year's Eve, December 31, 1862, when the Battle of Murfreesboro, or Stones River, began in earnest. On Bragg's left, or southwestern, flank, McCown's and Cleburne's divisions smashed the Union right flank. But difficulties began as the sequential Confederate attacks from left to right reached the center of the Federal line, which was held by the division of a tough, rising officer, Brigadier General Philip H. Sheridan. Here, through untimely casualties, the command of the leftmost brigade of Withers's front line division devolved onto a junior colonel. Amid this command breakdown, confusion permeated rightward along the line as one brigade after another of Withers's front line attacked in a piecemeal manner.[15]

Finally it was the turn of Chalmers's brigade, the rightmost unit of Withers's front-line division. The conditions under which Chalmers's brigade charged were brutal. In front of them lay 800 yards of open field that belonged to a family named Cowan, with a brick farmhouse, outbuildings, and fences located near the center. At the far edge of the field, the Union line waited in the protection of a cedar brake that became known as the Round Forest. The Federals met Chalmers's charge "with a murderous fire of artillery and infantry." Advancing past the buildings, the brigade was split, separating its right two regiments from the rest of the brigade. Chalmers, who was leading the main group, was struck in the head by a shell fragment and carried unconscious from the field. The senior colonel, leading one of the wayward regiments farther off toward the right, could not be notified that the command had passed to him. Thus, yet another brigade floundered in leaderless disorder as Union volleys strewed the Cowan fields with Confederate bodies.[16]

Meanwhile, Donelson advanced his brigade forward to occupy Chalmers's original starting position in "obedience to the foregoing orders," although he did not specify whether they came from Withers or Polk. He placed the time at 10:00 a.m. Colonel John Savage's Sixteenth Tennessee Infantry Regiment to Donelson's far right served as the "directing regiment" with the railroad as "the line of direction" for the entire brigade. To the left of Savage was the Fifty-first Tennessee Infantry Regiment commanded by Colonel John Chester, then next the Eighth Tennessee Infantry Regiment commanded by Colonel William L. Moore, with its left resting on the Wilkinson Turnpike, and extending beyond there, the Thirty-eighth Tennessee Infantry Regiment commanded by Colonel John Carter. Donelson's recent acquisition, the Eighty-fourth Tennessee Infantry Regiment under command of Colonel Sidney Stanton, is described by Donelson as "being a new and small one, and having received its arms only the day before," and thus, Donelson explains, "I deemed it best to leave it in the rear, in support of Captain Carnes' battery." Still, Donelson's decision displeased its commander and men, who were eager to prove themselves.[17]

From where he sat on his horse, Donelson watched Chalmers's attack in front of him first falter and then fall apart under the intense Union fire. As he reported, Chalmers's "brigade was broken and the greater part of it fell back in disorder and confusion." Donelson was ordered, this time directly by corps commander Polk, "to move forward" to support the remnants of Chalmers's brigade. In response, "I immediately advanced my brigade to its support, and, indeed," in such dire circumstances, admitted Donelson, also to "its relief, under a shower of shot and shell of almost every description."[18]

Already whittled down considerably by attrition from one-and-a-half years of service, Donelson's brigade advanced with only about 1,400 men, but they were hardened, disciplined veterans, and still enthusiastic. "We moved forward at a double-quick, under a perfect hail of shot, shell, and grape," reported Lieutenant Colonel John H. Anderson of the Eighth Tennessee Infantry Regiment. Observers marveled at the sight of how resolutely Donelson's men conducted themselves. "The brigade of General Donelson . . . moved with steady step upon the enemy's position and attacked it with great energy," Polk reported. Division commander Cheatham pointed out that Donelson's men "pressed forward . . . under a terrific fire of twenty pieces of artillery and a heavy infantry force."[19]

Donelson's men advanced across the field, with the Cowan house in the middle now afire, and toward the Union line that was well-positioned along the cedar brake. At the northern end of the line, on the far right, Savage's Sixteenth Tennessee Infantry Regiment advanced along the railroad, with the two rightmost companies to the right of the rails, while the eight left-wing companies advanced between the railroad and the Nashville-Murfreesboro Turnpike "without the slightest protection, engaging a battery and the enemy's infantry in the woods at a distance of less than 150 yards."[20]

If Savage groaned that the open field offered no protection for his men, then just to the left, or south, neither did the structures of the Cowan farm improve conditions for the next units in the line. "In advancing upon and attacking the enemy under such a fire," Donelson reported, "my brigade found it impossible to preserve its alignment, because of the walls of the burnt house known as Cowan's and the yard and garden fence and picketing left standing around and about it." On the far right, Savage's regiment was able to march cleanly past the Cowan house but Chester's Fifty-first Tennessee Infantry Regiment, advancing to the immediate left, was heading directly toward the house, outbuildings, and fences. Worse, Chester's men found the Cowan house and yard filled with the men of Chalmers' brigade, huddling and milling about "in great confusion." As a consequence of these impediments, Chester admitted, "my regiment became somewhat scattered." He had put it mildly. The three righthand companies passed to the north of the Cowan house alongside the left of Savage's regiment. Under the circumstances, these three companies fought with Savage's Sixteenth Regiment through the remainder of the battle. Chester took the remaining seven companies and advanced through the field on the left of the Cowan house toward the woods.[21]

Donelson was experiencing his own difficulties. While the Cowan house was a serious obstruction, its central location and commanding view of that section of the battlefield also bestowed upon it a clearly strategic importance; that was why the Confederates became so determined to take it and the Yankees in the Round Forest beyond it were so determined to oppose their attempts. For that reason, Donelson chose to lead his brigade's attack by placing himself with the Fifty-first Tennessee Infantry Regiment. As he rode toward the Cowan house "under a shower of shot and shell," his horse was shot out from underneath him. Donelson fell heavily but picked himself up, apparently unhurt; so, too, his horse again stood and was still capable of being ridden. He remounted and continued to lead his men. When he reached the Cowan house, however, his horse went down a second time, permanently. Thrown a second time, Donelson was obliged to command the rest of the attack on foot.[22]

To Donelson's left, the Eighth Tennessee Infantry Regiment advanced, with the "gallant Colonel Moore leading." Moving forward "at a double-quick, under a perfect hail of shot, shell, and grape," the regiment was the first to arrive at the burned-out Cowan house. Once there, the regiment was thrown into "some confusion" caused by the buildings and fences, and also Chalmers's huddling men, which obliged "some four of the companies on the right of the regiment to pass round and through the best way they could." While the regiment negotiated these obstructions, Moore's horse also went down. Thus, amid the horrific chaos, Lieutenant Colonel Anderson "supposed" that Moore "was either killed or wounded." The leftmost unit of Donelson's brigade, the Thirty-eighth Tennessee Infantry Regiment, passed well south of the Cowan house but then "advanced over an open field and under a terrific fire."[23]

The Eighth Tennessee Infantry Regiment, entangled among the obstructions of the Cowan house, was exposed to "a powerful enemy in our front and on the right and left—" With the regiment's commander Colonel Moore having gone down with his horse, the second-in-command, Lieutenant Colonel Anderson, took charge. "Seeing the condition in which the regiment was placed . . . and seeing so many of my young men falling around me," Anderson could think of no other way to extricate them from this dire situation than to order them "forward at a double-quick with fixed bayonets." The charging regiment was just entering the woods when Moore, who it turned out had not been hurt when his horse fell, "came up with sword in hand." Moore had just begun to urge his men forward, however, when he fell dead, "shot through the heart with a minie ball."[24]

For all the ferocity of the fighting and the resulting bloodshed around the Cowan house, Savage's Sixteenth Tennessee Infantry Regiment, along with the three companies of Chester's Fifty-first that had passed north of the house, "held, in my judgment," Donelson soon decided, "the critical position on that part of the field." But, as Savage's men advanced with Stones River on their right, the railroad to the left of the river and the Nashville-Murfreesboro Turnpike to the left of the railroad steadily diverged from one another, which meant that his lines had to spread out dangerously thin to cover their widening front. Worse, due to the bulk of Chester's regiment having gone to the left of the Cowan house, Savage complained, "I was without the expected support on my left." Though his men succeeded in disabling the battery in front of them by shooting the gunners and horses, they could not advance farther without being outflanked by a battery on their right. The dead and wounded mounted, but Savage's "men maintained the fight against superior numbers with great spirit and obstinacy." "Unable to advance, and determined not to retire," Donelson reported proudly of their stubbornness, "I ordered Colonel Savage to hold his position at all hazards," while Polk promised support and reinforcements. "I felt it to be my duty to remain with that part of the brigade," Donelson explained, which was "holding so important and hazardous a position as that occupied by" Savage and his men.[25]

Reinforcements came in dribbles, and occasionally from unexpected sources. Polk spied the Eighty-fourth Tennessee Infantry Regiment, which was still guarding Carnes's battery in the rear, where Donelson originally had thought best to place it. Green and understrength though it was, right now every musket counted. Polk ordered the unit to advance upon the Federal battery to the right that was impeding Savage's men. Thus, the new little regiment got its baptism by fire on one of the worst sectors of the battlefield but acquitted itself well in guarding Savage's right flank along the river. Also advancing with its guardian regiment was Carnes's battery, which lent strong support to the right wing. At this point in the right-wing's crisis, the Thirty-ninth North Carolina Infantry Regiment "came up in my rear," Savage reported with equal surprise and pleasure, for it was an act of pure serendipity. The regiment had arrived at

Murfreesboro only that morning, just as the battle began, and was trying to find its assigned brigade. With no authority but without hesitation, Savage ordered it into the line of battle.[26]

Despite these reinforcements, Savage's line remained "entirely too long for the number of men under his command," Donelson reported, and was in danger of being flanked by a Federal force that might cross the river to their right. Savage therefore ordered his men to fall back to the river, where they formed two retracted lines to the right and front. To shore them up, Savage again tapped unassigned troops, ordering forward Blythe's Mississippi Regiment, which "had collected near the railroad." In this way, Savage "held his position, with characteristic and most commendable tenacity," Donelson reported, "for over three hours."[27]

All this time, Donelson's regiments that had passed to the left of the Cowan house, while they were sustaining horrific casualties, were nevertheless enjoying success. Anderson, who was now in command of the Eighth Tennessee Infantry Regiment after Moore was killed, boldly continued the attack into the woods. Against the onslaught of Anderson's Eighth and Carter's adjacent Thirty-eighth Tennessee Infantry regiments, the Federals in the Round Forest, as Carter reported, soon "broke and fled in confusion." Their efforts were aided by a timely attack to their left by Stewart's brigade. The combined forces chased the Federals entirely through the cedar forest, to an open cotton field on the far side.[28]

Meanwhile, to the far right of Donelson's brigade and still under his watchful eye, the patchwork force comprised of Savage's Sixteenth Tennessee, the three right-hand companies of the Fifty-first Tennessee, Stanton's green Eighty-fourth Tennessee, and Thirty-ninth North Carolina Infantry regiments, and also Blythe's Mississippi Regiment, all grimly held their position against attempted Federal advances. But, with Union artillery and small-arms fire steadily whittling them to a skeleton, reinforcements more significant than just a regiment here and there were desperately needed.

Northeast of Stones River, Bragg had posted the division of Major General John C. Breckinridge from Hardee's Corps to guard against a feared attack on his right flank by a Union column, said to be approaching from the north down the Lebanon Turnpike. All morning, Breckinridge's entire division sat idle, charged with meeting an attack from a nonexistent enemy, while Chalmers's and Donelson's brigades fought furiously just on the other side of the river. Finally, about midday, the brigade of Brigadier General John K. Jackson was ordered to cross Stone's River and report to Polk. Pointing beyond the Cowan house, Polk directed Jackson to support Donelson's brigade "where the battle was raging fiercely." The beleaguered Donelson, who had been seeking such a large body of troops for assistance for hours, was at first thrilled when Jackson's brigade advanced to his support, then watched in helpless frustration as, "instead of going to the right of the Cowan house and to the support of Colonel Savage," it veered to the left as had Donelson's other regiments. Jackson's brigade joined Donelson's left regiments and Stewart's brigade in the cedar woods, "doing fine service," but not where it was desperately needed. Donelson's beleaguered little command on the far right continued to hold, still awaiting support.[29]

They waited for more than another hour. Once Donelson and Polk realized that Jackson's brigade had marched in the wrong direction, the brigade of Brigadier General Daniel W. Adams was ordered to do what Jackson's brigade had failed to accomplish. This time the charge was in the right direction. Savage's beleaguered regiment and the associated units were at last receiving the support for which they had been waiting for hours. Adams's attack even reinvigorated Savage's exhausted men. Savage collected the men of the Sixteenth and the three companies of the Fifty-first Tennessee Infantry regiments, and advanced them to the front of Chalmers's original position.[30]

Alas, although Donelson reported that Adams's brigade "attacked the enemy with spirit," it was "checked by a terrible fire" from the Union battery. Grimly, Adams's men held their ground for about an hour until they could take no more. Donelson and Savage, observing what happened, did not resort to euphemisms. Donelson reported that Adams's brigade was "driven back in disorder and confusion," while Savage was characteristically even blunter in reporting that "it broke and fled in confusion." For Donelson's ragged survivors on the right, the rout of Adams's men signaled the end of the battle on that body-strewn field. As Adams's brigade retired, Donelson ordered Savage's exhausted men to retire along with it. Having received its baptism by fire, the green Eighty-fourth Tennessee Infantry Regiment was ordered to return to the safer duty of guarding Carnes's battery. As for the Thirty-ninth North Carolina Infantry

Regiment, which was not part of Donelson's brigade and which, in his desperate hour, Savage had appropriated, once Donelson's right wing retired, it disappeared whence it came.[31]

By the time these battered, exhausted units cleared the field, it was about 4:00 p.m. With the short winter day and dreary, overcast weather, light was fading fast. Polk made one last attempt to drive the Federals from their position. Two last brigades had arrived from Breckinridge, those of Brigadier Generals Joseph B. Palmer and William Preston. Polk sent them forward together. The results were discouragingly familiar: Palmer's brigade veered to the left into the cedar forest. Worse, as Donelson reported, almost shaking his head, Preston's brigade split at the Cowan house, with one regiment going to the right, which was repulsed, while the rest of the brigade veered to the left of the Cowan house and "over the same ground which a part of my brigade and all of Jackson's had already traversed."[32]

Donelson had done all that he could in that sector, as the crisis that had engulfed his units had passed with their retirement from the battlefield. He rejoined his left regiments, the Eighth, Thirty-eighth, and seven companies of the Fifty-first Tennessee Infantry regiments. He found them in a good position, drawn up in line of battle on the right side of Stewart's brigade at the edge of the cotton field. "Here we remained under a very heavy fire from the enemy's artillery, both of shell and shot, until dark."[33]

For Donelson's brigade, the worst of the fighting at Murfreesboro was over—and what fighting it had been! "There was no instance of more distinguished bravery exhibited during this battle than was shown by the command of General Donelson," Polk reported with pride, and he then added, "In the charge which it made it was brought directly under the fire of several batteries, strongly posted and supported, which it assaulted with eager resolution."[34]

It was the casualties that riveted attention. Both sides suffered horrendously, but casualties in Donelson's brigade were almost in a category of their own. Unit strengths upon entering the battle, plus numbers of killed, wounded, and missing, may often differ somewhat from report to report, but such slight discrepancies do not obscure the overall toll. For the Sixteenth Tennessee Infantry Regiment, Savage reported that he carried about 400 officers and men into action. Polk's report enumerated 402 while an organizational report stated 474. The 36 men who were reported as killed, 155 wounded, and 16 missing, totaling 207 casualties, is sobering by any measure and supports Polk's claim that the Sixteenth Tennessee Infantry Regiment lost "more than half its number."[35]

The Eighth Tennessee Infantry Regiment suffered even greater numbers of casualties, both absolutely and relatively. Polk reported that 425 officers and men entered battle while the organizational report enumerated 474 "actually engaged." The 41 men who were reported as killed and 265 wounded, a total of 306 casualties, represents a casualty rate of two-thirds and possibly nearly three-quarters of the regiment's total strength; to its credit, not a single man was reported as missing, meaning that none had been captured. For Company D, Donelson reported that "out of 12 commissioned and non-commissioned officers and 62 men who went into the fight only 1 corporal and 20 men escaped." This represents a casualty rate of 72 percent. "Other companies suffered almost as heavily," he added. Indeed, the standard modern study of the battle pronounces that the losses sustained by the Eighth Tennessee Infantry Regiment were "the heaviest suffered by a Confederate regiment in any single battle of the war."[36]

Donelson's other two regiments that fought around the Cowan farm and in the Round Forest also suffered heavily. The Thirty-eighth Tennessee Infantry Regiment carried 282 officers and men into battle and reported 12 killed and 73 wounded (again, none missing), or 85 total casualties, a 30 percent casualty rate. The Fifty-first Tennessee Infantry Regiment carried 293 officers and men into battle and reported 11 killed, 72 wounded, and 3 missing, or 86 total casualties, a 29 percent casualty rate. The green Eighty-fourth Tennessee Infantry Regiment initially was so successfully kept out of harm's way that it reported no casualties on the day of battle. Altogether, Donelson reported total casualties (varying slightly between reports) between 691 and 700 which, out of the total 1,456 officers and men of the four main infantry regiments that he led into battle, represents a staggering casualty rate of 48 percent. By any measure, Donelson's brigade was shattered at Murfreesboro.[37]

Yet despite the frightful losses, Donelson's brigade had distinguished itself. "The enemy was now driven from the field at all points occupied by him in the morning," Polk bragged of the results of Donelson's assaults. Only the Union line's "extreme left alone held its position." But even there, on the Confederate far right end, where Savage and his redoubtable Sixteenth Tennessee Infantry Regiment had struggled so indefatigably if fruitlessly, there was cause for pride. "I claim for my command great gallantry in action," Savage crowed, then further boasted "that it engaged and held in check superior forces of the enemy, who were attempting to turn our right—forces that afterward drove off Adams' and Preston's brigades."[38]

Finally, in terms of the measurable spoils of war, Donelson's brigade achieved commendable success. As Anderson conceded, "It is generally the case in battles that every regiment that passes a battery claims to have taken it." Thus, several regiments reported capturing the same cannons. Sifting carefully through his subordinates' regimental reports, conducting "a full conversation with them all," his own "knowledge of the ground" over which his regiments had passed, "and the position and movements of the other troops upon the same field," Donelson was "satisfied" that his brigade had captured, in all, "at least eleven pieces of artillery and over 1,000 prisoners."[39]

As for Donelson, no one set him apart for dash and brilliance, but he cemented his reputation for aggressive leadership and dogged tenacity. Personally brave and heedless of his own safety, he led at the front of his brigade in its initial charge. His horse was twice shot from under him, throwing him twice to the ground, but each time this oldest field general in the Confederate States Army picked himself up and continued the charge. He was lucky not to have been killed or wounded by enemy fire, or seriously hurt from his two falls. Active and alert throughout, he went to whichever part of the field was the most important at a given stage of the fight. He focused initially on taking the strategic Cowan house, appreciating its dominance of the surrounding field across which his regiments were advancing. Then, as Savage's command struggled on the right, Donelson went there, it being, "in my judgment, the critical position of that part of the field." For hours, he worked with Savage and Polk to locate and send reinforcements into the fight. Only after he saw to it that Savage and the battered survivors of the far-right line retired safely with Adams's beaten brigade was Donelson assured that he was free to return to his left regiments. For all of their own hard fighting, he knew that they were never at risk of annihilation, as had been Savage's command.[40]

As night settled over the bloody fields and forests west of Murfreesboro on that cold, damp New Year's Eve, Donelson continued to work, this time to reassemble his scattered command and see to the needs of his men—the dead, wounded, and unhurt. He withdrew his brigade about 200 yards from where it had ended the day's fighting in the cedar wood, but carefully posted "a strong picket for its protection." The green Eighty-Fourth Tennessee Infantry Regiment still had not received any blankets, so he directed that the men be moved back to a point where they could make fires for protection from the cold.[41]

Dawn of New Year's Day, January 1, 1863, brought no cheer to the exhausted men of both armies. On the Confederate side, Bragg was so pleased with the results of the previous day's battle that he dispatched a victory telegram to Richmond. On the Union side, however, Rosecrans made the critical decision not to retreat and instead to strengthen his position. As did the other commanders of their units on both sides, Donelson spent the day organizing his line, seeing to the care of his men, and preparing for whatever might come next. In short, he wrote of keeping "my men (under an occasional shelling) in line of battle and on the alert. . . . During this interval my dead were buried, and my wounded, which had not already been cared for, properly attended to." To clear his sector of obstructions in case the battle was resumed over the same ground, Donelson assigned the Eighty-fourth Tennessee Infantry Regiment the task of tearing down the offending ruins of the Cowan house, its outbuildings, and fences. While it was at this task, the regiment was shelled, with two being wounded, its only reported casualties of the campaign. Under these conditions, along with the officers and men also resenting being used for menial labor, nerves became frayed. The regiment's commander, Colonel Stanton, became involved in a fight with one of Polk's staff officers and "was ordered to the rear, under arrest," although the resolution was never recounted in the records.[42]

January 2 dawned with rain that soon turned to sleet. Worse, Bragg became aware that Rosecrans had moved troops and artillery to the northeast side of Stones River and now occupied a ridge, from which they could rain an enfilading fire on the men of Polk's corps in the very positions that they had won during the battle of December 31. Ignorant of the threat that loomed from across the river, Donelson's men, as did all in Cheatham's division, continued their routines from the relatively quiet preceding day. That afternoon, Cheatham ordered Donelson to advance his brigade and relieve Maney's brigade on the front line. "There we remained," Donelson reported, "with a strong picket thrown out in front, and skirmishing with the enemy's pickets nearly all the while," although his brigade suffered no casualties.[43]

Bragg determined that the Union force on the northeast side of the river would have to be driven away. Breckinridge's division constituted the only available infantry for the attack, but Bragg also tapped the artillery batteries from Cheatham's division on the west bank. Carnes's battery was given the honor of firing the signal gun for Breckinridge's attack. Despite early successes, Breckinridge's forces were repulsed.[44]

January 3 saw more cold rain. On the southwest bank of Stones River, the stalemate continued. Donelson's pickets skirmished with their Yankee counterparts most of the day but he reported no casualties. That evening, Federal artillery opened "a powerful fire" on Carnes's battery, killing one man and wounding four others, the last casualties that Donelson's brigade suffered during the army's stay in Murfreesboro.[45]

Cheatham and Withers were already urging Bragg that the army must retreat. With the move of Hardee's corps to the northeast side of Stones River to face the Federal force there, the seven decimated brigades of Cheatham's and Withers's two divisions were all that remained to face the main Union army on the west side. As the incessant rain was causing the river to rise, their commands risked becoming isolated if Rosecrans launched a full attack against them. Moreover, captured Federal papers had convinced Bragg that his army, reduced by a third from the battles of the preceding week, faced a Union force of seventy thousand. The Army of Tennessee began its retreat that night. At 1:00 a.m. in the wee hours of January 4, 1863, Donelson's brigade "took up the line of March to Shelbyville."[46]

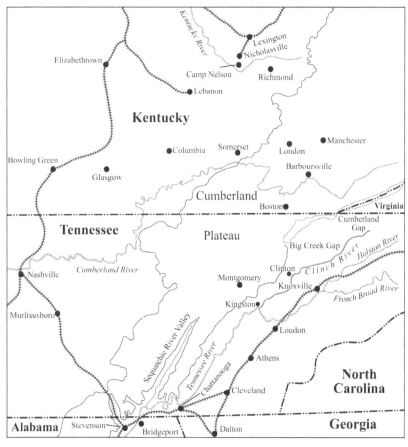

East Tennessee. From Earl J. Hess, *The Knoxville Campaign: Burnside and Longstreet in East Tennessee.*

CHAPTER EIGHT

"An Irreparable Loss"

EAST TENNESSEE,
JANUARY 1863–APRIL 1863

General Braxton Bragg directed the retreating Army of Tennessee southward. Polk's Corps settled a few miles north of Shelbyville while Hardee's Corps camped at Tullahoma. This was about as far south as Bragg could go and still plausibly claim to hold a section of Middle Tennessee. Bragg's popularity with the troops was as low as their morale, and his critics among the corps and divisional commanders renewed their attacks on him.[1]

Fortunately, Daniel Donelson was spared the risk of being drawn into taking sides by the timely arrival of orders from Richmond, dated January 17, 1863: "Brig. Gen. D.S. Donelson is assigned to the command of the Department of East Tennessee," which would be augmented to include several counties in southwestern Virginia.[2]

The announcement came seemingly as a surprise, but there were foundations. Why President Jefferson Davis had earlier rejected Donelson's name for promotion to major general remained unexplained. If the decision had been based on nothing more than the absence of a suitable command, then the Department of East Tennessee now provided one. The department had been commanded by Edmund Kirby Smith. Bragg's second major defeat at Murfreesboro and consequent revival of criticisms of him precipitated another crisis in the command structure of the western Confederate States armies. General Joseph E. Johnston, the overall commander of the Trans-Allegheny theater, decided to retain Bragg as commander of the Army of Tennessee but Kirby Smith was transferred to command of the Trans-Mississippi Department. Although Brigadier General Henry Heth was initially appointed to succeed Kirby Smith in

East Tennessee, Heth was so highly regarded by General Robert E. Lee that as soon as Lee heard of the changes, he requested Heth for the Army of Northern Virginia. This made the Department of East Tennessee available for Donelson.[3]

Less happily, Donelson, nearing sixty-two, was again suffering from the rigors of field duty. The year before, he had complained that the cold, wet weather in western Virginia had afflicted him in his "Bowels & stomach." Just recently, he took those two hard falls as his horse was twice shot from under him at the battle of Murfreesboro. He rose, apparently uninjured, but there may have been lingering aftereffects. At any rate, almost as soon as the army evacuated Murfreesboro, Donelson was stricken with "Chronic Diarrhea," according to a surgeon's diagnosis. "Contracting disease by exposure during the bloody field of Stone's River" is the way General William B. Bate diplomatically phrased how Donelson's medical affliction so quickly followed the battle. "Hoping that rest would restore his health" is how Donelson's earliest biographer W. W. Clayton reported the reason he accepted the departmental command. Even so, the timing and justification that account for Donelson's appointment to command the Department of East Tennessee were a combination of promotion and health.[4]

The formal notification of his departure from the Army of Tennessee emphasized the new appointment as being a promotion. "Brig. Gen. D. S. Donelson having been assigned by the War Department to duty in East Tennessee," Bragg's headquarters announced, "is relieved from the command he has so gallantly and ably led in this army, and will proceed to Knoxville in execution of his orders. He bears with him the confidence and esteem of his old companions in arms of every grade, whose regret at parting with him is partly relieved, however, by a knowledge of the transfer to a higher and more important command." Brigadier General Marcus J. Wright succeeded Donelson in command of his brigade. The brigade's senior colonel, the irascible John Savage, was so angered at being passed over for promotion to the command, which he believed he deserved, that he resigned his commission and left the army, and as always, blaming a conspiracy that included Donelson.[5]

The local Confederate population also hailed Donelson's appointment. "We are pleased to notice," wrote the *Chattanooga Daily Rebel*, hinting that it knew of the unaccountable prior delay in Donelson's promotion, "that he has at length grown in favor with 'the powers that be' to the extent that his services are required in a higher and more responsible trust. The Department of East Tennessee could not be entrusted to a more sagacious commander." On February 4, 1863, the Chattanooga headquarters of theater commander Johnston announced that "Brig. Gen. D.S. Donelson having been assigned . . . to the command of the Department of East Tennessee, will enter immediately upon the discharge of his duties." Donelson took command of his department by February 10, establishing his headquarters not in Chattanooga, as the *Athens Post* originally reported, but in more forwardly located Knoxville, which symbolized the paper's hope "that a more rigorous and efficient policy will be inaugurated." *The Daily Register* of Knoxville welcomed the new commander: "From Gen. Donelson's high character . . . we hope much good from his administration, and hail, as auspicious his entrance upon the difficult and delicate duties of his new command." He retained on his staff his assistant adjutant-general and son-in-law, Major James G. Martin, and his son Lieutenant Samuel Donelson as his aide-de-camp. Best of all, his wife Margaret again soon joined him, presumably bringing the two youngest children, Branch and Dan.[6]

Despite its geographic isolation, East Tennessee held great strategic, military, political, and symbolic importance. Its mountainous topography had kept it a region of small farms and towns whose people owned few slaves and who had voted against secession in 1861. Once the war began, many of its inhabitants remained strong Unionists, or, at best, surly, reluctant Confederates. Consequently, East Tennessee constituted a weak link in the Confederate States, a fact that riveted attention both in Washington and Richmond. President Abraham Lincoln badgered his generals to undertake military campaigns to liberate the thousands of loyal Unionists whom he imagined being oppressed by the rebels. The inaccessibility of the region stymied these efforts. Conversely, the region was important to the Confederate States to hold but presented similar problems to the authorities in Richmond. The Virginia and Tennessee Railroad, running northeast through Chattanooga and Knoxville into southwestern Virginia, was the only railroad link through the Appalachian Mountains between the eastern and western states in the Upper South. The Confederate States government therefore dedicated considerable resources to defend East Tennessee from external invasion and internal insurgency. Aggressive Confederates also looked on East Tennessee as providing a base for launching military operations into areas that were held by Union forces, especially neighboring Kentucky.[7]

Donelson had hardly settled into his office when he received just such a proposal from Brigadier General Humphrey Marshall. A onetime Whig congressman, Marshall's ambitions to redeem his native Kentucky for the Confederate States were not matched by his military abilities. Nevertheless, in January 1863, he proposed a plan to Major General Samuel Jones, commander of the Department of Western Virginia, for mounting a raid through the Cumberland Gap into eastern Kentucky by several thousand infantry and cavalry whose provisions would be carried by a thousand pack mules. When the Virginia counties under Marshall's command were transferred to the Department of East Tennessee upon Donelson's appointment, he forwarded the proposal to his new superior. Donelson then forwarded Marshall's proposal to the headquarters of his own superior, theater commander Johnston. "Having just entered on my duties, and having no knowledge of the causes inducing the order," he explained, "I have not thought [it] proper to take action until properly advised."[8]

Donelson learned that Brigadier General John Pegram was already carrying out a foraging raid in southeastern Kentucky. He accordingly directed Marshall, through his Assistant Adjutant General James G. Martin, to send "some 500 cavalry" to create "a diversion to cover and favor" Pegram's expedition. Johnston then passed word to Donelson that a series of Union pack mules were being driven to Nashville to supply Major General William S. Rosecrans's army. "Would it not be well to give this information" to Pegram, Johnston asked, that he might appropriate those badly needed mules?[9]

When Donelson directed Marshall to assist Pegram, he was obliged to add "that as you have as yet made no report of the strength of your command you must use some discretion in the execution of the above order, not weakening your cavalry force too much for the safety of your position." That Donelson granted such discretion to Marshall was based less on magnanimity than necessity, for he found his new department in a woeful state of administrative disorder. He even lacked records of which units were assigned to his command. As he groused, "respectfully," in his first report to Johnston's headquarters, "as far as my investigations have gone, I find the army here in the worst possible condition, on the score of discipline and efficient military government; no [field] returns made, no reports of brigades, &c., giving data upon which reliable returns can be made and forwarded to headquarters; great complaint in getting the necessary forage."[10]

Donelson immediately set about putting his new department into a state of order. Within a few days, he had complete lists of all the units that were under his command, where they were stationed, and most important, the numbers of "aggregate present and absent." In addition to Marshall's force in southwestern Virginia, from Cumberland Gap to towns and hamlets scattered throughout East Tennessee, in total, Donelson commanded in his department 11,875 troops designated "Aggregate present" or, more revealingly, 18,761 "aggregate present and absent." As a measure of the disorganization, nearly 7,000 troops, over one-third of Donelson's command, were absent.[11]

The last subject to catch Donelson's eye on the first survey of his new department was the persistent Unionism among the region's inhabitants, something that a staunch Confederate such as Donelson deplored. "The disloyal spirit of East Tennessee seems not to have been improved by the lenient course hitherto pursued," he frowned to headquarters. "I am of the opinion more stringent measures should be adopted." He advised that "all persons of the proper age" be conscripted into the army and the "disaffected disloyal portion" be sent south. "In this way you rid East Tennessee of a population that always has and will give aid and comfort to our enemies." He further advised that "some of the prominent leaders be arrested, put in prison, and held as hostages" to ensure the good behavior of the locals.[12]

Marshall was not the only Kentuckian who was interested in redeeming his strategically important state. On February 14, Secretary of War James A. Seddon wrote Donelson that Brigadier General John S. Williams and the "Kentucky Representatives in Congress" thought that a cavalry force could make "a rapid dash ... into the fertile and abundant districts of Kentucky." Although Kentucky's Confederate congressmen anticipated "important political consequences" from the proposed "enterprise," Seddon could see it only as being "a mere raid," and therefore it "is to my mind very questionable." He therefore sought Donelson's "superior knowledge and judgment on the feasibility and expediency" of the "expedition."[13]

Merits of the proposed raid aside, the secretary of war, revealingly, addressed his communication to "Maj. Gen. D.S. Donelson." Indeed, two days later, on February 16, Seddon submitted a list to President Davis of officers who had been recommended for promotion. On the list was Donelson, with his long-delayed promotion to major general now being revived. Political friends were now helping. As soon as his appointment to command the Department of East Tennessee had been announced, Tennessee's two senators in the Confederate States Congress, Landon C. Haynes and Gustavus A. Henry, wrote a joint letter to Davis urging that "Brig. [General] D.S. Donelson be promoted to the rank of Maj. General."[14]

Meanwhile, his theater commander Johnston doubted that Donelson could spare troops from his department to support the raids into Kentucky proposed by Marshall and Williams. Johnston opined to Adjutant and Inspector General Samuel Cooper in Richmond that the force in Donelson's department "is now quite inadequate—not more than sufficient to deal with internal enemies—" The mention of "internal enemies" also brought Donelson's views on "disloyal" Tennesseans to the attention of the Richmond government. "Concurring in your general views," Secretary of War Seddon wrote on February 27, in another letter addressed to "Maj. Gen." Donelson, "the President and myself repose full confidence in your energy, judgment, and discretion" but "would only suggest" that, before he implement any "measures of severity against leading Unionists," Donelson first gain "the countenance and approval" of Tennessee governor Isham G. Harris, "as it will strengthen you in public support and prevent some causeless clamors."[15]

Samuel Jones, commander of the Department of Western Virginia, averred to Donelson that Marshall's proposed "expedition" could well produce "important political and military results." Meanwhile, Donelson was growing impatient, grousing to Johnston that, since he had told Marshall to prepare his cavalry for the expedition, "I have not heard one word from him upon the subject." Writing to Jones, Donelson tried to balance cautious support for a combined expedition with the real difficulties that it would face. If Pegram and Marshall could advance simultaneously into Kentucky, then "the two movements might result in brilliant success to one or both expeditions, and corresponding beneficial results to our cause." Within days, however, the authorities in Richmond began to think that Marshall's force could be better used to reinforce Bragg.

Seddon thus telegraphed "Major-General Donelson" regarding whether Marshall should lead a Kentucky raid or reinforce Bragg, but added, "I do not intend to interfere with any movement you have ordered."[16]

Thus reassured from Richmond, Donelson wrote Johnston's headquarters that Pegram "is ready to start at once." Marshall, who was now in Knoxville appealing to Donelson directly, "says that he can start in three days with a cavalry force of from 1,500 to 2,000. . . . Shall such permission be given?" inquired Donelson. Before the end of the day, however, with the pesky Marshall gone but his inspector-general having "just returned from a thorough inspection" of the department, Donelson's patience snapped. That same day, in a second letter to Johnston's headquarters, he admitted bluntly "that I have no confidence in an expedition headed by Brigadier-General Marshall." Based on the inspector-general's report, Marshall's command was in "a most deplorable condition, undisciplined and scattered." Donelson therefore decided that Marshall and his command should instead reinforce Bragg, "provided an equal or even less number of forces be given me to supply his place." The last phrase was Donelson's devastating assessment that Marshall was more trouble than he and even his troops were worth.[17]

When Marshall got wind of Donelson's opinion of his proposed expedition, his "soldierly sensibility" was offended. He wrote an angry letter directly to President Davis, who attempted to smooth things over. "Although it is admitted that you have apparent grounds for complaint," Davis replied, "yet I am satisfied that no intentional disrespect or disregard of your feelings or rights was meant by General Donelson."[18]

Marshall had now involved the meddlesome president. "General Marshall proposed to go into Kentucky," Davis wrote Johnston. "Can you so arrange the forces in the Department of East Tennessee . . . as to obtain any valuable aid?" The prickly Johnston was jealous of his prerogatives and protective of his subordinates. He would not prod the commander of the Department of East Tennessee into relinquishing troops that could not be spared, for an expedition in which neither Johnston nor Donelson had any confidence. "That department is too weak to do more than control the disloyal (about 7,000 [sic])," Johnston explained to Davis. Donelson had no troops to spare for unnecessary glory-raids.[19]

The decision had already been made, however. While Davis and Johnston exchanged letters, Cooper wrote directly to Donelson, again addressing him as "Maj. Gen.," that Marshall's proposed expedition "has been favorably considered by the Department. . . . It is hoped that favorable political results may follow this movement." Cooper thus instructed Donelson to give Marshall the necessary orders "so that he may commence the expedition with the least practicable delay." Johnston bristled at Richmond bypassing the proper chain of command. "If the Department will give me timely notice when it intends to exercise my command," he snapped to the meddling authorities in Richmond, "I shall be able to avoid such interference with its orders."[20]

On April 1, Donelson forwarded to Johnston copies of all the communications with the War Department regarding Marshall's raid into Kentucky, which had finally commenced on March 13. Significantly for the first time, he signed after his name "*Major-General, Commanding.*" He must have heard by this time that on March 5, "Agreeably to the recommendation of the Secretary of War," President Davis had finally forwarded to the Confederate States Congress Seddon's list of officers who had been nominated for promotion, including Donelson. A Tennessee congressman assured the Knoxville *Register* that the "administration of General Donelson in East Tennessee 'is by far more promising than any we have had in the past.'" By now even Donelson felt comfortable using his new rank.[21]

The long, grinding issue of Marshall's Kentucky expedition had thus hardly been settled when the other issue arose which Donelson also had been facing: Unionists and other shirkers of the Confederate cause. The problem was not unique to East Tennessee; indeed, it was endemic throughout all Appalachian regions of the Confederate States. On March 27, Secretary of War Seddon wrote Donelson that Governor Zebulon Vance of North Carolina and others were complaining "of the presence and depredations of marauding deserters and refugees lurking in the mountains of North Carolina, near Asheville, and in the neighboring mountainous districts. Send, if you can, an efficient detachment to sweep the country of such bands, conscripting all of proper age."[22]

Donelson would never act on Seddon's request nor, for that matter, have the opportunity to enjoy formally his promotion to major general. On April 7, only a week after Donelson tentatively signed his impending new rank, Johnston surprised Cooper in Richmond with another of his characteristically terse messages: "Brigadier-General Donelson applies for a leave of absence, on surgeon's certificate."[23]

Alas, if Donelson's health had precipitated being relieved from his field command, neither had his subsequent office duties alleviated his condition. Whatever respite he gained was brief, for within a short time his digestive maladies had returned. Although the departmental medical inspector, E. Woodward, noted that Donelson initially "required but little medical attention," he was "totally without appetite" and not properly nourished by "any description of diet." Consequently, Donelson rapidly lost weight and strength. Remarkably, as evidenced by his huge work output, his physical incapacity had not compromised his attention to duty. Nevertheless, as Dr. Woodward noted, much of his time was "spent in bed or in a reclining position." Margaret no doubt ministered to her husband with her characteristic attention but, by early April, Woodward diagnosed that "it is absolutely necessary for the restoration of his health that he be relieved from all care and business." Woodward further recommended that "leave of absence be granted him for sixty days, as in my opinion he will not be able to resume his duties in a less period."[24]

Donelson's superiors scrambled to fill the gap. "It is important at this juncture to have a man of ability in his place," Johnston urged upon Cooper. The next day, Cooper telegraphed Johnston in reply, "Can you not send a ranking officer to command Department of East Tennessee." Johnston suggested Major General Richard S. Ewell, in what was seen as a temporary appointment until Donelson could resume his duties. Ewell had lost a leg below the knee at the Second Battle of Manassas in August 1862. Although he had not yet recovered sufficiently to resume a field command, Johnston considered him to be available for a desk job in Donelson's absence. "There is no officer in the department [of East Tennessee] at all competent," he sighed, revealingly. In the end, Ewell did not yet feel up to an independent command anyway, and preferred to wait on a full recovery in hopes of resuming his field command in the Army of Northern Virginia.[25]

For various reasons, the other officers who were suggested to command in place of Donelson were either unavailable or unacceptable. Brigadier General William S. Preston, whom Cooper suggested to Johnston, was already in temporary command of John C. Breckinridge's division in Bragg's army. Brigadier General Alfred E. Jackson, whom Donelson had initially assigned to command in his stead, was junior to Brigadier General William G. M. Davis, raising possibilities of offended pride among sensitive Southern officers. As for Davis, Donelson had already complained that he was absent from his command, which Donelson described as "necessarily in a scattered and bad condition, and his brigade suffering for the want of a commander." This could hardly be taken as an endorsement. Nevertheless, Davis was assigned to temporary command until Major General Dabney H. Maury, who commanded a division in Pemberton's army near Vicksburg, was given the permanent command in Donelson's place.[26]

Meanwhile, Donelson, accompanied by Margaret and presumably the boys, retired to Montvale Springs, a nearby mountain resort in Blount County, hoping to restore his health. Instead, his decline continued. Only ten days after taking leave of absence, Daniel Smith Donelson died of "Chronic Diarrhea and extreme prostration" on April 17, 1863, "at half past nine o'clock A.M." According to W. W. Clayton, who may have gotten the information from one of Donelson's children, his last words were, "Justice and mercy."[27]

Donelson's funeral was held on April 20 in Knoxville, and he was buried there "with military honors." Colonel Jesse J. Finley, commander of the Sixth Florida Infantry Regiment, headed the "funeral escort," while General Davis, as Donelson's temporary successor, directed that "as a mark of respect to the memory of the deceased, all business will be suspended between the hours of 11 o'clock A.M. and 2 o'clock P.M." Lieutenant James A. Wallace reported to his family, "A few days ago I attended the funeral and barrial [sic] of Genl. Donalson," adding that "The procession was very large."[28]

To Margaret, her husband of more than thirty years and father of their eleven children "was a man of education, honest in all his words & actions, beloved by all who knew him." In announcing Donelson's death, the Knoxville *Daily Register* led with the local implications. When he had been assigned to the Department of East Tennessee, "great good was hoped for from his administration of the complicated affairs of this section; but his declining health prevented him from carrying out the measures his experienced mind had devised." The obituary then waxed more expansively: "Both as a soldier and a civilian Gen. Donelson ranked among the leading spirits of Tennessee, and not only this his native State, but the whole country will experience in his death an irreparable loss." In announcing

Donelson's death to the Army of Tennessee, Bragg similarly paid him a sincere and appropriate tribute:

> The general commanding announces to the army the death of Brig. Gen. D.S. Donelson. . . . The regret with which his death is announced will be felt by the army and his country. He was an educated soldier, of great purity of character, singleness of purpose, and goodness of heart. Conspicuous for gallantry on the field, after the excitement had passed he was foremost in providing for the wants of his command, and devoted to the sick and wounded. His comrades in this army, and those who served under his orders, will long remember his deeds and his virtues.

In Donelson's old brigade, on April 27 the officers gathered in their camp near Shelbyville, Tennessee, to honor him. "The officers and men of this brigade have received with deep sensibility and melancholy intelligence of the death of Maj. Gen. Dan'l S. Donelson," began the "Tribute of Respect" that they drafted. The brigade could "testify of his worth as a patriot, a soldier and man . . . and witnessed his heroic and self-sacrificing devotion to his country and the holy cause, in the defense of which, he periled everything, and in the vindication of which, he sacrificed his life." They closed by adopting a resolution to tender "the warmest sympathies of his brothers in arms . . . to Mrs. Donelson."[29]

Donelson's death provides a revealing example by this time of the difficulties of conveying news across the war-torn Confederate States. On the day after he died, Marshall reported to him from Harlan County, Kentucky, on the progress of his raid, clearly still uninformed that eleven days earlier Donelson had stepped down as commander of the Department of East Tennessee. "In obedience to your order," Marshall reported, he had advanced "all my available cavalry" into Kentucky. The results, however, were disappointing. "I have not procured any recruits," Marshall pouted. "The people manifest no desire to rise against Lincoln's rule." If Donelson could have desired a little posthumous vindication, then Marshall's expedition proved to be as fruitless as he had so diplomatically forewarned.[30]

In other ways, news of Donelson's death traveled slowly enough that actions continued even in ignorance of the event. Most important, on April 22, the Congress of the Confederate States voted at last to confirm

"Brig. Gen. D.S. Donelson, of Tennessee, to be major-general, to rank [from] January 17, 1863," the date of his appointment to command the Department of East Tennessee. At the time of the confirmation of his promotion, the Congress was unaware that Donelson had been dead for five days.[31]

Newspapers were similarly slow to receive and print notification of Donelson's death. The news took a week to reach the *Southern Confederacy* in Atlanta, which published it largely by reprinting the original obituary from the Knoxville *Daily Register*. Not until eleven days after Donelson's death did the *Nashville Dispatch* print the news, in the process revealing its Union stance through lack of timely information: "He entered the Rebel service as a Brigadier-General but was, we believe, promoted to a Major-General, and was, a short time previous to his death, in command of the department of East Tennessee."[32]

The scarcity of family correspondence makes it impossible to know when or how Donelson's extended family learned of his death or their reactions to it. News traveled haphazardly and often arrived garbled. At the Hermitage, the wife of Andrew Jackson Jr., heard, inaccurately, that both Donelson brothers had died. "Genl. Donelson I hear is dead," she wrote her son, "also Major Andrew J.D." Little-noticed but no less tragic were two other actual family deaths. On January 4, 1863, as her husband's brigade began its retreat from Murfreesboro, Margaret's father, John Branch, died at Enfield in North Carolina. On April 22, five days after the death of his namesake grandfather, Daniel Donelson Horton, the son of daughter Emily and her husband James E. Horton, died only four days after his first birthday.[33]

The war continued to rage, and Donelson's two oldest sons remained faithful to the Confederate cause. As Sam wrote his uncle William Branch that summer, "in the language of my dear lamented Father, 'We must fight until the last man fall[s].'" He was first appointed onto the staff of Leonidas Polk, but eventually became aide-de-camp on the staff of cavalry commander Lieutenant General Nathan Bedford Forrest. James remained with the Seventh Tennessee Infantry Regiment, which saw action with the Army of Northern Virginia in the great campaigns in the eastern theater—Chancellorsville, Gettysburg, the Overland Campaign, and the siege of Petersburg—before surrendering at Appomattox. Fortunately, both brothers survived the war; they were luckier than many of their family and friends.[34]

In his will, Daniel left Margaret the Hazel Path farm "on which he was born & lived for many years & after my death to be divided between our children." He also bade her "to raise and educate our younger children in the same manner which our older children have been raised and educated." These provisions could not be fulfilled so long as the war raged. Hazel Path was repeatedly ransacked. "Cousin Daniels place is a perfect [w]reck," cousin Harry Smith reported to Andrew Donelson, "though the houses are still standing."[35]

On the day after her husband's funeral, Margaret Donelson appeared before a justice of the peace of Knox County to claim his back pay, which was calculated at $1,029.29 and eventually was paid to her. Thereafter, she and the children traveled to Tallahassee to wait out the war while living with her Branch relatives. "Ma," Sam wrote to his uncle William Branch, after visiting her in August 1863, "bears her inseparable loss with a Christian spirit, and is fully aware of the responsibility resting upon her in the management of her affairs." In late 1864, Margaret applied to Union occupation authorities for permission to return to live in Davidson County with her daughter and to have the possession of Hazel Path restored to her, but both requests were denied. Once the war was over, she and the children returned to Hazel Path in July 1865 to find that "their dwelling, barn &c, are greatly damaged, Most of the fences are burned, every tree of any size has been sawed into lumber." In addition, the Freedmen's Bureau had settled over four hundred freed slaves on the farm. It took several appeals directly to President Andrew Johnson, reminding him that her husband "was for many years a warm personal & political friend of yours," for Hazel Path to be restored to her.[36]

The family adjusted to the new social dynamics of the Reconstruction South. In December 1865, "Samuel Donelson, Attorney at Law," opened an office in Nashville. Just after the New Year, 1866, Sam announced his candidacy for attorney general of the judicial district comprising Davidson, Sumner, and Williamson counties. "Mr. D. is a son of the late General Daniel S. Donelson," beamed the Nashville *Daily Union and American*, now fully redeemed and already steeped in the mythos of the Lost Cause, "and is a gentleman of fine legal attainments," although he was barely twenty-one.[37]

Happy family events soon resumed. On September 25, 1866, Susan ("Sue") married Marcus Lafayette Dismukes. On August 17, 1867, Sam married Jessie L. Walton. On October 28, 1867, in a double ceremony,

Rebecca married David J. Dismukes, the brother of Sue's husband, and Martha married John M. Shute. There were sad events, also. In 1869 (date unrecorded), daughter Sarah Bradford died at the age of about thirty-three in Florida, where she was buried in her husband's family cemetery.[38]

In November 1868, Margaret put Hazel Path up for sale. "This farm has the Gallatin turnpike in front," ran the advertisement, "Drake's creek on one side, the Depot of the Louisville railroad in view," thanks to her husband's efforts, during his service in the General Assembly, to bring the railroad through Sumner County, "and is unsurpassed by any other in the State." She was unable to sell the place, but the next year the family saw through a happier accomplishment. In December 1869, Sam traveled to Knoxville, where he oversaw the disinterment of his father's remains from their original burial site during the war. Daniel Smith Donelson was reburied permanently, near his home and where he had been born, in the cemetery of the Hendersonville Presbyterian Church. On April 15, 1871, daughter Sue Dismukes died at the age of twenty-two, after five years of marriage and three children, and was buried near her father. Margaret Branch Donelson lived only another month. She died at Hazel Path on May 10, 1871, some three months shy of her sixtieth birthday. The "particulars" of her death were not known to her family, who knew "only that it was very sudden." She was buried beside her husband.[39]

In her will, Margaret bequeathed "to my two youngest sons John Branch Donelson and Daniel S. Donelson my plantation in Florida and all interest I have in my Father's estate, to be equally divided between them." Branch received the portrait of Margaret's father John Branch, for whom he was named. Dan received his father's portrait and the watch that Old Hickory had given to Daniel upon his departure from the Hermitage for West Point half a century earlier. Daughter Rebecca Dismukes received Margaret's portrait while Mary Ann Martin received "Mother Sander[s]'s" portrait. Margaret divided "all my silver, Furniture, and bed clothing" between Rebecca and Martha Shute. Her silver cake knife, pickle stand, and token mementos went straight to her granddaughter Margaret Horton, bypassing daughter Emily Horton. In a sentence which obscures as much as it informs regarding Margaret's relations with the remaining living children—Margaret ("Lizzie") Williams, Emily, and Sam—she stated briefly, "To each of my other children I give one dollar."[40]

In the years that followed, the two youngest sons married—Branch to Jennie Alexander on July 16, 1874, and Dan to Florence Hood on October 9, 1890. So far as the documentary records reveal, all of the Donelson children lived out respected lives in their communities. Dan served as mayor of Gallatin. Sam eventually moved to Washington, D.C., where, as "Col. Sam" Donelson, he served as the popular sergeant-at-arms in the House of Representatives during the speakership of John G. Carlisle of Kentucky, 1883–1889. Among so many Donelson children, there were innumerable grandchildren.[41]

After their mother's death, while they were settling their father's estate, Daniel Donelson's children sold Hazel Path to Judge John Kincaide. Upon his death, the house and property were inherited by Kincaide's daughter, Mrs. Mary Ann Weisiger. In 1886, Donelson's cousin Harry Smith, who lived at Rock Castle, purchased Hazel Path from the Weisiger family, thus restoring ownership of the house and property at least to the extended Donelson family. Smith's daughter, Nannie Smith Berry, lived there with her husband and three children, and there Nannie died in 1961, at the age of one-hundred. In 1978, the Berry family sold the mansion and surrounding grounds for commercial development. Today, Hazel Path is a well-known Hendersonville landmark, listed on the National Register of Historic Homes, open to the public, and used for office space as well as a popular scenic backdrop for weddings and other social events.[42]

EPILOGUE

★

"Something Peculiarly Appropriate in the Man for the Time"

In 1855, when his friends were pushing him for the speakership of the State House of Representatives, "MIDDLE TENNESSEE" had written of Daniel Smith Donelson in the *Nashville Union and American*, "there is something peculiarly appropriate in the man for the time." The pseudonymous writer made the inevitable connection to Old Hickory and took the obligatory swipe at the apostate brother Andrew in explaining how Daniel Donelson "was raised at the feet of ANDREW JACKSON, imbibed from him the political sentiments which now he advocates so ably, and the integrity of which, in these days of apostacy [sic], is doubly dear to every patriot."[1]

"MIDDLE TENNESSEE" thus established the criteria by which the life and career of Daniel Smith Donelson may be evaluated. In so many ways, his character, beliefs, and actions were outgrowths of his relations with his uncle and brother. In particular, it is instructive to consider how the two brothers, though both were raised at the Hermitage and initially pursued such similar trajectories of life and career, in the long run so differently applied what they had learned from their uncle and in the end took such divergent paths. Each brother always maintained that he remained the true disciple of their uncle Andrew Jackson, founder of the Democratic party and unbending defender of the Union. Yet Daniel's brother Andrew ultimately broke with the party and remained loyal to the Union, while Daniel remained loyal to the party but broke with the Union. What was it that made Daniel Donelson the brother who proved to be "peculiarly appropriate" for his time and led him to choose the course that he did?

Unfortunately, any full assessment of the life and career of Daniel Smith Donelson is hampered by the scarcity of his own words. No collection of his personal papers is known to exist. Most likely, whatever records and files he maintained were lost or destroyed when Union forces occupied and ransacked his home, Hazel Path. Aside from his military correspondence during the Civil War, only about fifty letters that were written by or to Donelson are known to exist, scattered among the collections of his correspondents.

In no area is the absence of personal records more deeply felt than in Donelson's domestic life. No letters that were exchanged between Daniel and Margaret Donelson, or with any of their children, are known. Even basic information such as birth, marriage, and death dates, as well as middle names are lacking for several of the children. Except for a few public records such as land and slave transactions, almost nothing is known about Donelson's farming activities, financial affairs, relations with his slaves, or his views regarding slavery as an institution. Few anecdotes survive that might illuminate or add charm to the family circle. And, amid the cacophony of his brother's financial crises, only silence suggests that Daniel's finances were in better shape. Future historians can only hope that a descendant may yet one day discover a trove of family records and letters in an old trunk.

Until such may occur, available information must suffice. The Donelson brothers began their lives and careers, with respect to one another and to their uncle Andrew Jackson, in almost identical ways, although divergences are discernible even early on. Orphaned, then at young ages estranged from their mother and stepfather, they spent much of their childhood at the Hermitage, but Daniel seems to have spent considerably more time with his Smith grandparents at Rock Castle. Once each brother returned from West Point, however, the differences in their relations with their uncle became more pronounced.

The most fundamental initiator of the divergence was simple proximity. Each brother settled on the property that their father had left them, and arranged through Grandfather Smith's will. Andrew thus lived only down the lane from the Hermitage. Unless travel separated them, Jackson and Andrew saw each other virtually every day. Beyond Andrew's formal duties in the White House during his years as President Jackson's secretary, the two men formed a unique symbiotic working relationship, exchanging hundreds of letters and notes. In contrast, Daniel settled on his father's farm outside Hendersonville in Sumner County. The distance to the Hermitage was barely six miles as the crow flies, but something more than just the winding Cumberland River intervened. In a telling statistic, although Jackson meticulously kept and filed the thousands of letters that he received throughout his life, only three are from Daniel Donelson. "Danl has never wrote me the scrape of a pen since he left here," was a typical Jackson complaint from the spring of 1831, after newlyweds Daniel and Margaret departed the White House for Tennesee.[2]

Both brothers were swept into the Eaton affair, but they suffered from Old Hickory's wrath at different stages, in different ways, and with different results. Andrew and his wife Emily had to endure living with Jackson's tirades in the White House during the height of the affair, even to the point of being accused of betrayal and disloyalty. Once the petticoat war ended, however, they resumed their former places in their uncle's affections with apparently never another word being said on the matter. By contrast, Daniel's marriage in the midst of the affair to the daughter of one of the men whom Jackson had fingered as agitating the scandal, produced only the happiest responses from Old Hickory, such was Jackson's romantic sentimentality and his ability to separate the purely personal from the political. Rather, Daniel suffered in the aftermath, using his resentment over the dismissal of his father-in-law John Branch from the Cabinet, to embarrass his uncle in the affair involving Robert Desha and Robert M. Burton. The cumulative result was that Daniel began to drift southward, politically. Although he never formally broke with his uncle's party, he sided with the nullifiers, opposed Martin Van Buren's nomination as vice president in 1832, and sympathized with the presidential movement for Hugh Lawson White.

Significantly, however, Daniel never lost his appreciation for all that his uncle had done for him. Even at the height of this trying period, he admitted to Andrew, "notwithstanding all that has been said and done, I can never forget what Genl Jackson has done for us, and shall always entertain for him the proper feelings of gratitude and respect—" But even here, tellingly, Daniel's reference was to "Genl Jackson," not "Uncle."[3]

The passing of these crises allowed Daniel Donelson to return to the orthodox Jacksonian fold, where he remained through the rest of Jackson's life and which even propelled his rise in Tennessee state politics. Indeed, when the sectional crises arose again in the 1850s, it was Daniel who better followed the drift of the Democratic party while Andrew found himself becoming the one who was at odds with the new political map.

Thus, it was Daniel, as "MIDDLE TENNESSEE" could assert, who kept his "integrity" in adhering to the "political sentiments" of Andrew Jackson, while Andrew became the apostate. Such was the winding path by which Daniel, rather than Andrew, became "peculiarly appropriate" as "the man for the time."[4]

Later, as the secession crisis unfolded, Daniel Donelson's course remained "peculiarly appropriate" for a man in his situation, that is, as a Democratic conditional Unionist of an upper South state. Few Tennesseans were openly secessionist, but what they viewed as Lincoln's coercion to bring the seceded states back into the Union precipitated their embrace of the Confederate cause. However much his earliest biographer W. W. Clayton knew that he "deplored" the dissolution of the old Union, Donelson did not hesitate in his choice.[5]

Not only did Donelson embrace the Confederate cause, he raised his sword against the old Union. Initially, he was little more than a political general who had never served a day of active duty in the United States Army. Yet, this oldest field general in the Confederate States Army quickly showed his mettle. His years at the highest levels of the Tennessee state militia had taught him the importance of organization and logistics, which he applied to the needs of his troops. From his earliest campaigns he impressed even the exacting Robert E. Lee with his prompt response to orders, ability to march his troops rapidly over difficult terrain, and aggressive perseverance in engaging the enemy. As a leader on the battlefield, no one credited Donelson with the tactical brilliance of Lee or Stonewall Jackson, or the flamboyance of Jeb Stuart and Nathan Bedford Forrest, but the commanders above him and troops below him noted his dogged tenacity. He advanced with his men, led them from the front, and was always to be found on the critical part of the field. His men appreciated Donelson "as a brave and patriotic man," recalled Captain H. H. Dillard, "and one who had our cause much at heart, but perhaps thought him lacking somewhat in military tact[ics] and generalship." Lee, Braxton Bragg, Leonidas Polk, and Frank Cheatham all learned to rely on Donelson and his hard-hitting brigade. For that, so many of Donelson's brave men paid the ultimate price. Nevertheless, as Dillard added, his men "much regretted his death."[6]

Had Donelson fallen on the battlefield as did Stonewall Jackson or Patrick Cleburne, or, conversely, had he survived the war long enough to become a regular at reunions and even to write his memoirs, he might be better remembered today among historians, Civil War buffs, and even the general public. Instead, it was his fate to suffer an inglorious death at a desk job when the war had run barely half its course. Nevertheless, his contemporaries fully appreciated his worth in both the political and military realms. "Conspicuous for gallantry on the field," went Bragg's heartfelt tribute, "His comrades . . . will long remember his deeds and his virtues." Indeed they did, at least for as long they could hold him in their living memory. In the years after the war, the Association of Confederate Soldiers of Tennessee organized the Daniel S. Donelson bivouac in Sumner County, named in his honor. The aging veterans of his brigade met regularly well into the twentieth century. A picture of the general adorned the bivouac's banner. "It was mine to know and admire him from [my] boyhood," said Confederate States General and Tennessee Senator William B. Bate thirty years after Donelson's death, in an address given at the unveiling of a Confederate monument in Knoxville, speaking of him "as a man eminently qualified for both civil and military command. For devotion to duty and nobleness of nature General Daniel S. Donelson was the peer of the purest and bravest."[7]

NOTES

Abbreviations

AJ	Andrew Jackson
AJD	Andrew Jackson Donelson
AJDJr	Andrew Jackson Donelson, Junior
AJDLC	Andrew Jackson Donelson Papers, Library of Congress
AJDTHS	Andrew Jackson Donelson Papers, Tennessee Historical Society
AJJr	Andrew Jackson, Junior
AJLC	Andrew Jackson Papers, Manuscript Division, Library of Congress
BDTGA	*Biographical Directory of the Tennessee General Assembly*, Eds. Robert M. McBride, Dan M. Robison, and Ilene J. Cornwell, 6 volumes (Nashville: Tennessee Historical Commission, 1975–1990).
BDUSC	*Biographical Directory of the United States Congress, 1774–1989, Bicentennial Edition: The Continental Congress, September 5, 1774, to October 21, 1788, and the Congress of the United States from the First to the One Hundredth Congress, March 4, 1789, to January 3, 1989, Inclusive*, Eds.-in-chief Kathryn Allamong Jacob and Bruce A. Ragsdale (Washington: United States Government Printing Office, 1989).
DAB	*Dictionary of American Biography*, Eds. Allen Johnson and Dumas Malone, 20 volumes (New York: Charles Scribner's Sons, 1928–1936).
DSD	Daniel Smith Donelson
Jackson Correspondence	*Correspondence of Andrew Jackson*, Ed. John Spencer Bassett, 6 volumes (Washington: Carnegie Institute of Washington, 1926–1933).

Jackson Papers	*The Papers of Andrew Jackson,* Eds. Sam B. Smith, Harold D. Moser, and Daniel Feller, et al., 11 volumes to-date (Knoxville: The University of Tennessee Press, 1980–2019).
LOC	Library of Congress, Washington, D.C.
MBD	Margaret Branch Donelson
OR	U.S. War Department, *The War of the Rebellion: A Compilation of the Official Records of the Union and Confederate Armies,* 130 serial volumes (Washington: Government Printing Office, 1880–1901).
SHCUNC	Southern Historical Collection, Louis Round Wilson Library, University of North Carolina, Chapel Hill, NC.
SOR	*Supplement to the Official Records of the Union and Confederate Armies,* Eds. Janet B. Hewett, Noah Andre Trudeau, and Bruce A. Sudrow, 100 volumes (Wilmington: Broadfoot Publishing Company, 1994).
TEHC	Carroll Van West, editor-in-chief, *The Tennessee Encyclopedia of History & Culture* (Nashville: Rutledge Hill Press, 1998).
THQ	*Tennessee Historical Quarterly*
THS	Tennessee Historical Society
TSLA	Tennessee State Library and Archives
West Point Biographical Register	George W. Cullum, *Biographical Register of the Officers and Graduates of the U.S. Military Academy at West Point, N.Y., from its Establishment, in 1802 to 1890, with the Early History of the United States Military Academy 3ed.*, 3 volumes (Boston: Houghton, Mifflin and Company, 1891).
WRHS	Western Reserve Historical Society, Cleveland, OH.

Preface

1. The earliest and most valuable of these brief biographies of DSD appears in W. W. Clayton, *History of Davidson County, Tennessee, with Illustrations and Biographical Sketches of its Prominent Men and Pioneers* (Philadelphia: J.W. Lewis & Co., 1880), 396–397. Clayton may have known DSD personally, and otherwise relates information that must have come from some of DSD's children. Next is evidently the one in Clement A. Evans, ed., *Confederate Military History* 8 (Atlanta:

Confederate Publishing Company, 1899), 307–308. Recent accessible brief biographies include those in: *Biographical Directory of the Tennessee General Assembly*, Eds. Robert M. McBride, Dan M. Robison, and Ilene J. Cornwell, 6 volumes (Nashville: Tennessee Historical Commission, 1975–1990), 1:206–207, hereinafter cited as *BDTGA*; Ezra J. Warner, *Generals in Gray: Lives of the Confederate Commanders* (Baton Rouge: Louisiana State University Press, 1959), 74–75; and Randy Bishop, *Civil War Generals of Tennessee* (Gretna: Pelican Publishing Company, 2013), 74–76.

Chapter One: "Fine Material for a Military Man"

1. John Donelson, quoted in: John Donelson to William Preston, October 1, 1778, letter, William Preston Papers, Lyman C. Draper Collection of Manuscripts, Historical Society of Wisconsin, Library Mall, University of Wisconsin-Madison, Madison, WI; Richard Douglas Spence, "John Donelson and the Opening of the Old Southwest," *Tennessee Historical Quarterly* 50, no. 3 (Fall 1991), 157–163, hereinafter cited as *THQ*.

2. J. G. M. Ramsey, quoted from *The Annals of Tennessee to the End of the Eighteenth Century* (Philadelphia: Lippincott, Grambo & Co., 1853), 197–202; Spence, "John Donelson," 163–165 (see previous note); John R. Finger, *Tennessee Frontiers: Three Regions in Transition* (Bloomington: Indiana University Press, 2001), 77–82.

3. Spence, "John Donelson," 165–169; Finger, *Tennessee Frontiers*, 82–103 (see prev. note).

4. Walter T. Durham, *Daniel Smith, Frontier Statesman* (Gallatin: Sumner County Public Library Board, 1976), *passim*; Mary Ann (Polly) Smith Donelson Sanders, birthdate from her tombstone, Rock Castle Cemetery, Hendersonville, Sumner County, Tennessee.

5. Walter T. Durham, *The Great Leap Westward: A History of Sumner County, Tennessee, From Its Beginnings to 1805* (Gallatin: Sumner County Public Library Board, 1969), 1-2, 55–58.

6. Walter Clark, ed., *The State Records of North Carolina*, [laws in] Vol. 24, 1777-1788 (Goldsboro: Nash Brothers, Book and Job Printers, 1895–1914), 975. For AJ's appointment, see Vol. 21, 1788-1790: 403, 412, 712, 714, 717; Durham, *Daniel Smith*, 96–103 (see note 4).

7. Hendrik Booraem, *Young Hickory: The Making of Andrew Jackson* (Dallas: Taylor Trade Publishing, 2001), passim; Marquis James, *The Life of Andrew Jackson* (New York: Garden City Publishing Co., Inc., 1940), 3–41; Robert V. Remini, *Andrew Jackson and the Course of American Empire, 1767–1821* (New York: Harper & Row Publishers, 1977), 1–36.

8. "Permission for Robards to sue for divorce," December 20, 1790, in *The Papers of Andrew Jackson*, Eds. Sam B. Smith, Harold D. Moser, and Daniel Feller, et al., 11 vols. to-date (Knoxville: The University of Tennessee Press, 1980–2019),

1:424, hereinafter cited as *Jackson Papers*. Divorce Decree, September 27, 1790, Ibid. 1: 427–428. Marriage Bond, January 17, 1794, Ibid. 1: 428. Marriage License, January 18, 1794, Ibid. 1: 44. It is beyond the present book to dissect the legalities and timing of the divorce and marriage episode; see Remini, *Andrew Jackson and the Course of American Empire*, 41–44, 57–69 (see note 7), and Andrew Burstein, *The Passions of Andrew Jackson* (New York: Alfred A. Knopf, 2003), 241–248.

9. Richard Douglas Spence, "Samuel Donelson: The Young Andrew Jackson's Best Friend," *THQ* 69, no. 2 (Summer 2010): 106–123; also Rodney Faulk, email to author, November 29, 2010. On p. 113, I reported Samuel Donelson's defeat for election as attorney general and thought that the episode was closed. After reading the *THQ* article, Rodney Faulk of the District Attorney's Office of Davidson County, Tennessee, contacted me with the story of Tatum's election, declination to serve, and Samuel Donelson's consequent appointment as attorney general *pro tempore*. I greatly appreciate Mr. Faulk providing me with this additional information. For Howell Tatum (1753–1822), see *Dictionary of North Carolina Biography*, Ed. William S. Powell, 6 volumes (Chapel Hill: The University of North Carolina Press, 1996), 6:5–6.

10. Silas Emmett Lucas Jr., ed., *Marriage Record Book I, January 2, 1789–December 13, 1837, Davidson County, Tennessee* (Easley: Southern Historical Press, 1979), 83; Mary Emily Donelson Wilcox, "Biographical Sketch of AJD," personal account, n.d., Andrew Jackson Donelson Papers, Manuscript Division, MSS 18721, Library of Congress, Washington, D.C., hereinafter cited as AJDLC and LOC, respectively; Pauline Wilcox Burke, *Emily Donelson of Tennessee* (Richmond: Garrett and Massie, Incorporated, 1941), 1:23–26; Durham, *Daniel Smith*, 80, 201–203; Durham, *Great Leap Westward*, 177 (see note 5); Curiously, AJD and DSD were uncertain of the date of their parents' marriage. A clause in the papers concerning *Donelson v. Sanders* refers to the marriage as taking place "sometime in the year 1796," *Donelson v. Sanders*, collected papers, AJDLC.

11. Joseph Anderson to AJ, August 4, 1796, *Jackson Papers* 1, 97; *Donelson v. Sanders*, AJDLC. John Samuel Donelson's birth date within 1797 is not known; Burke, *Emily Donelson*, 1:26–27 (see prev. note); Durham, *Daniel Smith*, 203; Richard Douglas Spence, *Andrew Jackson Donelson: Jacksonian and Unionist* (Nashville: Vanderbilt University Press, 2017), 6; For Joseph Anderson (1757–1837), see *Dictionary of American Biography*, Eds. Allen Johnson and Dumas Malone, 20 volumes (New York: Charles Scribner's Sons, 1928–1936), 1:267–268, hereinafter cited as *DAB*.

12. DSD, birth date from his tombstone, First Presbyterian Church of Hendersonville Cemetery, Hendersonville, Sumner County, Tennessee; Durham, *Daniel Smith*, 211.

13. The exact circumstances and date of Samuel Donelson's death are not known and even the year has been variously reported. For a discussion of the issue, see Spence, "Samuel Donelson," 116–117 (see note 9).

14. Daniel Smith to AJ, letters, February 19, and April 12, 1806; AJ, notes on the back of letter, J. Mason Campbell to AJ, August 13, 1838, Andrew Jackson Papers, Manuscript Division, Library of Congress, Washington, D.C., hereinafter cited as AJLC; Statement from *Donelson v. Sanders,* AJDLC; Estate of Samuel Donelson, Inventory, September 19, 1804, and also, record of posting bond. Both calendared in *Jackson Papers* 2: 525; Burke, *Emily Donelson* 1: 29; Durham, *Daniel Smith*, 231.

15. Deed to the Hermitage; AJ to James Stephenson, letter, March 11, 1804, AJLC; For the birth date and adoption of AJJr., a matter of some confusion, see the discussion in *Jackson Papers* 2: 218; also see Robert V. Remini, *Andrew Jackson and the Course of American Freedom, 1822–1832* (New York: Harper & Row, Publishers, 1981), 395, n 6.

16. Marriage between James Sanders and Molley [*sic*] Donelson, February 26, 1806, as cited in *Marriages of Sumner County, Tennessee, 1787–1838,* Comp. Edith Rucker Whitley (Baltimore: Genealogical Publishing Co., Inc., 1981), 14; Burke, *Emily Donelson* 1: 93; Sanders's surname is frequently spelled Saunders, e.g., James Saunders (1764–1836), in *BDTGA* 1: 648–649 (see Preface, note 1).

17. William Ballard to AJ, letter, March 24, 1807; January 3, 1808; George M. Deaderick to AJ, letter, January 15, 1808; account between AJ and John Caldwell, April 25, 1808, AJLC; AJ to Smith, letter, November 28, 1807, *Jackson Papers* 2: 176; R. Beeler Satterfield, *Andrew Jackson Donelson: Jackson's Confidant and Political Heir* (Bowling Green: Hickory Tales, 2000), 3.

18. AJ's campaigns during the War of 1812 are chronicled in Remini, *Andrew Jackson and the Course of American Empire,* 187–297.

19. "University of Nashville," *The Republican Banner and Nashville Whig,* April 17, 1850; John F. Woolverton, "Philip Lindsley and the Cause of Education in the Old Southwest," *THQ,* 19, no. 1 (March 1960): 4; John H. Thweatt, "James Priestley: Classical Scholar of the Old South," *THQ* 39, no. 4 (Winter 1980): 436; Burke, *Emily Donelson* 1: 50; Spence, *Andrew Jackson Donelson,* 8–9.

20. Owen, quoted from W. Purnell Owen to Smith, February 28, 1817, letter, in compendium "Papers of Gen. Daniel Smith," Ed. W. R. Garrett, *The American Historical Magazine* (Nashville) 6, no. 3 (July 1901): 235; Ibid., AJ to Smith, March 27, 1817, 235; Mary Sanders to AJD, letter, May 19, 1817, Miscellaneous Manuscripts, TSLA.

21. Smith to AJD, May 6, 1817; AJ to AJD, December 16, 1817; DSD to AJD, March 22, 1818, all in: Dyas Collection of John Coffee Family Papers, TSLA; DSD to AJD, letter, September 20, [1818], Bettie Mizell Donelson Papers, THS. There is no year on the letter but the content places it in 1818; Durham, *Daniel Smith,* 263.

22. DSD to AJD, letter, September 20, [1818], Bettie M. Donelson Papers, THS; DSD to AJD, letter, January 2, 1819, photocopy, in possession of Dr. Andrew Jackson "Jack" Donelson of Bowling Green, Kentucky. Location of the original letter is unknown; AJ to AJD, letter, May 17, 1819, *Jackson Papers* 4: 299; DSD to

AJD, letter, March 12, 1819, Dyas Collection, TSLA; "University of Nashville," *Republican Banner and Nashville Whig*, April 17, 1850.

23. Mary Emily Donelson Wilcox, "superb," quoted from biographical sketch of AJD, AJDLC; description of DSD, cited from W. W. Clayton, *History of Davidson County, Tennessee, with Illustrations and Biographical Sketches of its Prominent Men and Pioneers* (Philadelphia: J.W. Lewis & Co., 1880), 397; "Daniel S. Donelson," The *Nashville Banner*, June 24, 1897; Spence, *Andrew Jackson Donelson*, 18.

24. Andrew Jackson, "Loan Office" Memorial, reprinted in "Tennessee Bank and Relief Law," *Niles' Weekly Register*, September 2, 1820: 9–11; James, *Life of Andrew Jackson*, 305–306.

25. AJ to John C. Calhoun, letter, December 21, 1820, *Jackson Papers* 4: 410. The most thorough biography of John Caldwell Calhoun remains: Charles M. Wiltse, *John C. Calhoun*, 3 vols. (Indianapolis: The Bobbs-Merrill Company, Inc., 1944–1951).

26. Calhoun to AJ, letters, January 13, 1821, and March 7, 1821, both in: *The Papers of John C. Calhoun*, Eds. W. Edwin Hemphill, Clyde N. Wilson, and Robert L. Meriwether (Columbia: University of South Carolina Press, 1959–2003), 5:553, 664, respectively; DSD's appointment to the United States Military Academy at West Point, signed by Calhoun, n.d., Bettie M. Donelson Papers, THS.

27. AJ to AJD, March 31, 1821, letter, *Jackson Papers* 5: 24; "Unveiling of Statue Highlights Hermitage Spring Outing Today," *Nashville Banner*, May 17, 1950: 14 (DSD's watch).

28. Calhoun to AJ, May 19, 1820 [*sic*, correct: 1821], *Papers of John C. Calhoun* 6: 130. Perhaps misled by Calhoun's misdating of the letter, W. Edwin Hemphill, an editor of this volume of *Papers*, identified the "Nephew" as AJD, but evidence within the letter places the correct date as 1821 and the correct nephew as DSD.

29. Sylvanus Thayer (1785–1872), *DAB* 18: 410–411 (see note 11); Stephen E. Ambrose, *Duty, Honor, Country: A History of West Point* (Baltimore: The Johns Hopkins Press, 1966), 41–68; George S. Pappas, *To the Point: The United States Military Academy, 1802–1902* (Westport: Praeger Publishers, 1993), 65–103; E.D. Mansfield, quoted in *Personal Memories, Social, Political and Literary, with Sketches of Many Noted People, 1803–1843* (Cincinnati: Robert Clarke & Co., 1879), 69.

30. Walter Lowrie and Matthew St. Clair Clarke, eds., "Rules and Regulations for the Government of the Military Academy at West Point," in *American State Papers, Documents, Legislative and Executive, of the Congress of the United States, From the First Session of the First to the Second Session of the Fifteenth Congress, Inclusive: Commencing March 3, 1789, and Ending March 3, 1819. Class V. Military Affairs* 2 (Washington: Gales and Seaton, 1832), no. 188, 78; AJ to AJD, March 31, 1821, *Jackson Papers* 5: 24.

31. "Rules and Regulations," *Military Affairs* 2, no. 188, 78 (see prev. note);

Distribution of the Daily Exercises at the Mil[itary] Academy, September 1, 1817, in *The West Point Thayer Papers, 1808–1872*, Ed. Cindy Adams, 11 vols. (West Point: Association of Graduates, 1965), 2:176.

32. AJD to Nicholas P. Trist, letter, February 19, 1822, Nicholas P. Trist Papers, LOC; Robert W. Drexler, *Guilty of Making Peace: A Biography of Nicholas P. Trist* (Lanham: University Press of America, Inc., 1991), 26–27; For Joseph King Fenno Mansfield (1803–1862), see George W. Cullum, *Biographical Register of the Officers and Graduates of the U.S. Military Academy at West Point, N.Y., from its Establishment, in 1802 to 1890, with the Early History of the United States Military Academy*, 3rd ed. (Boston: Houghton, Mifflin and Company, 1891), 1:276–278, hereinafter cited as *West Point Biographical Register*. Also see Ezra J. Warner, *Generals in Blue: Lives of the Union Commanders* (Baton Rouge: Louisiana State University Press, 1964), 309–310; Isaac Ridgeway Trimble (1802–1888), cited in Cullum, *West Point Biographical Register* 1: 285–286, and in Ezra J. Warner, *Generals in Gray: Lives of the Confederate Commanders* (Baton Rouge: Louisiana State University Press, 1959), 310–311.

33. Sylvanus Thayer to AJ, February 4, 1822, and AJ to Thayer, March 9, 1822, letters, both in AJLC; *West Point Biographical Register* 1: 342. Spence, *Andrew Jackson Donelson*, 21–24.

34. AJ to AJD, April 26, 1822, and AJ to AJD, August 6, 1822, both in *Jackson Papers* 5, 177 and 214, respectively.

35. "Rules and Regulations," *Military Affairs* 2, no. 188, 78; AJ to AJD, October 11, 1822, *Jackson Papers* 5: 220.

36. DSD to AJ, letter, November 20, 1822, a copy in AJ's handwriting, subsequently enclosed in AJ to AJD, December 16, 1822, including AJD's undated reply written and returned on the same letter, both in AJLC; AJ, quoted in letter, AJ to AJD, December 23, 1822, *Jackson Papers* 5: 230.

37. AJ to AJD, letter, January 8, 21, 1823, AJDLC; AJ to AJD, letter, March 5, 1823, quoted from *Correspondence of Andrew Jackson*, Ed. John Spencer Bassett, 6 vols. (Washington: Carnegie Institute of Washington, 1929–1933), 3:190–191. Hereinafter cited as *Jackson Correspondence*.

38. Thayer to AJ, August 4, 1823; also DSD to AJ, September 27, 1823; both in AJLC.

39. AJD to Thayer, July 19, 1823, in Adams, *West Point Thayer Papers* 4: 3 (see ch. 1, note 31); DSD to AJ, September 27, 1823, AJLC; AJ to AJD, February 26, 1824, *Jackson Papers* 5: 367; DSD to AJ, June 22, 1824, AJLC; "Rules and Regulations," *Military Affairs* 2, no. 188, 72; Ambrose, *Duty, Honor, Country*, 25–26, 45–46, 71–72 (see note 29).

40. For Tennessee politics during this period, see Thomas P. Abernethy, *From Frontier to Plantation in Tennessee: A Study in Frontier Democracy* (Chapel Hill: The University of North Carolina Press, 1932), 164–181. And also Remini, *Andrew Jackson*

and the Course of American Freedom, 42–50, and Kristopher Ray, *Middle Tennessee 1775–1825: Progress and Popular Democracy on the Southwestern Frontier* (Knoxville: The University of Tennessee Press, 2007), 43–54, 124–134.

41. Remini, *Andrew Jackson and the Course of American Freedom*, 42–50; Lynn Hudson Parsons, *The Birth of Modern Politics: Andrew Jackson, John Quincy Adams, and the Election of 1828* (New York: Oxford University Press, 2009), 69–110; Spence, *Andrew Jackson Donelson*, 25–31.

42. AJD to AJ, November 23, 1818, AJLC; Ambrose, *Duty, Honor, Country*, 97–98; *West Point Biographical Register* 1: 245, 342; Clayton, *History of Davidson County, Tennessee*, 397.

43. "Alexander Dallas Bache [1806–1867]," listed in Cullum, *West Point Biographical Register* 1: 337–341; Ibid., "Robert Anderson [1805–1871]," 347–352; Warner, *Generals in Blue*, 7–8; "Charles Ferguson Smith [1807–1862]," listed in Cullum, *West Point Biographical Register* 1: 353–357; Warner, *Generals in Blue*, 455–456.

44. "Albert Sidney Johnston [1803–1862]," listed in Cullum, *West Point Biographical Register* 1: 368; Ibid., "Leonidas Polk [1806–1864]," 391, and "Jefferson Davis [1808–1889]," 416.

Chapter Two: "I Would Sooner See Revolution"

1. Statement of DSD, n.d., probably August 1825, and AJD to James Sanders, August 24, 1825, both in: AJDLC; Daniel Smith's will, July 22, 1816, with postscript dated October 17, 1817, Loose Will no. 757, Sumner County Loose Wills, Sumner County Archives, Gallatin, Sumner County, Tennessee.

2. AJD to Sanders, August 24, 1825, and also statement of DSD, n.d., probably August 1825, both in AJDLC.

3. AJD to Sanders, August 24, 1825, AJDLC.

4. AJD to Sanders, September 10, 1825, AJDLC.

5. AJD to Sanders, n.d., probably late October 1825, copy in AJD's handwriting, AJDLC. Cullum, *West Point Biographical Register* 1: 342.

6. AJD to Sanders, n.d., probably late October 1825; Sanders to AJD, November 4, 1825; statement of arbitration agreement signed by Sanders, AJD, DSD, and Ephraim H. Foster, November 11, 1825, AJDLC. The judges agreed upon were William L. Brown and Henry Crabb, who both served on the state Supreme Court of Errors and Appeals during the 1820s. Both are described in Clayton, *History of Davidson County, Tennessee*, 94 (see ch. 1, note 23); For John C. McLemore (1790–1864), see Marvin Downing, "John Christmas McLemore: 19th Century Land Speculator," *THQ* 42, no. 3 (Fall 1983): 254–265, and also Marvin Downing, "An Admiring Nephew-in-Law: John Christmas McLemore and His Relationship to 'Uncle' Andrew Jackson," *The West Tennessee Historical Society Papers*, 44 (December 1990): 38–47; For Ephraim Hubbard Foster (1794–1854), see

Carroll Van West, editor-in-chief, *The Tennessee Encyclopedia of History and Culture* (Nashville: Rutledge Hill Press, 1998), 333–334, hereinafter cited as *TEHC*.

7. For the marriages of the Sanders sisters, see Edith Rucker Whitley, comp., *Marriages of Sumner County, Tennessee, 1787–1838* (Baltimore: Genealogical Publishing Co., Inc., 1981). Therein as follows: Robert Caruthers and Sally Saunders [sic], January 15, 1827, 67; Thomas G. Watson and Martha Sanders, February 25, 1829, 89; James W. Hoggatt and Mary Ann Saunders [sic], October 17, 1831, 89; and M.P. Gentry and E[mily] Sanders, February 17, 1838, 106; For Robert Looney Caruthers (1800–1882) and Meredith Poindexter Gentry (1809–1866), see *BDTGA* 1: 132–133 (Caruthers), and 279 (Gentry). Also for Caruthers and Gentry, see Kathryn Allamong Jacob and Bruce A. Ragsdale, eds. in chief, *Biographical Directory of the United States Congress, 1774–1989, Bicentennial Edition: The Continental Congress, September 5, 1774, to October 21, 1788, and the Congress of the United States from the First to the One Hundredth Congress, March 4, 1789, to January 3, 1989, Inclusive* (Washington: United States Government Printing Office, 1989), 751 (Caruthers), and 1052 (Gentry). The *Biographical Directory* is hereinafter cited as *BDUSC*.

8. *West Point Biographical Register* 1: 342.

9. Daniel Smith Donelson House, Eventide. National Register of Historic Places Inventory–Nomination Form, United States Department of the Interior, National Park Service. The Eventide house, restored and updated but otherwise little-altered, now has the street address 178 Berrywood Drive, in a subdivision of Hendersonville; Sumner County Tax Lists, 1826–1830, 1777 (page), Sumner County Archives.

10. AJ to AJD, May 20, 1822, *Jackson Papers* 5: 188–189; Richard Douglas Spence, "John Donelson and the Opening of the Old Southwest," *THQ* 50, no. 3 (Fall 1991): 168–169; *Annals of the Congress of the United States: Eighteenth Congress, First Session, December 1, 1823, to May 27, 1824* (Washington: Gales and Seaton, 1856), 617, 750, 772, 2675, 2682.

11. AJD, quoted, from letters to John Coffee, April 16 or 18 (the reading of the date is uncertain) and May 3, both in 1826, and also April 6, 1827, all in: AJDLC; For John Coffee, see Gordon T. Chappell, "The Life and Activities of General John Coffee," *THQ* 1, no. 2 (September 1942): 125–146.

12. *West Point Biographical Register* 1: 342. I found no documentation on when and where AJD and DSD were commissioned into the Tennessee state militia. Marylin Bell Hughes, archivist at TSLA, similarly found no listing for DSD's commission as major in the Tennessee State Militia Commission Books, Record Group 195. Marylin Bell Hughes, letter to author, August 2, 2005; "Division Orders," *National Banner and Nashville Whig*, November 1, 1828; For the social role of the state militia in early Tennessee, see Kristofer Ray, *Middle Tennessee 1775–1825: Progress and Popular Democracy on the Southwestern Frontier* (Knoxville: The University of Tennessee Press, 2007), 42–47.

13. "Dinner to Gen Jackson at Lebanon," *National Banner and Nashville Whig,* July 11, 1828; AJ to Nathaniel W. Williams, February 23, 1828. Also Williams to AJ, February 27, 1828. Both in: *Jackson Papers* 6:421–422 and 423, respectively; Sally Smith, "Jackson's Marriage: Sworn Statement of Mrs. Sally Smith," witnessed by DSD, December 10, 1826, *Jackson Correspondence* 3:322–323; *The United States' Telegraph,* June 22, 1827; Robert V. Remini, *Andrew Jackson and the Course of American Freedom, 1822–1832* (New York: Harper & Row, Publishers, 1981), 105–144.

14. DSD to "Dear Sam," November 16, 1828, AJLC. The identities of the men in this letter are the author's conjectures. William Gibbes Hunt was editor of the *National Banner and Nashville Whig, DAB* 9: 396. For William Preston Anderson, who was a critic of AJ over the controversial duel in 1806 in which AJ killed Charles Dickinson, see *Jackson Papers* 6: 328–329, 518–519. "Sam" is not further identified in the letter, and DSD refers to him by no tighter relation than "Kinsman and Friend." The letter is catalogued in AJLC as though it is addressed to Samuel Donelson, albeit marked with an asterisk (*) as "a doubtful reading of name," in *Index to the Andrew Jackson Papers* (Washington: Library of Congress, 1967), xxvi. The only other Samuel Donelson who is plausible is Samuel Rucker Donelson—a son of Severn Donelson, brother of DSD's father and Rachel Jackson, and thus DSD's cousin—but this Samuel Donelson was no more than eighteen years old at this time. The genealogical chart in *Jackson Papers* 1: 421 places his birth ca. 1817, although *Jackson* Papers 9: 665 places his birth in 1810. A better possible candidate is another cousin, Samuel Jackson Hays (son of Robert and Jane Donelson Hays, a sister of DSD's father and Rachel Jackson), who was closer to DSD's age (b. 1800) and simultaneously involved in other aspects of AJ's campaign difficulties. See AJ to William B. Lewis, August 16, 1828, *Jackson Papers* 6: 498–499; John H. Eaton to AJ, September 25, 1828, *Jackson Papers* 6: 509.

15. Rachel Jackson's illness, death, and funeral are recounted in Remini, *Andrew Jackson and the Course of American Freedom,* 150–155.

16. Pauline Wilcox Burke, *Emily Donelson of Tennessee,* 2 volumes (Richmond: Garrett and Massie, Incorporated, 1941), 1:163; Remini, *Andrew Jackson and the Course of American Freedom,* 157, 159; Spence, *Andrew Jackson Donelson: Jacksonian and Unionist,* 35–39 (see ch. 1, note 11).

17. Every biographer of Sam Houston has struggled with the marriage episode. For the range of treatments, see, for example: Marquis James, *The Raven: A Biography of Sam Houston* (Indianapolis: The Bobbs-Merrill Co., 1929), pp. 71–82, which is still the most readable, if not the most reliable, of the major Houston biographies. For a more recent scholarly treatment, see James L. Haley, *Sam Houston* (Norman: University of Oklahoma Press, 2002), 49–61, which nevertheless leaves holes inadequately filled. Walter T. Durham, *Old Sumner: A History of Sumner County, Tennessee, from 1805 to 1861* (Gallatin: Sumner County Public Library

Board, 1972), 186–210, treats the marriage episode in great detail with emphasis on the interconnecting local political intrigues.

18. DSD to AJD, May 22, 1829, Dyas Collection of John Coffee Family Papers, TSLA, printed in Stanley F. Horn, "An Unpublished Photograph of Sam Houston," *THQ* 3, no. 4 (December 1944): 349–351; Haley, in *Sam Houston*, 62–63 (see prev. note), in my opinion correctly refutes the rumor that Houston's marriage was a cruel sham on his way to revolutionize Texas, but from that point proceeds into unfounded conjecture. He does not quote any part of DSD's letter, and from the absence of a citation it is unclear whether he had ever seen it. On page 62, he describes DSD as being the "point man in Jackson's effort to purchase Texas and not a friend of Houston anyway." The first part of this statement is unsupported by any evidence that Haley presents or that I have seen. In his review of Haley's book, Mark R. Cheathem, *THQ* 62, no. 3 (Fall 2003): 286, is also unaware of such evidence. As for the second part, DSD clearly disapproved of Houston's behavior during and after the marriage scandal, but he was hardly alone; otherwise, he was not fundamentally unfriendly to Houston then or later, e.g., as in: DSD to AJD, June 23, 1845, Bettie Mizell Donelson Papers, THS. Yet, from this initial statement Haley builds an entire framework, pp. 65ff., in which both DSD and AJD are part of an anti-Houston cabal, although this is unsubstantiated by any evidence that Haley cites.

19. David Twopence to AJ, August 24, 1829, *Jackson Papers* 7: 391; DSD's election to brigadier general is attested, in John W. Simpson to William Carroll, December 29, 1829, photocopy, Military Elections Record Group 131, TSLA. The photocopy is kindly provided by TSLA archivist Marylin Bell Hughes; Allamong, et al., "Robert Desha" (1791–1849) in *BDUSC*, 901 (see ch. 1, note 7); Walter T. Durham, *Josephus Conn Guild and Rose Mont: Politics and Plantation in Nineteenth Century Tennessee* (Franklin: Hillsboro Press, 2002), 2; Twopence's statement that he was "Not allow'd a vote" is curious. The constitution of 1796, adopted when Tennessee became a state, allowed all freemen the vote, and thus by implication even free blacks. Not until the adoption of the 1834 state constitution was the right to vote specifically reserved for whites. See Robert E. Corlew, *Tennessee: A Short History*, 2ed. (Knoxville: The University of Tennessee Press, 1981), 98, 167, 219; Paul H. Bergeron, Stephen V. Ash, and Jeanette Keith, *Tennesseans and Their History* (Knoxville: The University of Tennessee Press, 1999), 65, 93. The difference may lie in the statements "not allowed a vote," as Twopence phrased it, and "not allowed *to* vote," as much of the history of the South has demonstrated.

20. DSD to "Dear Sir," letter, June 15, 1830, Military Elections, Record Group 131, 1829, Sumner County. See also DSD to Samuel Smith, October 17, 1831, R.G. 131, 1831, and DSD to Smith, March 26, 1832, R.G. 131, 1832. All in: Military Elections, Record Group 131 [Sumner County], TSLA, photocopies courtesy of TSLA archivist Marylin Bell Hughes; "Brigade Orders," *National Banner and*

Nashville Whig, August 23, 1830; DSD to Sylvanus Thayer, May 7, 1830, in Adams, *The West Point Thayer Papers* 5: 26; Walter T. Durham, *Balie Peyton of Tennessee: Nineteenth Century Politics and Thoroughbreds* (Franklin: Hillsboro Press, 2000), 10.

21. DSD to AJD, February 13, 1830, Bettie M. Donelson Papers, THS; DSD to Dixon Allen, February 26, 1830, Campbell Family Papers, David M. Rubenstein Rare Book & Manuscript Library, Duke University, Durham, NC.

22. John Branch (1782–1863), *DAB* 2: 596–597; Ermine Palmer Branch, *"Live Oak" Branches: A Genealogy,* unpublished typescript, 1971, John Branch Papers, North Carolina State Archives, Raleigh, NC; MBD, birth date from her tombstone, First Presbyterian Church of Hendersonville Cemetery, Hendersonville, Sumner County, Tennessee; W.W. Clayton, quoted, from Clayton, *History of Davidson County, Tennessee,* 396.

23. John F. Marszalek, *The Petticoat Affair: Manners, Mutiny and Sex in Andrew Jackson's White House* (New York: The Free Press, 1997), 22–41.

24. Emily Donelson to Mary Coffee, March 27, 1829, AJDLC; Remini, *Andrew Jackson and the Course of American Freedom,* 203–208; Marszalek, *Petticoat Affair,* 76–84 (see prev. note); Mark R. Cheatham, *Old Hickory's Nephew: The Political and Private Struggles of Andrew Jackson Donelson* (Baton Rouge: Louisiana State University Press, 2007), 64–68; Spence, *Andrew Jackson Donelson,* 39–42.

25. Richard B. Latner, *The Presidency of Andrew Jackson: White House Politics, 1829–1837* (Athens: The University of Georgia Press, 1979), 59–63; Remini, *Andrew Jackson and the Course of American Freedom,* 159–166, 203ff. As a biography, Donald B. Cole, *Martin Van Buren and the American Political System* (Princeton: Princeton University Press, 1984), *passim,* emphasizes Van Buren as a political creature.

26. Richard E. Ellis, *The Union at Risk: Jacksonian Democracy, States' Rights, and the Nullification Crisis* (New York: Oxford University Press, 1987), 1–56; Remini, *Andrew Jackson and the Course of American Freedom,* 233ff.

27. AJ to John C. McLemore, April 30, 1830, *Jackson Papers* 8: 219; AJ, check to DSD for $100, April 24, 1830, *Jackson Papers* 8: 762; DSD, quoted, from letter DSD to AJD, May 28, 1830, Bettie M. Donelson Papers, THS; DSD, quoted, from letter DSD to Mary Eastin, May 28, 1830, Yeatman-Polk Collection, TSLA.

28. AJ to Samuel Jackson Hays, undated letter fragment, located as though May 31, 1830, *Jackson Papers* 8: 332.

29. DSD to AJD, May 28, 1830, Bettie M. Donelson Papers, THS; DSD to Mary Eastin, May 28, 1830, Yeatman-Polk Collection, TSLA. AJ to William B. Lewis, August 10, 1830, *Jackson Papers* 8: 470; AJD to John Branch, August 10, 1830, AJDLC; Burke, *Emily Donelson of Tennessee* 1: 235–242.

30. Margaret Branch to Mary Eastin, September 6, 1830, Yeatman-Polk Collection, TSLA; AJ to John Overton, September 30, 1830, *Jackson Papers* 8: 534–535; Also AJ, check to DSD for $300, October 9, 1830, 790, and AJ to Mary Eastin,

October 24, 1830, concerning postponement, 578; both in *Jackson Papers* 8; AJD to John Pendleton Kennedy, October 14, 1830, John Pendleton Kennedy Papers, Maryland Center for History and Culture, Baltimore, MD; Marriage license, *District of Columbia Marriage Licenses Register 1, 1811–1858*, Comp. Wesley E. Pippenger (Westminster: Family Line Publications, 1994), 167. Records date the marriage license October 17, 1830; *National Banner and Nashville Whig,* November 8, 1830.

31. AJ to Mary Eastin, October 24, 1830, and: AJ to Emily Donelson, November 28, 1830, both in: *Jackson Papers* 8, 581 and 640, respectively; MBD, quoted, all in MBD to Mary Eastin, November 28, 1830, Yeatman-Polk Collection, TSLA.

32. Mary Eastin to AJ, December 5, 1830, *Jackson Papers* 8: 649; AJ to AJJr, "nutts," n.d., *Jackson Correspondence* 4: 214fn ; MBD to Mary Eastin, November 28, 1830, Yeatman-Polk Collection, TSLA; AJD to Emily Donelson, December 20, 1830, AJDLC; Burke, *Emily Donelson* 1:263–264, stated that DSD and Margaret left Washington on December 13, 1830, but DSD was the bearer of the letter AJD to Emily Donelson, December 20, 1830.

33. Sumner County, "pleasure carriage" (DSD's tax records), *Tax Lists, 1831–1834*, Sumner County Archives, Gallatin, Sumner County, Tennessee, 2195, 2293; Remini, *Andrew Jackson and the Course of American Freedom,* 306–316; Marszalek, *Petticoat Affair,* 157–162.

34. "Conspiracy" (against Eaton), quoted from AJ to Emily Donelson, November 28, 1830, *Jackson Papers* 8: 639; "Impolitic course," quoted from Robert L. Caruthers to Messrs, Allen & Wade, January 28, 1831, Campbell Family Papers, David M. Rubenstein Rare Books and Manuscript Library, Duke University, Durham, NC; Caruthers to DSD, February 5, 1831, and: DSD to Caruthers, February 20, 1831, both in: Robert Looney Caruthers Papers, SHCUNC. Hereinafter cited as Caruthers Papers, SHCUNC; Walter T. Durham, *The Life of William Trousdale: Soldier, Statesman, Diplomat, 1790–1872* (Gallatin: United Daughters of the Confederacy, 2001), 2–4; "Robert M. Burton" (1800–1843), *BDTGA* 1: 104–105.

35. AJ to Robert M. Burton, May 29, 1830, *Jackson Papers* 8: 304. Burton to AJ, October 16, 1830, 561–562, and: James Gwin to AJ, December 18, 1830, 697, both in *Jackson Papers* 8; "William Hall," *TEHC,* 396 (see ch. 2, note 6).

36. "Calhounite . . . hostility," quoted from AJ to McLemore, December 25, 1830, *Jackson Papers* 8: 711; Ibid., AJ to Hardy M. Cryer, October 18, 1830, 565; David Burford to AJ, December 4, 1831, *Jackson Papers* 9: 725–726; "David Burford" (1791–1864), *BDTGA* 1: 101–102.

37. Caruthers to DSD, February 5, 1831, Caruthers Papers, SHCUNC; AJ to AJD, May 5, 1831, *Jackson Papers* 9: 232.

38. AJ to Cryer, May 10, 1831, *Jackson Papers* 9:239; also AJ to Mary Eastin, May 10, 1831, 9:240, and: AJ to Coffee, May 13, 1831, 9:245, and: AJ to Emily Donelson, May 25, 1831, 9:262–263.

39. David Burford, first quotation, from Burford to AJ, July 3, 1831, *Jackson Papers* 9: 364; AJ to AJD, July 27, 1831, Ibid. 9: 439; Second Burford quotation, from Burford to AJ, December 4, 1831, Ibid. 9: 726; Burton to AJ, October 5, 1831, Ibid. 9: 608.

40. Burford to AJ, December 4, 1831, *Jackson Papers* 9: 726–727.

41. Caruthers to Allen & Wade, January 28, 1831, Campbell Family Papers, David M. Rubenstein Rare Book and Manuscript Library, Duke University, Durham, NC; AJ to Cryer, May 20, 1831, reprinted in W.R. Garrett, ed., "Unpublished Letters of Andrew Jackson," *The American Historical Magazine* 4, no. 3 (July 1899): 234.

42. DSD to AJD, August 11, 1831, Bettie M. Donelson Papers, THS. According to the information in the letter, Martha Sanders Watson was born March 15, 1811, and died February 5, 1830.

43. Elizabeth Branch Donelson Williams, August 25, 1831–August 30, 1918, date of birth, from tombstone epitaph, Spring Hill Cemetery, Nashville, Tennessee; Clayton, *History of Davidson County, Tennessee*, 396.

44. DSD, first quotation (Eaton's actions), in DSD to AJD, October 31, 1831, Coffee Family Papers, THS; DSD, last quotation, in DSD to AJD, August 7, 1832, Bettie M. Donelson Papers, THS; Marszalek, *Petticoat Affair*, 201–207; Jonathan M. Atkins, *Parties, Politics, and the Sectional Conflict in Tennessee, 1832–1861* (Knoxville: University of Tennessee Press, 1997), 29–31; J. Roderick Heller III, *Democracy's Lawyer. Felix Grundy of the Old Southwest* (Baton Rouge: Louisiana University Press, 2010), 209–214.

45. DSD, first two quotations, in DSD to AJD, August 7, 1832, and: last quotation, in December 16, 1832. Both in: Bettie M. Donelson Papers, THS; DSD to the Editor, *Nashville Union and American*, September 8, 1857 (Barbour meeting); William S. Belko, *Philip Pendleton Barbour in Jacksonian America: An Old Republican in King Andrew's Court* (Tuscaloosa: The University of Alabama Press, 2016), 169–175; For the presidential election, see Remini, *Andrew Jackson and the Course of American Freedom*, 374–380, 389–392.

46. Fourth Annual Message, in *A Compilation of the Messages and Papers of the Presidents, 1789–1897*, Ed. James D. Richardson, 10 volumes (Washington: Government Printing Office, 1895–1899), 2:597–599; Proclamation, December 10, 1832, Ibid., 640–656; Ellis, *The Union at Risk*, 74–76, 102–157 (see ch. 2, note 26).

47. DSD to AJD, February 1, 1833, Bettie M. Donelson Papers, THS; DSD to AJD, February 25, 1833, Jackson-Donelson Collection, Jean and Alexander Heard Library, Special Collections, Vanderbilt University, Nashville, TN.

48. Durham, *Old Sumner*, 213 (see note 17).

49. Force Bill, January 16, 1833, *Messages and Papers of the Presidents* 2: 610–632; Ellis, *The Union at Risk*, 158–177.

Chapter Three: "A Substantial Farmer of Old Sumner"

1. DSD to AJD, November 24, 1833, Bettie Mizell Donelson Papers, THS.

2. For land sales and purchases during this period, see Sumner County, Tennessee, Direct Deed Index, 1787–1947: Grantee C to D, 63, in Sumner County Archives, Gallatin, Sumner County, Tennessee; Edward E. Baptist, *Creating an Old South: Middle Florida's Plantation Frontier Before the Civil War* (Chapel Hill: The University of North Carolina Press, 2002), 29–30.

3. Juanita Patton, abstractor, entry of February 12, 1834, "Lands, Slaves, and Other Courthouse Transactions 1808–1863," *Abstracts of Sumner County, Tennessee* (Gallatin: Sumner County Archives, 2005), 10; Henry Smith (grantor) to DSD and William Donelson (grantees), February 20, 1834, *Sumner County Original Loose Deeds, 1786 to 1914*, deed case no. 974, Sumner County Archives, Gallatin, Tennessee; *The Tennessean* (Nashville), January 29, 1835; Mary Ann Donelson, August 14, 1834–July 13, 1916, date of birth, from her tombstone epitaph, First Presbyterian Church of Hendersonville Cemetery, Hendersonville, Sumner County, Tennessee.

4. DSD to Robert L. Caruthers, March 12, 1835, Robert Looney Caruthers Papers, SHCUNC; Adam Rothman, *Slave Country: American Expansion and the Origin of the Deep South* (Cambridge: Harvard University Press, 2005), 165–216.

5. DSD to Caruthers, March 12, 1835, Caruthers Papers, SHCUNC; DSD to AJD, July 9, 1835, Bettie M. Donelson Papers, THS.

6. DSD to AJD, July 9, 1835, Bettie M. Donelson Papers, THS; Conevery Bolton Valenčius, *The Health of the Country: How American Settlers Understood Themselves and Their Land* (New York: Basic Books, 2002), 22–23.

7. DSD to AJD, July 9, 1835, Bettie M. Donelson Papers, THS; Valenčius, *Health of the Country*, 232–240 (see prev. note).

8. DSD to AJD, July 9, 1835, Bettie M. Donelson Papers, THS.

9. DSD to AJD, October 26, 1835, Bettie M. Donelson Papers, THS; Robert E. Corlew, *Tennessee: A Short History*, 2ed. (Knoxville: University of Tennessee Press, 1981), 178–195; Paul H. Bergeron, *Antebellum Politics in Tennessee* (Lexington: University Press of Kentucky, 1982), 2–4; Atkins, *Parties, Politics, and the Sectional Conflict in Tennessee*, 26–36 (see ch. 2, note 44).

10. Joseph Howard Parks, *John Bell of Tennessee* (Baton Rouge: Louisiana State University Press, 1950), 58–75; Charles G. Sellers, *James K. Polk: Jacksonian, 1795–1843* (Princeton: Princeton University Press, 1957), 197–199, 234–242; Bergeron, Ash, and Keith, *Tennesseans and Their History*, 94–99 (see ch. 2, note 19).

11. Jonathan M. Atkins, "The Presidential Candidacy of Hugh Lawson White in Tennessee, 1832–1836," *The Journal of Southern History*, 58, no. 1 (February 1992): 27–56, and "pure," quoted from 33; Parks, *John Bell*, 90 (see note 9); Sellers,

James K. Polk, 253–255; Bergeron, *Antebellum Politics in Tennessee*, 35–37 (see note 9); Atkins, *Parties, Politics, and the Sectional Conflict in Tennessee*, 36–39; "Hugh Lawson White" (1773–1840), *TEHC*, 1053–1054.

12. DSD to Caruthers, March 12, 1835, Caruthers Papers, SHCUNC; Parks, *John Bell*, 87–91; Sellers, *James K. Polk*, 257. And also Ibid., John Tyler, quoted, 264.

13. AJ to Mary Eastin Polk, March 14, 1836, George Washington Polk Papers, SHCUNC; AJD to Caruthers, November 10, 1835; and also Robert M. Burton to Caruthers, November 29, 1835; both in: Caruthers Papers, SHCUNC.

14. *The Nashville Republican*, July 28, September 1, 8, and 15, 1835; AJD to James K. Polk, September 29, 1835, in *Correspondence of James K. Polk*, eds. Herbert Weaver, et al., 14 vols. (Nashville: Vanderbilt University Press, 1967–1989 and Knoxville: University of Tennessee Press, 1993–2021), 3:315; "Washington Barrow" (1807–1866), *DAB* 1: 651.

15. DSD to AJD, October 26, 1835, Bettie M. Donelson Papers, THS; Spence, *Andrew Jackson Donelson: Jacksonian and Unionist*, 65–66, 78–79.

16. *The Union* (Nashville), August 26, 1835; Parks, *John Bell*, 111–114; Sellers, *James K. Polk*, 283–284, 289–290, 295; Atkins, *Parties, Politics, and the Sectional Conflict in Tennessee*, 42–43.

17. DSD to AJD, July 9, October 26, 1835, Bettie M. Donelson Papers, THS; "Unknown Donelson," tombstone epitaph, Bradford-Eppes Cemetery, Leon County, Florida. For the effects of acclimation among new settlers on infant mortality, see Valenčius, *Health of the Country*, 35, 99, 219.

18. Stockley Donelson to AJD, June 5, 1836, Bettie M. Donelson Papers, THS; The tombstone epitaph of Sarah Smith Donelson Bradford, in the Bradford-Eppes Cemetery, Leon County, Florida, lists only the years of her birth and death (1836–1869). Sarah Michie Smith died April 2, 1831. Noted in: AJ to AJD, April 20, 1831, *Jackson Papers* 9: 200.

19. James Sanders, date of death from his tombstone epitaph, Rock Castle Cemetery, near Hendersonville, Sumner County, Tennessee; AJ to AJJr, August 23, 1836, *Jackson Correspondence* 5: 422–423; AJ to AJJr, August 26, 1836, AJLC; Samuel H. Laughlin to Polk, September 8, 1836, *Correspondence of James K. Polk* 5: 721; Laughlin to Polk, September 15, 1836, Ibid., 730; Burke, *Emily Donelson of Tennessee* 2:111; Spence, *Andrew Jackson Donelson*, 82–83.

20. AJD to Emily Donelson, October 13, 1836, AJDLC; DSD to Emily Donelson, October 19, 1836, Bettie M. Donelson Papers, THS; AJD to AJ, December 23 [22?], 1836, AJLC; Burke, *Emily Donelson* 2: 116–130; Spence, *Andrew Jackson Donelson*, 84–88.

21. Quotations from Clayton, *History of Davidson County, Tennessee*, 396; *Welcome to Hazel Path*, information sheet available to the public, provided at Hazel Path historic mansion, Hendersonville, Sumner County, Tennessee. Facts mentioned

are taken from a copy that I picked up on my first visit there, July 26, 2010. DSD was still calling his home Elm Tree as late as 1856; see DSD to Alfred Royal Wynne, March 9, 1856, George Winchester Wynne Collection of Wynne Family Papers, TSLA. Patton, *Land, Slaves, and Other Courthouse Transactions 1808–1863, Sumner County*, 42, 57, 59 (quotation "as security" regarding Watson), 60, 71; U.S. Bureau of the Census, *Population Schedules of the Sixth Census of the United States, 1840. Tennessee*, Volume 9 (214–433): Smith, Stewart, and Sumner Counties. NARA Mf. Publication M704 (580 rolls), Record Group 29, mf rolls 533-535 (Washington, D.C.: National Archives Records Administration), microfilm roll 534: 386; The Watson sale is not recorded in Sumner County, Tennessee, Direct Deed Index, 1787–1947, where it likely would be found, had the sale gone through.

22. DSD to AJD, October 15, 1837, Bettie M. Donelson Papers, THS; AJD to DSD, October 20, 1837, AJDLC; DSD to Caruthers, May 14, 1838, Caruthers Papers, SHCUNC.

23. Bergeron, *Antebellum Politics in Tennessee*, 47–53; Atkins, *Parties, Politics, and the Sectional Conflict in Tennessee*, 62–65, 72–78; Sellers, *James K. Polk*, 350–355, 366–377.

24. W.B. Preston et al., to Polk, December 23, 1840, and DSD et al., to Polk, May 14, 1841 (in DSD's handwriting), petitions, both in: Governor James K. Polk Papers, TSLA. The latter petition is also calendared in *Correspondence of James K. Polk* 6: 577, but incorrectly dated as 1840.

25. For Polk's governorship and the bracketing elections, see Bergeron, *Antebellum Politics in Tennessee*, 75–77. Atkins, *Parties, Politics, and the Sectional Conflict in Tennessee*, 116–118. Charles G. Sellers, *James K. Polk: Jacksonian, 1795–1843* (Princeton: Princeton University Press, 1957), 378–380, 385–399, 430, and: campaign rival described in quotation, 444. "James Chamberlain Jones" (1809–1859), *TEHC*, 492–493.

26. DSD quotations, from letter regarding Andrew's legal matters arising October 1, in DSD to Caruthers, November 24, 1839, Caruthers Papers, SHCUNC; Spence, *Andrew Jackson Donelson*, 95–96.

27. Robert Henderson to DSD, January 22, 1842, and note in AJD's handwriting on the envelope, AJDLC; Spence, *Andrew Jackson Donelson*, 100–101, 103.

28. Emily Donelson Horton, date of birth from her tombstone epitaph, February 19, 1838–December 29, 1931, Athens City Cemetery, Athens, Limestone County, Alabama; Rebecca (Williams) Donelson Dismukes, year of birth from her tombstone epitaph (no month or day) 1840–1911, Gallatin City Cemetery, Gallatin, Tennessee; James Branch Donelson, date of birth from his tombstone epitaph, July (no date) 1842–February 3, 1912, Oak Hill Cemetery, Birmingham, Alabama; James Branch, date of death from tombstone epitaph, October 30, 1839, Bradford-Eppes Cemetery, Tallahassee, Leon County, Florida; DSD to Caruthers, January 12, and August 14, 1843, Caruthers Papers, SHCUNC.

29. Daniel Graham to Polk, August 11, 1842, *Correspondence of James K. Polk* 6: 91; *The Nashville Union,* quoted respectively, on: August 9, and September 14, 1842; *The Republican Banner* (Nashville), September 12, 1842; "Daniel Smith Donelson" (1801–1863), *BDTGA* 1: 206; "Thomas R. Barry" (1807–1891), Ibid., 31.

30. *Republican Banner,* September 2, 1842; Bergeron, *Antebellum Politics in Tennessee,* 69–70; Atkins, *Parties, Politics, and the Sectional Conflict in Tennessee,* 120–123.

31. For near-verbatim accounts of the sessions of the General Assembly, see *Republican Banner,* October 5–November 18, 1842, and also *Nashville Union,* October 4–November 18, 1842. For DSD in the General Assembly, see *Nashville* Union, petition, October 14, inquiry, October 20, memorials, October 27, and remonstrance, November 10, all in 1842; Bergeron, *Antebellum Politics in Tennessee,* 70; Mary Ellen Gadski, "The Tennessee State Capitol: An Architectural History," *THQ,* 157, no. 2 (Summer 1988): 67–68.

32. AJ to Martin Van Buren, December 15, 1842, Martin Van Buren Papers, LOC; AJD to Van Buren, December 21, 1842, AJDTHS.

33. Armstrong, quoted from Robert Armstrong to Polk, December 20, 1842, *Correspondence of James K. Polk* 6: 153.

34. Armstrong, comparing Trousdale and DSD, quoted from Armstrong to Polk, February 16, 1843, *Correspondence of James K.* Polk, 6:211; Burton, quoted, advocating DSD, from Burton to Polk, February 18, 1843, Ibid., 6:216; Durham, *The Life of William Trousdale,* 4–5 (see ch. 2, note 34).

35. *Nashville Union,* January 27 (first quotation), February 14, and February 24 (second quotation), 1843; Van Buren, quoted from Van Buren to AJ, April 13, 1843, and: AJ, quoted from AJ to Van Buren, April 21, 1843, both in: Van Buren Papers, LOC.

36. Armstrong to Polk, March 31, 1843, *Correspondence of James K. Polk* 6: 260; Polk to Van Buren, August 18, 1843, Ibid., 6:332; *Nashville Union,* March 17, 1843 (quotations about first debate); *Republican Banner,* March 15, 1843 (quotations, last debate); "Joseph Hopkins Peyton" (1808–1845), *BDUSC,* 1640; Durham, *Balie Peyton of Tennessee,* 16–55, 75–92 (see ch. 2, note 20).

37. Gubernatorial and Eighth Congressional District election races and debates, reported in *Nashville Union,* May 26, 30, and June 2, 1843, and in *Republican Banner,* June 2, 7, 16, and 30, 1843. See also "DANIEL S. DONELSON," quoted from *Nashville Union,* August 1, 1843. And: "Sumner," quoted under the heading titled "Gen. D.S. Donelson," *Nashville Union and American,* February 16, 1859; Armstrong to Polk, May 22, 1843, *Correspondence of James K. Polk* 6:313; Armstrong to Polk, June 12, 1843, ibid., 6:316. For the campaign, see Sellers, *James K. Polk,* 472–487. Also Bergeron, *Antebellum Politics in Tennessee,* 75–77. And: Atkins, *Parties, Politics, and the Sectional Conflict in Tennessee,* 120–125.

38. Election results, *Nashville Union,* August 8, 11, 1843; DSD, quoted from DSD to Caruthers, August 14, 1843, Caruthers Papers, SHCUNC. DSD is negating

Julius Caesar's brief report to the Roman Senate following his easy victory at the Battle of Zela in Asia Minor in 47 B.C., *"Veni, vidi, vici."* "I came, I saw, I conquered."; "Sumner," quoted under the heading "Gen. D.S. Donelson," *Nashville Union and American*, February 16, 1859; Sellers, *James K. Polk*, 488–491; Bergeron, *Antebellum Politics in Tennessee*, 75–77; Atkins, *Parties, Politics, and the Sectional Conflict*, 125–127.

39. *Nashville Union*, November 25, 1843.

40. DSD to AJD, May 22, 1829, Dyas Collection of John Coffee Family Papers, TSLA; Jesse S. Reeves, *American Diplomacy under Tyler and Polk* (Baltimore: Johns Hopkins University Press, 1907), 118–125; Charles G. Sellers, *James K. Polk: Continentalist, 1843–1846* (Princeton: Princeton University Press, 1966), 87–98; Robert V. Remini, *Andrew Jackson and the Course of American Democracy, 1833–1845* (New York: Harper & Row, Publishers, 1980), 492–506; Spence, *Andrew Jackson Donelson*, 108–113, 118–120.

41. AJ to AJD, n.d., February (?), 1845, *Jackson Correspondence* 5: 368; Elizabeth Donelson to Nicholas P. Trist, February 5, 1845, Nicholas P. Trist Papers, LOC; Elizabeth Donelson to AJD, January 1, 17, 1845, Jackson-Donelson Collection, Jean and Alexander Heard Library, Special Collections, Vanderbilt University, Nashville TN; AJ, quoted from letter to Elizabeth Donelson, January 16, 1845, in St. George L. Sioussat, ed., "Selected Letters, 1844–1845, from the Donelson Papers," *Tennessee Historical Magazine* 3, no. 2 (June 1917): 149. AJ to AJD, February 10, 1845, also in: Sioussat, "Selected Letters, 1844–1845," 151–152; Spence, *Andrew Jackson Donelson*, 130–131.

42. AJ to AJD, November 19, 1844, *Jackson Correspondence* 5: 329–330; DSD, quotations from letter, DSD to Polk, June 1, 1845, James K. Polk Papers, LC; DSD to AJD, June 23, 1845, Bettie M. Donelson Papers, THS. For sutlers of the period, see Richard Bruce Winders, *Mr. Polk's Army: The American Military Experience in the Mexican War* (College Station: Texas A&M University Press, 1997), 19–20, 120–121.

43. Elizabeth Donelson to AJD, June 3, 1845, Jackson-Donelson Collection, Vanderbilt University, Nashville, TN.

44. Elizabeth Donelson to AJD, June 9, 1845, Jackson-Donelson Collection, Vanderbilt University, Nashville, TN; DSD to AJD, June 23, 1845, Bettie M. Donelson Papers, THS. The word I render as "already" is partially mutilated by a tear in the page; Remini, *Andrew Jackson and the Course of American Democracy*, 523–525.

45. DSD to AJD, June 23, 1845, Bettie M. Donelson Papers, THS.

46. DSD to AJD, April 18, 1846, mis-filed as 1844. Also August 3 and September 4, 1846, and July 3, 1847. All in: Bettie M. Donelson Papers, THS; James G. Martin Jr., to Elizabeth Donelson, November 11, 1848, Jackson-Donelson Collection, Vanderbilt University, Nashville, TN; Spence, *Andrew Jackson Donelson*, 163–165, 169, 175, 195–196.

47. DSD to AJD, July 3, 1847, Bettie M. Donelson Papers, THS; Samuel Donelson (December 15, 1844–July 23, 1906), date of birth from his tombstone epitaph, Rock Creek Cemetery, Washington, D.C.; Zella Armstrong, comp., *Notable Southern Families* (Chattanooga: The Lookout Publishing Co., 1922), 2:105. Armstrong gives Samuel Donelson's middle name as Davis, which is found nowhere else; Martha Bradford Donelson Shute (February 19, 1847–January 8, 1893), and Susan Branch Donelson Dismukes (October 18, 1848–April 15, 1871), dates of birth from their tombstone epitaphs, in the First Presbyterian Church of Hendersonville Cemetery, Hendersonville, Sumner County, Tennessee; Clayton, *History of Davidson County*, 396; Groom and bride listings for William Williams and Elizabeth ("Lizzie") Branch (married May 9, 1849), in Byron and Barbara Sistler, *Early Tennessee Marriages*, 2 vols. (Nashville: Byron Sistler & Associates, Inc., 1988), Grooms 1: 593, and Brides 2: 151.

48. For the Sumner County units in the Mexican War, see Walter T. Durham, *Old Sumner: A History of Sumner County, Tennessee, from 1805 to 1861* (Gallatin: Sumner County Public Library Board, 1972), 357–384; Durham, *The Life of William Trousdale*, 6–9, 25.

49. *Republican Banner*, October 23, 1846; and also quoted from March 12, 1847.

50. DSD to AJDJr, January 14, 1850, Bettie M. Donelson Papers THS; Spence, *Andrew Jackson Donelson*, 195–196, 200.

Chapter Four: "Still a Democrat of the Jackson School"

1. U. S. Bureau of the Census, *Population Schedules of the Seventh Census of the United States, 1850. First Series: White and Free Colored Population, Tennessee*: Sullivan, Sumner, Tipton, and Van Buren Counties. NARA Mf. Publication M432 (1009 rolls), Record Group 29 (Washington, D.C.: The National Archives Records Administration, n.d.), microfilm roll 897, 490. Also U.S. Bureau of the Census, *Population Schedules of the Seventh Census of the United States, 1850. Tennessee (Slave Schedules)*: Smith, Stewart, Sullivan, Sumner, Tipton, Van Buren, Warren, Washington, Wayne, Weakley, White, Williamson, and Wilson Counties. NARA Mf. Publication M432 (1009 rolls) (Washington, D.C.: The National Archives), microfilm roll 907, 311–312. A piece of tape binding the pages obscures the last two lines (41–42) on page 311, making it unclear whether there are entries on those lines, thus the exact number of slaves could vary from 49 (if there are not) to 51 (if there are); DSD, quoted from DSD to AJDJr, January 14, 1850, Bettie Mizell Donelson Papers, THS; Durham, *Old Sumner*, 395–396.

2. DSD quotations in DSD to John Branch, February 24, 1850, Branch Family Papers, SHCUNC; DSD to Robert L. Caruthers, March 27, 1850, Caruthers Papers, SHCUNC; For accounts of the cholera epidemic, see *Nashville Daily Union*, August 20, 21, 23, and 25, 1849; Durham, *Old Sumner*, 165–167, 388, 429; Amy S.

Greenberg, *Lady First: The World of First Lady Sarah Polk* (New York: Alfred A. Knopf, 2019), 182–184.

3. The literature on the westward expansion and sectional crisis is enormous. The venerable work by Allan Nevins, in *Ordeal of the Union*, 2-volume set (New York: Charles Scribner's Sons, 1947), *passim*, remains an exhaustive standard starting point, supplemented by more specific references cited below.

4. *Nashville Daily Union*, May 7, 25, 1850; *The Republican Banner and Nashville Whig*, May 7, 1850; St. George L. Sioussat, "Tennessee, the Compromise of 1850, and the Nashville Convention," *Tennessee Historical Magazine* 4, no. 4 (December 1918): 219–223; Durham, *Old Sumner*, 397; Thelma Jennings, *The Nashville Convention: Southern Movement for Unity, 1848–1851* (Memphis: Memphis State University Press, 1980), 57–79, 94–95; Bergeron, *Antebellum Politics in Tennessee*, 104; Atkins, *Parties, Politics, and the Sectional Conflict in Tennessee*, 163–167.

5. Accounts of the Nashville Convention in *Nashville* Union, June 4–8, 10, 13–15, 1850; *Republican Banner and Nashville Whig*, June 4, 5, 7, 13, 1850; Sioussat, "Tennessee, the Compromise of 1850 and the Nashville Convention," 230–232, 235–238; Jennings, *Nashville Convention*, 107–138, 140–142, 144–154, 178–186 (see prev. note). Spence, *Andrew Jackson Donelson: Jacksonian and Unionist*, 202–204.

6. DSD to John Branch, February 24, 1850, Branch Family Papers, SHCUNC. In addition to the census data and slave transaction records that have been cited in the notes above to this and preceding chapters, comparisons to AJD can be made from Spence, *Andrew Jackson Donelson*, 90–91, 229, 254–256.

7. DSD to Branch, February 24, 1850 (see prev. note); "Chancery Sale," *The Republican Banner and Nashville Whig*, August 26, and reprinted in every issue through September 20, 1856.

8. For the second Nashville convention, see *Daily Nashville Union*, November 14–16, 18, 19, 22, 1850; *Republican Banner and Nashville Whig*, November 14–16, 18, 1850, and: AJD, quoted from November 19, 1850; Jennings, *Nashville Convention*, 192–195; Spence, *Andrew Jackson Donelson*, 205–207; The tombstone epitaph of J. Branch Donelson, Elmwood Cemetery, Birmingham, Alabama, has only his birth and death years, 1850–1918.

9. Mark R. Cheathem, *Old Hickory's Nephew*, 262–282 (see ch. 2, note 24); Spence, *Andrew Jackson Donelson*, 209–227.

10. "Railroad Meeting," *Republican Banner and Nashville Whig*, March 8, 1851. Also reported in: *Daily Nashville Union*, November 22, 1851; Margaret Branch Williams Davis (May 3, 1850–October 4, 1877), tombstone epitaph, Spring Hill Cemetery, Nashville, Tennessee. Also Eliza Branch (January 1, 1787–January 19, 1851), tombstone epitaph, Bradford-Eppes Cemetery, Tallahassee, Leon County, Florida; For the marriage of Mary Ann Donelson, see Sistler, *Early Middle Tennessee Marriages*, Grooms 1: 346, and Brides 2: 151 (see ch. 3, note 45); John Donelson Martin to AJD, October 26, 1851, AJDTHS; Margaret Branch Martin Shute

(May 13, 1853–May 29, 1937), date of birth from her tombstone epitaph, Spring Hill Cemetery, Nashville; For Daniel Smith "Dan" Donelson (November 15, 1853–December 1, 1914), death certificate, filed December 1, 1914, by W.C. Headrick, Registrar, Hamilton County, Tennessee, and also from tombstone epitaph, Forest Hills Cemetery, Chattanooga.

11. Allan Nevins, *Ordeal of the Union: Fruits of Manifest Destiny 1847–1852* (New York: Charles Scribner's Sons, 1947), 346–411 (see note 3); Michael F. Holt, *Rise and Fall of the American Whig Party: Jacksonian Politics and the Onset of the Civil War* (New York: Oxford University Press, 1999), 551–554, 633–634.

12. Roy Franklin Nichols, *The Democratic Machine, 1850–1854* (New York: Columbia University Press, 1923), 131–168; Bergeron, *Antebellum Politics in Tennessee*, 134–135, 146; Atkins, *Parties, Politics, and the Sectional Conflict in Tennessee*, 184–185.

13. For the three Grand Divisions, from a general description of their geography to their economic, social, and political characteristics during the antebellum period, see: "Geologic Zones," *TEHC*, 355–356; John R. Finger, *Tennessee Frontiers: Three Regions in Transition* (Bloomington: Indiana University Press, 2001), 3–7; Bergeron, *Antebellum Politics in Tennessee*, 7–8; Atkins, *Parties, Politics, and the Sectional Conflict in Tennessee*, 14–21; Anita Shafer Goodstein, *Nashville, 1780–1860: From Frontier to City* (Gainesville: University of Florida Press, 1989), 157–165.

14. For Tennessee state politics during the antebellum period in general, see Bergeron, *Antebellum Politics in Tennessee*, 76–112; Atkins, *Parties, Politics, and the Sectional Conflict in Tennessee*, 138–188; Philip Langsdon, *Tennessee: A Political History* (Franklin: Hillsboro Press, 2000), 99–131.

15. Allan Nevins, *Ordeal of the Union: A House Dividing 1852–1857* (New York: Charles Scribner's Sons, 1947), 88–159, 322–323 (see note 3); Michael A. Morrison, *Slavery and the American West: The Eclipse of Manifest Destiny and the Coming of the Civil War* (Chapel Hill: The University of North Carolina Press, 1997), 141–156; Christopher Childers, *The Failure of Popular Sovereignty: Slavery, Manifest Destiny, and the Radicalization of Southern Politics* (Lawrence: University Press of Kansas, 2012), 204–233.

16. Nevins, *Ordeal of the Union: A House Dividing*, 88–159, 272–286, 322–323 (see prev. note); Tyler Anbinder, *Nativism and Slavery: The Northern Know Nothings and the Politics of the 1850s* (New York: Oxford University Press, 1992), 3–22, 31, 43, 52–74.

17. W. Darrell Overdyke, *The Know-Nothing Party in the South* (Baton Rouge: Louisiana State University Press, 1950), 16–33; Mark W. Summers, *The Plundering Generation: Corruption and the Crisis of the Union* (New York: Oxford University Press, 1987), 65–68; Bergeron, *Antebellum Politics in Tennessee*, 124–125; Atkins, *Parties, Politics, and the Sectional Conflict in Tennessee*, 196–197; Goodstein, *Nashville*, 194–196 (see note 13).

18. AJD, quoted from letter, AJD to E.G. Eastman, May 22, 1855, printed in

Nashville Republican Banner, May 25, July 21, 1855; Spence, *Andrew Jackson Donelson*, 231–233.

19. *Nashville Union and American*, February 12, 16, March 21, 27, 28, June 6, 1855; "Meredith P. Gentry," biographical entry, *BDTGA* 1: 279. Gentry's wife Emily Sanders Gentry, who was also the Donelson brothers' half-sister, had died in 1842 and Gentry had subsequently remarried.

20. *Nashville Union and American*, DSD candidacy report (first quotation) from July 17, 1855. And July 18, 1855. Also reprint of "CIRCULAR To the Voters of Sumner County," signed by DSD, July 17, 1855, accompanied by DSD's explanatory disclaimer (all other quotations), ibid., July 26, 1855.

21. DSD, quotations from article regarding "CIRCULAR" (signed by DSD, July 17, 1855, and reprinted), *Nashville Union and American*, July 26, 1855 (also see prev. note); Durham, *Old Sumner*, 405–406.

22. Events, quoted from reports in *Nashville Union and American*: Walton's Campground rally, July 19, barbeques, July 20; also Shallow Ford rally and "Spectator," both in July 27, and: Castalian Springs and second quotation by "Spectator," both in August 1, 1855; Atkins, *Parties, Politics, and the Sectional Conflict in Tennessee*, 202–203.

23. "SUMNER COUNTY," quoted from *Nashville Union and American*, August 4. Also *Nashville Union and American*, August 7–9, 1855; Hans L. Trefousse, *Andrew Johnson: A Biography* (New York: W.W. Norton & Company, 1989), 95–98; Atkins, *Parties, Politics, and the Sectional Conflict in Tennessee*, 205.

24. Quoted respectively: Headline, "GEN. DANIEL S. DONELSON," September 4, 1855, and "Middle Tennessee," September 22, 1855. Both in: *Nashville Union and American*.

25. *Nashville Union and American*, October 2, 1855; Mary Ellen Gadksi, "The Tennessee State Capitol: An Architectural History," *THQ* 157, no. 2 (Summer 1988): 76.

26. *The Daily Nashville True Whig*, October 2, 1855; *Nashville Union and American*, "failed" quotation from October 2. Also cited: October 3 and 4. And: DSD, quoted from October 5, and 13 (*True Whig* quotation), 1855; *Republican Banner and Nashville Whig*, October 5, 1855; "Conduct" quotation from James Vaulx Drake, *Life of General Robert Hatton, Including His Most Important Public Speeches; Together, with Much of His Washington & Army Correspondence* (Nashville: Marshall & Bruce, 1867), 47; "Neill Smith Brown" (1810–1886), biographical entry, *TEHC*, 96.

27. *Nashville Union and American*, October 9, 1855; Ibid., October 13, 1857; DSD, quoted from DSD to Alfred Royal Wynne, March 9, 1856, and also DSD to A.R. Wynne, February 27, 1857, George Winchester Wynne Collection of Wynne Family Papers, TSLA.

28. *Nashville Union and American*, October 9, 10, November 25, 29, and December 13, 15, 1855; Also January 10, 18, 1856, and: quotation from January 31. Also

see February 6, 1856; *The Daily Nashville Patriot*, February 1, 1856; Hartsville was then still in Sumner County, as Trousdale County, of which it is now the county seat, was not established until 1870. In: "Trousdale County," encyclopedia entry, *TEHC*, 993–994.

29. *Nashville Union and American*, October 26, December 11, 1855; Also DSD, quoted from a speech paraphrased in third person, *Nashville Union and* American, January 25, 1856; Robert E. Corlew, *Tennessee: A Short History*, 2ed. (Knoxville: The University of Tennessee Press, 1981), 202–208.

30. For DSD and bills, amendments, and remarks concerning the Louisville and Nashville Railroad, see *Nashville Union and American*, October 28, November 3, 14, 29, 30, 1855. Also exchange between DSD and a fellow House member, regarding the railroad, quoted from January 25. And the paper's paraphrase of DSD in the third person ("bargains," "log-rolled"), January 31, 1856.

31. DSD is reported as being in the chair during the sessions of November 21 and December 18, 1855, and January 31, 1856, in: *Nashville Union and American*, November 22, December 19, 1855, and February 2, 1856, respectively. Also "indebted" quotation, from Editorial, December 1, 1855; House resolution acknowledging Brown, quoted from March 2, 1856. Also see March 4 and 5, 1856; Trefousse, *Andrew Johnson*, 99–102.

32. *Nashville Union and American*, February 29, March 4, 1856. Also newspaper's remark on "Legislative proceedings" quoted from March 5, 1856; *Nashville Republican Banner*, February 28, 29, 1856. Trefousse, *Andrew Johnson*, 100, 102; Spence, *Andrew Jackson Donelson*, 237–239.

33. *Nashville Union and American*, quotation in two parts, from January 6, 1856. Also cited: January 10, 1856.

34. *Nashville Union and American*, June 20, and August 30, 1856. Also "invited" quoted from September 5 (first quotation), "patriotic letter" from October 3 (second quotation), and "Gen. Donelson" from October 19 (third quotation), 1856; "Aaron V. Brown" (1795–1859), encyclopedia entry, *TEHC*, p. 92.

35. Quotations from *Nashville Union and American*, October 15 and 23, 1856. The unnamed "Miss Donelson" was probably Emily, who was at that time eighteen and the oldest unmarried daughter.

36. AJD to AJDJr, September 3, 1856, AJDLC; Mary Trousdale, quoted from: Mary Trousdale to William Trousdale, October 15, 1856, William Trousdale Papers, THS; Spence, *Andrew Jackson Donelson*, 246.

37. *Nashville Union and American*, March 8, April 16, 1857; Bergeron, *Antebellum Politics in Tennessee*, 113–114, 127–128; Trefousse, *Andrew Johnson*, 105–106; Sam Davis Elliott, *Isham G. Harris of Tennessee: Confederate Governor and United States Senator* (Baton Rouge: Louisiana State University Press, 2010), 35–36.

38. Bergeron, *Antebellum Politics in Tennessee*, 129–131; Atkins, *Parties, Politics, and*

the Sectional Conflict in Tennessee, 203–207, 209–213, 215–216; Holt, *Rise and Fall of the American Whig Party*, 959–961 (see note 11).

39. "To the Democrats of Sumner County," June 2, 1857, newspaper announcement (card), printed in *Nashville Union and American*, June 4, 1857.

40. "Great Rally" campaign event reported, in *Nashville Union and American*, July 12; *Daily Nashville Patriot*, "esteemed" quotation from June 10 (first quotation), "constituents" from June 29 (second quotation). Also July 3, 1857; *Nashville Union and American*, July 23, August 4, 12, 13, 16, 23, and October 8, 11, 21, 27, 1857; Bergeron, *Antebellum Politics in Tennessee*, 114, 128–130. Also Table 5.1, 188, and Table 5.2, 122; Atkins, *Parties, Politics, and the Sectional Conflict in Tennessee*, 212; Elliott, *Isham G. Harris*, 36–40 (see note 37).

41. "Sumner" (pen name), quoted from *Nashville Union and American*, August 29. And: "sterling Democrat" (last quotation) from September 9. Also cited: September 22, 1857.

42. *Daily Nashville Patriot*, unsigned reply, quoted from September 3, 1857.

43. Editor, "causeless" quotation, and DSD, quoted excerpts from his letter to the editor, both in: *Nashville Union and American*, September 8, 1857.

44. "Anti-Nullifier" (pen name), "The Sham Democracy and its Sham General Donelson," *Daily Nashville Patriot*, October 2, 1857; DSD, reply, "To the Public," *Nashville Union and American*, October 4, 1857, and reprinted in the *New York Times*, October 17, 1857.

45. "To the Public," *Daily Nashville Patriot*, October 5, 1857, reprinted in *New-York Times*, October 17, 1857, also including an extract of letter, DSD to AJD, February 1, 1833, with "revolution itself" italicized. Original letter in Bettie Mizell Donelson Papers, THS, in which the phrase is not underlined.

46. Randal W. McGavock, quoted in *Pen and Sword: The Life and Journals of Randal W. McGavock*, ed. Herschel Gower (Nashville: Tennessee Historical Commission, 1960), entry of October 5, 1857. For this episode, see also Spence, *Andrew Jackson Donelson*, 254–255.

47. House speaker election proceedings, and DSD's address as Speaker, both quoted from: *Nashville Union and American*, October 6, 1857; "William Claiborne Dunlap" (1798–1872), biographical entry, *BDUSC*, 937; "George Washington Rowles" (1808–1869), biographical entry, *BDTGA* 1: 640–641; Ibid., "John Watkins Richardson" (1809–1872), biographical entry, 618.

48. *Nashville Union and American*, October 6, 7. Quotations on Legislature and Donelson's leadership, from October 8. Also cited: October 9, 10, 11, 1857; Bergeron, *Antebellum Politics in Tennessee*, 114; Trefousse, *Andrew Johnson*, 107.

49. *Nashville Union and American*, October 6, 28, 29, 1857; *Daily Nashville Patriot*, quoted from October 7, 1857; Bergeron, *Antebellum Politics in Tennessee*, 114–116; Alfred Osborne Pope Nicholson (1808–1876), encyclopedia entry, *TEHC*, 689–690.

50. *Nashville Union and American*, October 14. Resolutions from October 19 meeting in Gallatin, quoted, from November 1, 1857; Kenneth M. Stampp, *America in 1857: A Nation on the Brink* (New York: Oxford University Press, 1990), 222–224; Larry Schweikart, "Tennessee Banks in the Antebellum Period, Part II," *THQ* 155, no. 3 (Fall 1986): 205–206; Bergeron, *Antebellum Politics in Tennessee*, 108–109; Trefousse, *Andrew Johnson*, 107; Elliott, *Isham G. Harris*, 40–41.

51. Bergeron, *Antebellum Politics in Tennessee*, 109; Elliott, *Isham G. Harris*, 40–42; Whether in its daily accounts of the legislative sessions or numerous editorials, almost every issue of the *Nashville Union and American*, October 1857–March 1858, tracks the banking debates.

52. *Nashville Union and American*, October 23, mention of clerks November 29, 1857, and October 1857–March 1858, *passim*.

53. AJD to AJDJr, November 30, 1857, AJDTHS; *Nashville Union and American*, November 29, December 1, 1857; Mary Sanders's will, November 28, 1857, probated January 1858, Loose Will no. 756, Sumner County Loose Wills, Sumner County Archives, Gallatin, Sumner County, Tennessee. Polly Sanders did leave one slave girl to her great-granddaughter, Mary Rachel ("Molly") Wilcox, the daughter of AJD's oldest daughter, Mary Emily, and her husband, John A. Wilcox. For Caruthers, see *BDTGA* 1: 133.

54. DSD, to General Assembly on Christmas adjournment resolution, quoted in *Nashville Union and American*, December 20, 1857. DSD "detained," House journal notation, cited in January 5, 1858. And: January 6, 7, 1858. Also DSD request for "leave of absence" cited January 26, 1858. DSD February 3 announcement of leave for "business," cited in February 10, 1858. And finally: February 12, 1858. Whether because of continuing indisposition or simply to conduct routine legislative business, DSD did not take the speaker's chair during the morning session of Monday, January 25, 1858, but his attendance is documented by several recorded votes, and he was apparently back in the chair by the evening session January 26, 1858. Mary Sanders, date of death from her tombstone epitaph, Rock Castle Cemetery, Hendersonville, Tennessee.

55. *Nashville Union and American*, October 13, 1857. Also "exciting day" quotation from January 29, 1858. Also February 2, 1858. "Bank question" quotation from February 10, and *passim*, 1858; Elliot, *Isham G. Harris*, 42–43.

56. *Nashville Union and American*, "sustained" quotation from March 13 (first DSD quotation), and "forego" quotation from March 20 (second DSD quotation), 1858. While he served as vice president of the United States and thus president of the Senate (1797–1801), Thomas Jefferson compiled a manual of parliamentary procedure that became a standard of practice throughout the nineteenth century. From: Dumas Malone, *Jefferson and the Ordeal of Liberty* (Boston: Little, Brown and Company, 1962), 317–318, 453–456.

57. *Nashville Union and American*, DSD, March 22 valedictory address quoted from March 23, Richardson's March 22 resolution of thanks quoted from

March 25, both in 1858; McGavock, "good speech" quotation from Gower, *Pen and Sword*, entry of March 22, 1858, 460.

58. *Nashville Union and American*, "Know-Nothing," quoted from February 20, and all other quoted passages from March 23, 1858; Elliott, *Isham G. Harris*, 44.

59. *Nashville Union and American*, December 12, 18, 1858. Also Gallatin *Examiner*, reprinted February 8, 1859; "Sumner," under the heading "Gen. D.S. Donelson," quoted from February 16, 1859. It is not known whether this "Sumner" was the same "Sumner" who had earlier advocated DSD for the speakership, in *the Union* August 29, 1857, issue, but the probability is high; Bergeron, *Antebellum Politics in Tennessee*, 130; Elliott, *Isham G. Harris*, 46.

60. *Nashville Union and American*, Marriage announcement, February 3, 1856, which prints Sarah's middle initial as C., March 18, 1859. For marriage of Sarah Donelson, see Sistler, *Early Middle Tennessee Marriages*, 1:56; 2:151. Both volumes give Sarah's middle initial as E. and misprint the groom's surname as Bradburn; For marriage of Emily Donelson, see Ibid., 1:269, 2:151. Both volumes give Emily's middle initial as B.; Tombstone epitaph of Sarah Jane "Nannie" Bradford Phelps (July 31, 1859–August 23, 1893), Phelps Cemetery, near Athens, Limestone County, Alabama; Two identical tombstones, with epitaphs "Infant son of Dr. & Mrs W.H. Bradford," n.d., Bradford-Eppes Cemetery, near Tallahassee, Leon County, Florida.

61. *Welcome to Hazel Path*, information sheet available to the public, Hazel Path, Hendersonville, Sumner County, Tennessee. Description of Hazel Path mansion from the historical markers on the front lawn, and from the author's visits to it, July 2010, and twice (May, July) in 2018; U.S. Bureau of the Census, *Population Schedules of the Eighth Census of the United States, 1860. Tennessee*, Volume 19 (1–342): Sullivan and Sumner Counties. NARA Mf. Publication M653 (1,438 rolls), Record Group 29, mf. roll 1275 (Washington: The National Archives and Records Administration), 109 handwritten, 214 stamped. And: U.S. Bureau of the Census, *Population Schedules of the Eighth Census of the United States, 1860. Tennessee (Slave Schedules)*, Volume 3 (312–613): Sumner, Tipton, Van Buren, Warren, Washington, Wayne, Weakley, White, Williamson, and Wilson Counties. NARA Mf. Publication M653, Record Group 29, mf roll 1286 (Washington: The National Archives and Records Administration), 48–49 handwritten, 335–336 in print.

62. *Nashville Union and American*, March 4, 14, 1860; Rachel Jackson Lawrence to Sarah Yorke Jackson, March 8, 25, 1860, Andrew Jackson Papers, TSLA; Linda Bennett Galloway, "Andrew Jackson, Junior," *THQ* 9, no. 4 (December 1950): 338, 341–342.

63. State Democratic convention, call to order, quoted from *Nashville Union and American*, January 18, 19, 1860; Trefousse, *Andrew Johnson*, 122–123.

64. *Nashville Union and American*, April 24, 1860, lists the Tennessee delegates who were in attendance at Charleston. J.W. Avant and John McGavock, the two regular delegates from the Fifth District, are listed, but DSD is not listed. For the

Democratic national convention at Charleston, see Allan Nevins, *The Emergence of Lincoln* 2 (New York: Charles Scribner's Sons, 1950), 203–228; Eric H. Walther, *The Fire-Eaters* (Baton Rouge: Louisiana State University Press, 1992), 71–75.

65. Nevins, *Emergence of Lincoln* 2: 228–260 and 266–268, *passim* (see prev. note); Parks, *John Bell*, 353; Spence, *Andrew Jackson Donelson*, 259.

66. *Nashville Union and American*, May 4, 15. Tennessee delegation, quoted from May 22, and June 22, 1860. The last issue lists the Tennessee delegates in attendance at the Baltimore convention, including "D.S. Donaldson."

67. *Nashville Union and American*, June 23, and: "disruption," of Democratic National Convention, quoted from June 24, 1860; Daniel Smith Donelson (1801–1863), biographical entry, *BDTGA* 1: 206; Nevins, *Emergence of Lincoln* 2: 268–272.

68. June 30 "Grand Rally" report, quoted from *Nashville Union and American*, July 1, 1860. A large section is torn from the top corner of the source copy in the TSLA, including the left side of the column, in which most of DSD's speech is printed. The words in square brackets are my own interpolations of missing words; *Daily Nashville Patriot*, July 2, 1860. The paper prints Harris's but not DSD's speech.

69. Nevins, *Emergence of Lincoln* 2: 312–335, 414–435; William C. Davis, *Jefferson Davis: The Man and His Hour* (New York: Harper Collins Publishers, 1991), 301–303.

70. Daniel W. Crofts, *Reluctant Confederates: Upper South Unionists in the Secession Crisis* (Chapel Hill: The University of North Carolina Press, 1989), 104–144, 147–149; Atkins, *Parties, Politics, and the Sectional Conflict in Tennessee*, 228–242, and Table 11, 241; Elliott, *Isham G. Harris*, 59. Also ibid., 63, cites a quoted description of Harris by an unnamed political colleague.

71. Atkins, *Parties, Politics, and the Sectional Conflict in Tennessee*, 237–238, 243–246; Crofts, *Reluctant Confederates*, 104–106, 126–127 (see prev. note); AJD, quoted from Spence, *Andrew Jackson Donelson*, 260.

72. Spence, *Andrew Jackson Donelson*, 260–261; Clayton, *History of Davidson County, Tennessee*, 396.

Chapter Five: "Send Donelson's Brigade"

1. Proclamations, April 15 and 19, 1861, in *A Compilation of the Messages and Papers of the Presidents, 1789–1897*, comp. James A. Richardson (Washington: Government Printing Office, 1897), 6:13–15; Daniel W. Crofts, *Reluctant Confederates*, 308–333, 340–345.

2. *Nashville Union and American*, April 19, 1861; Atkins, *Parties, Politics, and the Sectional Conflict in Tennessee*, 244–247, and Table 12, 248.

3. Gideon J. Pillow, quoted from *Nashville Union and American*, April 19, 1861; Also cited from the *Union*: "people of Sumner," April 25, and "Sumner boys," May 4, 1861; Walter T. Durham, *Rebellion Revisited: A History of Sumner County*,

Tennessee, from 1861 to 1870 (Franklin: Hillsboro Press, 1999), 5, 18–21; "William Brimage Bate" (1826–1905), *TEHC*, 50; Nathaniel Cheairs Hughes Jr., and Roy P. Stonesifer Jr., *The Life and Wars of Gideon J. Pillow* (Chapel Hill: The University of North Carolina Press, 1993), 157–162.

4. May 8 General Assembly defense bill, quoted from *Nashville Union and American*, May 9; also May 10 (which misspells DSD's surname as "Donaldson"), both 1861; *The Republican Banner* (Nashville), May 10, 1861, which spells DSD's name correctly; Hughes and Stonesifer, *Life and Wars of Gideon J. Pillow*, 162, 171 (see prev. note). For Samuel Read Anderson (1804–1883), see Warner, *Generals in Gray*, 10–11 (see ch. 1, note 32).

5. For James Branch Donelson, see Stanley F. Horn, Chairman, *Tennesseans in the Civil War: A Military History of Confederate and Union Units with Available Rosters of Personnel*, Parts 1 & 2 (Nashville: Civil War Centennial Commission, 1964–1965), pt.1: 188–190, and pt.2: 132; William Thomas Venner, *The 7th Tennessee Infantry in the Civil War: A History and Roster* (Jefferson: McFarland & Company, Inc., Publishers, 2013), 178; For James Edwin Horton: tombstone epitaph, Athens City Cemetery, Athens, Limestone County, Alabama. For AJD's sons, see Horn, *Tennesseans in the Civil War*, Part 1, 308, and Part 2, 132). For AJ's grandsons: Ibid., 1: 118, 271, and 2: 221.

6. Provisional Army of Tennessee Records, Record Group 4: Records, Military Board of Tennessee, 8, TSLA; DSD to John Branch, December 8, 1861, Branch Family Papers, SHCUNC.

7. DSD to Gideon J. Pillow, May 31, 1861, Frederick M. Dearborn Collection of Military and Political Americana, Houghton Library, Harvard University, Cambridge, MA; Edwin C. Bearss, "The Construction of Fort Henry and Fort Donelson," *The West Tennessee Historical Society Papers*, no. 21 (1967): 24–47; Lewright B. Sikes, "Gustavus Adolphus Henry: Champion of Lost Causes," *THQ* 50, no. 3 (Fall 1991): 173–182; Elliott, *Isham G. Harris*, 74–75.

8. Isham G. Harris to Jefferson Davis, July 13, 1861, in U.S. War Department, *The War of the Rebellion: A Compilation of the Official Records of the Union and Confederate Armies*, 130 serial volumes (Washington: Government Printing Office, 1880–1901), Ser. 4, vol. 1, 474–475; hereinafter cited as *OR*; Harris to Leroy P. Walker, August 1, 1861, Ibid., 527–528; *Nashville Union and American*, July 9, 16, 1861; Jefferson Davis to the Congress of the Confederate States, list of nominations, August 1, 1861, *Journal of the Congress of the Confederate States of America, 1861–1865*, 7 volumes (Washington: Government Printing Office, 1904), 1:307; Daniel S. Donelson, Compiled Military Service File, *Compiled Service Records of Confederate Generals and Staff Officers, and Nonregimental Enlisted Men*, Civil War Records: Confederate Records, NARA Mf. Publication 331, RG 109 (Washington: National Archives and Records Administration, 1962); "Cousin Mary" to Pauline Wilcox Burke, May 8, 1943, AJDLC, relates the intoxicated AJD story. If this episode really took place,

it more likely occurred in Nashville than in Memphis; no corroborating evidence suggests that DSD was ever in Memphis during the secession crisis, but AJD was frequently in Nashville. For Benjamin Franklin Cheatham (1820–1886), see Christopher Losson, *Tennessee's Forgotten Warriors: Frank Cheatham and His Confederate Division* (Knoxville: The University of Tennessee Press, 1989).

9. Samuel R. Anderson to Leroy P. Walker, July 24, 1861, *OR*, ser. 1, vol. 51, pt.2: 197–198; Walker to Anderson, July 25, 1861, Ibid., 198; Also Samuel R. Anderson, quoted from Anderson to Walker, July 25, 1861, 198; and: General Samuel Cooper, quoted from Samuel Cooper to DSD, July 27, 1861, 203. Both in: *OR*, ser. 1, vol. 51, pt.2; James G. Martin Jr., to Elizabeth Donelson, November 30, 1861, Jackson-Donelson Collection, Vanderbilt University, Nashville, TN. For Samuel Cooper (1798–1876), see Warner, *Generals in Gray*, 62–63. Cooper was the ranking general in the Confederate States Army and, as adjutant and inspector general, was effectively chief of staff, although that term did not then exist.

10. "From Gen. Donelson's Brigade," *Nashville Union and American*, September 6, 1861. Many of the brief biographical sketches of DSD state with various phrasing that he was the oldest general to have a field command in the Confederate States army, but to state it with full accuracy requires qualification. Warner, *Generals in Gray*, profiles four, perhaps five, men who held general rank and were older than DSD. The oldest, David E. Twiggs (Warner, on 312), born in 1790, was appointed directly from the "old Army" to major general in the Provisional Army of the Confederate States after he surrendered Texas, but being "too old for active field service," he retired almost immediately. Adjutant and Inspector General Samuel Cooper (Warner, on 62–63), born in 1798, "was never in field command." Brigadier General John Henry Winder (Warner, on 340–341), born 1800, served as provost marshal in Richmond. William "Extra Billy" Smith (pp. 284–285), born 1797, who served at the rank of colonel while commanding the Forty-ninth Virginia Infantry Regiment, from the Peninsula Campaign to Gettysburg, was not promoted to brigadier general until January 31, 1863—as it happened, the day after DSD was formally relieved of his field command and assigned to command the Department of East Tennessee. See Special Orders, No. 24, January 30, 1863, *OR*, ser. 1, vol. 23, pt.2: 621. The questionable case, William Lindsey Brandon (Warner, *Generals in Gray*, 32) was born in either 1800 or 1802, so he may or may not have been older than DSD, but anyway, he served at the rank of lieutenant colonel with the Twenty-first Mississippi Infantry Regiment, losing a leg at Malvern Hill, and was not promoted to brigadier general until June 1864, upon which he commanded the Bureau of Conscription. So, it may correctly be stated that throughout the period of his field service, July 1861 through January 1863, DSD was the oldest officer of general rank in Confederate States service to hold a field command.

11. Charles Todd Quintard, quoted from *Doctor Quintard: Chaplain C.S.A. and Second Bishop of Tennessee, Being His Story of the War (1861–1865)*, ed. Arthur Howard

Noll (Sewanee: The University Press of Sewanee, Tennessee, 1905), 17; For the eastern-western divisions in Virginia, see William A. Link, *Roots of Secession: Slavery and Politics in Antebellum Virginia* (Chapel Hill: The University of North Carolina Press, 2003), 23–24, 159–160, 224–225, 250–254.

12. Field returns of C.S. troops in Northwest Virginia, July 8, 1861, *OR*, ser.1, vol. 2: 293; Robert E. Lee to William W. Loring, July 20, 1861, Ibid., 986; S. to "Messrs. Editors," August 13, 1861, and also "Donnleson," cited from *Nashville Union and American*, August 23, 1861; Douglas Southall Freeman, *R.E. Lee: A Biography*, published in 4 vols. (New York: Charles Scribner's Sons, 1934–1935), 1:532–535, 546; Jack Zinn, *R.E. Lee's Cheat Mountain Campaign* (Parsons: McClain Printing Company, 1974), 1–100, *passim*; Clayton R. Newell, *Lee vs. McClellan: The First Campaign* (Washington: Regnery Publishing, Inc., 1996), 161–187; William Wing Loring (1818–1886), Warner, *Generals in Gray*, 193–194.

13. R. E. Lee to Mary Custis Lee, August 9, 1861, in *The Wartime Papers of R.E. Lee*, eds. Clifford Dowdey and Louis H. Manarin (New York: Little, Brown & Co., Inc., 1961), 63; Cooper to Lee, September 4, 1862, *OR*, ser.1, vol. 5, 828–829; Freeman, *R.E. Lee* 1: 537–560 (see prev. note).

14. General Orders, No. 10, September 8, 1861, *OR*, ser. 1, vol. 51, pt.2: 283–284; Horn, *Tennesseans in the Civil War*, Part 1: 190–192, 208–209; "Surgeon J.W. Gray," *Nashville Union and American*, December 5, 1861; "The Cheat Mountain Affair— Letter from a Tennessean," the initials "J.C.C.," printed below the letter dated September 17, 1861, in *Nashville Union and* American, October 15, 1861; H.H. Dillard, "Sixteenth Tennessee Infantry," in *The Military Annals of Tennessee. Confederate. First Series: Embracing a Review of Military Operations, with Regimental Histories and Memorial Rolls, Compiled from Original and Official Sources*, ed. John Berrien Lindsley (Nashville: J.M. Lindsley & Co., Publishers, 1886), 342; John Houston Savage (1815–1904), biographical entry, *BDUSC* 1770.

15. Robert Hatton, "hogpen," quoted from Hatton to "My Dear Sophie," August 23, 1861, printed in Drake, *Life of General Robert Hatton*, 375 (see ch. 4, note 260 "From Gen. Donelson's Brigade" ("compelled"), quoted from *Nashville Union and American*, September 6, 1861; Dillard, "Sixteenth Tennessee Infantry," *Military Annals of Tennessee*, 335 (see note 14); DSD, quoted, in John H. Savage, *The Life of John H. Savage: Citizen, Soldier, Lawyer, Congressman, Before the War Begun and Prosecuted by the Abolitionists of the Northern States to Reduce the Descendants of the Rebels of 1776, who Defeated the Armies of the King of England and gained Independence for the United States, Down to the Level of the Negro Race* (Nashville: Printed for the Author, 1903), 91–94; Freeman, *R.E. Lee* 1: 555–557.

16. Orders, September 8, 1861, *OR*, ser. 1, vol. 51, pt.2: 282–283; William Starke Rosecrans (1819–1898), biographical entry, Warner, *Generals in Blue*, 410–411; Albert Rust (1818–1870), biographical entry, Warner, *Generals in Gray*, 266–267.

17. Thomas A. Head, *Campaigns and Battles of the Sixteenth Regiment, Tennessee Volunteers, in the War Between the States, with Incidental Sketches of the Part Performed by*

other Tennessee Troops in the same War, 1861–1865 (Nashville: Cumberland Presbyterian Publishing Company House, 1885), 33–34. Ibid., quotation referencing Oscar Butcher, 34; J.C.C., "The Cheat Mountain Affair," (see note 14); "From Col. Fulton's Regiment," *Fayetteville Observer* (Tennessee), October 3, 1861; *Cheat Mountain; or, Unwritten Chapter of the Late War. By a Member of the Bar, Fayetteville, Tenn.* (Nashville: Albert B. Tavel, Stationer and Printer, 1885), 63; Dillard, "Sixteenth Tennessee Infantry," in *Military Annals of Tennessee*, 336–337; J.H. Moore, "Seventh Tennessee Infantry," in *The Military Annals of Tennessee. Confederate. First Series: Embracing a Review of Military Operations, with Regimental Histories and Memorial Rolls, Compiled from Original and Official Sources*, ed. John Berrien Lindsley (Nashville: J.M. Lindsley & Co., Publishers, 1886), 227–228, 260; Zinn, *Lee's Cheat Mountain Campaign*, pp. 128–132 (see note 12).

18. Freeman, quoted from page 565 of Freeman, *R.E. Lee* 1, 565–566; Brigadier-General Daniel Smith Donelson, September 17, 1861, Report, in *Supplement to the Official Records of the Union and Confederate Armies*, eds. Janet B. Hewett, Noah Andre Trudeau, and Bryce A. Sudrow, 100 vols. (Wilmington: Broadfoot Publishing Company, 1994), 1:380; hereinafter cited as *SOR*. Head, *Sixteenth Tennessee Regiment*, 36–42 (see prev. note); "From Western Virginia," *Fayetteville Observer,* October 10, 1861; J.C.C., "The Cheat Mountain Affair"; "Surgeon J.W. Gray," December 5, 1861 (see note 14); *Cheat Mountain; . . . Unwritten Chapter*, 63 (see note 17); Zinn, *Lee's Cheat Mountain Campaign*, 132–138.

19. Quintard, *Doctor Quintard*, 24 (see note 11); Savage, *Life of John H. Savage*, 97–98 (see note 15); Freeman, *R.E. Lee* 1: 566–567; Zinn, *Lee's Cheat Mountain Campaign*, 146.

20. "Surgeon J.W. Gray" *Nashville Union and American*, December 19, 1861; Dillard, "haystacks," quoted from "Sixteenth Tennessee Infantry," in *Military Annals of Tennessee*, 337; Savage, *Life of John H. Savage*, 99–100. Freeman, *R.E. Lee* 1: 567; Zinn, *Lee's Cheat Mountain Campaign*, 154–156.

21. DSD, Report, September 17, 1861, *SOR* 1: 381 (see note 18); DSD's orders to "charge," quoted from article "From Our Army in Western Virginia," *Nashville Union and American*, September 28, 1861; J.C.C., "The Cheat Mountain Affair," October 15, 1861; "Surgeon J.W. Gray," account of exchanges between DSD and Lee, cited from December 19, 1861 (see previous note); Head, *Sixteenth Tennessee Regiment*, 46–49; Freeman, *R.E. Lee* 1: 567–568.

22. Freeman, *R.E. Lee* 1: 568–571; Zinn, *Lee's Cheat Mountain Campaign*, 171–201.

23. DSD, Report, September 17, 1861, *SOR* 1: 381; "Our Army in Western Virginia—The Cheat Mountain Fight," regarding Donelson's field conduct, quoted from an unsigned extract of a letter, dated September 16, 1861, published in *Nashville Union and American*, September 27, 1861; An officer in Anderson's brigade, quoted in "Tennessee," from letter of October 2, 1861, published in *Nashville Union and American*, October 13, 1861; "From Col. Fulton's Regiment," quoted from *Fayetteville Observer*, October 3, 1861 (third quotation); For an analysis of the

Cheat Mountain campaign and Lee's generalship, see Freeman, *R.E. Lee* 1: 572–577, and also Newell, *Lee vs. McClellan*, 232–233, 262–264 (see note 12).

24. J.C.C., "The Cheat Mountain Affair"; For Lee's style of seeking proven and removing incompetent officers, see Freeman, *R.E. Lee* 2: 245–247, 477–478, and: Douglas Southall Freeman, *Lee's Lieutenants: A Study in Command*, published in 3 vols. (New York: Charles Scribner's Sons, 1942–1944), 2:506–507.

25. Freeman, *R.E. Lee* 1: 574; John Buchanan Floyd (1806–1863), biographical entry, Warner, *Generals in Gray*, 89–90; Henry Alexander Wise (1806–1876), Ibid., 341–342.

26. Abstract from Return of the Army of the Northwest, October 1861, *OR*, ser. 1, vol. 5, 933; Cooper to Loring, November 5, 1861, Ibid., 938; Quoted, from Cooper to Floyd, November 5, 1861, *OR*, ser. 1, vol. 5, 937–938; DSD to Henry R. Jackson, October 16, 1861, Dearborn Collection, Houghton Library, Harvard University, Cambridge, MA; Alfred Abernathy, quoted from letter to his wife, October 11, 1861 (second quotation), Alfred Abernathy Letter, TSLA; Henry Rootes Jackson (1820–1898), biographical entry, Warner, *Generals in Gray*, 149–150.

27. Judah P. Benjamin to John B. Floyd, November 15, 1861, *OR*, ser. 1, vol. 5, 955; DSD to J. Lucius Davis, November 19, 1861, *OR*, ser. 1, vol. 51, pt.2: 383–384; DSD to Floyd, November 20, 1861, Ibid., 385; Dillard, "Sixteenth Tennessee Infantry," *Military Annals of Tennessee*, 339.

28. Dillard, "Sixteenth Tennessee Infantry," *Military Annals of Tennessee*, 339; Quoted from "Gen. Donelson's Brigade," article with extract from a letter, n.d., by Captain C.C. Brewer, in *Nashville Union and American*, December 8, 1861; DSD to John Branch, December 8, 1861, Branch Family Papers, SHCUNC; William Edwin Starke (1814–1862), biographical entry, in Warner, *Generals in Gray*, 289.

29. Cooper to M.G. Harman, December 2, 1861, *OR*, ser. 1, vol. 5, 976; DSD to Branch, December 8, 1861, Branch Family Papers, SHCUNC (see prev. note).

30. Special Orders, No. 258, December 6, 1861, *OR*, ser. 1, vol. 51, pt.2: 406; Cooper to DSD, December 10, 1861, *OR*, ser. 1, vol. 5, 992; George Deas to Cooper, December 10, 1861, Ibid., 992; James J. Womack, *The Civil War Diary of Capt. J.J. Womack, Co. E, Sixteenth Regiment, Tennessee Volunteers (Confederate)*, entry of December 8, 1861 (McMinnville: Womack Printing Company, 1961), 27.

31. DSD to Branch, December 8, 1861, Branch Family Papers, SHCUNC.

32. Cooper, quoted from Cooper to Floyd, December 16, 1861, *OR*, ser. 1, vol. 5, 1000. "Anderson's brigade" is in error and has been corrected to Donelson's with square brackets in the text, to read as "Anderson's [Donelson's] brigade."

33. Freeman, *R.E. Lee* 1: 606–608; Thomas West Sherman (1815–1879), biographical entry, Warner, *Generals in Blue*, 440–441.

34. Special Orders, No. 206, November 5, 1861, *OR*, ser. 1, vol. 6, 309; Benjamin to Lee, December 8, 1861, Ibid., 340; Savage, *Life of John H. Savage*, 108–109.

35. *Edgefield Advertiser* (South Carolina), December 18, 1862; *The Memphis Daily Appeal*, December 22, 1861; "Camp Notes," *Yorkville Enquirer* (South Carolina),

January 2, 1862; T.A. Washington to DSD, December 13, 1861, *OR*, ser. 1, vol. 6, 346; Lee to Benjamin, December 16, 1861, and Special Orders, No. 24, December 23, 1861: Ibid., 347 and 349, respectively.

36. Special Orders, No. 17, December 10, 1861, *OR*, ser. 1, vol. 6, 344–345; Michael B. Ballard, *Pemberton: A Biography* (Jackson: University Press of Mississippi, 1991), 83–89.

37. Brig. Gen. Thomas W. Sherman, Report, January 2, 1862, *OR*, ser. 1, vol. 6, 44–45, and the enclosed reports, 45–66; James Jones to DSD, battle report, January 4, 1862, Ibid., 69–70; John C. Pemberton to Washington, quoted, from battle report, January 10, 1862, Ibid., 67; "News from the Coast," *The Lancaster Ledger* (South Carolina), January 8, 1862; "Camp Near Stoney Creek, S.C., January 5, 1862," *Yorkville Enquirer*, January 9, 1862.

38. Pemberton, battle report, January 10, 1862, *OR*, ser. 1, vol. 6, 67; W.E. Martin to DSD, battle report, January 4, 1861 [misdated *sic*: 1862 is correct], Ibid., 74. ("local"). Martin to J.H. Morrison, battle report, January 4, 1862, Ibid., 75; Jones to DSD, battle report, January 4, 1862, Ibid., 70–71; And: other quotations from: DSD to Pemberton, battle report, January 5, 1862, Ibid., 68–69; "Assumed," in the text, quoted from "Camp Near Stoney Creek, S.C., January 5, 1862," *Yorkville Enquirer*, January 9, 1862; Head, *Campaigns and Battles of the Sixteenth Regiment*, 60–61, 195.

39. The *OR* section heading devoted to the action is "Engagement at Port Royal Ferry, Coosaw River, S.C.," *OR*, ser. 1, vol. 6, 44–75, *passim*. Jones to DSD, battle report, January 4 1862, Ibid., 71. Pemberton to Washington, battle report, January 10, 1862, Ibid., 67; T.A. Head, "Campaigns and Battles of the 16th Tennessee Regiment," McMinnville *Southern Standard*, June 28, 1884.

40. Head, "Campaigns and Battles," *Southern Standard*, June 28, 1884 (see prev. note); Christopher C. McKinney to his wife, Mary, February 16, 1862, Christopher C. McKinney Letters, Hesburgh Library, University of Notre Dame, South Bend, IN.

41. Dillard, "Sixteenth Tennessee Regiment," *Military Annals of Tennessee*, 341.

42. DSD, quoted from letter, DSD to Branch, December 8, 1861, Branch Family Papers, SHCUNC; Thomas R.S. Elliott, quoted from letter, "to Father," February 4, 1862, Elliott and Gonzales Family Papers, SHCUNC; Diary of George Washington Winchester, entry of July 23, 1862, typescript, James Winchester Papers, TSLA; For a list of DSD's staff, see Marcus J. Wright, comp., *Tennessee in the War, 1861–1865* (New York: Ambrose Lee Publishing Company, 1908), 33.

43. Thomas Lawrence Connelly, *Army of the Heartland: The Army of Tennessee, 1861–1862* (Baton Rouge: Louisiana State University Press, 1967), 96–99; Kent T. Dollar, Larry H. Whiteaker, and W. Calvin Dickinson, eds., *The Border Wars: The Civil War in Tennessee and Kentucky* (Kent: Kent State University Press, 2015), 162–166, 275; Felix Kirk Zollicoffer (1812–1862), biographical entry, Warner, *Generals*

in Gray, 349–350; Randy Bishop, *Civil War Generals of Tennessee* (Gretna: Pelican Publishing Company, 2013), 231–235.

44. *Nashville Union and American*, February 1, 1862; Durham, *Rebellion Revisited*, 59–60 (see note 3); Durham, *Balie Peyton of Tennessee*, 203–205; George Henry Thomas (1816–1870), biographical entry, Warner, *Generals in Blue*, 500–502.

45. Connelly, *Army of the Heartland*, 99 (see note 42); Durham, *Rebellion Revisited*, 60; Dillard, "Sixteenth Tennessee Infantry Regiment," *Military Annals of Tennessee*, 341.

46. For the events described, see Timothy B. Smith, *Grant Invades Tennessee: The 1862 Battles for Forts Henry and Donelson* (Lawrence: University Press of Kansas, 2016). Also see Walter T. Durham, *Nashville: The Occupied City, 1862–1863* (Knoxville: University of Tennessee Press, 2008), 1–3, 6–54, 177–180, and Durham, *Rebellion Revisited*, 66–71. And: Stephen V. Ash, *Middle Tennessee Society Transformed, 1860–1870: War and Peace in the Upper South* (Baton Rouge: Louisiana State University Press, 1988), 84–95; Daniel S. Donelson (son of AJD) to AJD, March 7, 1862, Jackson-Donelson Collection, Vanderbilt University Special Collections, Jean and Alexander Heard Library, Vanderbilt University, Nashville, TN; AJD, quoted, from letter to Elizabeth Donelson, March 22, 1862, AJDLC; MBD to Andrew Johnson, July 10, 1865, in *The Papers of Andrew Johnson*, eds. Leroy P. Graf, Ralph W. Haskins, and Paul H. Bergeron, in 16 volumes (Knoxville: The University of Tennessee Press, 1967–2001), 8:379.

47. Dillard, quoted from "Sixteenth Tennessee Regiment," in *Military Annals of Tennessee*, 341.

48. Davis to Lee, March 2, 1862, *OR*, ser. 1, vol. 6, 400; General Orders, No. 6, March 4, 1862, Ibid., 402, and Special Orders, No. 59, March 14, 1862, Ibid., 407; also Special Orders, No. 44, March 19, 1862, Ibid., 414; MBD, quoted, in "the girls," from letter to John Branch, April 10, 1862. And: William Branch to John Branch, November 4, 1862. Also Mary Branch to William Branch, January 18 [misdated 1862], February 22, 1863. All in: Branch Family Papers, SHCUNC; Savage, *Life of John H. Savage*, account of arrest, 108–114, and Savage, quoted, from Ibid., 109; Ballard, *Pemberton*, 89–90 (see note 35).

49. Lt. Col. John H. Jackson, Report, March 25, 1862, *OR*, ser. 1, vol. 6, 101–103; Brig. Gen. Thomas F. Drayton, Report, March 23, 1862, Ibid., 103–104; [J.R. Waddy] to DSD, March 20, 1862, Ibid., 109; Pemberton to DSD, March 20, 1862, Ibid., 109–110; [Blank] to DSD, March 21, 1862, Ibid., 110; Waddy to DSD, March 22, 1862, *OR*, series 1, vol. 6, 111.

50. For the Shiloh campaign, see Timothy B. Smith, *Shiloh: Conquer or Perish* (Lawrence: University Press of Kansas, 2014), *passim*.

51. Lee to Pemberton, April 10, 1862, quoted *in toto*, *OR*, ser. 1, vol. 6, 432; Pemberton's headquarters to DSD, quoted from Special Orders, No. 20, April 10, 1862, *OR*, ser. 1, vol. 6, 433.

52. MBD to John Branch, April 10, 1862, Branch Family Papers, SHCUNC.

Chapter Six: "A Most Determined Courage"

1. Edmund Kirby Smith to D. Leadbetter, April 14, 1862, *OR*, ser. 1, vol. 10, pt.2: 420; Thomas Jordan to DSD, April 22, 1862, Ibid., 433. The addressee of this communication is misprinted as "Brig. Gen. Daniel S. Johnson," a mistake that was evidently made at the printing stage of this volume of the *OR*. To trace the route of Donelson's brigade, see Womack, *The Civil War Diary of Capt. J.J. Womack*, entries April 11-23, 1862, 42–43 (see ch. 5, note 30).

2. Jordan to DSD, April 22, 1862, *OR*, ser. 1, vol. 10, pt.2: 433; Special Orders, No. 42, April 22, 1862, Ibid., 434. DSD's name is also misprinted as "D.S. Johnson" in these orders; Special Orders, No. 41, April 26, 1862, Ibid., 642; Field Returns, Army of the Mississippi, April 30, 1862, *OR*, ser. 1, vol. 10, pt.2: 475; DSD to Benjamin F. Cheatham, May 6, 1862, Ibid., 498; T. Harry Williams, *P.G.T. Beauregard: Napoleon in Gray* (Baton Rouge: Louisiana State University Press, 1955), 120–121, 150–151; Connelly, *Army of the Heartland*, 150, 175.

3. The standard biography of Polk is Joseph H. Parks, *General Leonidas Polk, C.S.A.: The Fighting Bishop* (Baton Rouge: Louisiana State University Press, 1962); Connelly, *Army of the Heartland*, 46–55, and Ibid., quoted in "mistakes," 50.

4. Isham G. Harris to Jefferson Davis, July 13, 1861, *OR*, ser. 4, vol. 1, 474–475; Losson, *Tennessee's Forgotten Warriors*, 2–59 *passim* (see ch. 5, note 8).

5. John F. Marzsalek, *Commander of All Lincoln's Armies: A Life of General Henry W. Halleck* (Cambridge: Harvard University Press, 2004), 121–125.

6. Abstract from Field Return of the Army of the Mississippi, April 22, 1862, *OR*, ser. 1, vol. 10, pt.2: 433; Organization of the Army of the Mississippi, May [26?], 1862, Ibid., 548; Horn, *Tennesseans in the Civil War*, Part 1: 174–175. And also see, for the following units: Second Tennessee Infantry Regiment, 174–175, Fifteenth Tennessee Infantry Regiment, 205–208, and One Hundred Fifty-fourth Senior Tennessee Regiment, 308–311, and Carnes's Battery, 136–138. Williams, *Beauregard*, 150–151 (see note 2).

7. W.C. Bacot to DSD, May 6, 1862, *OR*, ser. 1, vol. 10, pt.2: 498–499; Bacot to DSD, May 6, 1862, Ibid., 499 (quotation); DSD, quoted from DSD to Cheatham, May 6, 1862, Ibid., 498; Cheatham, quoted from Cheatham to Leonidas Polk, undated endorsement, Ibid., 498.

8. *Daily Nashville Union*, May 15, 16, 1862; Durham, *Rebellion Revisited*, 79; Ash, *Middle Tennessee Society Transformed, 1860–1870*, 85–91 (see ch. 5, note 45); Stephen V. Ash, *When the Yankees Came: Conflict and Chaos in the Occupied South, 1861–1865* (Chapel Hill: The University of North Carolina Press, 1995), 78–90.

9. John Branch to William Branch, May 17, 1862, Branch Family Papers, SHCUNC.

10. Thomas A. Head, *Campaigns and Battles of the Sixteenth Regiment*, 72–73 (recollection of Donelson's speech, quoted from 73); Williams, *Beauregard*, 151–152.

11. William L. Moore to DSD, May 29, 1862, *OR*, ser. 1, vol. 52, pt.1, 36–37.

12. Womack, *Civil War Diary of Capt. J.J. Womack*, entry of June 3, 1862, 49; Williams, *Beauregard*, 152–158; Connelly, *Army of the Heartland*, 176–181.

13. Isham G. Harris to Andrew Ewing, July 28, 1862, *OR*, ser. 1, vol. 16, pt.1: 710; Connelly, *Army of the Heartland*, 190–191; Marszalek, *Commander of All Lincoln's Armies*, 126ff (see note 5); Sam Davis Elliott, *Isham G. Harris of Tennessee*, 118–119 (see ch. 4, note 37).

14. General Orders, No. 116, August 15, 1862, *OR*, ser. 1, vol. 16, pt.2: 759; Organization of the Right Wing, Army of the Mississippi, August 18 and 20, 1862, Ibid., 764; Womack, *Civil War Diary of J.J. Womack*, entries of July 22–27, 1862, 53–54; Horn, *Tennesseans in the Civil War*, Part 1, Thirty-eighth Tennessee Infantry Regiment, 255–258, and Fifty-first Tennessee Infantry Regiment, 288–291; Harris D. Riley Jr., "A Gallant Adopted Son of Tennessee–General John C. Carter, C.S.A.," *THQ*, 158, no. 4 (Winter 1989): 195–208; Grady McWhiney, *Braxton Bragg and Confederate Defeat* (Tuscaloosa: The University of Alabama Press, 1969), 266–271; Connelly, *Army of the Heartland*, 196–204.

15. Womack, *Civil War Diary of Capt. J.J. Womack*, entries of August 7–8, 1862, 55.

16. George Williamson to Cheatham, August 22, 1862, *OR*, ser. 1, vol. 16, pt.2: 770; Connelly, *Army of the Heartland*, 202–203; Stephen D. Engle, "Don Carlos Buell: Misunderstood Commander of the West," in *The Border Wars: The Civil War in Tennessee and Kentucky*, eds. Kent T. Dollar, Larry H. Whiteaker, and W. Calvin Dickinson (Kent: Kent State University Press, 2015), 179–184 (see ch. 5, note 43).

17. Special Orders, No. 142, August 5, 1862, *OR*, ser. 1, vol. 16, pt.2: 744–745; Connelly, *Army of the Heartland*, 209; DSD to Marcus J. Wright, October 26, 1862, report on the Battle of Perryville, William P. Palmer Collection of Civil War Manuscripts, Western Reserve Historical Society, Cleveland, Ohio, hereafter cited as WRHS; Earl J. Hess, *Banners to the Breeze: The Kentucky Campaign, Corinth, and Stones River* (Lincoln: University of Nebraska Press, 2000), 20–22; Kenneth W. Noe, *Perryville: This Grand Havoc of Battle* (Lexington: The University Press of Kentucky, 2001), 33–34.

18. Head, *Campaigns and Battles of the Sixteenth Regiment*, 199–201. Mention of DSD, quoted from 201; Connelly, *Army of the Heartland*, 221–224; Noe, *Perryville*, 39–64, *passim*.

19. Braxton Bragg to Polk, September 7, 1862, *OR*, ser. 1, vol. 16, pt.2: 799–800 (quotation); Also see George G. Garner to Polk, September 10, 1862, 806, and: Williamson to Cheatham, September 10, 1862, 808, and also Lovell H. Rousseau to J.B. Fry, September 13, 1862, 512. All in: *OR*, ser. 1, vol. 16, pt.2; L.G. Marshall, "Jackson's Battery–Carnes's Battery–Marshall's Battery," in *The Military Annals of Tennessee. Confederate. First Series: Embracing a Review of Military Operations, with Regimental Histories and Memorial Rolls, Compiled from Original and Official Sources*, ed. John Berrien Lindsley (Nashville: J.M. Lindsley & Co., Publishers, 1886), 811;

McWhiney, *Braxton Bragg and Confederate Defeat*, 282–283 (see note 14); Connelly, *Army of the Heartland*, 221–224, 227; Noe, *Perryville*, 39–66.

20. George Washington Winchester Diary, entry of September 13, 1862 (see ch. 5, note 41); Marshall, "Jackson's Battery–Carnes's Battery–Marshall's Battery," *Military Annals of Tennessee*, 811 (see prev. note); Connelly, *Army of the Heartland*, 227–229; Noe, *Perryville*, 67–70.

21. General Orders, No. 8, September 28, 1862, *OR*, ser. 1, vol. 16, pt.2: 886; General Orders, No. 9, September 28, 1862, Ibid., 886; Abstract from Daily Returns, October 1, 1862, Ibid., 896; Connelly, *Army of the Heartland*, 229–242; McWhiney, *Braxton Bragg and Confederate Defeat*, 285–292; Noe, *Perryville*, 70–79.

22. Polk, quoted from Polk to Bragg, October 3, 1862, *OR*, ser. 1, vol. 16, pt.2: 901; Polk to Bragg, October 5, 1862, Ibid., 911; McWhiney, *Braxton Bragg and Confederate Defeat*, 300–308; Connelly, *Army of the Heartland*, 243–250; Noe, *Perryville*, 124–129.

23. Bragg's orders to join Kirby Smith, quoted from George W. Brent to Polk, October 7, 1862, *OR*, ser. 1, vol. 16, pt.1: 1095; Bragg's orders to support Hardee, quoted from Bragg to Polk, October 7, 1862, Ibid., 1096; McWhiney, *Braxton Bragg and Confederate Defeat*, 307–311; Connelly, *Army of the Heartland*, 252–259; Noe, *Perryville*, 124–140; Nathaniel Cheairs Hughes Jr., *General William J. Hardee: Old Reliable* (Baton Rouge: Louisiana State University Press, 1965), 120, 125–126.

24. Report of Maj. Gen. Leonidas Polk, November [n. d.], 1862, quoted from *OR*, ser. 1, vol. 16, pt.1: 1109; Donelson's brigade known as Cheatham's, cited from "Brig.-General Preston Smith's Brigade," *The Memphis Daily Appeal*, November 12, 1862; For James Patton Anderson (1822–1872), see Warner, *Generals in Gray*, 7–8; also see Ibid., for Jones Mitchell Withers (1814–1890), 342–343; Whether for simplicity or from forgetting, as did Bragg, that DSD was its temporary commander, Noe refers to the unit as Cheatham's division. Noe, *Perryville*, 140.

25. Polk, quoted regarding troop placements, and number of force, from Polk Report, November 1862, *OR*, ser. 1, vol. 16, pt.1: 1110 (see prev. note); Simon Bolivar Buckner (1823–1914), biographical entry, Warner, *Generals in Gray*, 38–39; Hughes, *William J. Hardee*, 125–128 (see note 23); Losson, *Tennessee's Forgotten Warriors*, 64–65.

26. Polk Report, November 1862, *OR*, ser. 1, vol. 16, pt.1: 1110. Even though Polk in his report punctiliously refers twice to it as "Donelson's division," p. 1109, and the "division . . . of General Donelson," p. 1110, this is the major primary source for the meetings. Again, perhaps for simplicity or forgetting that at this time of the morning, DSD was still in command of the First Division, none of the secondary accounts that name generals who ostensibly attended this meeting, name DSD. McWhiney, *Braxton Bragg and Confederate Defeat*, 312, fn 37, names Hardee, Anderson, Buckner, and Cheatham. Connelly, *Army of the Heartland*, 259, retains the distinction between the wing and division commanders by writing "Hardee, Cheatham, and the division commanders."

27. Hess, *Banners to the Breeze*, 86–87 (see note 17); Noe, *Perryville*, 145–156; Alexander McDowell McCook (1831–1903), biographical entry, Warner, *Generals in Blue*, 294–295; Also see Ibid. for: Charles Champion Gilbert (1822–1903), 173–174, and: Thomas Leonidas Crittenden (1819–1893), 100–101; Noe, *Perryville*, is the most detailed major study of the Battle of Perryville, and the principal source for the general description of the battle in the following account. I am grateful to Chuck Lott, a park ranger at the Perryville Battlefield State Historic Site, for giving me a copy of an unpublished booklet, *Battle of Perryville: Movement Maps Showing the Fighting Ground of the Union Left and Centre, 12:00 PM to 8:00 PM*, compiled by Kurt Holman as of Monday, May 9, 2016 (Perryville: Friends of Perryville Battlefield, Perryville, Kentucky, 2016), which has been extremely helpful in informing my description of the battle, as follows.

28. Report of General Braxton Bragg, October 12, 1862, *OR*, ser. 1, vol. 16, pt.1: 1087; Polk Report, November 1862, Ibid., 1109; McWhiney, *Braxton Bragg and Confederate Defeat*, 311–314; Hess, *Banners to the Breeze*, 87–88; Noe, *Perryville*, 170–171.

29. "Suggested," from Bragg Report, October 12, 1862, *OR*, ser. 1, vol. 16, pt.1: 1087; Polk, orders to Cheatham, quoted from Polk Report, November 1862, Ibid., 1110; McWhiney, *Braxton Bragg and Confederate Defeat*, 314; Hess, *Banners to the Breeze*, 87–88; Noe, *Perryville*, 160–169, 171–172.

30. DSD Report, October 26, 1862, Palmer Collection, WRHS; "Double quick," quoted from McWhiney, *Braxton Bragg and Confederate Defeat*, 315; Noe, *Perryville*, 181; Sterling Alexander Martin Wood (1823–1891), biographical entry, Warner, *Generals in Gray*, 344–345.

31. W.W. Carnes, quoted from "Artillery at the Battle of Perryville, Ky.," *Confederate Veteran* 33, no. 1 (January 1925): 8; Marshall, "Jackson's Battery-Carnes's Battery-Marshall's Battery," *Military Annals of Tennessee*, 813–814; Noe, *Perryville*, 181.

32. Geographic description and placement of Cheatham's division, taken from Noe, *Perryville*, 182, and from Holman, comp., *Battle of Perryville: Movement Maps* (see note 29); John H. Savage, in *The Life of John H. Savage: Citizen, Soldier, Lawyer, Congressman* (Nashville: Printed for the Author, 1903), 118, asserts that he "never had command of Donelson's brigade for a moment at the battle of Perryville." As Savage maintained, the claim that he was in command of the brigade was a conspiracy to "shift the responsibility" of the heavy casualties that the brigade incurred "from Cheatham's and Donelson's shoulders so as to wrongfully charge it on" him. All quoted from 118; Sam Davis Elliott, *Soldier of Tennessee: General Alexander P. Stewart and the Civil War in the West* (Baton Rouge: Louisiana State University Press, 1999), 54–55; George Earl Maney (1826–1901), biographical entry, Warner, *Generals in Gray*, 210.

33. DSD, Report, October 26, 1862, Palmer Collection, WRHS; Polk Report, November 1862, *OR*, ser. 1, vol. 16, pt.1: 1110; Cheatham to Wright, November 19, 1862, Report on the Battle of Perryville, Palmer Collection, WRHS; Connelly, *Army of the Heartland*, 263; Hess, *Banners to the Breeze*, 88–89; Noe, *Perryville*, 182–183;

John Archer Wharton (1828–1865), biographical entry, Warner, *Generals in Gray*, 331–332; I am much obliged to Chuck Lott, a park ranger at the Perryville Battlefield State Historic Site, and Ren Hankla, a local resident who now owns the property of Walker Bend, which is located outside the park boundary. On May 29, 2018, they very kindly treated Dr. Jose A. Meza, his son Mason (then twelve), and me to an extensive tour of the Walker Bend area and the Walker house.

34. DSD Report, October 26, 1862, Palmer Collection, WRHS.

35. DSD, quoted from Report, October 26, 1862, Palmer Collection, WRHS; Head, quoted in "consulted," from *Campaigns and Battles of the Sixteenth Regiment, Tennessee Volunteers*, 36; Womack, *Civil War Diary of Capt. J.J. Womack*, entry of October 8, 1862, 62; Savage, *Life of John H. Savage*, 119–120; Losson, *Tennessee's Forgotten Warriors*, 66; Noe, *Perryville*, 193–195; On the tour of Walker Bend described above in note 33, Mr. Hankla pointed out where DSD's brigade crossed the Chaplin River and climbed the bluff on the west bank, which is still heavily wooded.

36. DSD Report, October 26, 1862, Palmer Collection, WRHS; Savage, *Life of John H. Savage*, 119–120; Noe, in *Perryville*, 195–196, at this stage of his narrative relates only Savage's account, but not DSD's report.

37. "Forward," quoted from Head, *Campaigns and Battles*, 95; "Victory," quoted from Womack, *Civil War Diary of J.J. Womack*, entry of October 8, 1862, 62; Cheatham Report, November 19, 1862, Palmer Collection, WRHS; Atlanta *Southern Confederacy*, November 13, 1862; Noe, *Perryville*, 196–197; DSD Report, October 26, 1862, Palmer Collection, WRHS.

38. DSD Report, October 26, 1862, Palmer Collection, WRHS. Connelly, *Army of the Heartland*, 263; Hess, *Banners to the Breeze*, 88, 92; Numbers estimated from Appendix I, "Order of Battle, October 8, 1862," in Noe, *Perryville*, 369 and 373–374.

39. DSD Report, October 26, 1862, Palmer Collection, WRHS; Womack, *Civil War Diary of J.J. Womack*, entry of October 8, 1862, 62–63; Savage, *Life of John H. Savage*, 120–121; Noe, *Perryville*, 198–199.

40. DSD Report, October 26, 1862, Palmer Collection, WRHS; Womack, *Civil War Diary of J.J. Womack*, entry of October 8, 1862, 63; Savage, *Life of John H. Savage*, 121–123. Savage, on pages 116, 122, 128 and 131, four times incorrectly refers to "Colonel Donelson," instead of the correct Lieutenant Colonel D. M. Donnell, as is correctly cited on page 123. The resulting confusion only weakens his later criticisms of DSD at the battle of Perryville. Noe, *Perryville*, 203. Not catching Savage's error, Noe incorrectly states in *Perryville* on page 203, that Savage "turn[ed] over command to Donelson," but a subordinate officer does not turn over a command to his superior commander. For D.M. Donnell, see Dillard, "Sixteenth Tennessee Infantry," *Military Annals of Tennessee*, 345.

41. DSD Report, October 26, 1862, and: Cheatham Report, November 19, 1862, both in: Palmer Collection, WRHS; George E. Maney to Wright, October 29, 1862, Report on the Battle of Perryville, *SOR* 94, 668–672; Stuart W. Sanders, *Maney's Confederate Brigade at the Battle of Perryville* (Charleston: The History Press, 2014), 36–50.

42. Hess, *Banners to the Breeze*, 93; Noe, *Perryville*, 214.

43. DSD Report, October 26, 1862. Cheatham Report, November 19, 1862. A.P. Stewart to Wright, October 28, 1862. And: Report on the Battle of Perryville. All in: Palmer Collection, WRHS; Womack, *Civil War Diary of J.J. Womack*, entry of October 8, 1862, 63; Savage, *Life of John H. Savage*, 122–123; Hess, *Banners to the Breeze*, 97–100; Noe, *Perryville*, 215–241.

44. Connelly, *Army of the Heartland*, 263–264; Hess, *Banners to the Breeze*, 96–102; Noe, *Perryville*, 254–267; Craig L. Symonds, *Stonewall of the West: Patrick Cleburne and the Civil War* (Lawrence: University Press of Kansas, 1997), 87; Losson, *Tennessee's Forgotten Warriors*, 70–71; John Calvin Brown (1827–1889), biographical entry, Warner, *Generals in Gray*, 35–36.

45. DSD Report, October 26, 1862. Cheatham Report, November 19, 1862. And: Stewart Report, October 28, 1862. All in: Palmer Collection, WRHS; Elliott, *Soldier of Tennessee*, 56–58; Sanders, *Maney's Confederate Brigade*, 95–98.

46. DSD Report, October 26, 1862, Palmer Collection, WRHS; Carnes, quotations from "Artillery," *Confederate Veteran* 33, no. 1 (January 1925):8 (see note 31); Head, *Campaigns and Battles of the Sixteenth Regiment*, 241–242; Losson, *Tennessee's Forgotten Warriors*, 70–71; Noe, *Perryville*, 247–254.

47. DSD Report, October 26, 1862, Palmer Collection, WRHS; Womack, *Civil War Diary of J.J. Womack*, entry of October 8, 1862, 63; Noe, *Perryville*, 245–246; "Army Letters," *Fayetteville Observer* (Fayetteville, Tennessee), November 13, 1862; Losson, *Tennessee's Forgotten Warriors*, 71.

48. DSD Report, October 26, 1862, Palmer Collection, WRHS; Noe, *Perryville*, 268; Hess, *Banners to the Breeze*, 102–103; Elliott, *Soldier of Tennessee*, 58.

49. Marshall, "Jackson's Battery–Carnes's Battery–Marshall's Battery," *Military Annals of Tennessee*, 814.

50. Connelly, *Army of the Heartland*, 264–266; Hess, *Banners to the Breeze*, 102–104; Noe, *Perryville*, 268–305.

51. Abstract from Daily Returns, October 1, 1862, *OR*, ser. 1, vol. 16, pt.2: 896. Incomplete return of Casualties in the Confederate forces at the Battle of Perryville, October 8, 1862, *OR*, vol. 16, pt.1: 1108. "Army Letters," *Fayetteville Observer*, November 13, 1862. Estimates of total regimental strength from Appendix 1, "Order of Battle, October 8, 1862," in Noe, *Perryville*, 369. There are slight discrepancies in numbers among these sources.

52. Polk, quoted from Polk Report, November 1862, *OR*, ser. 1, vol. 16, pt.2: 1111; DSD Report, October 26, 1862, and: Cheatham, quoted from Cheatham Report,

November 19, 1862. Both in: Palmer Collection, WRHS; Colonel Tyler, quoted from "Details of the Recent Battle in Kentucky," *The Daily Bulletin* (Winchester, Tennessee), October 24, 1862.

53. At this point in the Notes, it is worth reprinting the full citation of Savage's autobiography, including the lengthy subtitle: John H. Savage, *The Life of John H. Savage: Citizen, Soldier, Lawyer, Congressman, Before the War Begun and Prosecuted by the Abolitionists of the Northern States to Reduce the Descendants of the Rebels of 1776, who Defeated the Armies of the King of England and gained Independence for the United States, Down to the Level of the Negro Race* (Nashville: Printed for the Author, 1903).

54. Savage, quoted in "no good feeling," and in subsequent quotations, from *Life of John H. Savage*, 123, and 128–129, respectively.

55. Savage, *Life of John H. Savage*, states on p. 136, that during the battle of Perryville he "did not know whether he [Cheatham] was drunk or sober." Yet, in other places he asserts "proof that they [Cheatham and DSD] were drunk," on 121, and similarly on 135 and 136. Losson, *Tennessee's Forgotten Warriors*, enumerates four drinking episodes for Cheatham: sharing a bottle of champagne with Ulysses S. Grant at a parley following the battle of Belmont, on page 38, and also during the battles of Murfreesboro, 89–91, Dalton, 130, and Atlanta, 140. He does not mention Cheatham being drunk at Perryville, 66–73. For DSD and the whisky episode during the march through Sparta and neighboring counties as related above, see Head, *Campaigns and Battles of the Sixteenth Regiment*, 201.

56. John Savage, quoted from Savage, *Life of John H. Savage*, referencing "a blank space," 116, assertion of no reports, cited on 116 and 129, claim of suppressed reports, cited on 126, and again quoted in "shot," from 129.

57. Savage, *Life of John H. Savage*, comparison to Tennyson poem, 129–130. Maney's report was eventually published in Hewett, *et al.*, *SOR* 94, 668–672, and contains nothing to substantiate Savage's charges. The reports of Cheatham, DSD, and Stewart remain unpublished but are located in the William P. Palmer Collection of Civil War Manuscripts, Western Reserve Historical Society, Cleveland, OH.

58. DSD Report, October 26, 1862, and Cheatham Report, November 19, 1862. Both in: Palmer Collection, WRHS; Savage, *Life of John H. Savage*, 119–120.

59. McWhiney, *Braxton Bragg and Confederate Defeat* 1: 320–323; Connelly, *Army of the Heartland*, 266–270, 279–280; Hess, *Banners to the Breeze*, 107–113; Noe, *Perryville*, 313–315, 327–338; Bruce Catton, *The American Heritage Pictorial History of the Civil War* (New York: American Heritage Publishing Co., Inc., 1960), includes the Perryville campaign, along with Lee's Maryland campaign, in the chapter entitled "Confederate High-Water Mark," 208–247. Similarly, Larry J. Daniel, in *Conquered: Why the Army of Tennessee Failed* (Chapel Hill: The University of North Carolina Press, 2019), entitles the chapter recounting the Perryville campaign as "High Tide," 32–48.

60. McWhiney, *Braxton Bragg and Confederate Defeat*, 323–334; Thomas Lawrence Connelly, *Autumn of Glory: The Army of Tennessee, 1862–1865* (Baton Rouge: Louisiana State University Press, 1971), 19–23; Christopher Losson, "Mutual Antagonists: Braxton Bragg, Frank Cheatham, and the Army of Tennessee," in *The Border Wars: The Civil War in Tennessee and Kentucky*, eds. Kent T. Dollar, Larry H. Whiteaker, and W. Calvin Dickinson (Kent: Kent State University Press, 2015), 214–237. Earl J. Hess, *Braxton Bragg: The Most Hated Man in the Confederacy* (Chapel Hill: The University of North Carolina Press, 2016), 80–92. There is not complete agreement as to whether some officers were Bragg supporters or detractors. McWhiney, *Braxton Bragg and Confederate Defeat*, 331, fn72; Noe, *Perryville*, 339; Daniel, *Conquered*, 50 (see note 59). All these sources list DSD among Bragg supporters, but without providing primary source evidence or elaboration.

61. General Orders, No. 145, November 8, 1862, *OR*, ser. 1, vol. 20, pt.2: 385; Bragg to Samuel Cooper, November 22, 1862, Ibid., 417. And also ibid., an enclosed list of general officers absent and detached from the Army of the Mississippi, 508; *Southern Confederacy*, November 23, 1862; McWhiney, *Braxton Bragg and Confederate Defeat* 1, 325–334; Connelly, *Autumn of Glory*, 14–15 (see prev. note).

62. List of general officers in the armies under General Johnston's command, November 27, 1862, *OR*, ser. 1, vol. 17, pt.2: 765; List of names submitted for general officers, *OR*, ser. 1, vol. 20, pt.2: 508–509, and: Bragg, quoted from Inclosure no. 5, in Bragg to Cooper, November 22, 1862, Ibid., 417–418; The most senior brigadier general, Charles Clark (1811–1877), had been so severely wounded, first at Shiloh in April, then at Baton Rouge in August 1862, that he was retired from the army; Warner, *Generals in Gray*, 51–52.

Chapter Seven: "More Distinguished Bravery"

1. List of names submitted for general officers, *OR*, ser. 1, vol. 20, pt.2: 508–509. Ibid., Inclosure no. 5 in Braxton Bragg to Samuel Cooper, November 22, 1862, 417–418. And: General Orders, No. 151, November 20, 1862, 411. And also organization of the infantry of the army of Tennessee, November 22, 1862, 418. This first organizational table does not list artillery batteries with their infantry brigades but subsequent tables do.

2. Connelly, *Autumn of Glory*, 13–15, 23–25; Walter T. Durham, *Nashville: The Occupied City, 1862–1863* (Knoxville: The University of Tennessee, 2008), 116–126 (see ch. 5, note 46); Earl J. Hess, "Braxton Bragg and the Stones River Campaign," in *The Border Wars: The Civil War in Tennessee and Kentucky*, eds. Kent T. Dollar, Larry H. Whiteaker, and W. Calvin Dickinson (Kent: Kent State University Press, 2015), 194–195, 198.

3. Womack, *The Civil War Diary of Capt. James J. Womack*, entries of October 31–November 24, 1862, 68–72.

4. Special Orders, No. 8, December 3, 1862, *OR*, ser.1, vol. 20, pt.2: 435; Circular, December 4, 1862, Ibid., 439; Report of Benjamin F. Cheatham, February 20, 1863, *OR*, ser. 1, vol. 20, pt.1: 705; "Stirring Times in Middle Tennessee," *The Memphis Daily Appeal*, December 17, 1862; Womack, *Civil War Diary of Capt. J.J. Womack*, entries of December 5 and 6, 1862, 73–74; Losson, *Tennessee's Forgotten Warriors*, 77; Larry J. Daniel, *Battle of Stones River: The Forgotten Conflict between the Confederate Army of Tennessee and the Union Army of the Cumberland* (Baton Rouge: Louisiana State University, 2012), 24–25. The town whose modern spelling is La Vergne was spelled Lavergne at the time. Ibid., xii.

5. "From Nashville," *Memphis Daily Appeal*, November 4, 1862; Durham, *Rebellion Revisited*, 103; For general pillaging by the United States occupation forces in the area, see Stephen V. Ash, *Middle Tennessee Society Transformed, 1860–1870: War and Peace in the Upper South* (Baton Rouge: Louisiana State University Press, 1988), 85–91.

6. Report of Daniel S. Donelson, January 20, 1863, *OR*, ser. 1, vol. 20, pt.1: 713; Peter Cozzens, *No Better Place to Die: The Battle of Stones River* (Urbana: University of Illinois Press, 1990), 12–28; Daniel, *Stones River*, 10–14, 20–22 (see note 4).

7. McWhiney, *Braxton Bragg and Confederate Defeat*, 344–345; Connelly, *Autumn of Glory*, 32–40; William C. Davis, *Jefferson Davis: The Man and His Hour* (New York: Harper Collins Publisher, 1991), 482–484.

8. Special Orders, No. 24, December 14, 1862, *OR*, ser. 1, vol. 20, pt.2: 449; Davis, *Jefferson Davis*, 482–483; McWhiney, *Braxton Bragg and Confederate Defeat*, 344; Craig L. Symonds, *Stonewall of the West: Patrick Cleburne and the Civil War* (Lawrence: University Press of Kansas, 1997), 101–102; Spence, *Andrew Jackson Donelson: Jacksonian and Unionist*, 223, 249, 263; In his journal, Colonel George William Brent, Bragg's assistant adjutant general, made comments, favorable or otherwise, regarding the promotions of several of these officers, but did not comment on why DSD was not promoted. In: George William Brent Journal, entry of December 14, 1862, Braxton Bragg Papers, WRHS; For Arthur Middleton Manigault (1824–1886), see Warner, *Generals in Gray*, 210–211.

9. Cheatham Report, February 20, 1863, *OR*, ser. 1, vol. 20, pt.1: 705; Connelly, *Autumn of Glory*, 44–46; Cozzens, *No Better Place to Die*, 48–59 (see note 6); Hess, *Banners to the Breeze*, 187–191; Daniel, *Stones River*, 33–46.

10. Cheatham Report, February 20, 1863, *OR*, ser. 1, vol. 20, pt.1: 705; Report of officers and men actually engaged in the battle of Murfreesborough, in Cheatham's division, Ibid., 709; DSD Report, January 20, 1863, Ibid., 710. For troop dispositions of the Army of the Tennessee, see Memoranda for general and staff officers, December 28, 1862, Ibid., 672–673; Cozzens, *No Better Place to Die*, 59-61; Daniel, *Stones River*, 50–51; Preston Smith (1823–1863), Warner, biographical entry, *Generals in Gray*, 283–284.

11. DSD Report, January 20, 1863, *OR*, ser. 1, vol. 20, pt.1: 710; Report of S.S.

Stanton, January 13, 1863, Ibid., 720; Horn, *Tennesseans in the Civil War*, Part 1, 207 (Fifteenth Tennessee Infantry Regiment), and 307–308 (Eighty-fourth Tennessee Infantry Regiment); Daniel, *Stones River*, 51.

12. Womack, *Civil War Diary of Capt. J.J. Womack*, entry of December 30, 1862, 77; Cheatham Report, February 20, 1863, OR, ser. 1, vol. 20, pt.1: 705; John Samuel Donelson to Elizabeth Donelson, February 2, 1863, AJDLC.

13. DSD Report, January 20, 1863, OR, ser. 1, vol. 20, pt.1: 710; Hess, *Banners to the Breeze*, 196; Daniel, *Stones River*, 68.

14. Divisional arrangements, quoted from Report of Jones M. Withers, May 20, 1863, OR, ser. 1, vol. 20, pt.1: 754; DSD, quoted, writing of Cheatham's orders, in DSD Report, January 20, 1863, Ibid., 710; McWhiney, *Braxton Bragg and Confederate Defeat*, 350–352; Losson, *Tennessee's Forgotten Warriors*, 80–81; Cozzens, *No Better Place to Die*, 72–76; Daniel, *Stones River*, 62–64; James Ronald Chalmers (1831–1898), biographical entry, Warner, *Generals in Gray*, 46.

15. Withers Report, May 20, 1863, OR, ser. 1, vol. 20, pt.1: 754–755; Losson, *Tennessee's Forgotten Warriors*, 81–87; Hess, *Banners to the Breeze*, 197–207; Cozzens, *No Better Place to Die*, 81–127; Daniel, *Stones River*, 72–129.

16. Report of Leonidas Polk, February 28, 1863, OR, ser. 1, vol. 20, pt.1: 689 (quotation). Cozzens, *No Better Place to Die*, 152–154; Daniel, *Stones River*, 153–154.

17. Quoted passages, all from DSD Report, January 20, 1863, OR, ser. 1, vol. 20, pt.1: 711. The placements of the regiments of DSD's brigade can be deduced from their commanders' battle reports, in OR, ser. 1, vol. 20, pt.1: Anderson, Eighth, 714–716; Savage, Sixteenth, 717–718; Carter, Thirty-eighth, 718–719; Chester, Fifty-eighth, 719–720; and: Stanton, Eighty-fourth, 720–721.

18. "Forward," quoted from Polk Report, February 28, 1863, OR, ser. 1, vol. 20, pt.1: 689; Other quoted passages from DSD Report, January 20, 1863, Ibid., 711; Cozzens, *No Better Place to Die*, 154.

19. DSD Report, January 20, 1863, OR, ser. 1, vol. 20, pt.1: 711; Anderson, quoted from Report of John H. Anderson, January 12, 1863, Ibid., 714; Polk, quoted from Polk Report, February 28, 1863, Ibid., 689; Cheatham, quoted from Cheatham Report, February 20, 1863, Ibid., 707; Cozzens, *No Better Place to Die*, 154.

20. Report of John H. Savage, January 8, 1863, OR, ser. 1, vol. 20, pt.1: 717.

21. DSD Report, January 20, 1863, OR, ser. 1, vol. 20, pt.1: 711; Report of John Chester, January 13, 1863, Ibid., 719.

22. DSD Report, January 20, 1863, OR, ser. 1, vol. 20, pt.1: 711; Cozzens, *No Better Place to Die*, 61, 65, 151–152, 154.

23. All quoted from Anderson Report, January 12, 1863, OR, ser. 1, vol. 20, pt.1: 714–715, excepting last quotation "open field," by Carter, from Report of John C. Carter, January 14, 1863, Ibid., 718.

24. Anderson Report, January 12, 1863, OR, ser. 1, vol. 20, pt.1: 715; Head, *Campaigns and Battles of the Sixteenth Regiment*, 205.

25. DSD Report, January 20, 1863, *OR*, ser. 1, vol. 20, pt.1: 712; John Savage, quoted from Savage Report, January 8, 1863, Ibid., 717; Savage, *The Life of John H. Savage*, 139–140.

26. Stanton Report, January 13, 1863, *OR*, ser. 1, vol. 20, pt.1: 720–721 (quotation); Report of L. G. Marshall, Carnes' battery, January 15, 1863, Ibid., 721–722; Savage Report, January 8, 1863, Ibid., 717; Organization of the Army of Tennessee, Ibid., 659; Organization of troops in the Department of East Tennessee, November 20, 1862, Ibid., ser. 1, vol. 20, pt.2: p. 414.

27. DSD Report, January 20, 1863, *OR*, ser. 1, vol. 20, pt.1: 712; Savage Report, January 8, 1863, Ibid., 717.

28. Anderson Report, January 12, 1863, *OR*, ser. 1, vol. 20, pt.1: 715; Carter Report, January 14, 1863, Ibid., 718; Chester Report, January 13, 1863, Ibid., 720; Report of Alexander P. Stewart, January 13, 1863, Ibid., 723; Organization of the Army of Tennessee, Ibid., 658; Sam Davis Elliott, *Soldier of Tennessee*, 69–71 (see ch. 6, note 32); Cozzens, *No Better Place to Die*, 157.

29. Report of W.J. Hardee, February 28, 1863, *OR*, ser. 1, vol. 20, pt.1: 776; Report of John K. Jackson, January 22, 1863, Ibid., 838; DSD, quoted from DSD Report, January 20, 1863, Ibid., 712; "Fine service," quoted from Stewart Report, January 13, 1863, Ibid., 725; Cozzens, *No Better Place to Die*, 61, 69, 159–161; Daniel, *Stones River*, 47–49, 55, 58, 69, 160–161; John King Jackson (1828–1866), biographical entry, Warner, *Generals in Gray*, 150–151.

30. Report of Daniel W. Adams, January 12, 1863, *OR*, ser. 1, vol. 20, pt.1: 793; Hardee Report, February 28, 1863, Ibid., 777; Savage Report, January 8, 1863, Ibid., 717–718; Savage, *Life of John H. Savage*, 140; Daniel Weisiger Adams (1821–1872), biographical entry, Warner, *Generals in Gray*, 1.

31. Adams Report, January 12, 1863, *OR*, ser. 1, vol. 20, pt.1: 793; "Attacked . . . checked . . . driven back," all quoted from DSD Report, January 20, 1863, Ibid., 712; Savage, quoted from Savage Report, January 8, 1863, Ibid., p. 718; Stanton Report, January 13, 1863, Ibid., 721; Savage, *Life of John H. Savage*, 140; Cozzens, *No Better Place to Die*, 162–164; Daniel, *Stones River*, 163–165.

32. DSD Report, January 20, 1863, *OR*, ser. 1, vol. 20, pt.1: 712; Report of William Preston, January 12, 1863, Ibid., 811–812; Cozzens, *No Better Place to Die*, 164–166; Daniel, *Stones River*, 166–168; Joseph Benjamin Palmer (1825–1890), biographical entry, Warner, *Generals in Gray*, 227–228; William Preston (1816–1887), Ibid., 246.

33. DSD Report, January 20, 1863, *OR*, ser. 1, vol. 20, pt.1: 712.

34. Polk Report, February 28, 1863, *OR*, ser. 1, vol. 20, pt.1: 689–690.

35. Return of casualties in the Confederate forces, *OR*, ser. 1, vol. 20, pt.1: 676; Polk Report, February 28, 1863, Ibid., 690; Report of officers and men actually engaged in the battle of Murfreesboro, in Cheatham's division, Ibid., 709; Ibid.,

718. In the Savage Report, January 8, 1863, 208 total casualties are reported, which is one more than other cited sources.

36. Polk Report, February 28, 1863, *OR*, ser. 1, vol. 20, pt.1: 690; DSD Report, January 20, 1863, Ibid., 713; Return of casualties in the Confederate forces, Ibid., 676; Report of officers and men actually engaged in the battle of Murfreesboro, in Cheatham's division, Ibid., 709; Cozzens, *No Better Place to Die*, 157. Cozzens's statement is true in terms of absolute numbers of casualties that were suffered from absolute regimental strengths, but a few other Confederate States regiments suffered greater casualties proportionally from smaller initial unit strengths. The regiment that suffered the highest proportional casualty rate in a single battle was the First Texas Infantry Regiment at the Battle of Antietam, or Sharpsburg, September 17, 1862, which suffered 186 casualties from a regimental strength of 226, a casualty rate of 82 percent. In: Report of . . . killed and wounded at . . . Sharpsburg (Antietam), *OR*, ser. 1, vol. 19, pt.1: 811. Also Burke Davis, *Our Incredible Civil War* (New York: Holt, Rinehart, and Winston, Inc., 1960), 218–219, recounts notable examples of high regimental losses.

37. Tabular statement showing the number present for duty on the morning of December 31, 1862, *OR*, ser. 1, vol. 20, pt.1: 674; Return of casualties in the Confederate forces, Ibid., 676; List of killed, wounded, and missing in Polk's corps in the battles before Murfreesboro, Ibid., 693. Report of officers and men actually engaged in the battle of Murfreesboro, in Cheatham's division, Ibid., 709. I have subtracted the men in Carnes's battery from this number.

38. Polk Report, February 28, 1863, *OR*, ser. 1, vol. 20, pt.1: 690; Savage Report, January 8, 1863, Ibid., 718; Carter Report, January 14, 1863, Ibid., 718; Chester Report, January 13, 1863, Ibid., 720; Anderson Report, January 12, 1863, Ibid., 715, 716; DSD Report, January 20, 1863, Ibid., 712.

39. Carter Report, January 14, 1863, *OR*, ser. 1, vol. 20, pt.1: 718; Chester Report, January 13, 1863, Ibid., 720; Anderson Report, January 12, 1863, Ibid., 715, 716; DSD Report, January 20, 1863, Ibid., 712.

40. DSD Report, January 20, 1863, *OR*, ser. 1, vol. 20, pt.1: 711, 712; Savage, *Life of John H. Savage*, 142–143. Savage again dissents, claiming against all the other evidence that DSD was absent from his sector until after the Union batteries had been captured. Otherwise, compared to his lengthy and vitriolic criticisms of DSD at the battle of Perryville, Savage's criticisms of DSD at Murfreesboro are brief and muted.

41. "Strong picket," quoted from DSD Report, January 20, 1863, *OR*, ser. 1, vol. 20, pt.1: 712; Stanton Report, January 13, 1863, Ibid., 721; Cozzens, *No Better Place to Die*, 167.

42. DSD, quoted in "my men. . . ." from DSD Report, January 20, 1863, *OR*, ser. 1, vol. 20, pt.1: 712; Col. Stanton, quoted in " . . . under arrest," from Stanton

Report, January 13, 1863, Ibid., 721; Connelly, *Autumn of Glory*, 61–62; Hess, *Banners to the Breeze*, 216–219; Cozzens, *No Better Place to Die*, 167–176; Daniel, *Stones River*, 169–177.

43. DSD Report, January 20, 1863, *OR*, ser. 1, vol. 20, pt.1: 712; Connelly, *Autumn of Glory*, 62; Hess, *Banners to the Breeze*, 218–219; Cozzens, *No Better Place to Die*, 174–176; Daniel, *Stones River*, 173, 175, 179–180.

44. Marshall Report, January 15, 1863, *OR*, ser. 1, vol. 20, pt.1: 723; Connelly, *Autumn of Glory*, 63–65; Hess, *Banners to the Breeze*, 220–224; Cozzens, *No Better Place to Die*, 181–196; Daniel, *Stones River*, 184–196.

45. DSD Report, January 20, 1863, *OR*, ser. 1, vol. 20, pt.1: 712; "Powerful fire," quoted from Marshall Report, January 15, 1863, Ibid., 723; Daniel, *Stones River*, 199.

46. DSD Report, January 20, 1863, *OR*, ser. 1, vol. 20, pt.1: 712; Connelly, *Autumn of Glory*, 66–68; Losson, *Tennessee's Forgotten Warriors*, 91–92; Hess, *Banners to the Breeze*, 225–226; Cozzens, *No Better Place to Die*, 199–201; Daniel, *Stones River*, 198–200.

Chapter Eight: "An Irreparable Loss"

1. McWhiney, *Braxton Bragg and Confederate Defeat*, 374–381; Connelly, *Autumn of Glory*, 69–76; Hess, *Braxton Bragg. The Most Hated Man of the Confederacy*, 103–109, 113–126; Daniel, *Conquered*, 89–93.

2. Special Orders, No. 14, January 17, 1863, *OR*, ser. 1, vol. 20, pt.2: 499.

3. Special Orders, No. 11, January 14, 1863, *OR*, ser. 1, vol. 15, 948; Special Orders, No. 14, January 17, 1863, *OR*, ser. 1, vol. 20, pt.2: 499; Connelly, *Autumn of Glory*, 76–85; Freeman, *Lee's Lieutenants*, 2:506–607 (see ch. 5, note 24); Daniel, *Conquered*, 57; For Henry Heth (1825–1899), see Warner, *Generals in Gray*, 133.

4. DSD to John Branch, December 8, 1861, Branch Family Papers, SHCUNC; Certificate by E. Woodward, Surgeon and Medical Inspector, April 2, 1863, in Daniel S. Donelson, Compiled Military Service File, U.S., *Compiled Service Records of Confederate Generals and Staff Officers, and Nonregimental Enlisted Men*, NARA Mf. publication M331A, 200 rolls, War Department Collection of Confederate Records, RG 109, National Archives, Washington, D.C. (Washington: National Archives and Records Administration [NARA], 1962); William B. Bate, *Our Confederate Dead: Oration by Maj. Gen'l Wm. B. Bate, U.S. Senator, on Occasion of Unveiling Confederate Monument at Knoxville, Tennessee, May 19, 1892* (Knoxville: S.B. Newman & Co., Printers and Binders, 1892), 45; Clayton, *History of Davidson County, Tennessee*, 396.

5. Special Orders, No. 24, January 30, 1863; and: Special Orders, No. 25, January 31, 1863. Both in: *OR*, ser. 1, vol. 23, pt.2: 621; John H. Savage, *The Life of John H. Savage*, 144–146; Daniel, *Conquered*, 57; Marcus Joseph Wright (1831–1922), biographical entry, *Generals in Gray*, 346–347.

6. *Chattanooga Daily Rebel*, February 3, 1863; Johnston, Chattanooga Headquarters, quoted from Special Orders, No. 16, February 4, 1863, *OR*, ser. 1, vol. 23, pt.2: 626; *The Athens Post* (Athens, Tennessee), January 30, 1863; *The Daily Register* (Knoxville), February 10, 1863; James G. Martin to Humphrey Marshall, February 11, 1863, *OR*, ser. 1, vol. 52, pt.2: 421; MBD to Andrew Johnson, July 10, 1865, in Graf, et al., *The Papers of Andrew Johnson* 8, 379 (see ch. 5, note 45); Clayton, *History of Davidson County, Tennessee*, 397; Durham, *Rebellion Revisited*, 182.

7. Oliver P. Temple, *East Tennessee and the Civil War* (Cincinnati: The Robert Clarke Company, Publishers, 1899), 432–463; Noel C. Fisher, *War at Every Door: Partisan Politics and Guerrilla Violence in East Tennessee, 1860–1869* (Chapel Hill: The University of North Carolina Press, 1997), 16–37, 51ff; Atkins, *Parties, Politics, and the Sectional Conflict in Tennessee*, 248–258; Donald Stoker, *The Grand Design: Strategy and the U.S. Civil War* (New York: Oxford University Press, 2010), 73–75, 91, 173–174.

8. Special Orders, No. 14, January 17, 1863, *OR*, ser. 1, vol. 20, pt.2: 499; Marshall to [C.S.] Stringfellow, January 25, 1863, *OR*, vol. 23, pt.2: 615–617; DSD, quoted from DSD to Benjamin. S. Ewell, February 10, 1863, Ibid., 631; Also see Humphrey Marshall (1812–1872), biographical entry, *BDUSC*, 1425, and also in: Warner, *Generals in Gray*, 212–213. And also Samuel Jones (1819–1887), biographical entry, Warner, Generals in Gray, 165–166.

9. Donelson, instructions through Martin, quoted from Martin to Marshall, February 11, 1863, *OR*, ser. 1, vol. 52, pt.2: 421; John Pegram (1832-1865), biographical entry, Warner, *Generals in Gray*, 231–232; Johnston, quoted from Joseph E. Johnston to DSD, February 11, 1863, *OR*, vol. 23, pt.2: 632.

10. Donelson's directions via Martin, quoted from Martin to Marshall, February 11, 1863, *OR*, ser. 1, vol. 52, pt.2: 421; DSD, first report to Johnston's headquarters, quoted from DSD to Ewell, February 10, 1863, *OR*, ser. 1, vol. 23, pt.2: p. 631.

11. Abstract from return of troops of the line, February 18, 1863, *OR*, ser. 1, vol. 23, pt.2: 638; Aggregate "Troops of the Line," February 18, 1863, Ibid., 639; Abstract from field return of the forces in the Department of East Tennessee, February 20, 1863, Ibid., 644; Organization of forces in the Department of East Tennessee, February 20, 1863, Ibid., 644–645.

12. DSD to Ewell, February 10, 1863, *OR*, ser. 1, vol. 23, pt.2: 631; Fisher, *War at Every Door*, 118 (see note 7).

13. James A. Seddon to DSD, February 14, 1863, *OR*, ser. 1, vol. 23, pt.2: 634–635; Seddon to Samuel Jones, February 13, 1863, Ibid., vol. 25, pt.2: 620–621; John Stuart Williams (1818–1898), biographical entry, Warner, *Generals in Gray*, 338–339.

14. Seddon to DSD, February 14, 1863, *OR*, ser. 1, vol. 23, pt.2: 634; Seddon to Jefferson Davis, February 16, 1863, *Journal of the Congress of the Confederate States of America, 1861–1865* (Washington: Government Printing Office, 1904), 3:136; Landon C. Haynes and Gustavus A. Henry to Davis, January 19, 1863, enclosed

in Daniel S. Donelson, Compiled Military Service File, National Archives and Records Administration, Washington, D.C. (see note 4). Also see biographical entries for Landon Carter Haynes (1816–1875), 348–349, and Gustavus Adolphus Henry (1804–1880), 360–361, both in *BDTGA*.

15. Johnston to Samuel Cooper, February 17, 1863, *OR*, ser. 1, vol. 23, pt.2: 637; Seddon to DSD, February 27, 1863, Ibid., 652; Fisher, *War at Every Door*, 118; Elliott, *Isham G. Harris of Tennessee*, 128, 136–137.

16. Jones to DSD, February 27, 1863, *OR*, ser. 1, vol. 25, pt.2: 643–644; DSD to Johnston, March 1, 1863, *OR*, ser. 1, vol. 23, pt.2: 655; DSD to Jones, March 1, 1863, Ibid., 656; Seddon to DSD, March 4, 1863, Ibid., 662; Connelly, *Autumn of Glory*, 96–97.

17. DSD, quoted from DSD to Ewell, March 4, 1863, and DSD to Ewell, March 4, 1863, both in: *OR*, ser. 1, vol. 23, pt.2: 661 and 662, respectively; Connelly, *Autumn of Glory*, 107.

18. Jefferson Davis, quoted from Davis to Marshall, March 11, 1863, *OR*, ser. 1, vol. 52, pt.2: 433.

19. Davis to Johnston, March 16, 1863, *OR*, ser. 1, vol. 23, pt.2: 713; Johnston to Davis, March 18, 1863, Ibid., 713. The [*sic*] is inserted in the printed text of the *OR* at that point. Johnston probably meant 70,000 disloyal in East Tennessee.

20. Cooper to DSD, March 17, 1863, *OR*, ser. 1, vol. 23, pt.2: 705–706; Johnston to Cooper, March 27, 1863, ibid., 726; Johnston to Davis, March 28, 1863, Ibid., 726–727.

21. DSD to Johnston, April 1, 1863, *OR*, ser. 1, vol. 23, pt.2: 735–736; Davis to the Congress of the Confederate States, March 5, 1863, *Journal of the Congress of the Confederate States* 3: 136; *The Memphis Daily Appeal*, April 3, 1863, recounting a report from *The Daily Register* (Knoxville), no copy of which seems to be extant.

22. Seddon to DSD, March 27, 1863, *OR*, ser. 1, vol. 23, pt.2: 726; Gordon B. McKinney, *Zeb Vance: North Carolina's Civil War Governor and Gilded Age Political Leader* (Chapel Hill: The University of North Carolina Press, 2004), 160–162.

23. Johnston to Cooper, April 7, 1863, *OR*, ser. 1, vol. 23, pt.2: 744.

24. Dr. E. Woodward, departmental medical inspector, quoted from Certificate of E. Woodward, April 2, 1863, enclosed in Daniel S. Donelson, Compiled Military Service File, National Archives and Records Administration, Washington, D.C.; Also see Jack D. Welsh, *Medical Histories of Confederate Generals* (Kent: Kent State University Press, 1995), 55.

25. Johnston to Cooper, April 7, 1863, *OR*, ser. 1, vol. 23, pt.2: 744; Cooper to Johnston, April 8, 1863, Ibid., 744; Johnston to Davis, April 10, 1863, Ibid., 745–746; Donald C. Pfanz, *Richard S. Ewell: A Soldier's Life* (Chapel Hill: The University of North Carolina Press, 1998), 257–272.

26. Special Orders, No. 27, January 16, 1863, *OR*, ser. 1, vol. 20, pt.2: 498; DSD to Ewell, March 4, 1863, *OR*, ser. 1, vol. 23, pt.2: 662; Special Orders, No. 92,

April 15, 1863, Ibid., 773; Johnston to John C. Pemberton, April 15, 1863, Ibid., 774; Cooper to Johnston, April 8, 1863, Ibid., 744; *Athens Post*, April 17, 1863; William George Mackey Davis (1812–1898), biographical entry, Warner, *Generals in Gray*, 69; Alfred Eugene Jackson (1807–1889), Ibid., 148–149.

27. DSD, cause of death, Certificate of E. Woodward, April 2, 1863, enclosed in Daniel S. Donelson, Compiled Military Service File, National Archives; DSD, time of death, quoted from Knoxville *Daily Register*, April 19, 1863; *Athens Post*, April 24, 1863; MBD to Johnson, July 10, 1865, *Papers of Andrew Johnson* 8: 379; DSD, attribution of last words, quoted, from Clayton, *History of Davidson County, Tennessee*, 397.

28. Knoxville *Daily Register*, April 19, 1863; James A. Wallace to "Emma," April 15, 24, 1863, James A. Wallace Letter, TSLA. The letter begins on April 15 and concludes April 24, the page on which Wallace recounts DSD's funeral; Jesse Johnson Finley (1812–1904), biographical entry, Warner, *Generals in Gray*, 89.

29. Margaret Branch Donelson, quoted from MBD to Johnson, July 10, 1865, *Papers of Andrew Johnson* 8: 379; DSD obituary, quoted from Knoxville *Daily Register*, April 19, 1863; Gen. Braxton Bragg, quoted passage, from announcement of DSD's death in General Orders, No. 85, April 24, 1863, *OR*, vol. 23, pt.2: 787–788; "Tribute of Respect," from the officers of Donelson's brigade, quoted in *Fayetteville Observer* (Tennessee), June 4, 1863.

30. Marshall to DSD, April 18, 1863, *OR*, ser. 1, vol. 23, pt.2: 777–778.

31. Donelson promotion confirmation, quoted from *Journal of the Congress of the Confederate States* 3: 324, 330.

32. Atlanta *Southern Confederacy* (Georgia), April 24, 1863; *The Nashville Dispatch*, April 28, 1863.

33. Sarah Yorke Jackson to Andrew Jackson III, June 22, 1863, Andrew Jackson Papers, TSLA; Mary Branch to William Branch, January 18, 1863 [misdated 1862], Branch Family Papers, SHCUNC; John Branch (November 4, 1782–January 4, 1863), Tombstone epitaph, Elmwood Cemetery, Enfield, Halifax County, North Carolina. John Branch (1782–1863), *DAB* 2: 596–597; Daniel Donelson Horton (April 18, 1862–April 22, 1863), Tombstone epitaph, Athens City Cemetery, Athens, Limestone County, Alabama.

34. Samuel Donelson to William Branch, August 11, 1863, Branch Family Papers, SHCUNC; For James Branch Donelson, see Horn, *Tennesseans in the Civil War*, 1: 188–190, and 2: 132. Also see William Thomas Venner, *The 7th Tennessee Infantry in the Civil War: A History and Roster* (Jefferson: McFarland & Company, Inc., Publishers, 2013), 178; For Samuel Davis Donelson, see Report of Nathan B. Forrest, July 1, 1864, *OR*, ser. 1, vol. 39, pt.1: 226; Ibid., Addenda, June 28, 1864, 230; "Col. 'Sam' Donelson is Called by Death," *Washington Post* (D.C.), July 24, 1906.

35. MBD, quoted from MBD to Johnson, July 10, 1865, *Papers of Andrew Johnson*

8: 379; Last Will and Testament of Daniel S. Donelson, February 26, 1863 (second quotation), probated February 1867, Loose Will no. 512, Sumner County Loose Wills, Sumner County Archives, Gallatin, Sumner County, Tennessee; Smith, quoted from Harry Smith to AJD, March 30, 1864, Miscellaneous Manuscripts, TSLA; Spence, *Andrew Jackson Donelson: Jacksonian and Unionist*, 264, 267–268.

36. To secure DSD's back pay, see MBD affidavit before George M. White, justice of the peace of Knox County, Tennessee, April 21, 1863; corroborating statements signed by William Craig, April 21, 1863, and W.G.M. Davis, April 21, 1863; auditor's certificate, Treasury Department, Confederate States of America, April 27, 1863; voucher payable to MBD, April 27, 1863; DSD's Compiled Military Service File, National Archives; Samuel Donelson, quoted from Samuel Donelson to William Branch, August 11, 1863, Branch Family Papers, SHCUNC; MBD, quoted from letter, MBD to Johnson, July 10, 1865, *Papers of Andrew Johnson* 8: 379–380; Johnson to Andrew J. Martin, August 29, 1865, Ibid., 669; Clinton B. Fisk to Johnson, September 1, 1865, *Papers of Andrew Johnson* 9: 6–7; MBD to Johnson, September 29, 1865, Ibid., 148; Johnson to Fisk, September 30, 1865, Ibid., 148n; Fisk to Johnson, October 3, 1865, Ibid., 176; "Confiscating Private Property: A Reminiscence Connecting Gen. Fisk and President Andrew Johnson," *Confederate Veteran* 1, no. 2 (February 1893): 43–44.

37. MBD to Johnson, July 10, 1865, *Papers of Andrew Johnson* 8: 379; *The Daily Union and American* (Nashville), December 20, 1865, and January 2, 1866.

38. For the marriages, see Double ceremony, reported in *The Republican Banner* (Nashville), November 2, 1867. Also see Byron and Barbara Sistler, *Early Middle Tennessee Marriages*, 1 [brides] and 2 [grooms], for: Susan Branch Donelson, 1: 147, and Marcus Lafayette Dismukes, 2: 151. Samuel Donelson, 2: 566, and Jessie L. Walton, 1: 149. Rebecca W. Donelson, 1: 147, and David J. Dismukes, 2: 151. And finally: Martha B. Donelson, 1: 492, and John M. Shute, 2: 151; Sarah Smith Donelson Bradford, grave, Bradford-Eppes Cemetery, Leon County, Florida.

39. "House and Land for Sale," *Nashville Union and American*, November 13, 1868; For DSD's efforts to bring the Louisville and Nashville Railroad through Sumner County, see Chapter 4; "Gone after His Remains," *Nashville Union and American*, December 7, 1869; *Republican Banner*, December 9, 1869; Amy Whitehead to William Branch, May 12, 1871, Branch Family Papers, SHCUNC; The *Nashville Union and American*, May 12, 1871, reported that MBD died "yesterday," and is perhaps the source of many incorrect statements that she died May 11, 1871; Tombstones with birth and death dates of DSD, MBD, and Susan Branch Donelson Dismukes, First Presbyterian Church, Hendersonville, Sumner County, Tennessee. At the time of the burials of these Donelsons, the name of the church was the Hendersonville Presbyterian Church, as named in the main text.

40. Excerpts, quoted from MBD's will, March 2, 1870, probated August 7, 1871, Loose Will no. 554, Sumner County Loose Wills, Sumner County Archives,

Gallatin, Tennessee; For AJ's gift of the watch to DSD, on the latter's departure for West Point, see Chapter 1.

41. For marriage of John Branch Donelson and Jennie S. Alexander, see Sistler, *Early Middle Tennessee Marriages*, 1 (grooms) and 2 (brides), respectively, 1: 149, and 2: 6; For marriage of Daniel ("Dan") Donelson and Florence Hood, see *Nashville Banner*, October 10, 1890; "Sam'l Donelson Dead," *The Evening Star* (Washington, D.C.), July 23, 1906; "Col. 'Sam' Donelson is Called by Death," *Washington Post*, July 24, 1906. The various sources listing the birth, marriage, and birth dates of DSD's children and grandchildren are often incomplete and occasionally contradictory. Zella Armstrong, comp., *Notable Southern Families* (Chattanooga: The Lookout Publishing Co., 1922), 2:95, 104–105, provides lists of DSD's children and grandchildren that were compiled when many of them were still living.

42. *Welcome to Hazel Path*, information sheet available to the public, Hazel Path, Hendersonville, Sumner County, Tennessee. Description of Hazel Path mansion and its history from the historical markers on the front lawn, and from the author's visits to it, July 2010, and twice (May, July) in 2018.

Epilogue

1. "MIDDLE TENNESSEE," under the headline "GENERAL D.S. DONELSON," *Nashville Union and American*, September 22, 1855.

2. Three, depending on how one counts the document that constitutes the third letter. Only two letters survive in the AJLC repository which were written directly from DSD to AJ: September 27, 1823, and June 22, 1824. Another letter, DSD to AJ, November 20, 1822, survives solely as a copy in AJ's hand, enclosed in AJ to AJD, December 16, 1822. Yet another letter, DSD to "Dear Sam," probably to Samuel Jackson Hays, November 16, 1828, is also in AJLC; AJ quotation from a printed footnote, for AJ to AJJr, undated but spring 1831, in *Jackson Correspondence* 4, 214 fn; In another telling statistic, the most recently published (2019) volume of *Jackson Papers*, volume 11, which covers the year 1833, does not list DSD's name in the index.

3. DSD to AJD, August 7, 1832, Dyas Collection of John Coffee Family Papers, TSLA; see also Spence, *Andrew Jackson Donelson: Jacksonian and Unionist*, 63–65.

4. "MIDDLE TENNESSEE," *Nashville Union and American*, September 22, 1855 (see note 1).

5. Clayton, *History of Davidson County, Tennessee*, 396.

6. Dillard, "Sixteenth Tennessee Infantry," in Lindsley, *Military Annals of Tennessee*, 342.

7. General Orders, No. 85, April 24, 1863, *OR*, vol. 23, pt.2: pp. 787–788; *The Daily American* (Nashville), February 26, 1889; Ibid., photo, May 22, 1890; Bate, *Our Confederate Dead*, 45 (see ch. 8, note 4).

BIBLIOGRAPHY

Primary Sources

MANUSCRIPTS

John Branch Papers. State Library of North Carolina, Government and Heritage Library, Raleigh, NC.
Campbell Family Papers. David M. Rubenstein Rare Book & Manuscript Library. Duke University, Durham, NC.
Compiled Service Records of Confederate Generals and Staff Officers, and Nonregimental Enlisted Men. Civil War Records, Confederate. Washington: National Archives and Records Administration.
Frederick M. Dearborn Collection of Military and Political Americana. Houghton Library. Harvard University, Cambridge, MA.
Lyman C. Draper Collection of Manuscripts. State Historical Society of Wisconsin. Library Mall, University of Wisconsin-Madison, Madison, WI.
Library of Congress, Manuscript Division, Washington, DC:
    Andrew Jackson Donelson Papers
    Andrew Jackson Papers
    James K. Polk Papers
    Nicholas Philip Trist Papers
    Martin Van Buren Papers
Jackson-Donelson Collection. Vanderbilt University, Nashville, TN.
John Pendleton Kennedy Papers. Maryland Center for History and Culture. Baltimore, MD.
Christopher C. McKinney Letters. Hesburgh Library. University of Notre Dame, Notre Dame, IN.
William Preston Papers. Lyman C. Draper Collection of Manuscripts. State Historical Society of Wisconsin. Library Mall, University of Wisconsin-Madison, Madison, WI.
Southern Historical Collection. University of North Carolina, Chapel Hill, NC:
    Branch Family Papers
    Robert Looney Caruthers Papers
    Elliott and Gonzales Family Papers
    George Washington Polk Papers

State Historical Society of Wisconsin. Library Mall, University of Wisconsin-Madison, Madison, WI.
Sumner County Archives. Gallatin, TN:
    Sumner County Direct Deed Index, 1787–1947
    Sumner County Original Loose Deeds 1786 to 1914
    Sumner County Loose Wills
    Sumner County Tax Lists, 1826–1830
    Sumner County Tax Lists, 1831–1834
    Sumner County Tax Lists, 1856–1867
Tennessee Historical Society. Tennessee State Library and Archives. Nashville, TN:
    Andrew Jackson Donelson Papers
    Dyas Collection of John Coffee Family Papers
    Bettie Mizell Donelson Papers
    Miscellaneous Manuscripts
    William Trousdale Papers
Tennessee State Library and Archives. Nashville, TN:
    Alfred Abernathy Letter
    Andrew Jackson Papers
    Military Elections Record Group. Record Group 131
    Miscellaneous Manuscripts
    Governor James K. Polk Papers
    Provisional Army of Tennessee Records. Record Group 4
    Tennessee State Militia Commission Books. Record Group 195
    James A. Wallace Letter
    James Winchester Papers
    George Winchester Wynne Collection of Wynne Family Papers
    Yeatman-Polk Collection
Western Reserve Historical Society Library. Cleveland History Center. University Circle, Case Western Reserve University, Cleveland, OH:
    Braxton Bragg Papers
    William P. Palmer Collection of Civil War Manuscripts

NEWSPAPERS

The Athens Post. Athens, Tennessee.
Chattanooga Daily Rebel. Chattanooga, Tennessee.
The Daily American. Nashville, Tennessee.
The Daily Bulletin. Winchester, Tennessee.
The Daily Nashville Patriot. Nashville, Tennessee.
The Daily Nashville True Whig. Nashville, Tennessee.
The Daily Register. Knoxville, Tennessee.

BIBLIOGRAPHY

Edgefield Advertiser. Edgefield, South Carolina.
The Evening Star. Washington, D.C.
Fayetteville Observer. Fayetteville, Tennessee.
The Lancaster Ledger. Lancaster, South Carolina.
The Memphis Daily Appeal. Memphis, Tennessee.
Nashville Banner. Nashville, Tennessee.
The Nashville Dispatch. Nashville, Tennessee.
National Banner and Nashville Whig. Nashville, Tennessee.
New York Times. New York, New York.
Niles' Weekly Register. Baltimore, Maryland.
The Nashville Republican. Nashville, Tennessee. Later, as *The Republican Banner*, *The Republican Banner and Nashville Whig*, and *Nashville Republican Banner*.
Southern Confederacy. Atlanta, Georgia.
Southern Standard. McMinnville, Tennessee.
The Tennessean. Nashville, Tennessee.
The Union. Nashville, Tennessee. Later, as *The Nashville Union*, *Nashville Daily Union*, *Nashville Union and American*, *Daily Nashville Union*, and *The Daily Union and American*.
The United States' Telegraph. Washington, D.C.
The Washington Post. Washington, D.C.
Yorkville Enquirer. Yorkville, South Carolina.

UNPUBLISHED DOCUMENTS

Battle of Perryville: Movement Maps Showing the Fighting Ground of the Union Left and Centre, 12:00 PM to 8:00 PM. Kurt Holmes, comp., as of Monday, May 9, 2016. Friends of Perryville Battlefield, Perryville, Kentucky.
National Register of Historic Places Inventory Nomination Form: Daniel Smith Doneslon House, Eventide, Hendersonville, TN. National Park Service. United States Department of the Interior, Washington, D.C.
Welcome to Hazel Path. Information sheet available to the public. Hazel Path, Hendersonville, Sumner County, Tennessee.

PUBLISHED CORRESPONDENCE, DIARIES, DOCUMENTS, MEMOIRS, AND STATISTICS

Adams, Cindy, ed. *The West Point Thayer Papers, 1808–1872.* 11 vols. West Point: Association of Graduates, 1965.
Annals of the Congress of the United States: Eighteenth Congress, First Session, December 1, 1823, to May 27, 1824. Washington: Gales and Seaton, 1856.
Bassett, John Spencer, ed. *Correspondence of Andrew Jackson.* 6 vols. Washington: Carnegie Institute of Washington, 1926–1933.
Bate, William B. *Our Confederate Dead. Oration by Maj. Gen'l Wm. B. Bate, U.S. Senator,*

on Occasion of Unveiling Confederate Monument at Knoxville, Tennessee, May 19, 1892. Knoxville: S.B. Newman & Co., Printers and Binders, 1892.

Carnes, W.W. "Artillery at the Battle of Perryville, Ky." *Confederate Veteran*, 33, no. 1 (January 1925): 8–9.

Cheat Mountain; or, Unwritten Chapter of the Late War. By a Member of the Bar, Fayetteville, Tenn. Nashville: Albert B. Tavel, Stationer and Printer, 1885.

Clark, Walter, ed. *The State Records of North Carolina*. 30 vols. Goldsboro: Nash Brothers, Book and Job Printers, 1895–1914.

"Confiscating Private Property. A Reminiscence Connecting Gen. Fisk and President Andrew Johnson." *Confederate Veteran* 1, no. 2 (February 1893): 43–44.

Dowdey, Clifford, and Louis H. Manarin, eds. *The Wartime Papers of R.E. Lee*. New York: Little, Brown & Company, Inc., 1961.

Garrett, W. R., ed. "Papers of Gen. Daniel Smith." *The American Historical Magazine* 6, no. 3 (July 1901): 213–235.

———. "Unpublished Letters of Andrew Jackson." *The American Historical Magazine* 4, no. 3 (July 1899): 229–246.

Gower, Herschel, ed. *Pen and Sword: The Life and Journals of Randal W. McGavock*. Nashville: Tennessee Historical Commission, 1960.

Graf, Leroy P., Ralph W. Haskins, and Paul H. Bergeron, eds. *The Papers of Andrew Johnson*. 16 vols. Knoxville: The University of Tennessee Press, 1967–2001.

Head, Thomas A. *Campaigns and Battles of the Sixteenth Regiment, Tennessee Volunteers, in the War Between the States, with Incidental Sketches of the Part Performed by other Tennessee Troops in the same War, 1861–1865*. Nashville: Cumberland Presbyterian Publishing House, 1885.

Hemphill, W. Edwin, Clyde N. Wilson, and Robert L. Meriwether, eds. *The Papers of John C. Calhoun*. 27 vols. Columbia: University of South Carolina, 1959–2003.

Hewett, Janet B., Noah Andre Trudeau, and Bryce A. Suderow, eds. *Supplement to the Official Records of the Union and Confederate Armies*. 100 vols. Wilmington: Broadfoot Publishing Company, 1994.

Horn, Stanley F., ed. "An Unpublished Photograph of Sam Houston." *Tennessee Historical Quarterly* 3, no. 4 (December 1944): 349–351.

Index to the Andrew Jackson Papers. Washington: Library of Congress, 1967.

Journal of the Congress of the Confederate States of America, 1861–1865. 7 vols. Washington: Government Printing Office, 1904.

Lindsley, John Berrien, ed. *The Military Annals of Tennessee. Confederate. First Series: Embracing a Review of Military Operations, with Regimental Histories and Memorial Rolls, Compiled from Original and Official Sources*. Nashville: J.M. Lindsley & Co., Publishers, 1886.

Lowrie, Walter, and Matthew St. Clair Clarke, eds. *American State Papers. Documents, Legislative and Executive, of the Congress of the United States, From the First Session of the First to the Second Session of the Fifteenth Congress, Inclusive: Commencing March 3, 1789, and Ending March 3, 1819. Class V. Military Affairs*. Washington: Gales and Seaton, 1832.

Lucas, Silas Emmett Jr., ed. *Marriage Record Book I: January 2, 1789–December 13, 1837, Davidson County, Tennessee*. Easley: Southern Historical Press, 1979.

Mansfield, E. D. *Personal Memories, Social, Political, and Literary, with Sketches of Many Noted People, 1803–1843*. Cincinnati: Robert Clarke & Co., 1879.

Patton, Juanita, abstractor. *Lands, Slaves, and Other Courthouse Transactions 1808–1863: Abstracts of Sumner County, Tennessee*. Gallatin: Sumner County Archives, 2005.

Pippenger, Wesley E., comp. *District of Columbia Marriage Licenses Register 1, 1811–1858*. Westminster: Family Line Publications, 1994.

Quintard, Charles Todd. *Doctor Quintard: Chaplain C.S.A. and Second Bishop of Tennessee, Being His Story of the War (1861–1865)*. ed. Arthur Howard Noll. Sewanee, Tennessee: The University Press of Sewanee, Tennessee, 1905.

Richardson, James D., editor and compiler. *A Compilation of the Messages and Papers of the Presidents, 1789–1897*. 10 vols. Washington: Government Printing Office, 1896–1899.

Savage, John H. *The Life of John H. Savage: Citizen, Soldier, Lawyer, Congressman, Before the War Begun and Prosecuted by the Abolitionists of the Northern States to Reduce the Descendants of the Rebels of 1776, who Defeated the Armies of the King of England and gained Independence for the United States, Down to the Level of the Negro Race.* Nashville: Printed for the Author, 1903.

Sioussat, St. George L., ed. "Selected Letters, 1844–1845, from the Donelson Papers." *Tennessee Historical Magazine* 3, no. 2 (June 1917): 134–162.

Sistler, Byron and Barbara. *Early Middle Tennessee Marriages*. 2 vols. Nashville: Byron Sistler & Associates, Inc., 1988.

Smith, Sam B., Harold D. Moser, and Daniel Feller, et al., eds. *The Papers of Andrew Jackson*. 11 vols. to-date. Knoxville: The University of Tennessee Press, 1980–2019.

U.S. Bureau of the Census. Washington, D.C. *Population Schedules of the Sixth Census of the United States, 1840. Tennessee*, Vol. 9 (214–433): Smith, Stewart, and Sumner Counties, 214-433. NARA Record Group 29, Microfilm Publication no. 704, roll 534. Washington: National Archives and Records Administration.

———. *Population Schedules of the Seventh Census of the United States, 1850. First Series: White and Free Colored Population, Tennessee*: Sullivan, Sumner, Tipton, and Van Buren Counties. NARA Record Group 29, Microfilm Publication no. M432, roll 897. Washington: National Archives and Records Administration.

———. *Population Schedules of the Seventh Census of the United States, 1850. Tennessee (Slave Schedules)*: Smith, Stewart, Sullivan, Sumner, Tipton, Van Buren, Warren, Washington, Wayne, Weakley, White, Williamson, and Wilson Counties. NARA Record Group 29, Microfilm Publication no. M432, roll 907. Washington: National Archives and Records Administration.

———. *Population Schedules of the Eighth Census of the United States, 1860. Tennessee*, Vol. 19 (1–342): Sullivan and Sumner Counties. NARA Record Group 29, Microfilm Publication no. M653, roll 1275. Washington: National Archives and Records Administration.

———. *Population Schedules of the Eighth Census of the United States, 1860. Tennessee (Slave Schedules)*, Vol. 3 (312–316): Sumner, Tipton, Van Buren, Warren, Washington, Wayne, Weakley, White, Williamson, and Wilson Counties. NARA Record Group 29, Microfilm Publication no. M653, roll 1286. Washington: National Archives and Records Administration.

U.S. War Department. *The War of the Rebellion: A Compilation of the Official Records of the Union and Confederate Armies*. 130 serial vols. Government Printing Office, Washington, D.C., 1880–1901.

Weaver, Herbert, et al., eds. *Correspondence of James K. Polk*. 14 vols. Nashville: Vanderbilt University Press, 1967–1989 and Knoxville: The University of Tennessee Press, 1993–2021.

Whitley, Edith Rucker, comp. *Marriages of Sumner County, Tennessee, 1787–1838*. Baltimore: Genealogical Publishing Co., Inc., 1981.

Womack, James J. *The Civil War Diary of Capt. J.J. Womack, Co. E, Sixteenth Regiment, Tennessee Volunteers (Confederate)*. McMinnville: Womack Printing Company, 1961.

Wright, Marcus J., comp. *Tennessee in the War, 1861–1865*. New York: Ambrose Lee Publishing Company, 1908.

Secondary Sources

Abernethy, Thomas P. *From Frontier to Plantation in Tennessee: A Study in Frontier Democracy*. Chapel Hill: The University of North Carolina Press, 1932.

Ambrose, Stephen E. *Duty, Honor, Country: A History of West Point*. Baltimore: Johns Hopkins Press, 1966.

Anbinder, Tyler. *Nativism and Slavery: The Northern Know Nothings and the Politics of the 1850s*. New York: Oxford University Press, 1992.

Armstrong, Zella, comp. *Notable Southern Families* 2. Chattanooga: The Lookout Publishing Co., 1922.

Ash, Stephen V. *Middle Tennessee Society Transformed, 1860–1870: War and Peace in the Upper South*. Baton Rouge: Louisiana State University Press, 1988.

———. *When the Yankees Came: Conflict and Chaos in the Occupied South, 1861–1865*. Chapel Hill: The University of North Carolina Press, 1995.

Atkins, Jonathan M. *Parties, Politics, and the Sectional Conflict in Tennessee, 1832–1861.* Knoxville: The University of Tennessee Press, 1997.
Ballard, Michael B. *Pemberton: A Biography.* Jackson: University Press of Mississippi, 1991.
Baptist, Edward E. *Creating an Old South: Middle Florida's Plantation Frontier Before the Civil War.* Chapel Hill: The University of North Carolina Press, 2002.
Belko, William S. *Philip Pendleton Barbour in Jacksonian America: An Old Republican in King Andrew's Court.* Tuscaloosa: The University of Alabama Press, 2016.
Bergeron, Paul H. *Antebellum Politics in Tennessee.* Lexington: The University Press of Kentucky, 1982.
Bergeron, Paul H., Stephen V. Ash, and Jeanette Keith. *Tennesseans and Their History* 1ed. Knoxville: The University of Tennessee Press, 1999.
Bishop, Randy. *Civil War Generals of Tennessee.* Gretna: Pelican Publishing Company, 2013.
Booraem, Hendrik. *Young Hickory: The Making of Andrew Jackson.* Dallas: Taylor Trade Publishing, 2001.
Burke, Pauline Wilcox. *Emily Donelson of Tennessee.* 2 vols. Richmond: Garrett and Massie, Incorporated, 1941.
Burstein, Andrew. *The Passions of Andrew Jackson.* New York: Alfred A. Knopf, 2003.
Catton, Bruce. *The American Heritage Pictorial History of the Civil War.* New York: American Heritage Publishing Co., Inc., 1960.
Cheathem, Mark R. *Old Hickory's Nephew: The Political and Private Struggles of Andrew Jackson Donelson.* Baton Rouge: Louisiana State University Press, 2007.
Childers, Christopher. *The Failure of Popular Sovereignty: Slavery, Manifest Destiny, and the Radicalization of Southern Politics.* Lawrence: University Press of Kansas, 2012.
Clayton, W.W. *History of Davidson County, Tennessee, with Illustrations and Biographical Sketches of its Prominent Men and Pioneers.* Philadelphia: J.W. Lewis & Co., 1880.
Cole, Donald B. *Martin Van Buren and the American Political System.* Princeton: Princeton University Press, 1984.
Connelly, Thomas Lawrence. *Army of the Heartland. The Army of Tennessee, 1861–1862.* Baton Rouge: Louisiana State University Press, 1967.
———. *Autumn of Glory: The Army of Tennessee, 1862–1865.* Baton Rouge: Louisiana State University Press, 1971.
Corlew, Robert E. *Tennessee: A Short History* 2ed. Knoxville: The University of Tennessee Press, 1981.
Cozzens, Peter. *No Better Place to Die: The Battle of Stones River.* Urbana: University of Illinois Press, 1990.
Crofts, Daniel W. *Reluctant Confederates: Upper South Unionists in the Secession Crisis.* Chapel Hill: The University of North Carolina Press, 1989.

Cullum, George W. *Biographical Register of the Officers and Graduates of the U. S. Military Academy at West Point, N. Y., from its Establishment, in 1802 to 1890, with the Early History of the United States Military Academy* 3ed., 3 vols. Boston: Houghton, Mifflin and Company, 1891.

Daniel, Larry J. *Battle of Stones River: The Forgotten Conflict between the Confederate Army of Tennessee and the Union Army of the Cumberland.* Baton Rouge: Louisiana State University Press, 2012.

———. *Conquered: Why the Army of Tennessee Failed.* Chapel Hill: The University of North Carolina Press, 2019.

Davis, Burke. *Our Incredible Civil War.* New York: Holt, Rinehart, and Winston, Inc., 1960.

Davis, William C. *Jefferson Davis: The Man and His Hour.* New York: Harper Collins Publishers, 1991.

Dollar, Kent T., Larry H. Whiteaker, and W. Calvin Dickinson, eds. *Border Wars: The Civil War in Tennessee and Kentucky.* Kent: Kent State University Press, 2015.

Drake, James Vaulx. *Life of General Robert Hatton, Including His Most Important Public Speeches; Together, with Much of His Washington & Army Correspondence.* Nashville: Marshall & Bruce, 1867.

Drexler, Robert W. *Guilty of Making Peace: A Biography of Nicholas P. Trist.* Lanham: University Press of America, Inc., 1991.

Durham, Walter T. *The Great Leap Westward: A History of Sumner County, Tennessee, From Its Beginnings to 1805.* Gallatin: Sumner County Public Library Board, 1969.

———. *Old Sumner: A History of Sumner County, Tennessee, from 1805 to 1861.* Gallatin: Sumner County Public Library Board, 1972.

———. *Daniel Smith, Frontier Statesman.* Gallatin: Sumner County Public Library Board, 1976.

———. *Rebellion Revisited: A History of Sumner County, Tennessee, from 1861 to 1870.* Franklin: Hillsboro Press, 1999.

———. *Nashville: The Occupied City, 1862–1863.* Knoxville: University of Tennessee Press, 2008.

———. *The Life of William Trousdale: Soldier, Statesman, Diplomat, 1790–1872.* Gallatin: United Daughters of the Confederacy, 2001.

———. *Josephus Conn Guild and Rose Mont: Politics and Plantation in Nineteenth Century Tennessee.* Franklin: Hillsboro Press, 2002.

———. *Balie Peyton of Tennessee: Nineteenth Century Politics and Thoroughbreds.* Franklin: Hillsboro Press, 2004.

Elliott, Sam Davis. *Soldier of Tennessee: General Alexander P. Stewart and the Civil War in the West.* Baton Rouge: Louisiana State University Press, 1999.

———. *Isham G. Harris of Tennessee: Confederate Governor and United States Senator.* Baton Rouge: Louisiana State University Press, 2010.

Ellis, Richard E. *The Union at Risk: Jacksonian Democracy, States' Rights, and the Nullification Crisis.* New York: Oxford University Press, 1987.
Evans, Clement A., ed. *Confederate Military History.* 12 vols. Atlanta: Confederate Publishing Company, 1899.
Finger, John R. *Tennessee Frontiers: Three Regions in Transition.* Bloomington: Indiana University Press, 2001.
Fisher, Noel C. *War at Every Door: Partisan Politics and Guerrilla Violence in East Tennessee, 1860–1869.* Chapel Hill: The University of North Carolina Press, 1997.
Freeman, Douglas Southall. *R. E. Lee: A Biography.* 4 vols. New York: Charles Scribner's Sons, 1934–1935.
———. *Lee's Lieutenants: A Study in Command.* 3 vols. New York: Charles Scribner's Sons, 1942–1944.
Goodstein, Anita Shafer. *Nashville, 1780–1860: From Frontier to City.* Gainesville: University of Florida Press, 1989.
Greenberg, Amy S. *Lady First: The World of First Lady Sarah Polk.* New York: Alfred A. Knopf, 2019.
Haley, James L. *Sam Houston.* Norman: University of Oklahoma Press, 2002.
Heller, J. Roderick III. *Democracy's Lawyer: Felix Grundy of the Old Southwest.* Baton Rouge: Louisiana State University Press, 2010.
Hess, Earl J. *Banners to the Breeze: The Kentucky Campaign, Corinth, and Stones River.* Lincoln: University of Nebraska Press, 2000.
———. *Braxton Bragg: The Most Hated Man of the Confederacy.* Chapel Hill: The University of North Carolina Press, 2016.
Holt, Michael F. *The Rise and Fall of the American Whig Party: Jacksonian Politics and the Onset of the Civil War.* New York: Oxford University Press, 1999.
Horn, Stanley F., Commission chairman. *Tennesseans in the Civil War: A Military History of Confederate and Union Units with Available Rosters of Personnel*, Parts I and II. Nashville: Civil War Centennial Commission, 1964–1965.
Hughes, Nathaniel Cheairs Jr. *General William J. Hardee: Old Reliable.* Baton Rouge: Louisiana State University Press, 1965.
Hughes, Nathaniel Cheairs Jr., and Roy P. Stonesifer Jr. *The Life and Wars of Gideon J. Pillow.* Chapel Hill: The University of North Carolina Press, 1993.
Jacob, Kathryn A., and Bruce A. Ragsdale, eds.-in-chief. *Biographical Directory of the United States Congress, 1774–1989. Bicentennial Edition. The Continental Congress, September 5, 1774, to October 21, 1788, and the Congress of the United States from the First to the One Hundredth Congress, March 4, 1789, to January 3, 1989, Inclusive.* Washington: United States Government Printing Office, 1989.
James, Marquis. *The Raven: A Biography of Sam Houston.* Indianapolis: Bobbs-Merrill Co., Publishers, 1929.
———. *The Life of Andrew Jackson.* New York: Garden City Publishing Co., Inc., 1940.

Jennings, Thelma. *The Nashville Convention: Southern Movement for Unity, 1848–1850.* Memphis: Memphis State University Press, 1980.
Johnson, Allen, and Dumas Malone, eds. *Dictionary of American Biography.* 20 vols. New York: Charles Scribner's Sons, 1928–1936.
Langsdon, Philip. *Tennessee: A Political History.* Franklin: Hillsboro Press, 2000.
Latner, Richard B. *The Presidency of Andrew Jackson: White House Politics, 1829–1837.* Athens: The University of Georgia Press, 1979.
Link, Willam A. *Roots of Secession: Slavery and Politics in Antebellum Virginia.* Chapel Hill: The University of North Carolina Press, 2003.
Losson, Christopher. *Tennessee's Forgotten Warriors: Frank Cheatham and His Confederate Division.* Knoxville: The University of Tennessee Press, 1989.
Malone, Dumas. *Jefferson and the Ordeal of Liberty.* Boston: Little, Brown, and Company, 1962.
Marszalek, John F. *The Petticoat Affair: Manners, Mutiny, and Sex in Andrew Jackson's White House.* New York: The Free Press, 1997.
———. *Commander of All Lincoln's Armies: A Life of General Henry W. Halleck.* Cambridge: Harvard University Press, 2004.
McBride, Robert M., Dan M. Robison, and Ilene J. Cornwell, eds. *Biographical Directory of the Tennessee General Assembly.* 6 vols. Nashville: Tennessee Historical Commission, 1975–1990.
McKinney, Gordon B. *Zeb Vance: North Carolina's Civil War Governor and Gilded Age Political Leader.* Chapel Hill: The University of North Carolina Press, 2004.
McWhiney, Grady. *Braxton Bragg and Confederate Defeat.* Tuscaloosa: The University of Alabama Press, 1969.
Morrison, Michael R. *Slavery and the American West: The Eclipse of Manifest Destiny and the Coming of the Civil War.* Chapel Hill: The University of North Carolina Press, 1997.
Nevins, Allan. *Ordeal of the Union.* 2 vols. New York: Charles Scribner's Sons, 1947.
———. *The Emergence of Lincoln.* 2 vols. New York: Charles Scribner's Sons, 1950.
Newell, Clayton R. *Lee vs. McClellan: The First Campaign.* Washington: Regency Publishing, Inc., 1996.
Nichols, Roy Franklin. *The Democratic Machine, 1850–1854.* New York: Columbia University Press, 1923.
Noe, Kenneth W. *Perryville: This Grand Havoc of Battle.* Lexington: The University Press of Kentucky, 2001.
Overdyke, W. Darrell. *The Know-Nothing Party in the South.* Baton Rouge: Louisiana State University Press, 1950.
Pappas, George S. *To the Point. The United States Military Academy, 1802–1902.* Westport: Praeger Publishers, 1993.
Parks, Joseph Howard. *John Bell of Tennessee.* Baton Rouge: Louisiana State University Press, 1950.

———. *General Leonidas Polk, C.S.A.: The Fighting Bishop*. Baton Rouge: Louisiana State University Press, 1962.
Parsons, Lynn Hudson. *The Birth of Modern Politics: Andrew Jackson, John Quincy Adams, and the Election of 1828*. New York: Oxford University Press, 2009.
Pfanz, Donald C. *Richard S. Ewell: A Soldier's Life*. Chapel Hill: The University of North Carolina Press, 1998.
Powell, William S., ed. *Dictionary of North Carolina Biography*. 6 vols. Chapel Hill: The University of North Carolina Press, 1996.
Ramsey, J.G.M. *The Annals of Tennessee to the End of the Eighteenth Century*. Philadelphia: Lippincott, Grambo & Co., 1853.
Ray, Kristofer. *Middle Tennessee, 1775–1825: Progress and Popular Democracy on the Southwestern Frontier*. Knoxville: The University of Tennessee Press, 2007.
Reeves, Jesse S. *American Diplomacy under Tyler and Polk*. Baltimore: Johns Hopkins University Press, 1907.
Remini, Robert V. *Andrew Jackson and the Course of American Empire, 1767–1821*. New York: Harper & Row, Publishers, 1977.
———. *Andrew Jackson and the Course of American Freedom, 1822–1832*. New York: Harper & Row, Publishers, 1981.
———. *Andrew Jackson and the Course of American Democracy, 1833–1845*. New York: Harper & Row, Publishers, 1984.
Rothman, Adam. *Slave Country: American Expansion and the Origin of the Deep South*. Cambridge: Harvard University Press, 2005.
Sanders, Stuart W. *Maney's Confederate Brigade at the Battle of Perryville*. Charleston: The History Press, 2014.
Satterfield, R. Beeler. *Andrew Jackson Donelson: Jackson's Confidant and Political Heir*. Bowling Green: Hickory Tales, 2000.
Sellers, Charles G. *James K. Polk: Jacksonian, 1795–1843*. Princeton: Princeton University Press, 1957.
———. *James K. Polk: Continentalist, 1843–1846*. Princeton: Princeton University Press, 1966.
Smith, Timothy B. *Shiloh: Conquer or Perish*. Lawrence: University Press of Kansas, 2014.
———. *Grant Invades Tennessee: The 1862 Battles for Forts Henry and Donelson*. Lawrence: University Press of Kansas, 2016.
Spence, Richard Douglas. *Andrew Jackson Donelson: Jacksonian and Unionist*. Nashville: Vanderbilt University Press, 2017.
Stampp, Kenneth M. *America in 1857: A Nation on the Brink*. New York: Oxford University Press, 1990.
Stoker, Donald. *The Grand Design: Strategy and the U.S. Civil War*. New York: Oxford University Press, 2010.
Summers, Mark W. *The Plundering Generation: Corruption and the Crisis of the Union*. New York: Oxford University Press, 1982.

Symonds, Craig L. *Stonewall of the West: Patrick Cleburne and the Civil War.* Lawrence: University Press of Kansas, 1997.
Temple, Oliver P. *East Tennessee and the Civil War.* Cincinnati: The Robert Clarke Company, Publishers, 1899.
Trefousse, Hans L. *Andrew Johnson: A Biography.* New York: W.W. Norton & Company, 1989.
Venner, William Thomas. *The 7th Tennessee in the Civil War: A History and a Roster.* Jefferson: McFarland & Company, Inc., Publishers, 2013.
Valenčius, Conevery Bolton. *The Health of the Country: How American Settlers Understood Themselves and Their Land.* New York: Basic Books, 2002.
Walther, Eric H. *The Fire-Eaters.* Baton Rouge: Louisiana State University Press, 1992.
Warner, Ezra J. *Generals in Gray: Lives of the Confederate Commanders.* Baton Rouge: Louisiana State University Press, 1959.
———. *Generals in Blue: Lives of the Union Commanders.* Baton Rouge: Louisiana State University Press, 1964.
Welsh, Jack D. *Medical Histories of Confederate Generals.* Kent: Kent State University Press, 1995.
West, Carroll Van, editor-in-chief. *The Tennessee Encyclopedia of History and Culture.* Nashville: Rutledge Hill Press, 1998.
Williams, T. Harry. *P.G.T. Beauregard: Napoleon in Gray.* Baton Rouge: Louisiana State University Press, 1955.
Wiltse, Charles M. *John C. Calhoun.* 3 vols. Indianapolis: The Bobbs-Merrill Company, Inc., 1944–1951.
Winders, Richard Bruce. *Mr. Polk's Army: The American Military Experience in the Mexican War.* College Station: Texas A&M University Press, 1997.
Zinn, Jack. *R.E. Lee's Cheat Mountain Campaign.* Parsons: McClain Printing Company, 1974.

JOURNAL ARTICLES

Atkins, Jonathan M. "The Presidential Candidacy of Hugh Lawson White, 1832–1836." *The Journal of Southern History* 58, no. 1 (February 1992): 27–56.
Bearss, Edwin C. "The Construction of Fort Henry and Fort Donelson." *The West Tennessee Historical Society Papers*, no. 21 (1967): 24–47.
Chappell, Gordon T. "The Life and Activities of General John Coffee." *Tennessee Historical Quarterly* 1, no. 2 (September 1942): 125–146.
Cheathem, Mark R. "'Sam Houston,' by James L. Haley." Book review. *Tennessee Historical Quarterly* 62, no. 3 (Fall 2003): 285–286.
Downing, Marvin. "John Christmas McLemore: 19th Century Land Speculator." *Tennessee Historical Quarterly* 42, no. 3 (Fall 1983): 254–265.
Downing, Marvin. "An Admiring Nephew-in-Law: John Christmas McLemore

and His Relationship to 'Uncle' Andrew Jackson." *The West Tennessee Historical Society Papers* 44 (December 1990): 38–47.

Gadski, Mary Ellen. "The Tennessee State Capitol: An Architectural History." *Tennessee Historical Quarterly* 47, no. 2 (Summer 1988): 67–120.

Galloway, Linda Bennett. "Andrew Jackson, Junior." *Tennessee Historical Quarterly* 9, no. 3 (September 1950): Part 1, 195–216 and no. 4 (December 1950): Part 2, 306–343.

Riley, Harris D. Jr. "A Gallant Adopted Son of Tennessee—General John C. Carter, C.S.A." *Tennessee Historical Quarterly* 48, no. 4 (Winter 1989): 195–208.

Schweikart, Larry. "Tennessee Banks in the Antebellum Period, Part II." *Tennessee Historical Quarterly* 45, no. 3 (Fall 1986): 199–209.

Sikes, Lewright B. "Gustavus Adolphus Henry: Champion of Lost Causes." *Tennessee Historical Quarterly* 50, no. 3 (Fall 1991): 173–182.

Sioussat, St. George L. "Tennessee, the Compromise of 1850, and the Nashville Convention." *Tennessee Historical Magazine* 4, no. 4 (December 1918): 215–247.

Spence, Richard Douglas. "John Donelson and the Opening of the Old Southwest." *Tennessee Historical Quarterly* 50, no. 3 (Fall 1991): 157–172.

Spence, Richard Douglas. "Samuel Donelson. The Young Andrew Jackson's Best Friend." *Tennessee Historical Quarterly* 69, no. 2 (Summer 2010): 106–123.

Thweatt, John H. "James Priestley: Classical Scholar of the Old South." *Tennessee Historical Quarterly* 39, no. 4 (Winter 1980): 423–439.

Woolverton, John F. "Philip Lindsley and the Cause of Education in the Old Southwest." *Tennessee Historical Quarterly* 19, no. 1 (March 1960): 3–22.

INDEX

Page numbers in **boldface** refer to illustrations.

acknowledgments, xii–xiii
Adams, Daniel W., 148, 151
Adams, John Quincy, 15
African Americans, 23, 37, 39, 57, 110, 132, 138
Alabama: and Army of the Ohio, 119; Buell's withdraw from, 120; and cultivation of cotton, 61–62; and Jackson's land speculation, 9; and Jacky's death, 7; and John Coffee as surveyor, 20; and Mobile, 115, 139; and Montgomery, 84; and settlement of Big Bend of Tennessee River, 19–20
Alexander, Jennie, 168–69
Allen, B. F., 71
Allen, Eliza, 22, 23
American Party, 63, 64, 65, 66–67, 68, 69, 70. *See also* Donelson, Andrew Jackson; United States
Anderson, Adna, 97
Anderson, James Patton, 122, 123
Anderson, John H., 144, 145, 147, 151
Anderson, Joseph, 5
Anderson, Robert, 16, 95
Anderson, Samuel R., 96, 97, 98, 100, 101, 102, 104
Anderson, William Preston, 21
Armstrong, Robert H., 44, 48, 49, 50
Avant, J. W., 83

Bache, Alexander Dallas, 16
Bacot, Captain W. C., 117

Bank of the United States, 40, 49
Barbour, Philip P., 33, 73
Barrow, Washington, 41, 42
Barry, Thomas R., 46, 48, 49
Bate, William B., 96, 156, 175
Beauregard, Pierre G. T., 99, 112, 113, 115, 116, 118, 119
Bell, John, 40–42 *passim*, 44, 49, 71, 76, 82, 83. *See also* Donelson, Andrew Jackson; Kentucky; Tennessee; Virginia
Benjamin, Judah P., 104–5, 107
Berrien, John M., 25, 29
Berry, Nannie Smith, 169
Bradford, Priestly, 45
Bradford, William Henry, 80
Bragg, Braxton: **92**; and Army of Tennessee, 137, 138, 139; and Battle of Mufreesboro, 142, 147, 152; and command of Army of Mississippi, 119, 120, 121–24, 125, 128, 130, 133–35; and Murfreesboro's geography, 140; and officers' promotions, 135
Branch, Eliza Foort, 24, 60
Branch, John: **89**; and Andrew Jackson, 72; and cabinet purge, 32; and Daniel Donelson, 57, 85, 88, 105, 106, 173; and daughter Margaret, 28, 35, 88, 113, 118; death of, 166; dismissal of, 31, 85; and Eaton affair, 88; and North Carolina's government, 24; and nullification controversy, 34; plantation of, 37;

Branch, John (cont.)
portrait of, 168; resignation of, 29, 88; as Secretary of the Navy, 24, 25, 28, 29, 88; and wife Eliza, 24
Branch, John (son), 47–48
Branch, Margaret, 24, 25–27. *See also* Donelson, Daniel Smith; Donelson, Margaret Branch
Branch, William, 166, 167
Breckinridge, John C., 83, 147, 149, 153, 163
Brewer, C. C., 105
Brown, Aaron V., 62, 69
Brown, John Calvin, 129
Brown, Neill S., 62, 66–67, 68, 69, 77
Buchanan, James, 71, 81, 82, 83, 104
Buckner, Simon Bolivar, 123, 128, 134, 139
Buell, Don Carlos, 116, 119, 120, 121, 122, 138
Burford, David, 30, 31–32, 49, 50
Burr, Aaron, 21
Burton, Robert M., 29–32 *passim*, 41, 48, 49, 54, 173
Butcher, Oscar, 101–2
Butler, Robert, 41–42

Caesar, Julius, 61
Calhoun, John C., 9, 10, 25, 29, 30, 32, 34. *See also* Jackson, Andrew; United States
California, 57–58, 70
Campbell, William B., 62
Cannon, Newton, 42, 44
Carlisle, John G., 169
Carnes, William W., artillery battery of, 117, 121, 124–25, 129, 130, 137, 143, 146, 148, 153; and Battle of Murfreesboro, 143, 146, 148, 153. *See also* Confederate States of America
Carr, Thomas, 20

Carroll, Willis G., 45
Carter, John C., 119, 126, 140, 143
Caruthers, Robert Looney, 19, 29–32 *passim*, 38, 41, 44–46, 69–70, 77. *See also* Donelson, Daniel Smith
Cass, Lewis, 61
Chalmers, James R., 141, 142, 143, 144, 145, 147, 148
Cheatham, Benjamin Franklin: **92**; battlefield conduct of, 92, 131, 132, 133; and Battle of Belmont, 116; and Battle of Murfreesboro (or Stones River), 140, 141, 142; and Battle of Perryville, 123, 124, 125, 126–27, 128, 129, 131, 132, 133; as brigadier general, 97, 116; and criticism of Bragg, 134; and Daniel Donelson, 97, 117, 174; and First Brigade of the Second Division, 116, 119, 120, 121, 122, 123, 125, 137; and Murfreesboro, 138; troops of, 119, 137, 138, 153
Chester, John, 119, 143, 144, 146
Civil War: and Antietam, 12; and Battle of Murfreesboro (or Stones River), xi, xii, **136**, 142–51; and Battle of Perryville, xi, xii, **114**, 122–33; and Battle of Shiloh, 16, 112, 115, 116, 117, 119; beginning of, 95; casualties from, 130, 131, 146, 147, 149–50, 152, 153; and Cowan house, 142, 144–46, 147, 148, 149, 150, 151, 152; and Daniel Donelson, 11, 85, 96, 97–98, 99, 100, 101–4, 109, 110–13, 115–16, 117, 118, 121–35, 142–53, 168, 172, 174–75; deaths from, 130–31, 146, 147, 149–50, 152, 153; and eastern theater campaigns, 166; and Engagement at Port Royal Ferry, 108–9; and Fort Sumter, 95; and freed slaves, 167; and General

Braxton Bragg, 133–34; and Gettysburg, 12; and James Martin, 129; military history of, xiii, 133–35; and Mill Springs clash, 110–11; and pillaging of Hazel Path, 90, 167, 172; popularity of, xi; prisoners of, 103, 151; and Second Battle of Manassas, 163; soldiers in, 11–12, 16, 90, 95, 96, 97, 98–105, 106, 107, 108, 110, 111, 112–13, 115–16, 119, 120–22, 123, 128–33, 134, 137–38, 141–51; songs of, 141; and surrender at Appomattox, 166; and Tennessee, 95, 97, 98, 99, 111, 137, 138, 141, 146, 157–58; and Tennessee forces, 143–46; and weather, 100, 102, 105, 106, 138, 141, 149, 152, 156; Western Theater in, **94**. *See also* Confederate States of America; Kentucky; Union; Virginia

Clay, Henry, 15, 25, 33, 35, 51, 52

Clayton, W. W., 9, 24, 43, 85, 156, 164, 174

Cleburne, Patrick R., 128, 135, 139, 142, 174

Coffee, John, 20, 22, 27, 31

Compromise of 1850, 59, 60–61

Confederate States of America: as aggressor in Civil War, 116; and Albert Sidney Johnston, 16, 105–6; and Alexander P. Stewart, 148, 149; Army of, 97–99, 104, 106, 110, 115, 116, 119, 122, 124, 125–35, 137–51, 152, 153, 155–56, 158–59, 165, 174; and Army of Northern Virginia, 163, 166; and Battle of Manassas (Bull Run), 99; and Battle of Murfreesboro (or Stones River), 140–51, 155; and Battle of Perryville, **114**, 123–33; and Battle of Shiloh, 117, 119; and Captain Felix Robertson, 141; and Carnes' battery, 153; cavalry of, 158, 159, 160, 161, 165; and Colonel John Savage, 120, 121, 126, 127, 128, 131–33, 140, 143, 144, 146, 147, 148, 150–51, 156; Congress of, 97, 134, 137, 159, 160, 165–66; and Daniel Donelson's sons, 166; and Danville depot, 122; and defeat at Mill Springs, 110–11; and Department of East Tennessee, 161, 163, 166; and Department of Western Virginia, 158, 160; and East Tennessee, 157–59, 161; and Eighth Tennessee Infantry regiment, 145–46, 147, 150; and Engagement at Port Royal Ferry, 108–9; and General Braxton Bragg, 92, 130, 133–34, 135, 137, 138, 139, 140, 142, 147, 152, 153, 155, 156, 160, 161, 163, 165, 174, 175; and General Daniel Donelson, **90**, **92**, 118, 151, 155, 159, 164, 165, 174; and General William Bate, 175; and Hardee's corps, 155; and James C. Jones, 108; and Jefferson Davis, 16, 84, 97, 155; and John C. Pemberton, 107–8; and Jones M. Withers, 153; and Joseph E. Johnston, 162, 163; and Kentucky, 120, 122, 128, 134, 135, 158, 159, 160, 161, 162; and killing of escaped slaves, 109–10; and leaders' battle reports, 131–33; and Leonidas Polk, 91, 116, 117, 123, 124, 125, 131, 134, 137, 138, 139, 140, 141, 142, 143, 146, 148, 149, 150, 151, 152, 155, 166, 174; and Lt. Colonel D. M. Donnell, 128; newspapers in, 134, 138, 156–57, 166; and North Carolina Infantry Regiment, 148–49; and Pittsburg Landing, 112; and Preston Smith's brigade, 140–41; and reinforcements for

Confederate States of America (*cont.*)
Beauregard, 112–13; and Richmond, 106, 119, 152, 155, 157, 160, 161, 162; and Sixteenth Tennessee Infantry regiment, 100, 115, 121, 129, 137, 138, 140, 141, 143, 146, 147, 148, 149, 150–51; and Tennessee, 119, 137–38, 161, 162, 163, 174; and Tennessee forces, 97–99, 100, 107, 115, 129, 130–31, 137–38, 140–41, 143, 145–49, 150, 153, 166; unionists in, 162; and Virginia, 98, 108; War Department of, 162. *See also* Davis, Jefferson; Donelson, Daniel Smith; Lee, Robert E.; Mississippi
Connecticut, 12
Cooper, Samuel, 98, 105, 106, 160, 161–62, 163
Crittenden, Thomas L., 123
Cryer, Hardy M., 31
Cumberland College, 7, 8

Daily Nashville Patriot (newspaper), 72, 73, 74, 75–76
Daily Union (newspaper), 60
Daughtrey, Joel H., 47
Davis, Jefferson: and Andrew Donelson, 139–40; character of, 139; and Daniel Donelson, 160, 162; as president of Confederate States of America, 16, 84, 97, 112, 116, 119, 139, 155, 160, 161, 162; and Robert E. Lee, 99. *See also* Confederate States of America
Davis, J. Lucius, 105
Davis, William G. M., 163–64
Democratic Party: and Alfred Osborne Pope Nicholson, 76; and Andrew Donelson, xii, 60, 63–64, 69, 70, 88; and Andrew Jackson, 71; and annexation of Texas, 51, 52; and B. F. Allen, 71; and Daniel Donelson, xii, 46–47, 48, 49, 50, 58, 64, 65, 69, 70, 71, 72–73, 74, 75, 82, 83, 88; and David Burford, 49, 50; and the Deep South, 62, 83; and Democratic House majority, 75–77; and Democratic National Convention, 51, 61, 81–83; factions of, 81; and Franklin Pierce, 61; and immigrants, 63; and Isham Green Harris, 71, 72; and Jacksonians, 45, 73; and James Buchanan, 71; and James K. Polk, 44–45, 46, 47, 48, 49, 50, 51; and Josephus Conn Guild, 48; and J. S. Dyer, 71; and Know-Nothing movement, 64, 65; and Martin Van Buren, 47, 51; moderate center of, 60; *Nashville Union* (newspaper), 47; and Northern free-soilers, 60; and presidential election of 1856, 70; rise of, 39; and Sam Houston, 53; and secession from the Union, 95; and slavery, 62–63; and Southern states' rightists, 60, 63, 82, 139; split in, 61; and Tennessee, 44–47, 48, 50, 61, 62, 64–66, 69–72, 75–77, 80; and Thomas R. Barry, 46; and turnpikes and railroads, 45; and unionists, 84
Desha, Robert, 23, 29, 30, 31, 32, 48, 49, 179. *See also* Donelson, Daniel Smith
Dillard, H. H., 99, 105, 109, 111, 174
Dismukes, David, 168
Dismukes, Marcus Lafayette, 167
Donelson, Andrew Jackson (brother): **89,** 166; and Andrew Jackson, xi–xii 6, 7, 10, 11, 12, 13–14, 15, 20, 21, 27, 28, 31, 51, 81, 171, 172; and *Andrew Jackson Donelson: Jacksonian*

and Unionist (Spence), xii; and aunt Rachel Jackson, 15; and Bank War, 40; as brigade major, 21; brothers-in-law of, 19; charges of sedition for, 139–40; children of, 53, 111; and Colonel John Donelson's land, 20; and Constitutional Union party, 82; and cotton plantations, 52, 77; and Cumberland College, 7; and *The Daily Union* (newspaper), 60; and Daniel Donelson, 33, 45–46, 52, 63, 65, 70, 72–73, 88, 97, 111; and Davidson tract of land, 17; and death of Martha Watson, 32; as a delegate, 48; and Democratic National Convention, 51; diplomatic career of, 53, 54, 55; early life of, 172; and the Eaton scandal, 25, 26, 27, 28, 29, 32, 173; education of, 6, 7, 8–9, 11; as Fillmore's running mate, 69; financial affairs of, 45–46, 51, 53, 55, 60, 81, 172; and Harry Smith, 167; and the Hermitage, 171, 172; and Hugh Lawson White, 41; and Jacky's death, 7; and James Sanders, 17–19, 43; and John Bell, 82; and land purchase, 38; as leading member of American Party, 139; letters of, 11, 14, 53; and mother's death, 77; naming of, 5; and Nashville Convention, 59–60; and nullification controversy, 34, 35; as a politician, xi, 69, 70, 72–73; and Poplar Grove, 43; as President Jackson's secretary, 22, 27, 41–42; and Republic of Texas, 51, 52; and secession from the Union, 85; and slaves, 59; sons of, 46, 96, 111, 141; and Sumner tract of land, 17–19; and Tennessee's rights, 84–85; and Tennessee state militia, 21, 23; and Transylvania University law school, 12, 14; and unionism, 59, 96, 139–40; and US Military Academy in West Point, 7, 8–9, 10, 11, 15, 172; and Washington, D.C., 24, 27, 44; and the Washington *Union* (newspaper), 139; and wife Elizabeth, 46, 51, 53, 60, 111; and wife Emily, 15, 22, 25, 27, 28, 43, 46, 173. *See also* Tulip Grove

Donelson, Captain John (uncle), 15, 20

Donelson, Daniel Smith, **87**; additional troops for, 116–17, 151; and Alfred Royal Wynne, 67; ancestry of, 1; and Andrew Donelson, 33, 34, 37, 38, 39, 41–42, 45–46, 51, 52, 53, 55, 65, 70, 73–74, 81, 139, 171, 173; and Andrew Jackson, xi–xii, 6, 10, 12, 13, 14, 21, 26, 27, 28, 33, 35, 48, 51, 52–53, 72–73, 74, 81, 171, 172, 173; and antebellum South, xiii, 38; and Army of the Northwest, 98; and Battle of Murfreesboro (or Stones River), 140–52, 156; and Battle of Perryville, 114, 123, 125, 126–29, 130–33; birth of, 5; birthplace of, 19, 43, 167, 168; and Branch family, 70, 80, 83; bravery of, 174; as brevet Second Lieutenant, 15, 17; as brigade commander, xi, xiii, xxi, 16, 21, 107, 109, 131, 132, 134–35, 146, 149, 151–52, 156–57; brigade of, 91, 92, 100–104, 105, 106, 107, 108, 109, 110, 113, 115–21, 124, 125, 126, 127–28, 129, 130, 131, 137–38, 140, 141–50, 151, 152–53, 156, 165, 174, 175; as brigadier general for Confederate States Provisional Army, 97, 98; as brigadier general of Tennessee militia, 23, 26, 49, 90, 116; brothers-in-law of, 19, 41, 44, 64, 69, 77;

Donelson, Daniel Smith (*cont.*)
and Burton-Desha episode, 54, 173; campaign of, 47; and captured artillery and prisoners, 151; character of, 54, 164, 165, 171; children of, 38, 42–43, 46, 53–54, 59, 60, 80, 97, 106, 111, 112, 118, 157, 164, 166, 167–68, 169, 172; and the Civil War, xi, 11, 16, 97–13, 117, 165; and Colonel John Donelson's land, 20; and command in South Carolina, 112; and command of Department of East Tennessee, 155–58, 160; and command of Fifth Military District, 113; and command of Third Brigade, 99–103, 104; committees of, 67; and Compromise of 1850, 60–61; construction of houses of, 19 (Eventide), 43–44 (Elm Tree), 44, 80–81 (Hazel Path); and crossing of "Alleghanies," 101; and Cumberland Valley, 54; and daughter Elizabeth, 33, 46; and daughter Emily, 80, 166; and daughter Mary, 80; and daughter Sarah, 42–43, 80; and Davidson tract of land, 17; death of, 164–65, 166, 167, 174, 175; and death of Rachel Jackson, 22; as a delegate to state convention, 70; and Democratic Party, 173; and Department of East Tennessee, 164, 165, 166; and devotion to Confederate cause, 118; early life of, 6, 172; and East Tennessee, 92, 158–59, 160, 164; and the Eaton scandal, xi, 26–27, 29, 33, 35, 173; education of, 6, 8, 9–16, 54; and Eighth District, 50; and Eighth Tennessee Infantry regiment, 99, 103, 108, 109, 113, 116, 145; and Elm Tree, 44, 45, 52, 64, 80–81, 90; estate of, 81; and Eventide, 19, 38, 43; and examining fort sites, 97; and Ex-Governor Brown, 70; and farming, 37, 38, 39, 42, 44, 51–52, 57, 58–59, 60, 81, 172; financial affairs of, 39, 45, 46, 51–52, 57, 81, 172; and the First Division, 121–22, 124, 131; and Florida, 54, 59; and fort on Cumberland River, 16; and funds for statues, 68; funeral of, 164, 167; grandchildren of, 60, 80; and Hazel Path, 44, 80–81, 97, 111–12, 117, 118, 138, 167, 168, 169, 172; headquarters of, 110; and Hendersonville, 19, 168; and the Hermitage, 50, 85, 166, 171, 172–73; and honoring Tennessee Volunteers, 55; House seat of, 48, 49; as a Jacksonian, 41, 44, 46, 49, 73, 79, 173; and Jacksonian Democracy, 74; and James G. Martin, 139, 157, 158; and James K. Polk, 45; and James Sanders, 17–19, 43; and John Savage, 112, 132, 133; land purchases of, 37, 44; letters of, xi, 8, 11, 12, 14, 24, 26, 33, 34, 42, 53, 54, 57, 59, 74, 105, 106, 160, 161, 172, 173; and Louisville and Nashville Railroad, 57, 60, 68, 69, 111, 168; as Major General Donelson, 160, 161, 162, 165; and March to Shelbyville, 153; and Margaret Branch, 24, 25–27, 30; and Martin Van Buren, 41, 44, 73; and Montvale Springs, 164; mother of, 77–78, 172; and Nashville Convention, 58, 59–60; and *Nashville Union and American*, 98; and Nicholas Philip Trist, 11; and North Carolina, 54; and nullification controversy, 34, 35, 73, 74, 85, 173, xi; and the petticoat war, 29, 35, 173; photographs of, **90**, **92**; plantation

house of, 43–44, 90; as a politician, 46, 47, 48–50, 54, 63, 64–65, 66, 67, 68–75, 76, 77, 78–80, 82, 83, 89, 171, 173, 175; and power of attorney, 53; and promotion to major general, 135, 137, 155, 160, 162, 165–66; and property in Middle Tennessee, 111; as a public citizen, 55; public records of, 172; and regiments under Polk's command, 115–16; and rented farm, 38; and resignation from US Army commission, 19, 20; and rights of the States, 34, 85; and Robert Caruthers, 45, 46, 50, 69–70, 77; and Rock Castle, 172; and Sam Houston, 22–23, 51, 53; and secession from the Union, 85, 174; and Secretary of War John Eaton, 33; sickness of, 57, 156, 162–63, 164; and Sixteenth Tennessee Infantry regiment, 99, 103, 113, 116, 120; and slaves, 37, 39, 44, 45, 57, 58–59, 81, 138, 172; son as aide of, 120, 139, 157; as Speaker of the House of Representatives (Tenn.), 75–76, 77, 78–79, 80, 82; and speaking at rallies, 69, 70, 83; and states' rights, 73; and Sumner County, 17, 18–19, 32, 49, 50, 54, 57, 59, 60, 64–65, 67, 68, 69, 70, 71–72, 74, 77, 80, 83, 89, 110, 111, 168, 172, 175; and Sumner County victory, 72; and Sumner tract of land, 17–18, 19; and support for Jackson's policies, 33; and Tennessee state militia, 20–21, 38, 49, 54, 67, 90; and Third Artillery Regiment, 15; troops of, 159, 160, 161, 174; and US Military Academy in West Point, 9–16, 17, 18, 19, 54, 95, 101, 105–6, 116, 135, 172; and Walker Bend, xiii, 126; and Washington,

D.C., 22, 23–24, 26, 27, 28, 30; and western Virginia campaign, 91, 98–99, 113; and wife Margaret, 27–29, 33, 35, 38, 42–43, 44, 46, 54, 59, 60, 93, 96–97, 106, 110, 112, 113, 115, 117, 118, 120, 157, 163, 164, 165, 167, 168, 172, 173; will of, 167. *See also* Civil War; Donelson, Andrew Jackson; Kentucky
Donelson, Daniel Smith II ("Dan") (son), 60, 112, 120, 157, 168, 169
Donelson, Daniel Smith (nephew), 46, 96, 111
Donelson, Elizabeth Anderson Martin Randolph (wife of AJD), 46, 51, 52, 53, 60, 111
Donelson, Elizabeth Branch ("Lizzie") (daughter), 33, 46, 54, 60, 168
Donelson, Elizabeth Rucker, 6
Donelson, Emily (wife of AJD), 15, 24–29 *passim*, 31, 143. *See also* Donelson, Andrew Jackson; Jackson, Andrew
Donelson, Emily (daughter), 46, 80, 96, 166, 168
Donelson, James Branch (son), 46, 96, 100, 166
Donelson, John (grandfather), 1–2, 3, 19–20
Donelson, John Branch ("Branch") (son), 59, 112, 113, 115, 130, 157, 168–69
Donelson, John Samuel ("Jacky"), 5, 6, 7, 8, 17
Donelson, John Samuel (nephew), 96, 117, 140–41
Donelson, Margaret Branch (wife): in Atlanta, GA, 115; and Balie Peyton, Jr.'s burial service, 110; and birth of Emily, Rebecca and James, 46; and birth of John Branch Donelson, 59;

Donelson, Margaret Branch (*cont.*)
and birth of Mary Ann, 38; and
Daniel Donelson's death, 165; death
of mother of, 60; and Elm Tree, 44;
first child of, 33; and fleeing Union
occupation, 111; and Hazel Path
farm, 117, 167, 168; and marriage
to Daniel Donelson, 27–29, 96–97,
106, 112, 113, 157, 163, 164, 172, 173;
and marriage of Elizabeth, 54; and
plantation near Tallahassee, 37;
portrait of, **93**; stays with father of,
118, 120; third daughter of 42–43.
See also Donelson, Daniel Smith;
Tennessee
Donelson, Margaret (grandchild), 60
Donelson, Martha, 29
Donelson, Martha Bradford (daughter), 54, 112, 168
Donelson, Mary Ann (daughter), 38, 60, 80, 168
Donelson, Rachel Stockley, 1, 3, 6
Donelson, Rebecca (daughter), 46, 112, 167–68
Donelson, Samuel (father), 4, 13, 17, 18, 19, 20, 29. *See also* Jackson, Andrew
Donelson, Samuel ("Sam") (son), 53, 112, 113, 120, 139, 157, 166–69 *passim*.
See also Tennessee; United States
Donelson, Sarah Smith (daughter), 43, 80, 168
Donelson, Stockley (cousin), 27, 42
Donelson, Susan Branch ("Sue") (daughter), 54, 112, 167–68
Donelson, William (uncle), 29,
Donelson, William (cousin), 37, 38, 81
Douglas, Stephen A., 61, 62, 82, 83
Dunlap, William C., 74
Dyer, J. S., 71

Earl, R. E. W., 87
Eastin, Mary Ann, 26, 28, 31. *See also* Polk, Mary Eastin
Eaton, John H., 14, 24, 26–27, 28, 29, 30, 33. *See also* Tennessee; United States
Eaton, Margaret O'Neale Timberlake, 24, 25, 27, 29. *See also* Branch, Margaret
Elliot, Thomas R. S., 110
Elm Tree, 43–44, 45, 52, 64, 80–81, 90
Eventide, 19, 23, 32, 37, 38, 43
Ewell, Richard S., 163
Examiner (Gallatin, Tennessee newspaper), 80

Federals. *See* Union
Fillmore, Millard, 69
Finley, Jesse J., 164
Florida: and children of Daniel Donelson, 42–43; and Daniel Donelson, 38–39, 42, 54, 59; and Margaret Donelson's brother, 46; and Margaret Donelson's plantation, 168; and Sarah Bradford, 168; sickness in, 38–39; and Tallahassee, 37, 38, 41, 60, 80, 167
Floyd, John B., 104, 105
Forrest, Nathan Bedford, 120, 121, 166, 174
Fort Donelson, 97, 111
Fort Henry, 97, 111
Foster, Ephraim H., 19
Franklin, Benjamin, 16
Freeman, Douglas Southall, 101
Fulton, Alfred S., 99, 100, 101, 104

Gentry, Meredith P., 19, 64, 66
Georgia, 19–20, 107, 112, 115, 119, 166
Gilbert, Charles C., 123

Graham, Daniel, 46–47
Grant, Ulysses S., 111, 112, 116, 119
Gray, J. W., 100, 101, 102
Great Britain, 1, 6, 132
Grundy, Felix, 33, 40
Guild, Josephus Conn, 23, 48

Hall, General William, 30, 31, 32
Hall, J. B., 44
Halleck, Henry W., 116, 117, 118, 119
Hardee, William J., 122–23, 128, 129, 134, 139, 140, 147. *See also* Confederate States of America
Harris, Isham Green: and Army's reinforcements, 119; as Democratic candidate for governor, 71, 80; and funeral of Balie Peyton, Jr., 110; as governor of Tennessee, 76–77, 78, 79, 81, 84, 95, 96, 97; and secession question, 84, 95; speech of, 83; and transfer of public lands, 72; and Unionist issue, 160
Harrison, William Henry, 45
Haynes, Landon C., 160
Hays, Samuel Jackson, 21, 26–27
Hazel Path, xi, xii, 44, 80–81, **90**, 97, 111. *See also* Donelson, Daniel Smith; Tennessee; Union
Henderson, Robert H., 46
Henry, Gustavus Adolphus, 97, 160
Henry, Patrick, 97
Hermitage, xii, 6, 14, 18, 22, 43, 44. *See also* Donelson, Andrew Jackson; Donelson, Daniel Smith; Jackson, Andrew; Tennessee
Heth, Henry, 155–56
Hoggatt, James W., 19
Hood, Florence, 169
Horton, Daniel Donelson, 166
Horton, James Edwin, 80, 96, 166
Horton, Margaret, 168

Houston, Sam, 22–23, 30, 51, 52, 53, 61
Hunt, William Gibbes, 21

Illinois, 82
Ingham, Samuel D., 25, 29
Ireland, 55

Jackson, Alfred E., 163
Jackson, Andrew: **88**, and adoption of children, 6, 41; and Andrew Donelson, 28, 29, 31, 32, 49, 85, 87, 172; Bank War of, 40; bill about reinterment of, 81; birthplace of, 3; and cabinet purge, 29, 31; and collection of debts, 9; as a congressman, 4; and the Creek War, 44; and Daniel Donelson, 12, 27, 30, 31, 32, 51, 52, 72–73, 87, 105, 168, 171, 172, 173; death of, 52–53; and Democratic Party, 65, 171, 173; and destruction of Second Bank of U.S., 76; and dismissal of Branch, 70, 85; and Donelson stockade, 3; early life of, 3; and the Eaton scandal, 24–27, 31, 32; and Eighth District, 49; and Emily Donelson, 24–25, 27, 31, 173; and federal government's authority, 25; and fighting against British, 6–7; financial affairs of, 51–52; and Force Bill, 35; as founder of Democratic Party, 171, xii; and friend John Coffee, 20, 22, 27, 31; and funds for statues, 68; as a general of Tennessee militia, 6; grandsons of, 96; and the Hermitage, 22, 51, 52, 53, 72, 74, 81, 87, 172; and Hunter's Hill home, 4, 5, 6; and Jacksonians, 15, 40, 74; and John Branch, 47–48, 88; and John C. Calhoun, 47; and John Donelson's children, 20;

Jackson, Andrew (*cont.*)
  as a lawyer, 3, 4; letters of, 6, 7, 8, 10, 12, 172, 173; and love for family, 26; and marriage to Rachel Robards, 3–4, 21, 22, 87; and Martin Van Buren, 33, 40, 51; and Mary Eastin Polk, 41; nickname of, 6; and the Nullification Proclamation, 34–35, 74; and the petticoat war, 29, 173; and Philip P. Barbour as running mate, 73; as a politician, 4, 14, 15, 21, 29, 30, 32, 33, 51, xi; popularity of, 39; presidency of, xi, 22, 23–24, 25, 27, 29, 30, 33–35, 39, 40, 41, 49, 172, 173; and presidential elections, 15, 21–22, 33, 52; principles of, 65; reelection of, 73; retirement of, 44; and Samuel Donelson, 26, 52; and Secretary of War John Eaton, 24, 27; and settling Samuel Donelson's affairs, 5–6, 17; as a U.S. Senator, 14, 15; and tariffs, 35; temper of, 18, 27, 31, 173; and Tennessee, 43, 58; and two-party system, 61; in U.S. Army, 6; and War of 1812, 6–7. *See also* Hermitage
Jackson, Andrew III, 96
Jackson, Andrew, Jr., 6, 28, 81, 166
Jackson, Henry R., 104
Jackson, John K., 148
Jackson, Rachel, 15, 21, 22, 25, 28, 29, **88**
Jackson, Samuel, 81, 96
Jackson, Stonewall, 174
Jefferson, Thomas, 11, 45, 65
Johnson, Andrew, 62, 64, 65–69 *passim*, 70, 75, 79, 167. *See also* Tennessee
Johnston, Albert Sidney, 16, 105–6, 110, 111, 112
Johnston, Joseph E., 99, 139, 155, 157, 158, 160–63. *See also* Confederate States of America
Jones, James, 108
Jones, James C., 45, 47, 62, 66, 75
Jones, Samuel, 158, 160
Jones, Thomas M., 128

Kansas, 62, 82
Kentucky: and Albert Sidney Johnston, 111; and Battle of Perryville, 122–33; and border with Tennessee, 97, 111, **154**; and Bowling Green, 105, 106, 111, 121; and capital of Frankfort, 121, 122; and the Civil War, 120, 121–33, 134, 137, 141, 158, 159; Columbus in, 116; and Confederate state governor, 122; and Cumberland River, 110; Daniel Donelson's retreat from, 138; and General Braxton Bragg, 137; and Daniel Donelson's greeting in Glasgow, 121; Harlan County in, 165; and Isaac R. Trimble, 12; and John Bell, 83; John C. Breckinridge of, 83; John Donelson's move to, 2; John G. Carlisle of, 169; Lexington in, 12, 121; line of, 3, 111; and Louisville, 68, 121, 122; and Louisville and Nashville Railroad, 111; raids into, 159, 160, 161, 162, 165; Robert Anderson of, 16; and settlement, 1; and Transylvania University, 12; and the Union, 97, 106, 122, 123; Versailles in, 122, 123, 124, 133
Kincaide, John, 169

Lane, Joseph, 83
Lee, Robert E.: **91**; and attacks on Federals, 100, 102–3, 104; and command of Virginia's forces, 98–99, 102, 104; as Davis's military

adviser, 99; description of, 102; and Donelson's and Starke's forces, 106, 107; and Donelson's brigade, 104, 107, 113, 115; and Heth for Army of Northern Virginia, 156; and instructions through Loring, 100; and John C. Pemberton, 108, 113; and organization of forces, 107; and Richmond, 112; tactical brilliance of, 174; and wife Mary, 98–99

Lewis, William B., 14, 39, 40

Lincoln, Abraham: and the Civil War, 118, 138, 165; as presidential candidate, 82; as president of United States, 138, 157, 174; and seceded states, 174; and suppression of insurrection, 95; victory of, 83–84

Loring, William W., 98, 99, 100, 103, 104

Louisiana, 6–7, 10, 14, 16, 51, 52, 116

Maney, George E., 125, 128, 133, 140

Manigault, Arthur M., 140

Mansfield, Joseph K. F., 12

Marshall, Humphrey, 158, 159, 160, 161, 162, 165

Martin, Alf, 103

Martin, Daniel Donelson, 80

Martin, James Glasgow, Jr., 53, 60, 80, 98, 102, 110, 125. *See also* Civil War

Martin, William E., 108, 109

Maryland, 1, 10, 83

Maury, Dabney H., 119, 164

McClellan, George B., 98, 100

McCook, Alexander McD., 123, 124

McGavick, Randal W., 74, 79

McKinney, Christopher C., 109

McLemore, John C., 18–19, 26, 27

Mexican War, 54–55, 57, 96, 99

Mexico, 54, 55, 108

Mississippi: Army of, 115, 119, 121, 124, 128, 133–34, 147; Bolivar County in, 77; and Chickasaw County, 52; and the Civil War, 115, 116, 117, 119; Corinth in, 112, 113, 115, 116, 118, 119; and cultivation of cotton, 61–62; and Daniel Donelson, 37, 39, 42, 52, 118; Jackson in, 58, 138; and Jefferson Davis, 16; and Negroes, 42; US Department of, 116

Missouri, 83

Moore, William L., 118, 143, 145–46, 147

Morgan, John Hunt, 120

Mott, Thomas R., 46

Nashborough settlement, 2

Nashville True Whig, 67

Nashville Union, 48–49, 50, 54

Nashville Union and American, 64, 65, 67, 68, 69, 70, 72. *See also* United States

National Banner and Nashville Whig, 21

native peoples, 1, 2, 6, 7, 22, 48

Nebraska-Kansas Act, 62, 69

New Jersey, 40

New York: and Daniel Donelson's honeymoon trip, 28; elections in, 40; and Martin Van Buren, 25, 41; and US Military Academy in West Point, 7, 10, 16, 23, 168

Nicholson, Alfred Osborne Pope, 76

North Carolina: and Asheville, 162; and boundary line with Virginia, 2; and Cumberland River, 1, 3; and Daniel Donelson, 83; Davidson County in (before Tennessee separated), 2, 3, 5; and District of Mero, 3, 4; Enfield in, 34, 74, 118, 166; Governor Zebulon Vance of, 162; and John Branch as governor, 24; Leonidas Polk of, 16;

North Carolina (*cont.*)
  and North Carolina Infantry Regiment, 148–49; and Sumner County, 3, 5, 6; and Waxhaws settlement, 3

Ohio, 98, 128, 133
Old Hickory. *See* Jackson, Andrew
Overton, John, 14, 39, 40
Owen, W. Purnell, 7

Palmer, Joseph B., 149
Payne, A. G., 44
Pegram, John, 158, 160
Pemberton, John Clifford, 107–8, 109, 112, 113, 164
Pennsylvania, 14, 15–16, 40, 61, 69
Perryville Battlefield State Historic Site, xiii
Peyton, Balie, 23, 49, 71, 110
Peyton, Balie, Jr., 110
Peyton, Joseph Hopkins, 49–50, 110
Pierce, Franklin, 61, 62, 63, 64
Pillow, Gideon J., 96, 97
Polk, James K., 40, 41, 44–53 *passim*, 57, 117. *See also* Tennessee; United States
Polk, Leonidas: and Army of the Mississippi, 119, 120, 121, 122, 123–24, 125; and command of corps, 16, 91, 116, 137, 140, 141, 143, 144, 152; headquarters of, 138; and reliance on Donelson's brigade, 174; and reports of dead and wounded, 149–50; staff of, 166; and support and reinforcements, 146, 148, 151. *See also* Confederate States of America
Polk, Lucius J., 41, 42
Polk, Mary Eastin, 41
Preston, William, 149, 151, 163
Price, Sterling, 119

Priestly, James, 8
Prussia, 53
Pryor, Reuben P., 23

Republican Banner, 49
Republican Party, 63, 82
Revolutionary War, 1, 3
Richardson, John Watkins, 74–75, 79
Robards, Lewis, 3–4, 21
Robertson, Felix, 141
Robertson, James, 1
Rock Castle, xii, 3, 4, 5, 6, 19, 172. *See also* Donelson, Daniel Smith
Rosecrans, William S., 100, 104, 138, 140, 141, 152, 153, 158. *See also* Union
Rowles, George W., 74
Rust, Albert, 100, 102, 103

Sanders, Emily, 19
Sanders, James: children of, 32, 77; as Daniel's stepfather, 6, 13, 17, 44; death of, 43; estate of, 44; and Sumner County, 18; and Sumner tract of land, 17–19
Sanders, Nathaniel, 45–46
Sanders, Polly, 17, 18, 43, 53, 77–78. *See also* Smith, Mary Ann (Polly)
Sanders, Sally, 19
Savage, John H.: arrest of, 112; and battle reports, 131–33, 149–50; and Captain James Womack's command, 120; and charging of enemy, 103, 127–28, 131, 133; as First Brigade commander, 121; as former veteran and congressman, 99; and relocation of encampment, 100; resignation of, 156; and Sixteenth Tennessee Infantry Regiment, 105, 107, 109, 112, 121, 126, 131, 140, 143, 144, 146–51; and swords of captured

INDEX 257

prisoners, 101–2. *See also* Confederate States of America
Scott, Winfield, 61
Seddon, James A., 159–60, 161, 162
Sevier, John, 68
Sheridan, Philip H., 142
Sherman, Thomas W., 107
Shute, John M., 168
slavery, 37, 38, 39, 44, 57, 58–59, 61. *See also* Donelson, Daniel Smith; Tennessee; Union; United States
Smith, Charles F., 16
Smith, Daniel, 2–3, 4, 5–8, 17, 77
Smith, Edmund Kirby, 120, 121, 122, 124, 134, 155
Smith, George, 2, 37
Smith, Henry (Harry), 37, 38, 169
Smith, Mary Ann (Polly), 2, 4, 5–6, 7, 32, 77–78. *See also* Sanders, Polly
Smith, Preston, 140
Smith, Sarah Michie, 2, 13, 21, 43
South Carolina: Charleston in, 82, 83, 95, 106, 107, 110, 111; coastal defenses of, 107; and command of Fifth Military District, 113; and Coosawhatchie, 107; and Daniel Donelson, 111, 112, 113, 116; and Fort Sumter, 16, 95; and Fourteenth South Carolina Infantry Regiment, 108; and John Pemberton as commander, 112; and the Nullification Proclamation, 34–35; and Port Royal Sound, 107, 108; secession from Union of, 84; and state nullification convention, 33–34; and Twelfth South Carolina Infantry Regiment, 108; and Union islands, 109; and Waxhaws settlement, 3
Stanton, Sidney S., 141, 143, 147, 152
Starke, William E., 105, 106, 107
Stewart, Alexander P., 125, 128, 129,
133, 140, 142, 147–49 *passim*. *See also* Confederate States of America
Stuart, Jeb, 174
Sumner, General Jethro, 3

Tatum, Howell, 4
Taylor, Zachary, 55, 58
Tennessee: and American Party, 71; and Andrew Jackson, 40; and Andrew Johnson, 76, 79, 82, 167; Army of, 91, 92, 137, 153, 155, 156, 165; and Association of Confederate Soldiers of Tennessee, 175; and Bank of Tennessee, 76, 77, 79; and border with Kentucky, 97, 111, **154**; capitol building of, 66, 67, 68, 78, 110; and charters for institutions, 67, 79; and Chattanooga, 115, 119, 120, 137, 139, 141, 157; cholera epidemic in, 57; and the Civil War, 96–97, 117, 134, 137, 139, 140–53, 155–58; and Clarksville, 63; counties of, 23, 32, 48, 49, 50, 57, 65, 74, 96, 99, 167; and cultivation of cotton, 61–62; and Cumberland River, 16, 62, 68, 97, 111; and Daniel Donelson, 28, 29, 30, 38, 39, 42, 43, 47, 48, 75–80, 89, 96, 164, 173–74; and Davidson County, 32, 47, 48, 50, 58, 65, 66, 69, 167; and "Declaration of Independence" from U.S., 95–96; and East Tennessee, 61, 84, 92, 96, 98, 99, 105, 120, **154**, 155–58, 159, 160, 162; and Eighth District, 49, 50; elections in, 42, 44, 45, 46, 47, 48, 50, 62, 65–66, 72, 74–75, 76, 80; electorate of, 62; financial issues of, 76–77, 78, 79; First Presbyterian Church in, xii; and First Regiment of Tennessee Volunteers, 55;

Tennessee (*cont.*)
  Gallatin in, 30, 34, 43, 45, 46, 49, 57, 64, 67, 71, 76, 77, 99, 110, 169; General Assembly of, 9, 14, 45, 46, 47, 48, 49, 57, 62, 66, 67, 72, 74, 75–79, 82, 84, 95, 96, 168; government of, 67–69, 70, 75–77, 78, 84, 119, 160; and Governor Isham Harris, 83, 84, 95, 96, 97, 110, 119, 160; and gubernatorial election, 48, 49, 50, 62, 65–66, 72; and Hazel Path, 168, 169; Hendersonville in, xi, xii, 70, 90, 111, 169, 172; and the Hermitage, 81, 168; and House of Representatives, 171; and Jacksonian Democracy, 61; and Jacksonians, 42; and Jackson's land speculation, 9; and James K. Polk, 45, 50, 57, 62, 68; and John Bell, 83; and John H. Eaton, 33, 40; and John W. Richardson, 74–75; and judge Nathaniel W. Williams, 21; and Know-Nothing movement, 63, 64, 65, 69; and Knoxville, 79, 141, 156, 157, 161, 164, 166, 168, 175; and Louisville and Nashville Railroad, 57, 60, 68; and Margaret Branch Donelson, **93**, 110, 111, 168, 169, 173; and Memphis, 62, 63, 79, 81, 97; and Middle Tennessee, 62, 84, 95, 96, 99, 111, 112, 117, 120, 137, 141, 155; and Murfreesboro, 111, 137, 138, 139, 140, 141, 150, 151, 153, 156, 166; and Nashville, 2, 3, 6, 7, 8, 14, 23, 40, 49, 50, 52, 57, 58, 59, 63, 64, 66, 68, 69, 70, 80, 81, 83, 87, 96, 99, 110, 111, 119, 120, 121, 137, 138, 140, 158, 167; and Nashville Convention, 58, 59, 62; and *Nashville Union and American*, 96; and the Nullification Proclamation, 34–35; officer corps of, 96; and the petticoat war, 27; politics in, 29–30, 32, 33, 35, 52, 58, 61, 64, 80, xi; and presidential elections, 52; Provisional Army of, 90, 97; railroad construction in, 68, 76; and representation in U.S. Senate, 47; and Revised Code of Laws, 78, 79, 80; and Sam Houston, 22, 53; and Samuel Donelson, 167, 168; and secession from the Union, 84, 90, 95–96, 157; and Shelbyville, 153, 155, 165; and slavery, 62, 157; and Smith County, 48, 49, 50; social structure in, 23; Sparta in, 120, 121; and state capitol, 81; and state Democratic convention, 80, 81–82; statehood of, 1, 4; state militia of, 23, 38, 96; and states' rights, 35; and Stones River, 140, 146, 147, 148, 152, 153, 156; and Sumner County, 22, 23, 29, 30, 32, 34, 45, 46, 47, 48, 49, 54, 54–55, 57, 58, 60, 64–65, 67, 68, 69, 70, 74, 77, 80, 83, 96, 99, 110, 111, 167, 172; Supreme Court of, 77; and telegraph lines, 68; and Tennessee River, 97, 111; and unionists, 84, 96, 157, 159, 160, 162, 166, 174; and Union occupation, 167; and West Tennessee, 61, 84, 95, 96, 112, 116; and William B. Bate, 96

Texas, 23, 50–51, 52, 53, 61, 80, 125
Thayer, Major Sylvanus, 10, 11, 12, 13, 19
Thomas, George H., 110
Timberlake, John B., 24
Treaty of Lochaber, 1
Trimble, Isaac R., 12
Trist, Nicholas P., 11
Trousdale, Mary, 70
Trousdale, William, 29, 30, 48, 55, 58, 62

INDEX

Tulip Grove, xii, 46, 52, 53, 81
Twopence, David, 23
Tyler, John, 40–41, 45, 51
Tyler, Robert C., 117, 126, 131

Union: and American Party, 63; and Andrew Donelson, xii, 35, 55, 85, 171; and Andrew Jackson, 34, 35, 58, 85, 171; Army of, 110, 111, 112, 115, 122–24, 127–28, 130, 131, 132, 133, 137, 138, 140, 145, 147, 152, 153, 158; and Battle of Murfreesboro (or Stones River), 140–51; and Battle of Perryville, **114**, 123–33; and Battle of Shiloh, 112; and Brigadier General George H. Thomas, 110; cavalry of, 102, 121; coastal islands of, 108; and Constitutional Union party, 82; and Coosaw River, 108; and *Daily Nashville Union* (newspaper), 117; and Daniel Donelson, xii, 35, 55, 65, 85, 171, 174; and the Deep South, 84; and Engagement at Port Royal Ferry, 108–9; and Fort Sumter, 95; future of, 81, 83; and future of slavery, 51, 57–58; gunboats of, 108, 109; Kentucky as member of, 122, 158; and movement from Huttonsville, 101; and Nashville Convention, 59; and the Nullification Proclamation, 34–35; pack mules of, 158; and pillaging of Hazel Path, 90, 138, 167, 172; and Port Royal Sound, 108; and slavery in territories, 57; and South Carolina, 34, 84, 112; southern loyalty to, 95; and Stones River, 153; and Tennessee, 84, 90, 95, 97, 111, 174; and unionists, 95; in Virginia, 101–3; and William S. Rosecrans, 158. *See also* United States

United States: 1840 Census of, 47; 1850 Census of, 57, 80; 1860 Census of, 81; and abolitionists, 63, 73, 74, 132; and American Party, 71; and Andrew Jackson, 22; and annexation of Texas, 51, 52, 53; Army of, 91, 116, 117, 174; and Brigadier General Thomas W. Sherman, 107; and civil and religious liberty, 69; and the Civil War, 106, 116; and "Col. Sam" Donelson, 169; Congress of, 20, 22, 24, 30, 34, 35, 40, 42, 44, 48, 49, 59, 62; Constitution of, 45, 67–68; and the Deep South, 38, 39; and drawing of legislative districts, 47; fleet of, 107; and Fugitive Slave Act, 59, 61; government of, 81, 84, 85; gunboats of, 111; and House of Representatives, 15, 33, 44, 69, 169; and immigrants, 63; independence for, 132; and Jacksonian Democrats, 67–68; and Jacksonians, 40, 41, 73; and John C. Calhoun, 35, 73; and John H. Eaton, 39; and Kansas-Nebraska Act, 62; Kentucky's attachment to, 116; and Know-Nothing movement, 63, 64, 79; and Mexican War, 54–55; and Mississippi, 116; and *Nashville Union and American*, 75, 78, 79–80, 82, 83, 171; newspapers in, 21, 41, 47, 48–49, 50, 54, 59, 60, 64–65, 67, 69, 72, 73–74, 75, 76, 78, 79–80, 82, 83, 117, 127, 139, 140, 162, 164, 167, 171, 174; and nullification controversy, 29, 33–34, 40, 73, 74; and Panic of 1837, 47; and Panic of 1857, 76; and the petticoat affair, 33; and Pierce administration, 62; politics in, 61–74; and presidential elections, 14, 15, 33, 45, 52, 61, 70, 71, 81–84;

United States (*cont.*)
and President James Polk, 52, 53, 117; and president's role, 30, 33; and public lands, 72; and Reconstruction South, 167; and Sam Houston, 23, 52; and secessionist Virginia, 98; and secession of Southern states, 59; Second Bank of, 33, 76; and the Seminole War, 48; Senate of, 20, 33, 47, 48, 75, 76; ships of, 108; and slavery, 62–63, 82, 83–84, 117–18, 172; and Southern society of planters, 44; sutlers in Army of, 52; and the "Tariff of Abominations," 25; and Tennessee's "Declaration of Independence," 95–96; and tensions between North and South, 81; and two-party system, 61, 62, 63; and US Military Academy in West Point, 81, 172; and War of 1812, 6, 20; and Washington, D.C., 29, 38, 43, 52, 60, 62, 157, 169. *See also* Bank of the United States; Union

United States Military Academy, 7, 8, 9–16, 17, 18, 23, 54. *See also* Donelson, Daniel Smith; Thayer, Major Sylvanus; United States

Van Buren, Martin: and Andrew Donelson, 48; campaign of, 45; and Daniel Donelson, 33, 44, 49, 73, 91, 173; as a Democrat, 51; as a New Yorker, 41; and the petticoat war, 25, 29; and the presidency, 40, 47, 73; as Secretary of State, 25; and Tennessee, 71; as Vice President, 33

Vance, Zebulon, 162

Van Dorn, Earl, 118, 140

Virginia: and Battle of Manassas (Bull Run), 99; and boundary line with North Carolina, 2; and Chancellorsville, 166; Charlottesville in, 2; Cheat Mountain in, 100, 102, 103, 104, 107, 109; and the Civil War, 91, 96, 97–99, 100, 101, 102–4, 106, 107, 166; counties of, 155, 158; and Daniel Donelson, 83, 98, 99, 106, 113, 155; Federals in, 99, 100–103, 104; and Gettysburg, 166; governors of, 104; and Greenbrier River valley, 104; and Huntersville, 98, 99, 100, 101; and John Bell, 83; and John Tyler, 40–41; Lewisburg in, 104, 105; and Lynchburg, 97; and Michie's Tavern, 2; and Philip P. Barbour, 33, 73; piedmont of, 1; politics in, 33; and Richmond, 112, 152, 155, 157, 160, 161, 162; Robert Henderson of, 46; and Sixtieth Virginia Infantry Regiment, 105, 107; southwestern region of, 159; and Stafford County, 2; Staunton in, 98; and unionists, 98; and Virginia and Tennessee Railroad, 157; western region of, 98–99, 113, 132, 155, 156, 157, 158, 160

Walker, Joseph Knox, 117

Wallace, James A., 164

Walton, Jessie L., 167

War of the Rebellion: A Compilation of the Official Records of the Union and Confederate Armies, The, 131, 132, 133

Washington, D.C., 10, 15, 22, 23, 24–25, 26, 27. *See also* Donelson, Daniel Smith; United States

Washington, George, 68

Watson, Martha Sanders, 19, 32

Watson, Thomas G., 19, 23

Watson, Thomas S., 23, 37, 43, 44

Weisiger, Mary Ann, 169

Wharton, John A., 125, 129
Wheeler, Joe, 140
Whig Party: and annexation of Texas, 51; in Congress, 40; division in, 61; and elections in New Jersey, 40; and elections in New York, 40; and elections in Pennsylvania, 40; factions of, 61; and gubernatorial elections, 66; and Henry Clay, 51; and immigrants, 63; and John Tyler, 45; and Nashville, 50; and presidential elections, 61; and President John Tyler, 51; and President Zachary Taylor, 55; rise of, 39; and secession from the Union, 95; and slavery, 62–63; and Tennessee, 44, 45, 47, 48, 49, 50, 62, 65, 66, 71, 76; and unionists, 84; and William Henry Harrison, 45; and Winfield Scott, 61
White, Hugh Lawson, 40, 41, 42, 44, 49, 68, 173

Williams, Colonel, 38
Williams, John S., 159, 160
Williams, Nathaniel W., 21
Williams, William, 54, 60
Winchester, George Washington, 110, 121
Wise, Henry A., 104
Withers, E. K., 44
Withers, Jones M., 123, 124, 133, 140–43 *passim*, 153. *See also* Confederate States of America
Womack, James J., 106, 120, 129, 137–38, 141
Wood, S. A. M., 124–25, 129, 130
Woodward, Dr. E., 163
Wright, Marcus J., 156
Wynne, Alfred Royal, 67

Yale College, 13

Zollicoffer, Felix K., 110